The Sha

This original and enlightening book casts fresh light on Shakespeare by examining the lives of his relatives, friends, fellow-actors, collaborators and patrons both in their own right and in relation to his life. Well-known figures such as Richard Burbage, Ben Jonson and Thomas Middleton are freshly considered; little-known but relevant lives are brought to the fore, and revisionist views are expressed on such matters as Shakespeare's wealth, his family and personal relationships, and his social status. Written by a distinguished team, including some of the foremost biographers, writers and Shakespeare scholars of today, this enthralling volume forms an original contribution to Shakespearian biography and Elizabethan and Jacobean social history. It will interest anyone looking to learn something new about the dramatist and the times in which he lived. A supplementary website offers imagined first-person audio accounts from the featured subjects.

PAUL EDMONDSON is Head of Research at the Shakespeare Birthplace Trust. He has authored and co-edited numerous articles and books on Shakespeare, including *Shakespeare's Sonnets* (with Stanley Wells, 2004), *The Shakespeare Handbooks: Twelfth Night* (2005) and *Shakespeare: Ideas in Profile* (2015).

STANLEY WELLS, CBE, FRSL, is Honorary President at the Shakespeare Birthplace Trust. His many books include *Shakespeare: For All Time* (2002), *Looking for Sex in Shakespeare* (2004), *Shakespeare & Co.* (2006), *Shakespeare, Sex, and Love* (2010), and *Great Shakespeare Actors* (2015). He edited *Shakespeare Survey* for almost twenty years, and is co-editor of *The Cambridge Companion to Shakespeare on Stage* (with Sarah Stanton, Cambridge, 2002) and *The New Cambridge Companion to Shakespeare* (with Margreta de Grazia, Cambridge, 2010). He is also the General Editor of the Oxford and Penguin editions of Shakespeare.

The Shakespeare Circle

An Alternative Biography

Edited by

PAUL EDMONDSON AND
STANLEY WELLS

CAMBRIDGE
UNIVERSITY PRESS

CAMBRIDGE
UNIVERSITY PRESS

University Printing House, Cambridge CB2 8BS, United Kingdom

Cambridge University Press is part of the University of Cambridge.

It furthers the University's mission by disseminating knowledge in the pursuit of education, learning and research at the highest international levels of excellence.

www.cambridge.org
Information on this title: www.cambridge.org/9781107699090

© Cambridge University Press 2015

First published 2015
Reprinted 2016

Printed in the United Kingdom by TJ International Ltd. Padstow Cornwall

A catalogue record for this publication is available from the British Library

Library of Congress Cataloguing in Publication data
The Shakespeare circle : an alternative biography / edited by Paul Edmondson and Stanley Wells.
pages cm
Includes index.
ISBN 978-1-107-05432-5 (Hardback) –
ISBN 978-1-107-69909-0 (Paperback)
1. Shakespeare, William, 1564–1616–Friends and associates.   I. Edmondson, Paul, editor.
II. Wells, Stanley, 1930– editor.
PR2911.S53 2015
822.3′3–dc23   2015015427

ISBN 978-1-107-05432-5 Hardback
ISBN 978-1-107-69909-0 Paperback

Additional resources for this publication at www.theshakespearecircle.com

Contents

PART II · FRIENDS AND NEIGHBOURS

PART III · COLLEAGUES AND PATRONS

Illustrations

Contributors

John H. Astington, *University of Toronto*

Susan Brock, *University of Warwick*

Margaret Drabble, *novelist*

Paul Edmondson, *Shakespeare Birthplace Trust*

David Fallow, *independent scholar*

Germaine Greer, *independent scholar*

Andrew Hadfield, *University of Sussex*

Tara Hamling, Shakespeare Institute, *University of Birmingham*

Graham Holderness, *University of Hertfordshire*

David Kathman, *independent scholar*

Andy Kesson, *University of Roehampton*

Lachlan Mackinnon, *independent scholar*

Lucy Munro, *King's College, London*

Alan H. Nelson, *University of California, Berkeley*

Catherine Richardson, *University of Kent*

David Riggs, *Stanford University*

Carol Chillington Rutter, *University of Warwick*

Duncan Salkeld, *University of Chichester*

Katherine Scheil, *University of Minnesota*

Cathy Shrank, *University of Sheffield*

Emma Smith, *Hertford College, Oxford*

Bart van Es, *St Catherine's College, Oxford*

René Weis, *University College London*

Greg Wells, *University of Warwick*

Stanley Wells, *Shakespeare Birthplace Trust*

Michael Wood, *independent scholar and television historian*

Preface and acknowledgements

In co-editing this book we have benefited from many kindnesses, not least from our colleagues Madeleine Cox and Helen Hargest in the Shakespeare Centre Library and Archive, and from Alec Cobbe and Tara Hamling.

Our contributors have responded generously to our editorial require-ments, especially our decision to use the Harvard author–date system which has allowed us to produce the book entirely without footnotes. Unless otherwise stated, all quotations from Shakespeare's work are taken from *The Oxford Shakespeare: The Complete Works*, edited by Stanley Wells and Gary Taylor, with John Jowett and William Montgomery (Oxford University Press, 1986; 2nd edn 2005). Quotations from early texts are given in modern spelling unless there is good reason to preserve the original. Earlier versions of many of the essays were presented at the kind invitation of Dominique Goy-Blanquet as a seminar in Paris which formed part of the Shakespeare 450 conference hosted by the Société Française Shakespeare.

This book forms part of the worldwide commemorations of the 400th anniversary of Shakespeare's death. In conjunction with its publication our friends and colleagues at Misfit Inc., A. J. and Melissa Leon, have produced a digital platform through which everyone can hear free of charge the re-imagined voices of the people in Shakespeare's life who were closest to him. You can find out more at www.theshakespearecircle.com.

Throughout our enterprise we have felt deep gratitude for the encour-agement and expertise of Sarah Stanton, who has guided the composition of the book from initial conversations through to completion. Rosemary Crawley at Cambridge University Press has been unfailingly helpful at all stages of production.

The following abbreviations are used for archival sources:

Folger	The Folger Shakespeare Library
SBTRO or SCLA	The Shakespeare Centre Library and Archive
TNA	The National Archives
WAAS	Worcestershire Archive and Archaeology Services

General introduction

PAUL EDMONDSON AND STANLEY WELLS

Imagination is needed if we are to bring the information we have about another human being to life. When the subject is Shakespeare, although we may continually lament that the facts we most desire do not exist, we may decide to broaden the scope of how to use what is available the better to imagine what his life was like.

Biographers of Shakespeare normally and understandably drive a direct trajectory from his birth to his death, writing about persons he knew mainly in relation to specific occasions when his life intersected with theirs. Relatives, friends, theatre practitioners, fellow writers, publishers and printers, patrons, business associates – people such as these all played significant roles in the dramatist's life. In this volume we have invited our contributors, instead of taking Shakespeare as the centre, to consider members of his circle – or rather of the intersecting circles of persons he encountered at various periods of his life – in their own right, as well as in relation to the ways in which their lives impinged on his and his on theirs. We hope that these explorations within the Shakespeare circle will both add to our knowledge of the society of his time and, more specifically, will cast reflected light back on Shakespeare himself, enriching our understanding of him by offering a fuller than usual picture of his personal and professional relationships, the people we know he was closest to.

The twin centres of Shakespeare's life are of course Stratford-upon-Avon and London. In his day Stratford, set on the River Avon in Warwickshire, was a thriving market town with around 2,000 inhabitants. It had a fine church and a well-established grammar school with Oxford-educated masters where all the boys of the town could receive a free, classics-based education with no expense to their parents. Many townsmen both spoke and wrote Latin. Girls, however, could be educated only at an elementary level. Daily life in the town is exceptionally well recorded because of the high survival rate of many of the corporation and other records, though some key documents are lost. The school's records, for example, are only preserved from the nineteenth century onwards. The town's affairs were regulated by its councillors and aldermen, presided over by the Bailiff, or mayor, an office held in 1568 by Shakespeare's father, John (Chapter 2). They were advised by lawyers such as Thomas Greene (Chapter 11), town clerk, who described himself as Shakespeare's 'cousin' (though they may not have been related by blood). The various trades practised by towns-people were organised into guilds which met in the Guildhall, which survives. It was both the centre of local government and a location that, under the patronage of the Bailiff and the Town Council, could host troupes of travelling players normally based in the metropolis. Officials and a town carrier were among those who travelled regularly between Stratford and London, a distance of just over 80 miles as the crow flies, but considerably more along the highways and byways of Elizabethan England; typically the journey took two or, more comfortably, three days on horseback, with overnight stops in, perhaps, Oxford and Aylesbury or Uxbridge.

London, with more like 200,000 inhabitants, was the centre of govern-ment and the Court, home of the monarch, a cosmopolitan city also, like Stratford, based on a river which gave it strong links with Europe and beyond; a centre of trade and commerce, but also a place where culture – music both sacred and secular, literature of many kinds, religion, painting and the other fine arts – thrived. The Inns of Court provided educational opportunities in the law. Crucially for Shakespeare, in the later part of the sixteenth century the city saw a rapid development of professional theatre, with permanent playhouses – the only ones in the country – increasing in number and in sophistication of design.

Many of the persons discussed here belong firmly to either Stratford or London. Most members of Shakespeare's immediate family – his parents Mary and John (Chapters 1 and 2), his surviving brothers Gilbert, Richard and Edmund (Chapter 3), his sister Joan (Chapter 4), his wife Anne and her relatives (Chapter 5), his children Susanna, Hamnet and Judith (Chapters 6, 8 and 9) – have left evidence of little if any direct contact with the capital, though Gilbert, a shadowy figure, may have worked there for a while, and his youngest brother, Edmund, followed in his footsteps in a brief acting career of which only faint traces survive. We can identify clear links between Shakespeare and a number of Stratfordians beyond his immediate family. He encountered the Quineys on both a public level, in his business dealings, and privately through the marriage of his daughter Judith to Thomas Quiney. The physician John Hall (Chapter 7), who came to live in Stratford when Shakespeare's London career was in full swing, married his other daughter, Susanna (Chapter 6), and fathered Shakespeare's granddaughter Elizabeth (Chapter 10). The lives of several members of another Warwickshire family, the Combes (Chapter 12), intertwined at various points with Shakespeare's: he had business dealings with some of them, received a legacy from one, and left his sword to another. One Stratford friend, Richard Field (Chapter 13), Shakespeare's schoolfellow, also made his career in London, becoming a distinguished printer and publisher associated with all Shakespeare's poems except the Sonnets.

References to parishes, streets and other London locations occur from time to among the essays. Readers seeking precise information about these locales and their scale in relation to each other may find it helpful to consult the on-going Map of Early Modern London project hosted by the University of Victoria, British Columbia, Canada at https://mapoflondon.uvic.ca/. Readers will find there an invaluable resource which allows them to zoom in to particular areas of the famous Agas map of the city from the 1560s. The project provides a searchable placeography, personography, bibliography, glossary and orgography (of organisations), as well as much other information. An overall effect of perusing a map of this kind is to be reminded of how close together the various communities and places were, a valuable insight into the geographical aspects of Shakespeare's London circles.

Shakespeare's closest identifiable personal links in London were with professional associates, fellow actors including Richard Burbage (Chapter 19), Will Kemp and Robert Armin (Chapter 20), John Heminges and Henry Condell (Chapter 25), and fellow dramatists such as Robert Greene, George Peele, Christopher Marlowe (Chapter 18), the deplorable George Wilkins (Chapter 22), Thomas Middleton (Chapter 23), John Fletcher (Chapter 24) and his admiring rival Ben Jonson (Chapter 15). Some of his fellow poets, such as Richard Barnfield, John Weever and William Basse, wrote about him (Chapter 16). We are lucky enough to know quite a lot about the Mountjoy family (Chapter 14), with whom Shakespeare lodged, becoming closely involved in their domestic affairs. Both the literary and the theatrical professions thrived on patronage. The evidence of the dedications to Shakespeare's narrative poems suggests that his relationship with the Earl of Southampton (Chapter 21) rapidly developed from formality to a close and loving intimacy.

We have restricted the subjects of this book almost entirely to persons for whose relationship with Shakespeare we have documentary evidence or with whom we can assume he had a close relationship, either personally or professionally. But the Shakespeare circle can always be widened. He knew composers, some of whom worked for his company, such as Thomas Morley, a near neighbour in London, Robert Johnson, who composed music for *The Tempest*, and John Dowland. He surely heard John Donne preach, and attendance at Court would have brought him into contact with a broad spectrum of Londoners from members of the royal family and the aristocracy through court officials such as Edmund Tilney, the Master of the Revels, to musicians, artisans and many other kinds of practitioners. Did he attend Edmund Spenser's funeral or see Essex's troops ride out on their way to the Irish wars (as Simon Forman did)? He certainly would have known other playwrights, poets and writers including Thomas Dekker, Thomas Heywood, John Marston, Thomas Nashe, Edmund Spenser and John Webster. Some of these would no doubt have been among his regular companions and associates. Together they form a litany of names that it becomes all too easy to imagine surrounding him as drinking companions in the Mermaid Tavern.

In the diary of the lawyer, John Manningham, we find the only surviving anecdote about Shakespeare's personal life:

Upon a time when Burbage played Richard the Third there was a citizen grew so far in liking with him, that before she went from the play she appointed him to come that night unto her by the name of Richard the Third. Shakespeare, over-hearing their conclusion, went before, was entertained and at his game ere Burbage came. Then, message being brought that Richard the Third was at the door, Shakespeare caused return to be made that William the Conqueror was before Richard the Third. (Schoenbaum 1975, p. 152)

Manningham's anecdote provides just the kind of insight which Shakespearian biography abundantly lacks: personally inflected and sensational, the account sounds as plausible today as it no doubt did 400 years ago. But Manningham seems to be writing at second-hand; it has a 'once upon a time' feeling to it. His contribution to Shakespearian biography is primarily to illustrate the kind of celebrity reputation Shakespeare had among trainee lawyers and the Inns of Court. Whilst Manningham's story is important, it does not warrant him a place among Shakespeare's intimates.

Much closer to home are all the other members of the Lord Chamberlain's Men (from 1594), later the King's Men (from 1603) who worked and acted alongside Shakespeare, for whom he was writing the parts in his plays, and whose names appear in what has long seemed like a roll call of honour at the front of the First Folio of 1623. Among these were his co-shareholders of these companies, along with the Globe and Blackfriars playhouses, men whom he trusted, respected and with whom he shared a passion for business. They all have ample qualification to be included in the Shakespeare circle but we have had to limit our attention to the major candidates. Augustine Phillips, for instance, was a loyal business colleague and fellow actor who left Shakespeare a legacy of a 30-shilling gold piece. It was Phillips who, in 1601, testified before the Privy Council about the Lord Chamberlain's Men's performance of *Richard II* on the eve of the ill-fated uprising led by the Earl of Essex.

We have been reminded in preparing this volume that biography, in its quest to tell the truth, articulates at the same time its own sense of longing, which makes itself felt, in part, through speculation. We have encouraged that longing to know as much as possible about Shakespeare's life among our contributors. Without wanting this book to be full of expressions such as 'he must have' and 'there can be little doubt that', we have not discouraged our contributors from going beyond narrowly documented evidence, relying on their familiarity with Shakespeare's life and times to exercise their imaginations in the attempt to illuminate obscure areas of his existence and experience. Some of them offer revisionist views. David Fallow, for instance, provides a fresh but reasoned perspective on John Shakespeare's career which has major implications for the sources of William's wealth; and Alan H. Nelson does not shrink from speculation about his sexuality. We have not attempted to impose uniformity on the volume, but present it as a collection of authoritatively engaged voices – some of whom are primarily historians, others literary scholars – who do not always agree, but who have been willing to think afresh about the lives that touched Shakespeare's most closely, as well as the kinds of experience those lives represent within the culture of the period.

All biographical discourse overlaps to a greater or lesser extent with fiction. Virginia Woolf explores the playfulness as well as the limits of biography in two novels. *Jacob's Room* (1922) is ostensibly about Jacob Flanders except that he never actually appears. Instead, the reader is presented with a series of impressions; the true subject, the heart of the matter, is tantalisingly deferred, refracted. In *Orlando: A Biography* (1928), Woolf teases the reader three times with the possible appearance of Shakespeare, whose name can be found in the index. On all three occasions, mention is made of his 'dirty ruff' and in the first two encounters he is described as being 'rather fat' (Woolf 1992, pp. 8 and 47). Here is his first appearance, a poet in the throes of composition, his eyes in what Theseus in *A Midsummer Night's Dream* describes as 'a fine frenzy rolling' (5.1.12):

He held a pen in his hand, but he was not writing. He seemed in the act of rolling some thought up and down, to and fro in his mind till it gathered shape or momentum to his liking. His eyes, globed and clouded like some green stone of curious texture, were fixed. He did not see Orlando. For all his hurry, Orlando stopped dead. Was this a poet? Was he writing poetry? 'Tell me', he wanted to say, 'everything in the whole world' – for he had the wildest, most absurd, extravagant ideas about poetry – but how to speak to a man who does not see you? Who sees ogres, satyrs, perhaps the depths of the sea instead? So Orlando stood gazing while the man turned his pen in his fingers, this way and that way, and gazed and mused; and then, very quickly, wrote half-a-dozen lines and looked up. (Woolf 1992, p. 8)

He remains anonymous until the third encounter, a memory, towards the end of the novel:

He sat at Twitchett's table ... with a dirty ruff on ... Was it old Mr Baker come to measure the timber? Or was it Sh-p-re? (for when we speak names we deeply reverence to ourselves we never speak them whole). (Woolf 1992, p. 204)

Little wonder that when Woolf visited Stratford-upon-Avon in search of Shakespeare on 9 May 1934 she described her visit to New Place in the following terms:

everything seemed to say, this was Shakespeare's, had [here?] he sat and walked; but you won't find me, not exactly in the flesh. He is serenely absent-present; both at once, radiating round one; yes; in the flowers, in the old hall, in the garden; but never to be pinned down. (Woolf 1978, pp. 264–5)

This is very much the spirit of the essays we have gathered to help form our sense of the Shakespeare circle. By trying to look their subjects in the eyes, we hope that our contributors have found something of Shakespeare, reflected – or perhaps refracted – back to them. It is our hope that the sum total of these biographical studies will enable you to think about Shakespeare from a range of different perspectives, 'serenely absent-present', but a presence which nevertheless haunts and moves across each and every one of these ensuing pages.

WORKS CITED

Schoenbaum, S. 1975. *William Shakespeare: A Documentary Life*. Oxford University Press

Woolf, Virginia 1978. *A Writer's Diary*. Leonard Woolf (ed.). London. Grafton Books

1992. *Orlando*. London. Vintage

PART I

§

Family

The closest members of the Shakespeare circle are his family. This section covers four generations. Starting with his mother, Mary Arden, the youngest of eight children, we are reminded by Michael Wood of a 'shift in wealth, education and opportunity which marked the later Tudor age'. It was Shakespeare's family who first stimulated his imagination and creativity by introducing him to the rhymes and folk tales of oral tradition. Helen Cooper, an authority on the late medieval influence on Shakespeare, has suggested to us that from his early years he knew tales such as those about Robin Hood and King Arthur as well as the romances of Guy of Warwick (all of which were widely disseminated orally and readily available through inexpensive editions). The presence of casual allusions to many of these tales in plays written much later in life – Edgar disguised as Poor Tom in *King Lear*, for example, alludes to the romances of Bevis of Hampton – suggests that they were deeply embedded in his imagination.

The medieval imagination was inextricably linked with the old faith, inevitably represented to Shakespeare by his parents. The Church of England, established during their formative years, was Catholic in the broadest sense of the term. The three Catholic creeds, along with 'The Song of the Blessed Virgin Mary' ('the Magnificat') and 'The Song of the Three' ('the Benedicite'), were printed in its foundational text, the Book of Common Prayer, first printed in 1549. It was always intended to be a broad church – one which was catholic and reformed and could accommodate a wide-range of spiritual and religious beliefs among those who were happy outwardly to conform. Overall Shakespeare and his family, like most other people of their time, seem to have done just that.

An interpretative clash in this section concerns John Shakespeare. David Fallow's revisionist view of the later part of his life and career finds a life of impressive prosperity deriving from his involvement with the thriving wool industry, whereas Michael Wood accepts the more traditional view that his withdrawal from his civic duties reflects a decline in his economic fortunes. In marrying into the Ardens, John Shakespeare allied himself with a junior branch of a prosperous land-owning family of good pedigree. William was also to marry into a farming family. He married young and in a hurry when he was just eighteen (the average age for men in Stratford-upon-Avon to marry was twenty-six), and his already pregnant bride was eight years his senior. Fallow plausibly suggests that he first went to London to further his father's business interests and only later became involved with the rising theatrical scene. Catherine Richardson points out that Shakespeare seems to have taken an almost paternal interest in his sixteen-year younger brother, Edmund, who followed him to London and became an actor.

Shakespeare's accrual of wealth by 1594 (when he was able to co-found and purchase shares in the Lord Chamberlain's Men) meant that all of his family members could have a roof over their heads. As Tara Hamling points out, there were rooms enough in New Place even for a lodger, Thomas Greene, Shakespeare's putative cousin. Evidence of the closeness of the Shakespeares is provided by the fact that his sister Joan Hart and her family lived in part of their late father's house which Shakespeare inherited in 1601. In writing about his wife, Anne Shakespeare, Katherine Scheil uses evidence from the 2010–13 archaeological investigations at New Place to demonstrate the lifestyle enjoyed in Shakespeare's family home, so substantial and handsome a house that it is reasonable to suppose that Shakespeare would have wished to spend as much time there as his professional commitments would permit.

The inheritor of New Place, Shakespeare's elder daughter Susanna, was brought up there, moved out on her marriage to the physician John Hall, and moved back from 1616 until her death in 1649. Greg Wells mentions what may be John Hall's first encounter with the Shakespeare family. William Covell, who refers to 'sweet Shakespeare' in his 1595 book *Polimanteia, or, the meanes lawfull and unlawful, to judge of the fall of a commonwealth*, was the signatory of Hall's Bachelor of Arts degree. There is a striking contrast between Shakespeare and his two sons-in-law. Thomas Quiney disappointed family hopes with his scandalous behaviour around the time of his marriage to Judith. This is reflected in changes to Shakespeare's will, which survives only in a revised draft. Although little is known about Shakespeare's younger daughter, Germaine

Greer is able fully to imagine her life in relation to the well-documented Quiney family. Shakespeare's other son-in-law, the eminent physician John Hall, was well known for his Puritan sympathies. In spite of these, there is reason to believe that the poet's daughter – whose father had made many appearances at Court with his acting companies – entertained the Roman Catholic Queen Henrietta Maria at New Place in 1643. She and King Charles (who as a young prince had seen many of Shakespeare's plays performed) were, as Lachlan McKinnon explains, passionate about the theatre. It is interesting to imagine the conversations that might have taken place between the poet's daughter and the wife of the theatre company's majestic patron.

The greatest sadness in Shakespeare's life was the death of his son, Hamnet, in 1596. He would have inherited the large house his father was about to buy, the rest of his estate, the family coat of arms, and Shakespeare's sword. Graham Holderness touchingly explores Hamnet's pathetic absence from the Shakespeare story. Mary Shakespeare, however, lived to see the arrival of her great-granddaughter, Elizabeth, who, by her second marriage would become Lady Barnard. Shakespeare's direct family-line died with her, but his DNA is still traceable through her mortal remains which, as René Weis tantalisingly mentions, were briefly uncovered in 1981.

1

His mother Mary Shakespeare

MICHAEL WOOD

§

When Nicholas Rowe published the first biographical notice of Shakespeare in 1709, the poet's mother did not figure in his account. Drawing on Thomas Betterton's investigations in Stratford parish documents and local traditions, Rowe says simply that William was the son of John Shakespeare who had 'bred him'. Even now the poet's mother is perhaps the least known of his circle. But Mary Arden's story, insofar as it can be recovered, casts interesting light on the poet's background, in both its social context and material culture, and, perhaps too, on his ways of seeing – what Emrys Jones called the 'mental world that is a person's natural inheritance' (Jones 1977, p. 3).

The poet's mother came from a prosperous peasant family. Her father was a husbandman, which, in the social gradations of the time, ranked him in rural society above a labourer, but below the status of yeoman. This is despite the family's submission to the College of Heralds in 1596 that Robert was 'a gentleman of worship' (Schoenbaum 1975, p. 167), a misrepresentation of the truth, though the story came down to Rowe. In reality Robert Arden, though better off than the poet's paternal grandfather, was a hundred-acre husbandman. His family's story is typical of a time which saw the rise of the gentry class, and the 'great rebuilding' of the sixteenth century; an example of how the daughter of a well-off peasant could move from a communal open hall in a village to a Stratford town house with thirty rooms and ten fireplaces at the end of Elizabeth's reign.

Mary's husband was a man of similar background; a small cultivator (described in an early document as an *agricola*) who apprenticed as glover (a craft in demand among the aspiring middle class in the mid-century) and rose in the world to become alderman bailiff and mayor in Stratford, eventually buying the title of 'gentleman'.

Mary's life as wife and mother is also typical of this time of transition. Like her father, Mary had eight children. In terms of family size in this class of people, such a large family would become unusual during the sixteenth century, as prudential marriage was more and more practised: increasingly it would be the rich, employing wet nurses, who had so many children. Of Mary's eight children, two daughters died in infancy and one aged seven, but those who lived to adulthood would be beneficiaries of the shift in wealth, education and opportunity which marked the later Tudor age. Her surviving daughter married a hatter; one son became a haberdasher, and two found jobs in the entertainment industry, one of them who attended grammar school rising to be the most successful poet writer in London with property there and in Warwickshire. For grandchildren of husbandmen, this is a fascinating example of social movement in the rural West Midlands in the sixteenth century. It is this social and cultural hinterland, the family memory as it were, on the poet's maternal side, which is the main subject of this chapter.

The sources for Mary's life, however, are as scanty as they are for all ordinary women in this period. She left no letters, no scribbles in books; no one wrote her story, recorded her words or even described her. With her husband, some sixty documents enable a fairly detailed discussion at least of his business career and financial dealings, but Mary's life only surfaces in the evidence of her father's will, the birth and death records of her children, and the leases and law suits to which her name is jointly attached in her middle years as her husband sank into financial trouble. The historian's task, then, is to piece her tale together from scraps. But as with almost all women's history before the modern age, that is how it has to be.

In any family history, memory goes back to the grandparents. They help create a person's cultural hinterland. In particular, it has been said, it is the twenty years before a person's birth that shape his or her mental horizons (Jones 1977, p. 5). Here, one or two clues in the documents suggest Mary's family's view of its past. Her father – so the family believed – belonged to a family of considerable standing in the West Midlands, the Ardens of Park Hall in Curdworth near Birmingham. There is, however, some doubt over her exact relation, if any, to the Park Hall Ardens. The evidence suggests she may have descended from Thomas Arden, one of several younger sons of Walter Arden of Park Hall, who recovered the family estates in the Wars of the Roses under Edward IV (Eccles 1961, pp. 13–15). Thomas held land in Wilmcote in Warwickshire, and at Snitterfield, and his son Robert had lands in both places. Though proof is lacking, most likely this Robert was Mary's father Robert Arden.

Robert must have been born before the battle of Bosworth, as he was of full age in 1501. He presumably married Mary's mother soon after 1517 when he was in his later thirties. (Her name is not known –possibly she was one of the Palmers who were friends and neighbours.) Given this date, it is interesting that the tree-ring dating of Robert's house in Wilmcote shows that the timbers were cut in 1513 and 1514; the construction of an open hall house a year or two later, after seasoning the wood, was perhaps with marriage and family in mind. Between around 1518 and the mid 1530s, he and his wife had at least eight children, all the surviving ones daughters, of whom Mary was the youngest. She was named after the Virgin, who is singled out in Robert's will as 'our bleside Laydye Sent Marye', the patron of the guild at Aston Cantlow (Eccles 1961, p. 18). As with Mary's other sisters, Alice, Margaret and Catherine, such naming is as might be expected in a rural Catholic community in the 1520s and 30s. These were the holy women of popular piety, as in the Gilte Legende, along with Mary Magdalene, dedicatee of the chapel in Wilmcote, which was attached to the Guild of the Holy Cross in Stratford.

The date of Mary's birth is not known. It is commonly assumed that she was seventeen or eighteen when she married, on the grounds that her last pregnancy began in summer 1579; but this is not certain. Though there are exceptions to the rule, women at this time generally married in their mid twenties, men in their late twenties. As Mary was executrix of her father's will in 1556, and probably married in 1557, she may have been born as early as 1535. An obstacle to this is the date of birth of her last child Edmund who was christened on 3 May 1580, but Mary may have been fertile into her forties: the gap between her earlier pregnancies was usually around two years (the period in which breast feeding helped prevent a new pregnancy), but the gap of more than six years since her previous pregnancy makes Edmund sound an unexpected surprise at a time when she thought she might no longer get pregnant. Be that as it may, as she lived to September 1608, she therefore died in her early seventies, by which time her eldest son was the leading playwright in London and a 'gentleman groom of the King's most honourable Privy Chamber'.

Mary grew up in Wilmcote, a chapelry of Aston Cantlow five miles north of Stratford, in 'champaine ground frutfull of corne and grasse' as Leland described it in 1543. There her father's presence as a well-off peasant cultivator is recorded in leases from 1501, and in the 1525 and 1545 subsidies, through to November 1556, when his will was drawn up. Aston was a prosperous village with its Guild of St Mary, which had a chapel in the parish church where, until 1535, two chaplains celebrated daily 'for the brethren and sisters of the Gild and their souls after death'. Women were active members of such fraternities, in traditional roles, watching over the dead, sewing liveries banners and vestments, preparing food for feasts. Though the guild was dissolved when Mary was in infancy, her older sisters must have known it, and some of its social and religious life may have survived into Edward's reign.

The guilds were part of the social ethos of late medieval rural society in Arden, fostering patterns of association, piety and charity, and also commercial contacts, down to the dissolution of Stratford's Guild of the Holy Cross in 1547–8. Robert's attachment to these values is indicated by his entry into the guild as 'Robert Arthern of Wyllmecott' in Stratford in 1517 along with Thomas Scharelett whose son would marry Robert's daughter Elizabeth (MacDonald 2007, p. 421). As 'Robert Arthern' he also seems to have joined the Knowle guild the same year (Bickley 1894, p. 236). All this suggests he already had connections with the main market town in south Arden, and that in his early thirties he was seen by his neighbours as a man of some substance. The guild books also hint at the connections between the extended families of the Ardens and Shakespeares and their neighbours in the rural community north of the Avon in the early sixteenth century, with its prosperous peasants and yeomen and the gentry of the shire.

This, then, was the late medieval society into which the poet's mother was born and grew up. The survival of the family house enables us to imagine something of her life (Alcock and Bearman 2002). The house in 1556 was still an open hall with a central fire and 'bacon in the roof'; there was a kitchen at one end with storerooms; Robert's bedchamber at the other with a sleeping platform above for daughters and maidservants. Outside were barns and outhouses. The inventory of Robert's goods attached to his will lists furnishings, utensils and possessions in the house, among them cushions, bolsters and mattresses – signs of comfort noted by

William Harrison in his *Description of England*, even among 'inferior artificers and many farmers, who, by virtue of their old and not of their new leases, have, for the most part, learned also to garnish their cupboards with plate, their joined beds with tapestry and silk hangings, and their tables with carpets and fine napery' (Harrison 1577, Book II, chapter 10). Among the fine cloths, some were perhaps those of 'Ypres work' later mentioned in Mary's sister's will. In the 1550s painted cloths and wall hangings were signs of middle-class aspirations, which are also indicated in the upward marriages Robert made for his older daughters.

The inventory also illuminates women's work in Mary's household. Between the mid fifteenth and mid seventeenth centuries the experience of the majority of working women was farmwork, housewifery and service (Whittle 2005, p. 51). This included manual work: later medieval rural women by and large 'belonged to a working class and participated in manual agricultural labour' (Hilton 1975, p. 97). This kind of work will change through the sixteenth century for prosperous peasantry like the Ardens, but the inventory shows it was still Mary's world. As the majority of young women between sixteen and twenty-five worked at some point as servants in other households, it is possible that Mary worked away for a time in her teens, even in Stratford. But in the 1550s, with no sons, Robert may have depended more than usual on women's labour. Many of the tasks on the Arden farm were women's jobs: brewing ale (a key part of the diet), milking, making butter, cheese and bread, feeding the pigs, tending the vegetable and herb gardens; all these are described in Fitzherbert's *Book of Husbandry* (1523) as the day-to-day routine of a rural housewife (Dyer 2001).

As Mary was the youngest, and four sisters had already left home by the time she was in her late teens, it is reasonable to assume she would have helped her father on all these tasks and perhaps in the fields too, especially as Robert was now in his sixties. Sixteenth-century engravings show women haymaking and winnowing. Robert also had an eight-ox ploughteam: and though he may have hired a day labourer for ploughing, his unmarried daughters may also have helped with the harrow, and even the plough – carrying the goad, for example.

Robert also had horses with which to ride to Stratford or Coventry, and no doubt Mary learned to ride early: she may have had use of a horse – her personal seal, still attached to her Snitterfield lease of 1579, has a horse as her emblem (SBT ER 30/1; Schoenbaum 1975, p. 38). When she went to Worcester, thirty miles away, in December 1556 to prove her father's will, we may assume she rode, if with a male neighbour like Adam Palmer; similarly on journeys to market in Stratford or to her father's land at Snitterfield.

Mary then grew up with a wide range of practical skills and deep knowledge of how a farm should be run; knowledge of seasonal planting and pruning, livestock health, and presumably traditional medicine too. Much of this she would have passed on to her children. For example, to cite a very simple instance, most of the words for farm implements, tools, utensils, linen and cloths in her father's inventory are part of her eldest son's vocabulary (Crystal 2002) . Other influences may be less obvious but no less important; a household full of women (Robert remarried in 1548–1550 Agnes Hill, who brought her own children into the house), where women did many tasks of work and 'business', and generally outlived their menfolk, cannot but have impressed itself on her attitudes, and through her those of her children.

But could Mary also read, or even write? The question might have relevance to her husband's business affairs and book keeping. But it could also throw light on the kind of reading her children might have encountered at home, if, as we might infer, they (or at least the boys?) had acquired basic reading skills before attending grammar school. Studies of wives of the lower yeomanry and well-off peasantry (Spufford 1974) suggest reading was becoming widespread among women – chapbooks, religious self-help and cheap romances – and simply to be named executrix of her father's will suggests Mary had the ability to read and add up. This should not be a surprise. Education has always been seen as conferring status as well as skills. The Virgin Mary is frequently depicted being taught to read by St Anne, and is usually shown reading when Gabriel arrives; heroines in popular romances were also readers. So in a competitive and acquisitive society, women wanting to get on in the world, or to help their husbands in business, would wish to do so too.

Elementary education was widespread in the early sixteenth century among the middling ranks of society – gentry, yeomanry, substantial tradesmen, shopkeepers – both for sons and daughters (Orme 2006, pp. 244–54). Elementary teaching took place mostly at home where there were literate parents. It was also available in some places for a small fee from a teacher in a private house. In the fifteenth century there are even references to schoolmistresses, who must have taught in their houses, and they must have existed in Mary's day too. Parish clerks and chantry priests seem to have often taught schools in churches (in the nave or a side-chapel, as at Aston) and there is no reason why they should not have taught girls as well as boys.

Reading then is possible for Mary. Writing is a different matter because it needs more lengthy and careful teaching and would therefore cost more, and hence was seen as primarily useful for men who handled business. Mary's use of mark and seal in her attestation of documents is therefore of great interest. There was a long tradition of using seals by peasants, even villeins; but on the Snitterfield lease of October 1579, SBT ER 30/1, the parchment endorsement attached to the seal, is a well-penned initial M, annotated by the clerk as 'the mark of Mary Shakespeare' (Schoenbaum 1975, p. 38; Honan 1998, pp. 14–15). Though her husband's mark is a crude cross, hers is a practised initial with a decorative flourish, which follows the standard pattern books of secretary hand. On the face of it, this could be her autograph. On a second document from the same day, SBT ER 30/2, the parchment tag bearing her seal also has Mary's mark, which appears to be less accomplished (though the nib has slipped over the crumpled parchment) but has clear traces of a similarly embellished M, beginning a longer word, presumably Mary. As things stand, then, it is not possible to be confident about Mary's literacy.

On Mary's religion more confidence is possible, at least for the first twenty-five years of her life, up to the beginning of Elizabeth's reign. Religion is a controversial aspect of the poet's background, but Mary's parents, born in the late fifteenth century, like all English people were Roman Catholics, and no doubt so was she. Modern re-evaluations have shown the Old Faith in rude health up to the 1530s and a very lukewarm response to the hardline policies of Edward before the return of Catholicism under Queen Mary in 1553 (Duffy 1992). Robert made his will in late November 1556 (when his daughter was perhaps twenty-one) and commends himself to 'Allmyghtye God and to our bleside Laydye Sent Marye and to all the holye companye of heven'. The formula is conventional, but it does not belong to a convinced Protestant; and the vicar who attests the will would soon be removed for his adherence to the Old Faith. This is to be expected in the time before Elizabeth's accession in rural Warwickshire; town and country, of course, were separate worlds, and the pace of change was faster in Stratford where we see accommodation to the government's demands by 1580 (Bearman 2007); but things were much slower in the countryside, as is shown by the 1585 Warwickshire Priests Survey ('How miserable the state of the church'). Of 186 priests, 120 are said to be 'dumbe' (unforthcoming) and 48 certain or suspected Catholics. As late as 1585 less than half of the parishes even had the authorised bible; a third didn't reply to the government's questions at all (Savage and Fripp 1929, pp. 2–8; Barratt 1955 and 1971).

Bearing this in mind we might conclude that Mary grew to adulthood in an old fashioned ritualised Catholicism of a kind found across much of rural England up to the mid sixteenth century. The murals she knew on the church walls at Aston Cantlow, showing Time with a scythe and Death as a skeleton with spade, have long disappeared, but it is the kind of faith we can see in the Guild Chapel murals in Stratford, whitewashed in winter 1563 when Mary was pregnant with her eldest son. Some only painted in the early sixteenth century, these give a vivid picture of local piety, the old stories and myths: St Helena and the finding of the True Cross; Thomas Becket; St George and the Dragon; the female saints Modwenna and possibly Ursula. Stories, thought worlds, images of the Golden Legend painted on plaster, these were the tales of Mary's childhood and youth.

So when Elizabeth came to the throne, the year Mary and John lost their first child, it is safe to assume Mary was still a traditional English Christian. More than that we are reduced to conjecture, but it may be significant that in 1585 the family chose as godparents for their grandchildren loyal old Catholics, or that as late as 1606 Mary's granddaughter, Susanna, joined them in refusing Easter communion (Brinkworth 1972, pp. 44–9). The possibility should at least be entertained that the women of the family retained some affection for the old religion.

A last aspect of this family hinterland is the life of the imagination, in which in a traditional society religion intermingles with folk story myth and legend. The old Christian culture of the countryside with its saints' tales, folk plays and festivals, Hock Day plays, St George and the Dragon street pageants, games and fairy tales – all this was part of the habit of mind in late medieval rural society. One local tale of especial interest is Guy of Warwick, a legendary ancestor of Thurkill of Arden and hence of Mary herself. Guy's tale was well known to William, who cites these stories from the early printed editions – had they been read to him? This and the related Bevis of Hampton and many other tales circulated in oral as well as written forms which enjoyed a surge of popularity in the early sixteenth century (Cooper 2012, pp. 170–203). Whether they were heard by the poet from his mother, we cannot prove, but it is likely.

To sum up, thin as the evidence is, it is enough to locate Mary's family in a village community on the cusp of great change, material, social and religious. The historian would naturally assume that this rural world between the 1530s and 50s was part of the family memory for her children, especially her oldest son, born early in the reign of Elizabeth I when the future course of the Reformation was not yet clear. The remainder of this chapter will briefly look at her married life.

In late 1556 Mary was still unmarried along with her sister Agnes, who would stay in the Wilmcote house with her stepmother's family. The wording of the provisions of her father's will suggests Mary and her sisters were not on good terms with their father's second wife, and within months Mary married. The marriage was perhaps already planned before Robert's death, which took place between 24 November and 9 December 1556. Mary's husband must have been long known to her. Among Robert's holdings had been 80 acres in Snitterfield. Here Richard Shakespeare leased land from Robert. It is worth emphasising the very similar social backgrounds of the two families. Richard was also a husbandman, who had been bailiff at the little nunnery at Wroxall where two of his kinswomen were nuns; Richard too is named in the Knowle guild book. So these were well-off peasant families of very similar horizons, old-fashioned, loyal to the places of local piety, the guilds and shrines. Richard had at least two sons, Harry, and John, who it may be assumed was a little older than Mary. Soon after Robert Arden's death, most likely in 1557, Mary married John.

In such a marriage, on a farm, Mary would have had to look forward to hard work in house, field and garden; her horizon that of thousands of her class: to be wife, mother, worker, cook; with visits to nearby markets to sell cheese, eggs and poultry. But John had apprenticed as a glover, and bought a town house in 1556: the couple had ambitions. Possibly Mary had married below her, compared, say, with her sister Joan, wife of Edmund Lambert at Barton on the Hill, but the interlocking circles of the two families offered many opportunities to get on in the world: her sisters and the Aston neighbours; the business partners of her husband in Stratford and Snitterfield, the Webbes, Skinners and Grants, the Shakespeares of Packwood: through them they had access to many yeomen and gentry of the region.

So the move to the town changed the family's fortunes. The small towns in the Arden were growing in prosperity: Stratford had only 1,500 people but had a thriving market with opportunities for luxury trades, glovers, haberdashers and drapers, to meet the demands of the new middle class. John's Henley Street house (though it had outhouses and a workshop) was typical of this new world, with an upper floor and separate bedrooms. Newly wed, Mary perhaps now had servants.

At this point we reach the well-known part of Mary's story. She had eight children. Joan the firstborn died in her first weeks, Margaret aged one, and Anne aged seven. The second Joan survived with the four boys. (The daughters all bore the names of Mary's sisters, who presumably stood as godparents.) Mary had seven children in the first fifteen years of marriage, about one pregnancy every two years. Then there was a six-year gap till Edmund, by which time she must have been in her forties. Whatever Mary and John's private beliefs, all their surviving children were baptised Protestants. But these religious distinctions were more fluid than is often assumed. The Stratford town books show that the townsfolk rubbed along with each other through the 1560s and 70s (Bearman 2007); while in the countryside the many old Marian priests were happy to accommodate traditional people on baptisms, marriages and deaths, and prayers for the dead (Savage and Fripp 1929, pp. 2–8).

More important perhaps to the family was getting on in the world. Tudor people were quite hard headed, not saints (Duffy 1992, p. 591). Early Elizabeth's reign was a good time for the family: in the 1560s John rose in the world and no doubt Mary's land and money helped. In Wilmcote they developed Asbies, building a house on the land in the early years of their marriage, to lease out to a tenant. By 1569 John had risen to be alderman, bailiff and finally mayor.

Meanwhile John was also making money on the side as a woolman. According to Rowe, John had been a 'considerable dealer in wool' and archive discoveries in 1984 showed this to be true (Thomas 1985, p. 3). But with very large sums of money disbursed on trust, there was great danger if it all went wrong. In the late 1570s the family was plunged into financial disasters and John lost office. (Rowe's story about William being withdrawn from school before completing his education at this time – in 1578? – is surely true.) At this time Mary also lost her seven-year-old daughter Anne. A little more about her life can be gleaned from legal cases involving her husband, especially her mortgaging of her inheritance in 1579 (Thomas 1985, p. 5). Mary raised cash on her Snitterfield and Wilmcote lands from her sisters and brothers-in-law, with further loans which were not repaid: the quarrel with the Lamberts was especially bitter. What strains this placed on the marriage, both as partners and as parents, is impossible to say, though the conception of Edmund in summer 1579 after more than six years shows that, in the midst of their trials, the couple were still intimate.

Of Mary's later life we know next to nothing. Whether the aftermath of the Somerville plot touched Henley Street is unknown – the interrogations around Stratford remain unexamined. In autumn 1582 her eighteen-year-old eldest son got the twenty-six-year-old daughter of a Shottery husband-man pregnant. Next year, Mary became a grandmother, first of a girl in 1583, then twins in 1585. Some of her own children were still at home: Richard eleven, her youngest Edmund only four, so we may imagine a house full of youngsters. Soon afterwards perhaps William moved to London, leaving his wife and family in Henley Street: Mary's role in their upbringing while supporting her debt-ridden husband may have been important. In the late 1580s John left public life forever; the 1592 recusancy returns show him unwilling to go out 'for fear of process for debt' (Savage and Fripp 1929, pp. 149, 161; Schoenbaum 1975, p. 39). But in the 1590s the couple's anxieties began to lessen and they recovered both money and status. The older children were now working; Gilbert apprenticed as a haberdasher and Richard (born 1574) possibly as a glover. John became solvent again, helped no doubt by William's money from the theatre.

In August 1596 the death of her only grandson must have been a great blow to the family for which the College of Heralds award of arms that autumn can have been no compensation. But her husband was now a gentleman 'of good wealth and substance': the herald's notes say he was worth £500 and had married 'the daughter and one of the heyres of Robert Arden of Wilmcoote ... esquire' (Schoenbaum 1975, p. 167.) For his remaining five years the records are virtually silent. In 1597 Mary and John associated with William made a new attempt in court to get the Asbies estate back (Poole 1980). This went on to September 1601 when the lease expired, but despite William's financial muscle the case was clear in English law; Lambert kept Asbies and leased it to a new tenant. Lambert's claim that John hadn't paid back other debts cannot but have soured family relations. Mary never got her land back. In September that year, her husband died after forty-four years of marriage.

Of Mary's last seven years we know nothing; perhaps she stayed with Joan's family in Henley Street, or with William in New Place, till her death in September 1608. The England of her last years was a very different place from that of her childhood. Mary had lived through part of the reign of Henry VIII, all of Edward, Mary and Elizabeth, and part of James. Of her eight children, five lived to maturity, though only Joan to old age. Her eldest son William had no more children after twenty; Joan married late and had four children in her thirties, two of whom died young; the eldest never married. Mary's sons Gilbert, Richard and Edmund never married. The pattern is unusual for a Tudor family. The Shakespeare boys were not perhaps great home makers.

It is reasonable to think that Mary carried down into James I's reign the thought world of the pre-Reformation countryside in Warwickshire, which seems constantly present in her son's language and imagination. Studies on Shakespeare's upbringing tend to focus on the influence of grammar school and Latin learning, but it is surely likely that at least as important in shaping his ways of seeing was his mother.

My thanks to Chris Dyer and Nicholas Orme for their generous help and advice, to Eamon Duffy, Helen Cooper and Mairi MacDonald, and to Paul Taylor and the staff of the Shakespeare Centre Library and Archive.

WORKS CITED

Alcock, Nat and Bearman, Robert 2002. 'Discovering Mary Arden's House', *Shakespeare Quarterly* 53.1: 53–82

Barratt, D. M. 1955 and 1971. *Ecclesiastical Terriers of Warwickshire Parishes*. Oxford. Dugdale Society

Bearman, Robert 2007. 'The Early Reformation Experience in a Warwickshire Market Town', *Midland History*: 68–109

Bickley, W. B. 1894. *The Register of the Guild of Knowle Birmingham*. Walsall. W. H. Robinson

Brinkworth, E. R. C. 1972. *Shakespeare and the Bawdy Court.* Chichester. Phillimore

Cooper, Helen 2012. *Shakespeare and the Medieval World.* London. Arden

Crystal, David 2002. *Shakespeare's Words.* London. Penguin

Duffy, Eamon 1992. *The Stripping of the Altars.* New Haven. Yale University Press

Eccles, Mark 1961. *Shakespeare In Wawickshire.* Madison. University of Wisconsin Press

Harrison, W. 1577. *A Description of England.* London. www.fordham.edu/halsall/mod/1577harrison-england.asp

Hilton, Rodney 1975. *The English Peasantry in the Later Middle Ages.* Oxford University Press

Honan, Park 1998. *Shakespeare: A Life.* Oxford University Press

Jones, Emrys 1977. *The Origins of Shakespeare.* Oxford University Press

MacDonald, Mairi 2007. *The Register of the Guild of the Holy Cross Stratford-upon Avon.* Stratford-upon-Avon. The Dugdale Society

Orme, Nicholas 2006. *English Medieval Schooling.* New Haven. Yale University Press

Poole, E. 1980. 'John and Mary Shakespeare and the Aston Cantlow Mortgage', *Cahiers Elisabéthains* 17: 21–41

1983. 'Shakespeare's Kinfolk and the Arden Inheritance', *Shakespeare Quarterly* 34.3: 311–24

Savage, Richard and Fripp, E. I. 1929. *Minutes and Accounts of the Corporation of Stratford-upon-Avon.* Vol. 1. Stratford-upon-Avon. The Dugdale Society

Schoenbaum, S. 1975. *William Shakespeare: A Documentary Life.* Oxford University Press

Spufford, Margaret 1974. *Contrasting Communities.* Cambridge University Press

Thomas, David 1985. *Shakespeare in the Public Records.* London. HMSO

Whittle, Jane 2005. 'Housewives and Servants in Rural England 1440–1650', *Transactions of the Royal Historical Society* 15: 51–74

2

His father John Shakespeare

DAVID FALLOW

§

The first biography of William Shakespeare in 1709 describes the play-wright's father as 'a considerable dealer in wool' (Rowe 1709, p. ii). Winnow out the subsequent speculative or anecdotal descriptions of John Shakespeare and what emerges is a successful self-made man, active in the business that then dominated the nation's economy. He lived almost two decades longer than his famous son, dying in 1601 aged 71 or so, still litigating on business debts in his final years.

John Shakespeare's apparent standing in the Stratford community changed over his lifetime, but there were solid financial reasons for this as legislation and regulation sought to restrict those who dealt in wool. Both father and playwright son died wealthy landed gentlemen, and the similarities in their handling of money rather than the differences in career choices have, remarkably, been largely ignored. Sufficient records exist to show how the Shakespeare fortune was accumulated, and understanding the economic necessities of their business illuminates much of the family's lives. William Shakespeare was never the romantic poor boy from an impoverished family. To better comprehend the son, we must understand the father. William Shakespeare's 'works' are poems and plays; John Shakespeare's 'work' was broking wool and lending money. Here I present a revisionist view of the father's business success through reference to Stratford-upon-Avon's borough records, his court cases and an analysis of English woolbroking in the sixteenth century. John Shakespeare was, in reality, a successful and astute individual who voluntarily left public life when his woolbroking business was threatened. Through an analysis of the social, political and economic contexts surrounding the 1576 Royal proclamation against woolbrokers or 'broggers', it can be shown that the Shakespeare family never experienced any economic adversity. This has significant implications for understanding William Shakespeare's prosperity, shifting the onus away from his artistic endeavours to the family business.

The peasant apprentice: John Shakespeare's rise in Stratford-upon-Avon

Neither John Shakespeare's birth date nor ancestry is certain. The probability is that he was born around 1530, the son of Richard, a tenant farmer in Snitterfield, a village four miles north-east of Stratford. He had at least one brother, Henry, and possibly two or more. Though financially quite successful for tenant farmers, having elder brothers meant no prospect of inheritance for John Shakespeare and his only chance for advancement lay in apprenticeship. A neighbour in Snitterfield was related to a local glover, Thomas Dickson, an Alderman on the first town council. It was probably under him that John Shakespeare undertook 'an apprenticeship of at least seven years to become a glover and whittawer, or dresser of white leather' (Schoenbaum 1975, p. 14).

No record survives of his schooling, numeracy or literacy. The harsh reality for an apprentice glover would have been labouring outdoors, beating cold stinking hides, and scraping filth from pieces of leather.

Entry into a Master's Guild remained far from automatic at the end of an apprenticeship. Only one in three ever rose to be 'freemen' – married householders and independent craftsmen. John Shakespeare was one that did. Parish records of the time are patchy, and the date and location of the nuptials of John Shakespeare to Mary Arden are unknown. Apprenticeships customarily started around sixteen for boys; add seven years and this suggests a wedding between 1556 and 1558.

For John Shakespeare to marry into even a humble branch 'of the ancient house of the Ardens of Park Hall' would certainly have needed the approval of both families (Chambers 1930, I, p. 12). Mary Arden was the 'daughter of that Robert from whom the [Shakespeare] grandfather had held land'. She was an heiress: 'in a small way ... Robert left her some land in Wilmcote called Asbies by his will of 1556, and had probably settled other property upon her' (Chambers 1930, I, p. 37). John Shakespeare bought property in the town and by 1590 owned two houses in Henley Street later known as the 'Birthplace' and the 'Woolshop', indicating success in business.

John Shakespeare's arrival in the town was timely (Fallow 2008, p. 253). Medieval governmental structures were replaced with borough status and a new class of successful, self-made citizen emerged between the labourers and the aristocracy. The borough operated as an autonomous hierarchical legal entity run by unpaid citizens nominated by their fellows. Executive authority sat with the annually elected Bailiff (Mayor), assisted by the Sub-Bailiff. Both men also served as Justices of the Peace (judges) in the town's permanent Court of Record. The governing body, the Corporation or (Town) Council, comprised fourteen Aldermen – senior town councillors, and fourteen Burgesses – junior councillors. To rise to Bailiff typically involved a series of civic posts of increasing importance. However, such status was usually matched by a successful career in business, and the senior members of the council were generally the town's principal merchants and tradesmen.

Civic responsibility was decidedly double-edged and more complex than today. Then, as well as granting seniority, it brought vulnerability to taxation, balanced by the opportunity for both legitimate and illegitimate financial gain. Many modern central government responsibilities were left to ordinary citizens. These included the quality control of food and beverages, financial management, local-level justice, sanitation, policing, fire-fighting, supervision of education, product quality control, licensing, and the equipping and training of soldiers.

John Shakespeare rose to Bailiff after holding numerous posts, some at personal risk of violence or disease. He accumulated goodwill, for following his voluntary withdrawal from public office (and public life) in 1576, the borough listed him as an Alderman for ten years afterwards. Moreover, they exempted him from taxation – an obvious advantage to any businessman, for Elizabethan taxes were many and varied at both national and borough level (Savage 1926, III, p. XXXVI).

In 1561, having been juror, taster and constable, he became a Chamberlain. Significantly, all of his posts linked into the legal process and he would have been habitually in the town's court. The expertise he acquired from this and his own numerous lawsuits clearly made him knowledgeable of the law.

Stratford-upon-Avon had two chamberlains, one senior in his second year in the role, the junior in his first. All borough-funded activity fell under their personal management; they were the town's 'general receiver[s]' (Wilkinson 1620, p. 137). In 1562, as Senior Chamberlain, John Shakespeare directed the protestantisation of the Chapel. Not under Episcopal jurisdiction, the Guild Chapel had been left intact, but as Edgar Fripp notes: 'It was not spared under the auspices of John Shakespeare' (Savage 1921, I, p. LI). However, C. J. Sisson suggests that Fripp's scholarship could be tainted by his personal beliefs, that his '"Protestant" and "Liberal" bias, the inevitable concomitant of Mr Fripp's own strong convictions', could lead to erroneous conclusions (Sisson 1939, p. 433). But setting his predilections aside, Fripp's factual understanding of Stratford-upon-Avon during the Shakespeares' time remains a valuable research tool.

Twelve months later John Shakespeare's term of office should have ended, but he continued in the role. At a Council meeting in January 1563 the minutes record the Corporation owing 'unto John Shakespeare £1 5s 8d' – suggesting he used his own money on the town's behalf (Savage 1921, I, p. 130).

'*Hic incepit pestis*' – 'here the plague begins' – wrote the Vicar in July 1564 (Savage 1921, I, p. LII). Minutes of 30 August show that 'money was paid towards the relief of the poor', John Shakespeare contributing a shilling. Additional levies followed; in September he paid 6d on two occasions, rising to 8d in October (Savage 1921, I, p. LIII). This is useful information for it places him in the lower half of the town's councillors by contribution. At the next civic elections, with the plague at its height, he remained Chamberlain for a fourth year and his third as Acting (Senior) Chamberlain. That week saw nineteen burials.

In 1565, acknowledging his service, John Shakespeare became 'Master Shakespeare'. The father of the then eighteen-month-old infant William became an Alderman. Nominated as Bailiff in 1567, he was elected the following year. His oath of office was 'to the uttermost of your cunning, wit and power [to] maintain and defend the liberties of the same borough and shall do equal right as well to the poor as to the rich' (Savage 1929, p. 352). As Bailiff and Justice of the Peace he presided at the borough's Court of Record. Justices of the Peace were the Crown's representatives in the town, a system that cost 'practically nothing to operate ... it exacted obedience not through force but through respect ... it typified that attachment of political obligation to social advantage ... the heart of Tudor political philosophy' (Bindoff 1950, p. 57).

In 1571 John Shakespeare became deputy to the new Bailiff, his friend, Adrian Quiney, and their 'first act ... was to dispose of the Romanist vestments remaining at the Gild Chapel' (Savage 1924, II, p. XXV). On 10 October the council resolved 'that Master Quiney should sell the copes and vestments here underwritten to the use of the Chamber and yield account of all such money' (Savage 1924, II, p. XXVI). Subsequently it was agreed 'that Master Adrian Quiney and Master John Shakespeare shall ... deal in the affairs of the borough [in London] according to their discretions' (Savage 1924, II, p. XXVI). John Shakespeare was representing the borough in London and dealing with senior aristocrats or their servants.

The brogger: wool dealing in sixteenth-century England

How did the glover's apprentice become 'a considerable dealer in wool'? Guilds vigorously patrolled their rights and in towns such as Stratford-upon-Avon a portion of all guild fees went to support the borough itself. Competition was simply not open to incomers. To understand the Shakespeares' rise to wealth requires an analysis of the wool market itself, for changes in the trade are reflected in both their business and personal lives.

By the early 1500s, a profound economic shift began away from the export of raw wool, previously the country's economic cornerstone, to the sale of woollen cloth. By 1565, cloth accounted for three-quarters of exports; raw wool slumped to just over 6 per cent (Stone 1949, p. 37). Rising demand and the switch to manufacturing created the opportunity for intermediaries among the growers, manufacturers and exporters.

Historically, control of the export trade was vested in the exclusive 'Company of Merchant Staplers' and only a Stapler could legally export wool through Calais (Unwin 1918, p. 221). Despite their efforts to depress domestic prices and maximise their gain, the demand for cloth outstripped wool availability, creating a scarcity that drove prices up while attracting new dealers lured by the prospect of profits from the higher prices. Short-term fluctuations aside, the century after John Shakespeare's birth saw wool prices increase fourfold (Bowden 1962, p. 82).

All this upheaval fuelled the wool broking business enabling 'A trend towards regional specialization ... due [principally] to the rise of classes of professional middlemen' (Bowden 1962, p. 77). This weakening of market structure permitted John Shakespeare to enter what had previously been a regulated market.

Foreigners trading in England with licences (some fraudulent) were one issue for the authorities, but locally three distinct groups of quasi-legal English traders emerged from this *mêlée* (Rich 1937, p. 10). First, there were the Staplers who, after the fall of Calais, pursued the English domestic market. Next came the professions whose activity involved hides – the glovers and leather traders who were traditionally permitted to sell wool removed from hides. Chief amongst these were the 'Glovers of the Central and East Midlands [who] were great wool dealers' (Bowden 1962, p. 82). Glovers such as John Shakespeare had sufficient wealth to finance purchases and contacts, created through service as bailiffs or mayors, to place the commodity with manufacturers and exporters. Last came the clothiers who bought for their own production needs. The term 'brogging' – the unlicensed trading in wool – applies in varying degrees to all three. However, 'brogger' with its disparaging connotation was more often applied to the smaller dealers who formed the bulk of the non-Staplers. The market was consolidating into fewer large traders and manufacturers, although smaller broggers were eventually acknowledged as vital to the smaller manufacturers in poor areas (Hewart 1900, p. 25).

Between 1550 and 1600, peaking in the 1570s, the selling of wool trading licences was a crucial source of Crown revenue. Licensees were irate when illegal traders went unpunished, but no consistent means of enforcing business regulation existed. The early 1570s saw the widespread sale of fraudulent licences and Proclamation 621/712 (Hampton Court) of November 1576 tried to resolve this by requiring all 'licences to be returned into the Exchequer for revision within two months' (Youngs 1976, p. 131). In 1577, supporting the proclamation, the Privy Council ordered Justices of the Peace in twenty counties to obtain £100 bonds from broggers 'that they would not buy for resale' (Youngs 1976, p. 131). But the local Justices (as John Shakespeare had been) proved reluctant to take action against their own wool middlemen (which John Shakespeare was) and accordingly the response remained a 'trickle' (Hewart 1900, p. 131).

Later in 1577 the Staplers lobbied unsuccessfully for a proclamation banning glovers from selling wool left on fleeces – directly aimed at putting broggers such as John Shakespeare out of business (Dasent 1894, p. 386;

1895, p. 24). However, by 1581 the Privy Council conceded the need for middlemen and let licences be used again, though this was no permit for unlicensed broggers.

Throughout John Shakespeare's career, rising prices fuelled the growth of the wool broking business and spawned groups of legal, quasi-legal and downright illegal traders. The authorities were ineffective in controlling the process while changes in markets forced a concentration of the export trade through London. To survive, the Shakespeare family business had to have a London representative. The probability is that business, not plays or poems, first took William Shakespeare to the capital.

Businessman: John Shakespeare the 'considerable dealer in wool'

In 1984, four court cases were highlighted where John Shakespeare was prosecuted as both usurer and illegal wool dealer – 'not titles which have traditionally been associated with Shakespeare's father' (Thomas and Evans 1984, p. 315).

Tudor Parliaments, unable to police tax levies, encouraged informers to bring cases to the courts in return for half the fine. This practice is often referred to in abbreviated form as '*qui tam*' cases from the Latin description which translates into, 'he who sues for the queen as well as for himself'. Trade already relied on credit, yet, reflecting earlier notions of interest as sinful, the law ran contrary to economic reality (Thomas and Evans 1984, p. 315). The Act of 1545 (TNA 37 Hen. 8, c.9) allowed interest up to 10 per cent per annum; however, pressure from religious quarters resulted in its replacement in 1552 (TNA 5 & 6 Edw. 6, c.20) that prohibited 'usury, a vice most odious'. In 1570, John Shakespeare was convicted under the 1552 Act (Wells and Dobson 2001). In 1571 the law was relaxed through a new statute (13 Eliz. 1, c.8), whereby lenders charging 10 per cent or less forfeited only their interest (previously principal and interest plus fines and imprisonment).

In 1570:

one of the barons [judges] of the exchequer exhibited an information by Anthony Harrison ... [who] claimed that John Shakespeare of 'Stratford upon Haven', Glover, had ... given to a certain John Mussum ... in Warwickshire the sum of £100. The principle was to be repaid ... to Shakespeare together with £20 interest . . . as the loan was a clear breach of a statute of 1552, Harrison demanded that Shakespeare forfeit the capital and interest and that he be imprisoned and fined . . . there is no further record after the accusation (Thomas and Evans 1984, p. 315).

This case was heard in the Court of Exchequer and the transcripts remain in The National Archives (TNA). John Shakespeare apparently avoided penalty, though he fared worse in another case (TNA E 159–359 Hil, p. 237). Self-appointed bounty hunters obtained money either by dragging their victims into court or by 'compounding' with them (Beresford 1957, p. 221; Thomas and Evans 1984, p. 315). The final adjudication of a two-pound fine was derisory given transactions of several hundred pounds that evidence a well-to-do merchant. But even a symbolic fine, when coupled with possible illegal compounding, surely made John Shakespeare more guarded in his business dealings.

Would professional informers in 1570 have bothered pursuing a minor trader through the London courts? One analysis shows that only 7 per cent of prosecutions involved wool (Beresford 1957, p. 221). Moreover, in the plague year of 1569 there were no brogging prosecutions at all and in 1570 only fourteen, with a modest twenty-five the following year.

John Shakespeare's cases permit a comparison with other large wool traders. The first involved buying 2,800 pounds of wool at sixpence per pound (weight) from the local aristocratic Grant family. Later that year 5,600 pounds of wool was bought from Walter Newsam, whose memorial now stands in the abandoned church of All Saints, Chadshunt near Stratford-upon-Avon. This was wool sourced from the biggest producers in villages and estates surrounding the town. In value terms these amount to £210 and are comparable to the activities of three other large traders: Thomas Adkins of Northampton, a glover who served as Bailiff; Richard Baynes, a Merchant of the Staple; and George Rugle a Suffolk clothier. Though their dealings post-date the John Shakespeare cases, the lot sizes, values and counterparties are similar to those in his indictments (Bowden 1962, p. 81). To buy 5,600 pounds of wool from one breeder meant that his flock would have been at least 1,600 sheep (Allison 1958, p. 100). Few farmers would have had such a flock and six pence per pound indicates premium pricing. A single transaction of £140 was very large in 1572 (Bowden 1962, p. 27).

Broggers usually bought a grower's entire wool clip, stored it, and then resold it in smaller lots. The goods were not standardised, nor were the terms of trade or the means of collection and delivery. Constant quality inspection and supervision against theft were necessary. Wagons to transport the wool needed more than just a driver, as breakdowns were regular occurrences. Even a regional level trader needed financial resources, trusted employees, equipment, and storage or distribution facilities. To prosper, a brogger needed help and sons were the logical choice. To suggest that the eldest Shakespeare boy, William, was exempt is most unlikely.

John Shakespeare's business and litigation span five decades. Known cases are incompletely documented, but they show the range of his commercial activities. In 1906 Thomas Carter writes: 'He [John Shakespeare] was one of the most litigious of men' but he tempers his enthusiasm by acknowledging that 'nearly every businessman in Stratford had been proceeded against in this way' (Carter 1906, 166; p. 200). Many suits in this period were, in reality, legal posturing, debt recording or plain commercial manoeuvrings. Later analyses have been more conservative than Carter's, but based on analysis of John Shakespeare's Court of Record appearances, his litigiousness does match that of a successful merchant 'of the middling sort' (Bearman 2005, p. 414). Robert Bearman notes seventeen suits between 1556 and 1570, eleven as plaintiff. Nor are the thirty-one years after 1570 void of legal activity, with his last case in 1599 being a suit against the former Mayor of Marlborough for £21 worth of wool. John Shakespeare's business activities were not small, either in scale or value. The Shakespeare family investments of the 1590s – land, titles and houses – had to be funded, and the family business is a far more credible source of funds than William's theatrical career, which was, at that time, in its infancy.

The fall from financial grace: did it happen?

After a council meeting in November 1576 John Shakespeare withdrew from public life. He ceased to attend council meetings, the only recorded exception being to vote for a friend in an election. He stopped paying taxes. His efforts to obtain 'gentlemanly' status were abandoned, even though these were already under way. Lastly, he stopped attending church and he and his family became recusants. The years after 1576 also brought a flurry of asset disposals into 'friendly' hands. The popular assumption is that unidentified business failure impoverished the family. One court entry of 1586 states John Shakespeare had nothing to be 'distrained' – capable of seizure to ensure. But in 1889 Halliwell-Phillipps refutes the 'sudden poverty' argument:

there can be no doubt whatever that the words ... *Johannes Shackspere nihil habet unde distringi potest* [John Shakespeare has nothing able to be distrained] are not to be taken literally, and that they merely belong to a formula that was in use when a writ of distringas [seizure for debt] failed in enforcing an appearance. (Halliwell-Phillipps 1889, II, p. 238)

Gamesmanship over debts, ignoring a case till the last moment or disregarding it until it was clear the other party would not give up, were common business tactics and this case was ultimately dropped or settled out of court. Moreover, John was placed on juries twice shortly afterwards and good standing in the borough can reasonably be inferred (Halliwell-Phillipps 1889, II, p. 238).

Scholars have either ignored Halliwell-Phillipps's caveat or find it more convenient to take the court statement as *prima facie* evidence. Opinions have hardened in recent years. In 1930, E. K. Chambers writes of 'indications of a decline in his fortunes', but he balances this with 'he was still in a position to spend £40 on property in 1575' (Chambers 1930, I, p. 14). F. E. Halliday considers that 'The twenty years 1576–96 appear to be years of adversity' (Halliday 1964, p. 441). Into the twenty-first century there are even more emphatic statements between 2002 and 2006 that John Shakespeare's financial problems become 'well documented' or his home exhibited 'grinding poverty' (Duncan-Jones 2001, p. 14). He supposedly feared 'arrest for debt' (Bearman 2005, p. 417) and lived 'in fear of being dunned for unpaid debts' (Pogue 2006, p. 2).

The courts relied heavily on co-guarantors for indemnification against failure to appear and in 1580 John Shakespeare was fined £40, half for his own non-appearance, the balance for not delivering another individual. This £40 is taken by some as proof of poverty while still failing to explain how, if insolvent, it was paid. In this particular case the effect of so many co-guarantors was confusion, as the jurisdictional limit of an individual court's authority was based on Church dioceses. In Elizabethan England the courts themselves simply had no means of co-ordinating fines in complex cases straddling numerous locations. Fripp observes:

The distribution of the security is striking ... John Shakespeare and his two sureties ... were in three dioceses under separate jurisdictions, and the procedure for the getting of the fines imposed would be so complex that we may well doubt whether they were [ever] paid (Savage 1924, p. XLI).

Friends, religion and literacy: three aspects of John Shakespeare's character

John Shakespeare had life-long friends who were both neighbours and fellow Aldermen. An examination of the town's records shows how tight some of these interpersonal relationships became, with children being named after neighbours and friendships becoming transgenerational. Moreover, these relationships transcend religious schism.

Among the 'middling sort' the sons customarily joined the family business and maintained the tradition of civic service. But John Shake-speare's sons do not fit the second part of the pattern, none ever serving on the council in any capacity whatsoever. Unusually, we have scant data (beyond buying property) on what the Shakespeare sons actually did in Stratford over the decades following 1576. This could be accidental, but it is more likely to reflect calculated caution around their finances. The Shakespeare family's tax manipulations are subjects in themselves; suffice to note here that William Shakespeare, like his father, avoided taxes (Chambers 1930, II, pp. 88–90).

No unequivocal evidence of the Shakespeare family's religious beliefs exists. Certainly the law forced nominal conformity to the Anglican church. But were they closet Catholics or even secret Puritans? On balance the Protestants have the slightly better claim, as John Shakespeare was active in the protestantisation of the Guild Chapel (Carter 1906, p. 70). For the Catholics there was the Borromeo Testament, a pamphlet (now lost) offered to Edmond Malone as a relic having John Shakespeare's name inscribed on the flyleaf. Malone himself rejected it as a forgery (Schoenbaum 1975, pp. 43–6). However, beyond doubt is the family's faith in money.

Equally perplexing is the question of John Shakespeare's literacy. There are some who take pains not to leave signatures or detailed financial records – sharp businessmen and tax dodgers among them. In stark contrast to Ben Jonson, aside from a few signatures, William Shakespeare left nothing (incontrovertibly) in his own script and neither did his father (Bland 2004, p. 393).

Schoenbaum questions whether John Shakespeare, despite managing the Stratford Town financial accounts for four years, could possibly have been unable to sign his name (Schoenbaum 1975, pp. 31–2). But the simplest explanations are that either he did sign, but just not in a manner common to contemporary eyes, or he chose not to leave a paper trail by ever suggesting he could write.

Borough officers often signed with a signum – a symbol. Chambers comments:

> In view of contemporary habits, it is no proof of inability to write that he [John Shakespeare] was accustomed to authenticate documents by a mark, which was sometimes a cross and sometimes a pair of glovers dividers. (Chambers 1930, I, p. 13)

C. J. Sisson comments:

> No survey of the subject can fail to observe the conflict between the ancientry and dignity of the mark and the newfangled qualifications for gentry or respectability by literacy. (Sisson 1928, p. 1)

John Shakespeare and his fellow Aldermen, true to their guilds, would always have made their mark. Reading was at the time viewed as an independent skill to penmanship; his writing skills remain simply unproven.

Stanley Wells, writing in 2002, comments:

> John Shakespeare also signed with a mark; it may seem hard to believe that one so able and successful in both public and business service was illiterate, but equally it is improbable that if he had indeed been able to write no document subscribed by him should have survived. (Wells 2002, p. 6)

William Shakespeare as a poor boy from an impoverished family bravely earning his extended family back to prosperity through participation in the Early Modern theatre makes a fine fable. But a broader study of his father challenges this myth. The examination of the Shakespeare family's financial affairs, borough records and the timing of the family's investments (virtually all made during John Shakespeare's lifetime and before the theatre could have supplied the funds) show the astute businessman and public figure. Both father and son were successful, self-made businessmen who made timely career choices while avoiding taxation. Chambers observes of Philip Henslowe – theatrical impresario and businessman – that his niceness was irrelevant; he was a 'capitalist' (Chambers 1923, I, p. 360). The same could be said of John Shakespeare.

The autocratic Elizabethan father had total sway over his family, who relied on him for their survival. Nothing suggests John Shakespeare deviated from this stereotype. The notion of employing men when he had healthy sons is simply not credible; his insisting they worked in the unregulated family business on an informal apprenticeship basis is therefore a logical possibility. William Shakespeare disappears from the record for seven years, the exact term of a traditional apprenticeship, and surfaces in London exactly where and when contacts in the wool trade would have been vital to the survival of the family business. Given John Shakespeare's relative market position in the English wool broking scene, the probability is that William first went to London as a businessman rather than as an impoverished poet.

WORKS CITED

Allison, K. J. 1958.'Flock Management in the Sixteenth and Seventeenth Centuries', *Economic History Review* 2.11: 98–112

Bearman, Robert 2005. 'John Shakespeare: A Papist or Just Penniless', *Shakespeare Quarterly* 56.4: 411–33

Beresford, M. W. 1957. 'The Common Informer, the Penal Statutes and Economic Regulation', *Economic History Review* 10.2: 221–38

Bindoff, S. T. 1950. *Tudor England*. London. Penguin

Bland, Mark 2004. 'Ben Jonson and the Legacies of the Past', *Huntington Library Quarterly* 67.3: 371–400

Bowden, Peter 1962. *The Wool Trade in Tudor and Stuart England*. London. Macmillan

Carter, T. 1906. *Shakespeare: Puritan and Recusant*. Edinburgh. Oliphant

Chambers, E. K. 1923. *The Elizabethan Stage*, 4 vols. Oxford University Press
   1930 *William Shakespeare*, 2 vols. Oxford. Clarendon Press

Dasent, J. R. (ed.) 1894. *Acts of the Privy Council of England Vol. 10*, 32 vols. London. HMSO
   1895 *Acts of the Privy Council of England Vol. 10*. London. HMSO

Duncan-Jones, Katherine 2001. *Ungentle Shakespeare*. London. Arden

Fallow, David 2008. 'Like Father Like Son: Financial Practices in the Shakespeare Family', *Studies in Theatre and Performance* 28.3 (2008): 253–63

Fripp, Edgar 1930. *Shakespeare Studies*. Oxford University Press

Halliday, F. E. 1964. *A Shakespeare Companion*. London. Penguin

Halliwell-Phillipps, J. O. 1889. *Outlines of the Life of Shakespeare*, 2 vols. London. Longmans

Hewart, Beatrice 1900. 'The Cloth Trade in the North of England in the Sixteenth and Seventeenth Centuries', *The Economic Journal* 10.37: 20–31

James, Mervyn 1974. *Family, Lineage and Civil Society*. Oxford University Press

Law, Jonathan, and Martin, Elizabeth E. 2009. *A Dictionary of Law*. Oxford University Press

Pogue, Kate Emery 2006. *Shakespeare's Friends*. London. Praeger

Rich, E. E. 1937. *The Ordinance of the Book of the Staple*. Cambridge University Press

Rowe, Nicholas 1709. *The Works of William Shakespear*. London. Tonson

Savage, Richard 1921–1929. *Minutes and Accounts of the Corporation of Stratford-upon-Avon and Other Records 1553–1620*, 4 vols. Oxford University Press

Schoenbaum, S. 1975. *William Shakespeare: A Documentary Life*. Oxford. Clarendon

Sisson, C. J. 1928. 'Marks as Signatures', *The Library* 9.1: 1–37. Oxford University Press

1939. 'Shakespeare Man and Artist by Edgar Fripp', *The Modern Language Review* (MHRA) 34.3: 433–4

Stone, Lawrence 1949. 'Elizabethan Overseas Trade', *The Economic History Review* 2.1: 30–58

Thomas, D. L., and Evans, N. E. 1984. 'John Shakespeare in the Exchequer', *Shakespeare Quarterly* 35.3: 315–18

TNA The National Archives

Unwin, George (ed.) 1918. *Finance and Trade Under Edward III* www.british-history.ac.uk/manchester-uni/london-lay-subsidy/1332/pp221-232 [accessed 6 May 2015]

Wells, Stanley 2002. *Shakespeare for All Time*. London. Macmillan

Wells, Stanley and Michael Dobson (eds.) 2001. *The Oxford Companion to Shakespeare*. Oxford University Press

Wilkinson, John 1620. *Court Leet*. London. Islip

Youngs, Frederic A. 1976. *The Proclamations of the Tudor Queens*. Cambridge University Press

3

His siblings

CATHERINE RICHARDSON

> Forasmuch as it hath pleased almighty God of his great mercy to
> take until him self the soul of our dear brother here departed: we
> therefore commit his body to the ground.   (1561, Piiii)

William Shakespeare had four siblings who survived into adulthood. Two
years after he was born a brother, Gilbert, arrived, and three years after that
a sister, Joan, about whom you can read elsewhere in this volume; in 1574,
when Shakespeare was 10, Richard arrived and finally, when he was 16,
Edmund.

Gilbert, who may have been named after Gilbert Bradley, a glover living
close to the family in Henley Street, apparently spent most of his life in
Stratford, where he often appears in the records, sometimes acting for
William. He did not marry, and died in 1612. There is also, however, a
record of a Gilbert Shackspere listed in 1597 as a haberdasher of St Bride's
in London, standing surety for William Sampson, a clockmaker from
Stratford-upon-Avon. This may be the same Gilbert, but new evidence
would be required to be sure.

About Richard we know next to nothing. Between his baptism on
11 March 1574 and burial on 4 February 1613, he made one appearance in
the ecclesiastical court in 1608 on an unspecified charge, and paid a fine of
12d to the poor for his fault (Schoenbaum 1975, p. 28).

Finally Edmund, probably named after Edmund Lambert, his mother's
brother-in-law, became an actor in London. In August 1607 a child who
appears to be his illegitimate son was buried in St Giles Cripplegate
(Schoenbaum 1975, p. 29). In the cruel winter which followed in which
the Thames froze before Christmas, Edmund himself was buried on
31 December in an expensive funeral in St Saviour's Southwark, between

40

London Bridge and the Globe. Someone, perhaps William, paid 20 shillings to have him buried in the church rather than the churchyard, and had him honoured 'with a forenoon knell of the great bell'. The words at the head of this chapter are part of the 'Order for the Burial of the Dead' which would have been spoken over his body. They invite us to think about the many meanings of that phrase 'dear brother'.

Brotherhood offered a model of behaviour for the male inhabitants of early modern towns. As well as referring to biological kin, 'brother' signalled various kinds of commonality such as fellow-Christian, its meaning in the burial service quoted above. But in an urban context it also meant 'a fellow-member of a guild, corporation, or order', or one of the same profession or trade. 'Brother' was the official title given to some members of livery companies and municipal corporations, and 'the brethren' referred to a company in general – theatre owner and manager Jacob Meade, for instance, gave his 'brethren the overseers of the Company of Watermen' 40 shillings to spend on his funeral day (*OED*; Honigmann and Brock 1993, p. 135). In Stratford the Guild of the Holy Cross, the medieval fraternity on which the town government was modelled after the Reformation, had required that 'every brother and sister that shall be received in this fraternity' be sworn to appropriately fraternal behaviour (Macdonald 2007, p. 37). In London, many of William and Edmund's fellow actors were apprenticed to masters who were both actors and guildsmen, including Andrew Cane who carried on his trade as a goldsmith, and many others who paid guild dues for parts of their working lives because they understood the benefits available to members of the brotherhood (Kathman 2004). The term, in other words, embodied the concept of working together as a group for mutual interest, rather than in a way that aimed at personal gain.

One brother who lived his life in Stratford, one in London, and one possibly between the two. I want to consider the part geography played in the strength and duration of Shakespeare's brotherly ties and to argue that thinking about the siblings as a circle, as this book encourages us to do, means focusing on how they may or may not have operated as a family, with a sense of their identity as the next generation of Shakespeares. When we consider an individual's familial position we usually look to the nuclear group of parents and children – the patriarchal relationships between the household head and his dependants. Thinking of Shakespeare as a brother, rather than a father or a son, helps us to understand him as part of a specifically middling-status family – one which might move up or down the social ladder from the position in which their father had set them, at the top of the urban administration of a medium-sized provincial town.

Work on the 'middling sort', as they were called in the early modern period, has shown them to be families in transition. Those who managed to rise to administrative prominence had a precarious hold on power: 'it remained rare in English towns for a single family to maintain its position at the top for more than a generation or two, three at the very most, before moving on in one social direction or another and being replaced' (Tittler and Jones 2004, p. 375). As William thought about his future, growing up amongst his brothers and sister in Stratford, there must have been a sense that the Shakespeares were poised, either to carry on in their influence there and the prosperity that went with it, or to move into the gentry as his father clearly intended. Not moving upwards might mean moving downwards, back into the ranks of less prosperous and influential traders and craftsmen. Focusing on siblings, therefore, means contemplating ambition and how it was managed in practical terms.

In this period reputation, honour and credit within one's society were the basis of social status – 'credit' had the dual senses of financial trust-worthiness and moral dependability, so the better your reputation the more money you might make. But these issues were not only, perhaps not even primarily *personal* ones: reputations belonged to families, and individuals added to or subtracted from the creditworthiness of their kin. Studying Shakespeare in relation to his siblings, then, means understanding him not as a strikingly unique individual, but as one of a group who might be expected to identify their futures in common.

We know much about the ways in which brothers were useful to one another, perhaps especially at death, because we have many records of them acting in one another's wills. Before death, the church courts that oversaw the moral health of the Midlands offer tiny vignettes that allow us to re-imagine the everyday sibling experiences that must have seemed normal to Shakespeare. The court's fundamental assumption was that brothers would be biased in some way in one another's affairs – witnesses in the courts are routinely asked what their relationship is with the parties in contention and brotherhood requires explanation: Richard Baker, for instance, says he is 'natural brother' to one of the parties 'and hath reason to favour and to be more familiar and conversant with him' than with the other party, 'And had rather wish him the victory for that he thinketh him to be wronged' (WAAS 794.052 Vol. 7, f.176). Wishing the victory to your brother was part of the ties of kinship that ensured a common purpose and shared set of goals.

These cases show different relationships between brothers close or far apart in age, a distinction that speaks to the gap between William and his younger siblings. As older brothers, independent householders in their own right, men might help one another in the administration of parish life: William Roe, yeoman of Halesowen, 'served a warrant for good behaviour on John Wood' in the supportive presence of his brother Henry, for example (794.052 Vol. 6, f.97v). Thomas Smith of Badsey stated that his neighbour came to his house and 'did withdraw this deponent into a private chamber with his brother Anthony Smith'. He entreated the brothers to witness his will, 'and withal desired their secrecy that his wife might not know thereof' (794.052 Vol. 6, f.87v). Working in pairs as equals, these older brothers gave one another various kinds of support, and offered gravitas and a greater authority than they could possess alone.

Some younger sons, on the other hand, were apprenticed formally or informally to their older brothers, who taught them their trade but also stood in the role of father to them. It was in the course of such instruction, while William Rose was working for his brother in his shop in Ilmington, for instance, that he heard one man say that another's 'wife was a whore and that one Richard Ballard had cried her a whore in Stratford' (794.052 Vol. 6, f.464). Anthony Best, seventeen years old, witnessed *his* brother's marriage from 'behind a bed', excluded from adult business: 'he liveth under his father and mother and his brother that instructeth him in his trade, and hath nothing as yet under his own hands' (794.052 Vol. 8, f.39v). If Edmund stood in such a dependent position in relation to his brother William, sixteen years his senior, within the London theatres, then we might imagine the latter both *in loco parentis* in their shared 'household' of the theatre and in the pedagogical role that he did not play with his own son.

Amongst these brief tales of brotherly assistance and familial identity, two strategies for sibling relationships linked to the geography of the individuals concerned are particularly prominent. One involves mature men who lived together relatively closely, keeping in touch often, both having reached the key early modern threshold of independent householder and therefore achieved a parity of status: John Rowland alias Stayner of the City of Worcester, gentleman, for example, states that he came 'oft times to see and visit the testator' his brother (794.052 Vol. 6, ff.448-v). At these times, the testator would usually complain to him of the 'miscarriage' of his son, Thomas Stayner, saying that if he left him his property he would spend it all 'to the utter undoing of his posterity and name'. The regular contact between these men allows them to support one another emotionally as well as professionally, offering an opportunity to discuss family outside its nuclear sense. Those Stratford brothers who worked together to further one another's careers in the same town often marked their closeness and their sense of the transfer of social identity between them by leaving one another their clothing in their wills. John Combe, for instance, gave his brother George 'my best suit of apparel and my second gown' as well as land (TNA PROB 11/126/415, 28/01/1613); John Smith gave his 'brother' Hamlet Sadler his gown, doublet and hat, and another 'brother' Richard Walker his jerkin of medley and his breeches (TNA PROB 11/101/512, 05/11/1601). These objects were worth money, but more importantly they demon-strated, in minute gradations of cloth and trimming, the urban status of their wearer. Bequeathing them allowed the absorption of a dead brother's visual identity back into the familial sibling reserves, even though his land and property might be passed to his sons. This is the model that Shakespeare's London move stretched geographically – close in age, Gilbert and William might have acted like this if the latter had stayed in Stratford. Had he not died before him, William might then have left his clothes to Gilbert instead of his sister Joan (who probably sold them).

In the other paradigm, brothers support one another from afar, often earlier in their lives, and that assistance is part of a wider family network which advances marriage prospects and secures career training. Historian Ilana Krausman Ben-Amos's work shows:

Ties of kin provided individuals with options for concentrating and distributing capital, entering careers and new social milieus, consolidating trusted networks and obtaining multiple forms of more casual help and support ... crucial to the sustenance of families among middling groups.

These networks included London contacts in trade, kin who 'supervised purchases and sales, safeguarded monetary transactions over long distances and provided intelligence and exclusive information on prices, markets and the credit value of customers' (Ben-Amos 2008, pp. 79, 53). In Chapter 2 of this volume you will see the possibility raised that Shakespeare originally came to London as a representative of his father's brogging business. The Records of London's Livery Companies Online (ROLLCO) show Warwickshire providing as much as 6 per cent of the annual number of apprentices in the early seventeenth century; Stratford neighbour Isabell Bardall writes 'To her loving kinsman' Quiney in London, commending herself 'most humbly unto you', to pray him 'for God's cause if possible you can to provide me a place in London for my eldest son with some handicraft man' (SBTRO ER1/97, ff.112v–113). Marriage and business were closely linked through family ties that fused the two. Hamnet Sadler's sister, Jane, married Ralph Ridley of London, coming back at the end of her life to be buried in Stratford. Robert Harvard of Southwark married Katherine Rogers of Stratford in her home town: both the Harvards and the Rogers were butchers and their son John, later famous as the founder of Harvard University, was baptised at Southwark on 29 November 1607, just under a month before Edmund Shakespeare was buried there, the coincidence emphasising the interpenetration of London and Stratford connections.

Gilbert seems to have come closest to this way of working amongst the Shakespeare brothers: he certainly acted as a kind of agent for William later in life. When he represents his brother in 1602 at a land transaction, the document is 'sealed and delivered unto Gilbert Shakespere to the use of the within named William Shakespere' (Schoenbaum 1975, p. 190). He is standing in for him in such a way that William can be administratively, *authoritatively* present although he is *physically* absent. The bias of brothers ensures that they can extend one another's social reach, representing each other in ways that connect interestingly with their transfers of clothing at death.

But the wider the familial 'brotherhood', the more effective the network. John Hall, Shakespeare's son-in-law, might have undertaken some of his medical training as an assistant with William Sheppard, who married his sister Sara, and you will have noticed that the clothing bequests discussed above were made to both brothers and brothers-in-law – a distinction that early modern men rarely made. These trajectories of brotherly influence make us realise that the failure of Shakespeare's brothers to marry

significantly curtailed the 'family circle' of his generation. Statistical work
on marriage in Stratford shows that 'bachelors aged more than thirty were
rare' (Jones 1996, p. 86), and the lack of documentary evidence for the
brothers of William's generation, in contrast with his uncles', suggests an
unwillingness or inability to expand their own circles of influence with
which they might have extended William's – to be active members of
the family in this sense. The Shakespeares' brotherly circle, then, employs
both strategies, of geographical closeness and distance, albeit sparingly and
in ways that seem from the evidence that remains to relate only from
William outwards. William appears to have taken primary responsibility
for securing the family's status.

Finally, then, I want to return to Edmund's burial in Southwark
in 1607, seeing it through the lens of these different kinds of brotherly
love. Edmund appears in the parish only briefly, his name flickering into
the books in which officials recorded sales of Easter tokens to households
in the parish, to be used when they attended church for communion.
Alan H. Nelson and William Ingram have made these sources more
widely available and helped me to interpret them, which makes it
possible to extend our understanding of his death (http://token
bookslma.cityoflondon.gov.uk/manual/introduction.php). In the first
quarter of the year the parish clerk copied the names of householders
into a book which the roundsmen took around the streets of Bankside as
they distributed tokens and collected money, tallying a 'best guess' about
the number of communicants per household based on last year's count
with what they found when they arrived. Edmund's name is entered
above the line in The Vine in Paris Garden liberty. The area housed
one larger property with seven communicants (including four servants),
but of the sixteen households that bought tokens that year, five had only
three communicants and the remaining ten consisted only of a husband
and wife. It looks as though Edmund was a new arrival in 1607, and
perhaps the wardens discovered him there on one of their searches
for newcomers, between the finalising of the books for the previous year
and the roundsman's perambulation. But before the number of his
household could be recorded he was already dead, his name crossed
through with no tokens sold.

Edmund's most solid appearance in Southwark is in the burial register, 'Edmund Shakspeare a player buried in the church with afore noon

knell of the great bell, 20s'. The payment was a standard one. It was not unheard of in Southwark, as it was in other parishes, for comparative strangers to buy their way into its holiest places at death – in March 1607/8, for instance, Alan H. Nelson tells me 25 shillings was paid for 'Thomas Barnes a man buried in the church: a stranger, with an hour's knell of the great bell' and a marginal note states that the churchwardens 'Mr Paine and Mr Yarwood agreed withal'. Edmund was more settled than Thomas Barnes, if only just. The two references to him seem to set the located identity of householder against the more mobile one of player, and suggest a man on the verge of achieving independence.

Our sense of the quality of Shakespeare's brotherhood probably hinges on our interpretation of the burial of Edmund, to whom he was geographically and professionally closest. If he paid the 20 shillings on Edmund's behalf, which he probably did unless Edmund had a lucrative by-employment in addition to his acting career or had recently found a wealthy wife, then that indicates an enduring relationship and a wider sense of brotherhood. By paying for the burial, William would have brought his younger sibling's status up in line with his own, concerned about family honour.

And if William did pay for the funeral, then we can imagine him in the first decade of the seventeenth century operating a muted version of those models of middling status brotherhood explored above. Geographically close to Edmund and working in the same business, he probably shaped his career. We know Gilbert worked on William's behalf in Stratford, and it may be that at some point in his life he was working or resident in London too, both brothers consolidating the Shakespeares' Stratford identity at a geographical remove. William's model of a life lived in London business but always orientated towards his home town was to an extent enabled by his brothers and lived in relation to them. We are familiar with the model of Dick Whittington, who went to London and made his fortune with no one but a cat to help him, but for an older brother of a middling status provincial family, success meant thinking as a sibling. Shakespeare's rapid rise on the public stage may have been unusual, but a more regular investment in brotherhood extended his theatrical achievements in social ways, underpinning that transition from playwright to gentleman.

WORKS CITED

1561. *The book of common prayer, and administration of the sacraments, and other rites and ceremonies in the Church of England*. London. STC / 2312:0

Ben-Amos, Ilana Krausman 2008. *The Culture of Giving, Informal Support and Gift-exchange in Early Modern England*. Cambridge University Press

Honigmann, E. A. J. and Brock, Susan (eds.) 1993. *Playhouse Wills*. Manchester University Press

Jones, Jeanne 1996. *Family Life in Shakespeare's England*. Stroud. Sutton

Kathman, David 2004. 'Grocers, Goldsmiths, and Drapers: Freemen and Apprentices in the Elizabethan Theater', *Shakespeare Quarterly* 55: 1–49

Macdonald, Mairi (ed.) 2007. *The Register of the Guild of the Holy Cross, Stratford-upon-Avon*. Vol. 42. Dugdale Society

OED (Oxford English Dictionary), online edition

Records of London's Livery Companies Online www.londonroll.org

Schoenbaum, S. 1975. *William Shakespeare, A Compact Documentary Life*. Oxford University Press

Shakespeare Birthplace Trust Record Office. Letter Book ER1/97

The National Archives. Prerogative Court of Canterbury Wills Registers PROB 11

The Token Books of St Saviour Southwark. http://tokenbookslma.cityoflondon.gov.uk/manual/introduction.php

Tittler, Robert, and Jones, Norman (eds.) 2004. *A Companion to Tudor Britain*. Oxford. Wiley-Blackwell

Worcestershire Archive and Archaeology Service. Ecclesiastical court depositions 794.052 Vols. 6–8

4

His sister's family: the Harts

CATHY SHRANK

§

William Hart, William Shakespeare's brother-in-law, is an instructive example as to just how invisible to the historical record someone of non-gentry status can be during the sixteenth and early seventeenth centuries. Particularly when vital records of baptism, marriage and burial are incomplete (as they often are), it becomes all too easy for someone to slip out of the purview of future generations if they are not badly behaved – or unfortunate – enough to show up in court records, or sufficiently wealthy and respectable to serve as a local office holder.

Shakespeare's younger sister, Joan, married Hart in the late 1590s. The date is uncertain because the Stratford-upon-Avon marriage registers are incomplete for that decade. This is especially unfortunate as William Hart may have come from somewhere other than Stratford, information which would have been recorded in the marriage register. Certainly, 'Hart' (or its variants, 'Harte', 'Hert', 'Herte') is not one of those family names that recur in the records for sixteenth-century Stratford (unlike 'Quiney' or 'Sadler'). There is a yeoman, Nicholas Hart, who – along with his wife Isabel – appears in various documents in 1558 and 1566 relating to the lease of land in Stivichall, circa seventeen miles from Stratford (Shakespeare Centre, Stratford-upon-Avon, DR10/785, DR10/796). However, the fact that after Nicholas's death (which occurred at some point before 1586) the lease passed to his widow would suggest that they had no male heirs and are therefore unlikely to be connected to William Hart (DR10/830).

Joan Shakespeare was five years William Shakespeare's junior, born in April 1569 and baptised on the 15th of that month (Schoenbaum 1975, p. 27). Assuming that Joan and William Hart's first child followed fairly quickly after their marriage (the eldest child, William, was born in August

49

1600), Joan would have been in her late twenties when she wed, at the upper end of the 'normal' age-range for making a first marriage in that period (MacFarlane 1980, p. 110). Three further children followed, at regular intervals, which speak to the fertility of both partners: Mary (born in 1603, and dying in 1607), Thomas (b. 1605), and Michael (b. 1608) (Schoenbaum 1975, p. 28).

In marrying William Hart, Joan Shakespeare does not seem to have made an impressive match. The first time that William Hart shows up in the surviving records is at the baptism of his son William on 28 August 1600, where he is described as a 'hatter', an occupation with obvious affinities to the glove business in which his father-in-law, John Shakespeare, worked. However, he does not appear to have been a particularly successful businessman. The only time that his name occurs with any regularity in the Stratford records is in 1600–1, when he was sued for debt in the Stratford Court of Record by a series of different creditors (Shakespeare Centre, BRU12/1). On 30 January 1600, the yeoman Richard Collins brought a plea of debt against him (Collins's status is given in BRU15/4/190, a writ for the general sessions of the peace, and in Shakespeare Centre, ER1/1/53, a recognisance). Hart defaulted on his essoins (that is, he failed to appear in court on the appointed day) on 15 March that year, the same day as Robert Cawdrey also sued him for debt. Hart again defaulted on his essoins and failed to appear in court on 24 April. Before the year was out, he was in financial difficulties again, with the shoe-maker Arthur Ange (or Ainge) suing him for debt on 17 December (Ange's occupation is stated in his will, made on 15 March 1606 and proved on 5 June that year; Shakespeare Centre, BRU3/1/1). It is possible that this debt changed hands, because when Hart defaulted on his essoins on 11 February 1601, it was the yeoman William Wyett who was named as creditor, not Ange, although there is no previous record of Hart being indebted to Wyett. Wyett (who was to become Bailiff, the highest office of the Stratford-upon-Avon corporation, in 1605) certainly figures prominently in the financial dealings of the town, making frequent appearances as a creditor in the registers of the Stratford Court of Record (BRU12/1). Wyett was also in the ascendant socially: whilst his status was recorded as that of 'yeoman' in 1601 (Shakespeare Centre, DR535/7), by 1604, he had acquired a coat of arms, as he is identified as 'gent' or 'Mr' on inventories of 1604, 1613 and 1614, for which he served as appraiser (Jones 2002–3, 1, pp. 227, 281, 285).

The information recorded about William Hart's debts is scant: no details are given of the amounts owed, for example, or the circumstances of the debt. The fact that, although he defaulted on his essoins, no further action seems to have been taken would suggest that the debts were settled out of court: he does not incur, for example, a fine or a distringas (a writ seizing property), as did Humphrey Underhill's debtor John Combes when he defaulted on his essoins on 15 September 1563 (an event also recorded in the registers of the Court of Record, BRU12/1). That being the case, it is nevertheless still peculiar that there is no mention in the records of an agreement having been reached, as happened with the debt that William Trowte owed Richard Hathaway in 1596, where the entry for 15 September in the same register notes that they are reconciled ('concordati sunt'). The omission of such information may, however, owe much to the patchiness of the records and to the idiosyncrasies of various clerks. What is clear is that any valid, outstanding debt would have been pursued.

William Hart's lack of 'credit' – a term which has reputational as well as financial heft (Muldrew 1998) – is probably further indicated by the fact that he does not seem to have participated as an office-holder in the civic and parochial life of Stratford; nor is he named as one of the appraisers on any of the extant Stratford inventories for this period, a role you would expect 'discreet' and 'reputable' friends and neighbours to perform: William Wyett, for example, is named as an appraiser on no fewer than thirteen extant inventories between 1593 and 1614 (Jones 2002–3, 1, pp. 138, 148, 160, 172, 181, 189, 223, 227, 265, 281, 285, 349; 2, p. 10). Unusually, after their marriage, the Harts also lived in Joan's family home, taking up residence in the west wing of the house in Henley Street ('Shakespeare's Birthplace'): that they did not establish their own independent household may further indicate William Hart's parlous financial state. The Harts stayed on there after the death of John Shakespeare in 1601, possibly along with his widow Mary. Katherine Duncan-Jones has even suggested that when Mary died in September 1608, it was the Harts who subsequently administered her estate, but gives no evidence for this (Duncan-Jones 2001, p. 199).

Joan Hart was William Shakespeare's sole surviving sibling when he died on 23 April 1616. Her own husband had died the previous week and was buried on 17 April 1616. However, Shakespeare could probably not have predicted this when he drafted his will in January 1616, or possibly even when he revised it on 25 March, and it is credible to read the omission of his brother-in-law from the list of beneficiaries as a deliberate 'snub' (Bevington 1999, p. 20), or as a means of protecting the family money from William Hart's seeming financial incompetence. Instead, he left £20 to Joan, along with the life tenancy of the western part of the Henley Street house where she lived, for a nominal rent of 12 pence a year, and all his 'wearing apparel', a gift which would have been of some financial worth: Adrian Quiney 'gent' – of a similar social status to Shakespeare and related to him by marriage (Judith Shakespeare married his younger brother) – left clothes valued at £6 13s 4d at his death in 1617 (Jones 2002–3, 1, p. 308), and there was a thriving trade in second-hand clothes in early modern England. The will further contained a clause stating that if Shakespeare's daughter Judith died without issue, Joan should inherit an additional £50. Shakespeare also made provision for his Hart nephews, leaving each of them £5 apiece. The will may hint that, although solicitous of their welfare, he was not that intimate with his sister's family, since he seems to have forgotten the name of the middle nephew (Thomas), which is left blank: that is how the gap has been generally interpreted by biographers (Duncan-Jones 2001, p. 199). However, as Susan Brock argues in this volume, a 'lack of attention to detail, haste and a surprising level of unconcern with outward forms' was 'typical' of the work of Francis Collins, the Stratford town clerk who drew up the document, and the omission of Thomas's name may be down to Collins's often slipshod practice rather than Shakespeare's amnesia.

The Henley Street house, where Joan lived most – if not all – of her life was, in its entirety, a three-bay timber-framed house, now known as 'Shakespeare's Birthplace', although the property that stands there now may be later Elizabethan or Jacobean and post-date the birth of John Shakespeare's children (Jones and Palmer 1999, p. 1). The house was close to a series of clay-lined tanning pits used in the production of leather (one of the more pungent industries in early modern England), whilst the large plot of land to the rear of the property ran down to the Guild (or 'Gil') Pits, which were used as a local rubbish tip and cess pit (Jones 1999, p. 1). The excrement gathered there would be sold for fertiliser: the inventory of one Henley Street resident, Lewis Hiccox, includes 40 shillings-worth of 'soil in the Gil Pits' (Jones 2002–3, 2, p. 16). Further up the street to the west was the Swan Inn, built on land which John Shakespeare had sold to George Badger in 1597 (Wheler 1824, p. 5). In the years immediately after John Shakespeare's death, while the Harts were occupying the west wing of the

Henley Street house, William Shakespeare (who had inherited the property), leased out the eastern part to Lewis Hiccox (the owner of the Gil Pit soil), with whom Shakespeare had other financial connections: around the same time, on 1 May 1602, William and John Combe transferred to Shakespeare a feoffment (grant of ownership) of land in Old Stratford, where Lewis Hiccox and his brother Thomas were tenants (Shakespeare Centre, ER27/1).

When exactly Hiccox took up occupation of Henley Street is not clear. He first appears on a list of victuallers in 1603 (Shakespeare Centre, ER2/25); although the location of his establishment is not noted, it is likely to have been the Henley Street property, as that is where he is listed as licensed to sell ale on 22 September 1606 (Shakespeare Centre, BRU15/12/75), and he was still resident there, as innkeeper, at his death in 1627 (Jones 1994, p. 498). From the early 1600s until her death, Joan Hart thus lived directly next door to an inn (known as the Maidenhead), located in the eastern wing of the Shakespeare property, and close to another (the Swan), built on land that once belonged to her father.

After Hiccox's death in 1627, his nephew Henry took over as innkeeper (Jones 2002–3, 2, p. 16). Henry Hiccox died in December 1638, leaving a widow (Jane) and two children, Thomas and Amy, as Joan Hart's neighbours (Shakespeare Centre, PR 293/95). The inn seems to have been run on their behalf by John Rutter, who was in charge during the Civil War when the inn was requisitioned by parliamentary forces for thirty-three months between 1642–5. Certainly, although Rutter was the licensee, the 1647 bill for compensation, for quartering soldiers and for various items removed from the inn, was made in the name of 'the orphan children of Jane Hiccox:-Thomas and Amy' (British Library Additional MS 28565). That Rutter ran the inn, but did not own the lease, is also suggested by the fact that the lease is not mentioned in his will and inventory of December 1648 (Worcester Records Office, 008.7 1649/128).

Situated close to the intersections of a number of principal thoroughfares (between London and Worcester; Gloucester and Coventry; and the Fosse Way, running from Exeter to Lincoln), Stratford-upon-Avon was a hub for trade and a good prospect for the would-be innkeeper (Styles 1945). The north-western end of Henley Street (where the Shakespeare property stood) was in turn perfectly positioned at the hub of the routes that ran into the town, as the setting up of two successful establishments – the Swan and the Maidenhead – in close proximity and within a couple of years of each other (between c. 1597 and 1603) would indicate. The Maidenhead was, in Jeanne Jones's words, 'a well-furnished and comfortable inn' in the seventeenth century (Jones 1994, p. 500): amongst the items allegedly purloined by parliamentary soldiers in the 1640s were seventeen silver spoons, two silver bowls and a double silver salt, items which suggest a fairly well-appointed establishment. The inventories of two of its early innkeepers, Lewis Hiccox and Rutter, also show them leaving substantial estates (worth £378 and £218 respectively), including a wide array of furniture and furnishings, including window curtains, cushions and rugs (Jones 2002–3, 2, pp. 13–16, 79–82). The inn was also sizeable: Hiccox's inventory lists ten rooms, excluding store-houses, comprising a hall, two parlours, a room over the cellar (which, from the contents of tables, benches, chairs and eating utensils, would seem to have been used for dining), Hiccox's lodging chamber, three other bedchambers ('the best', 'the stairhead', 'the third'), a servants' chamber (which may have been in the attic) and a kitchen. Even making allowance for the subsequent remodelling of the house, the number of rooms apportioned to the inn would have meant that Joan Hart's share of the property was 'small indeed, being, at the most, three rooms' (Jones 1994, p. 500). (There are eleven rooms in the Birthplace as it stands today.) However, as Jones notes, this was not necessarily an indication that Joan Hart was impoverished, nor that she lived in discomfort. By 1627, her household would probably have been small in number, since her two surviving children – William and Thomas, then aged twenty-seven and twenty-two – would have been likely to lodge elsewhere, and 'other inventories of the period reveal that larger households than that of Joan Hart were living in two or three rooms and these inventories were of the goods of people who were, by no means, among the poorest' (Jones 1994, p. 500). It was also possible that her household used some of the other buildings belonging to the property: it is striking, for example, that there is only one kitchen in the Henley Street house in its current layout, whereas two would have been needed during Joan Hart's day, with one servicing the inn (Jones 1994, p. 500).

Joan Hart lived for more than her three score years and ten: she died in autumn 1646, aged seventy-seven, after spending a good proportion of her final years living next to a billet of parliamentary soldiers, and she was buried on 4 November. She outlived all but one of her children: the eldest, William (sometimes mistaken for the Jacobean actor of the same name), died the same year as his mother; Michael, aged ten, in 1618; only Thomas Hart survived her, dying in 1661, in his mid-fifties (Schoenbaum 1975, p. 28). On 15 December 1653, along with Walter Jilkes, Thomas acted as surety for his son, Thomas junior, who had been bound over to keep the peace; in that document Thomas senior is listed as 'yeoman', his son as a shoemaker (BRT4/1/1/126). It was Thomas junior (Joan Hart's grandson) who inherited the property from Lady Elizabeth Barnard (née Hall), Shakespeare's granddaughter and his last lineal descendant, at which point the eastern half was still operating as an inn, under the occupation of a Michael Johnson (Shakespeare Centre, ER2/78). The Harts then remained in possession of the whole Henley Street house until 1806 (Schoenbaum 1975, p. 319). Their connection with Shakespeare was commemorated through George Hart (Shakespeare's great-nephew) christening his son 'Shakespeare Hart' in 1666 (Jordan 1790).

WORKS CITED

Bevington, David 1999. 'Shakespeare the Man' in David Scott Kastan (ed.), *A Companion to Shakespeare*. Oxford. Blackwell, pp. 9–24

British Library Additional MS 28565. 'A Booke of Such Damages as hath beene sustained by such persons of the said Burrough as have put in their bills, from the Parliament forces, by free quarter, contribucion & otherwise'

Duncan-Jones, Katherine 2001. *Ungentle Shakespeare*. London. Arden

Jones, C. and Palmer, N. 1999. *Archaeological Investigation at Shakespeare's Birthplace*, Henley Street, Stratford-upon-Avon. Warwick. Warwickshire County Council

Jones, G. C. 1999. *Archaeological Observation at 8/9 Henley Street*, Stratford-upon-Avon, Warwickshire. Warwick. Warwickshire County Council

Jones, Jeanne 1994. 'Lewis Hiccox and Shakespeare's birthplace', *Notes and Queries*, n.s. 41.4: 497–502

Jones, Jeanne (ed.) 2002–3. *Stratford-upon-Avon Inventories, 1538–1699*, 2 vols. Bristol. Dugdale Society

Jordan, John 1790. 'Memoirs and historical accounts of the families of Shakespeare (alias Shakespere) and Hart', Stratford-upon-Avon, Shakespeare Centre, ER 1/91

MacFarlane, Alan 1980. 'The Informal Social Control of Marriage in Seventeenth-Century England: Some Preliminary Notes' in Vivian C. Fox and Martin

H. Quitt (eds.), *Loving, Parenting and Dying: The Family Cycle in England and America, Past and Present*. New York. Psychohistory Press, pp. 110–21

Muldrew, Craig 1998. *The Economy of Obligation: The Culture of Credit and Social Relations in Early Modern England*. London. Palgrave Macmillan

Schoenbaum, S. 1975. *Shakespeare: A Compact Documentary Life*. Oxford University Press

Styles, Philip 1945. 'The borough of Stratford-upon-Avon: Historical Account', *A History of the County of Warwick*, vol. 3, *Victoria County History*, pp. 234–55

Wheler, R. B. 1824. *Historical and Descriptive Account of the Birthplace of Shakspeare*. Stratford-upon-Avon. James Ward

5

His wife Anne Shakespeare and the Hathaways

KATHERINE SCHEIL

Anne Hathaway is arguably the closest member of the Shakespeare circle, but the details about her life have been problematic from her first entry into the history of Shakespeare biography. Though her epitaph was included in William Dugdale's *Antiquities of Warwickshire* in 1656, Nicholas Rowe's 1709 biography was the first to include her as part of Shakespeare's life story. Rowe writes that Shakespeare's 'wife was the daughter of one Hathaway, said to have been a substantial yeoman in the neighbourhood of Stratford' (1709, p. v).

The source of Rowe's information was the retired actor Thomas Betterton, who apparently travelled to Holy Trinity Church in Stratford and looked at the parish records. However, there is no surviving parish record of Anne Hathaway's parentage, birth or marriage. In fact, the only parish record is of her burial; according to her gravestone, she was born before records began in Stratford. Betterton's information must have come from oral tradition rather than parish records, thus the 'said to have been' phrase, unless he was privy to parish documents that no longer survive. Later research has confirmed Rowe's account of Anne Hathaway, despite the ambiguity of Betterton's sources. If Betterton did visit Holy Trinity Church in Stratford, he would probably have stood on Anne's grave in order to see the Shakespeare monument (which Rowe mentions). Nevertheless, he omits Anne's birth or death dates in favour of verbal lore. This would not be the last time information about her came to be muddled.

This chapter revisits the various factual details associated with Anne Hathaway and her family, in order to give a clearer picture of realistic possibilities for her life story and for her role in the innermost ring of the Shakespeare circle. The uncertain nature of many of these facts has led to assumptions about Shakespeare's wife that fit with the desires of readers, audiences and tourists for particular 'Shakespeares' that build on a particular construction of his wife, but that may obscure other equally plausible narratives. Thus, rather than offer conclusions where there are alternatives, this chapter instead allows various interpretative possibilities to resonate when more than one explanation is possible.

The Hathaway family

The Hathaways were long-standing residents of the village of Shottery just outside Stratford, both before and after Shakespeare's time. Anne's grandfather John Hathaway was a tenant of Hewlands Farm as early as 1543, and held a number of leadership roles in the community (Pogue 2008, p. 57; Eccles 1961, p. 67). In numerous historical records, the name Hathaway appears as 'Hathaway alias Gardner', or even just 'Gardner', probably denoting their occupation or profession. Anne's father and several of her siblings were listed as 'Hathaway alias Gardner' in parish records, and it is likely that the family would have been identified as Gardners just as much as Hathaways until the end of the sixteenth century.

The location of the present Anne Hathaway's Cottage, one of the centrepiece Shakespeare Birthplace Trust properties, is the same site as Hewlands, the Hathaway family farm dating back to the sixteenth century, estimated at between fifty and ninety acres (Schoenbaum 1975, p. 66). Anne's father Richard was a tenant on Hewlands, and the property was not actually owned by the Hathaways until Anne's brother Bartholomew purchased it in 1610. It is likely that Anne lived at Hewlands until her marriage to Shakespeare in 1582, but no evidence survives to confirm this.

Anne's father Richard Hathaway (d. 1581) was a Shottery yeoman farmer, who seemed well connected in his community, as the relationship between the Hathaways and the neighbouring Burman family attests. Stephen Burman was executor of Richard Hathaway's will (along with Fulke Sandells, whose name appears on Shakespeare's marriage bond), and Richard Burman served as a witness to the will. Other members of the Burman family had connections with both the Hathaways and the Shakespeares; Stephen Burman was executor to Anne's brother Bartholomew Hathaway's will, along with Shakespeare's son-in-law John Hall. A later Richard Burman owed money to Thomas Nash, the husband of Elizabeth, Shakespeare's granddaughter. The impressive memorial tablet in Holy Trinity Church testifies to the influence that the Burman family had in Stratford and Shottery for over 300 years, and their many links to the Hathaways and to the Shakespeares suggest that all three families were closely knit and were influential in the larger community of Stratford (Horsler 2010, p. 49). The numerous connections between the families both before and after the marriage of William and Anne underline the fact that their union was a match between two families of long-standing relationships. John Shakespeare paid some of Richard Hathaway's debts as early as 1566, and they were likely to have been close friends; the marriage of Anne and William may have even been arranged before Richard Hathaway died (Pogue 2008, p. 57).

According to the inscription on her grave, Anne was born in 1555 or 1556, and was the eldest of seven children (three of whom died in infancy). There is some speculation that Richard Hathaway may have married twice, though if so, the name of a first wife does not survive. His wife Joan, named in his will, outlived him by fifteen years, dying in 1599. No details remain about Joan's relationship with Anne, although it is likely that Anne lived with her at Hewlands until her marriage in 1582.

We know very little about most of Anne's siblings, except for her brother Bartholomew, who purchased Hewlands in 1610; Shakespeare's lawyer Francis Collins drew up the deed. In Richard Hathaway's will, he instructs Bartholomew to 'be a guide to my said wife in her husbandry' and 'also a comfort unto his brethren and sisters to his power' (Lewis 1940, pp. 155–60). Like his sister, Bartholomew also married in November of 1582, and both marriages had an uncanny similarity. His wife Isabella Hancocks of Tredington died in 1617, just a year later than Shakespeare. Bartholomew and Isabella had five children: a daughter (coincidentally?) named Anne in 1584, an unnamed infant who died in 1588, and three sons: Richard (1583–1636), John (b. 1586) and Edmund (1590–1648). Though he farmed for a year or so in nearby Tysoe in the 1580s, Bartholomew later remained active in Stratford civic life (serving as a churchwarden for Holy Trinity from 1605 to 1609, for example), until his death in 1624, a year after his sister.

Bartholomew and Isabella's eldest son Richard was the one most likely to be in close contact with the Shakespeares in Stratford, since he became a baker based at the Crown in Bridge Street, just around the corner from New Place, and held several positions in Stratford civic life. In 1623, he supplied bread for seven communions, including one on 3 August, just a few days before his aunt Anne died (Fripp 1928, p. 69 n1). Anne's brother William may have had a more complicated relationship with her family. He was involved in an anti-Puritan riot over removal of a maypole in Stratford, sanctioned by the appointment of the new Puritan vicar Thomas Wilson in 1619 (Whitfield 1964, p. 259). Though Wilson was not well liked, his 'most passionate adherent' was John Hall, which may have caused conflict with his wife's uncle William Hathaway, who protested the new vicar's practices (Greer 2007, p. 332).

Further links between the Hathaways and the Shakespeares extended well into the eighteenth century. John Hall was the executor of Shakespeare's will as well as Bartholomew Hathaway's will in 1624. Hall was also a trustee in the marriage settlement of Bartholomew Hathaway's granddaughter Isabel in 1625, daughter of Richard Hathaway of Bridge Street (Halliwell-Phillipps 1887, p. 186). Richard Hathaway and his cousin Susanna were both born in 1583, so the fact that Susanna's husband had a role in the marriage of Richard's daughter comes as no surprise. In 1647, Anne's cousin Thomas Hathaway owned the house on No. 20 Chapel Street, just a few doors away (No. 23 Chapel Street) from New Place (Mitchell and Colls 2011, p. 65). That same year, members of the Hathaway family appear in the 1647 resettlement statement of Shakespeare's estates, which was undertaken by Elizabeth Nash and her mother Susanna Hall to prevent Thomas Nash's estate from going to his cousin Edward. In her will, Elizabeth Nash gives money to the daughters of Thomas Hathaway, and a later Hathaway cousin, Edmund Hathaway, relied on Shakespeare Hart, a grandson of William Shakespeare's sister Joan, as a trustee for his will in 1729.

The long-running associations between the Shakespeares and the Hathaways were further enriched as the tourist trade developed in Stratford. When Samuel Ireland visited Shottery in 1793, he commented that the cottage was still in the hands of the Hathaway family (1795, pp. 206–9). Ireland was referred to the cottage by Thomas Hart (c. 1729–1794), son of George Hart, a descendant of Shakespeare's sister Joan, who lived in the Birthplace on Henley Street and sold family relics. Even several generations after the death of Anne, the descendants of both families collaborated to take advantage of the tourism income from their famous relative.

One additional surviving document related to Anne, the will of Hathaway family shepherd Thomas Wittington, corroborates several facts about her. First, while there were several Hathaway families living in Shottery around the time of Anne, Whittington makes clear that Anne was descended from the family of Richard Hathaway. Whittington's 1602 will leaves money to the poor, which he had left 'in the hand of Ann Shakespeare wife unto Mr William Shakespeare' (Schoenbaum 1975, p. 69). The fact that Whittington entrusted Anne with funds suggests the influential role she had in her family.

Married life

Although numerous scholars have confirmed that Shakespeare's marriage to Anne Hathaway was not only typical for his day, but was also a good match for the poet, inconsistencies in the historical records have inspired much speculation. In November of 1582 the marriage licence obtained from the Bishop of Worcester, 'inter Wm Shaxpere et Annam whateley de Temple grafton', gave permission for William and Anne to wed with only one asking of the banns. The marriage bond for £40 from 28 November was backed by family friends Fulke Sandells and John Rychardson, for a marriage between 'William Shagspere' and 'Anne hathwey of Stratford in the Dioces of Worcester maiden'. It is unclear why two different names appear on these documents (Anna Whateley and Anne Hathaway), or why two different locations are mentioned (Temple Grafton and Stratford). It is possible that Anne was then living at Temple Grafton, though records of that village do not survive. Most likely, as Schoenbaum puts it, the Worcester clerk was 'fairly incompetent – careless at least – for he got a number of names wrong in the Register' (1975, p. 71). Both Fulke Sandells and John Rychardson were Shottery husbandmen; Sandells was described as a 'trusty friend and neighbor' in Richard Hathaway's will, and he also was a supervisor of the will (Schoenbaum 1975, p. 65). After their marriage, the Shakespeares would probably have lived with William's family in the house on Henley Street, as was the custom in Stratford (Lewis 1940, pp. 117, 239), though no evidence confirms this.

The birth of Susanna Shakespeare in May of 1583, and of the twins Hamnet and Judith two years later, are the clearest testament to Anne's position in the first ring of the Shakespeare circle. The epitaph on her gravestone eulogises her as a mother, underlining the fact that this was a role she took seriously throughout her life. No details survive about the death of her only son Hamnet in 1596, but the eulogy on her grave is an unequivocal tribute to a devoted and successful mother. Some have speculated about why the Shakespeares did not have additional children, perhaps due to physical conditions after the birth of twins, or due to the long-distance relationship between the Shakespeares (Bearman 1994, pp. 7–8). It is worth pointing out that other women of the Shakespeare family were not especially prolific either; Susanna Shakespeare Hall, who by all accounts lived with her husband in Stratford for all of their married life together (as opposed to her mother's situation), only had one daughter, Elizabeth, who even though she was married twice, never had any children. Daughter Judith Shakespeare Quiney had three sons, but none lived to adulthood.

New Place

In 1597, Shakespeare purchased New Place, the second largest house in Stratford, and this likely remained Anne's home until the end of her life; George Vertue described New Place as 'where [Shakespeare] lived and died with his wife after him 1623' (Simpson 1952). Given the discoveries at New Place in the 'Dig for Shakespeare', it is worth contemplating what family life at New Place could have looked like in the first decades of the seventeenth century, particularly if this was where Shakespeare wrote some of his plays. Exactly who lived at New Place during the time of Anne's life is uncertain, though the size of the house confirmed by the 'Dig', with ten chimneys and twenty to thirty rooms, suggests a large household. As Paul Edmondson puts it, 'New Place was too fine a house for Shakespeare to have been most of his time away from it' (2013, p. 98).

The Shakespeare family home on Henley Street may have been damaged by fire in 1594–5, and there is evidence that by April of 1602 it had already been converted to a tavern. Robert Bearman points out that Shakespeare's purchase of New Place may have been 'an effort by a man conscious of family obligations to provide a suitable home for his dependants in the wake of misfortune' (Bearman 2012, p. 485). John Shakespeare could have lived at New Place from 1597 until his death in 1601; Mary Arden until her death in 1608; and Shakespeare's brothers Gilbert and Richard until their deaths in 1612 and 1613 respectively. Hall's Croft was not built before 1613, so it is likely that Susanna and John Hall lived in New Place from their

FIGURE 1: Pat Hughes's impression of New Place showing the five-gabled frontage, the gardens to the rear, the courtyard and an inner dwelling, the main site of the Shakespeare family home.

marriage in 1607, during daughter Elizabeth's birth in 1608, and probably from 1616 onward, after Shakespeare's death. Judith Shakespeare may have lived there until her marriage to Thomas Quiney in 1616. Thus, there could have been a relatively large Shakespeare circle at New Place from the start of Shakespeare's ownership.

In addition to the extended Shakespeare family, New Place was also the home for Stratford town clerk Thomas Greene and his wife Lettice, at least in 1609 but probably longer. The Greenes had several connections with Anne Hathaway's family. Richard Hathaway, Anne's nephew, lent £20 to Thomas Greene in 1616 (Greer 2007, p. 327). In 1611 Greene and his wife witnessed a deed with Anne's daughter Judith Shakespeare (Lewis 1940, p. 456). Two of Greene's children were named Anne and William, perhaps not coincidentally. Greene also travelled back and forth to London, and had connections with the theatre community there; he may have even kept Anne 'informed of her husband's triumphs' on the London literary scene (Greer 2007, p. 234), and would have brought news of both local and London events to the New Place community.

It is likely that Susanna Hall and her mother had a close relationship, since Susanna probably lived at New Place with her mother after Shakespeare's death in 1616 and may have even taken on a supervisory role there. In 1614, a visiting clergyman was entertained at New Place; a surviving record lists 'one quart of sack and one quart of claret wine given to a preacher at the New Place' (Halliwell-Phillipps 1864, p. 26), which Susanna may have helped with. Susanna later lived in New Place with her daughter Elizabeth and son-in-law Thomas Nash after the death of John Hall in 1635; in 1642, Thomas Nash referred to 'my mother-in-law Mrs. Hall who lives with me' in New Place (Lewis 1940, pp. 245, 583), so there may have been something of a family tradition of mothers and daughters at New Place.

There is no evidence that any members of the Hathaway family lived in New Place, though the families must have remained close, since Susanna's husband John Hall was involved with the Hathaways until his death. As a physician, it is likely that Hall treated members of the Hathaway family, as he often travelled to Shottery, though no references survive to family members (other than his wife and daughter) in his casebook (Lane 1996, p. xviii).

Life at New Place for Anne included a large circle of family members and friends, but it was also the site of cottage industries which she probably managed. The discovery of 'an oval pit, possible oven/kiln, brick storage pit and possible quarry pit' prove that 'the back plots were being used for more than just gardens over an extended period of time' (Mitchell and Colls 2012, p. 11). There are several possibilities for activities that are likely to have occupied Anne. Stratford was well known for its brewing industry; in 1598 Shakespeare was hoarding malt at New Place, perhaps for a malt brewing business (Greer 2007, p. 217). Shakespeare also paid for a load of stone in 1598, probably for repairs or renovations to New Place. Given that in 1598 Shakespeare was probably in London most of the time, both the repairs and the brewing business may have been carried out by Anne (Bearman 2012, p. 482). The cloth trade seems to have been in decline in the late sixteenth century, even though some items from that industry have been found at New Place (Styles 1946, p. 25; Mitchell and Colls 2012, p. 55). Shakespeare's brother Gilbert was a haberdasher, dealing in the clothing trade, so it is possible he was involved in this type of cottage industry at New Place until his death in 1612 (Greer 2007, pp. 175–7).

Other archaeological discoveries at New Place give hints of the lifestyle there: pig bones from animals slaughtered before maturity suggest suckling pig prepared for a special feast; and venison was associated with the well-off (Bowsher and Miller 2009, p. 151; Joan Fitzpatrick, personal communication). Some of the pottery findings also confirm an upper-class status. One shard of Rhenish Stoneware contains remnants of a legend which was probably either 'When God wills it, so is my goal' or 'When God wills it, my time is up', a maxim that dates from the second half of the sixteenth century. Ceramic findings, including sixteenth-century Tudor Green wares, indicate 'reasonably prosperous bourgeois occupation' during Anne's lifetime (Mitchell and Colls 2011, p. 33).

Remembering

Of all the surviving documents related to Anne Hathaway, the twelve words in Shakespeare's will have received the most extended conjecture. Anne appears only once, on the third and last page of the will, in an interlineated line most likely reading 'Unto my wyf I gyve my second best bed with the furniture'. The fact that Anne is not mentioned by name (only as 'wyf') and in an interlineated line have been fodder for much wild speculation, yet closer inspection of the will should urge greater caution in assigning this line a single interpretative meaning, or even one directly connected to Shakespeare.

First, the three pages of the will are in different stages of finality. The first page has likely been corrected, but the third page was not. Given that the interlineated line is the only alteration on the third page, it may not be a change in the will in connection with daughter Judith's tumultuous marriage, which most scholars agree was the reason for the revisions that took place on the other pages of the will in March of 1616. Thus, all of the changes to Shakespeare's will may not date from the same time, nor derive from the same cause; the three sheets of paper that comprise the will are all composed on different makes of paper as well (Lewis 1940, p. 471).

Further, the origin of the interlineation is by no means certain. Did Shakespeare himself realise that he forgot to include his wife, and only added her at the last minute? Eighteenth-century editor Edmond Malone advances this argument, later picked up by biographer Stephen Greenblatt, among others. Yet, the interlineation could have absolutely nothing to do with Shakespeare, and could be attributed to the copier of the will, who may have been interrupted and may have missed his place; Francis Collins, Shakespeare's clerk, was known for producing imperfect and uncorrected wills. In Shakespeare's playtexts, scholars allow for a variety of accidental omissions in the printing process and in the transmission of texts that have nothing to do with Shakespeare, but are a result of secondary circumstances. Multi-spectral analysis has yet to be done on Shakespeare's will, but such a study might be able to reveal more details about the dating of the interlineations relative to the body of the will, and of the possible relationship between the hands on each of the three pages.

The question of whether the 'second best bed' is an insult or a term of endearment has been dealt with elsewhere (Rogers 1993; and see Chapter 12 of this volume), but it is worth underlining the uncertainty of interpretation that still remains, and pointing out the fallacies involved in taking one interpretation at the expense of another. In their desire to capture traces of Shakespeare's personal life in the surviving historical documents, many scholars have looked to the will for inspiration, overlooking its textual instability. One biographer has even used Anne's enigmatic reference in the will to construct a narrative of marital hostility: 'When Shakespeare lay dying, he tried to forget his wife and then remembered her with the second-best bed' (Greenblatt 2004, p. 147). But there is no evidence that these were Shakespeare's last words, or that they were added in rather than accidentally omitted in the transcription process. While it is possible that Anne Hathaway's position in Shakespeare's will is a result of his wishes, it is just as likely that Shakespeare had nothing to do with the interlineated line, and fully intended his wife to have her rightful and legal share in his estate upon his death, as many scholars have noted. In the end, we simply cannot know one way or another whether Shakespeare intended his will to be a statement of endearment or of dismissal to Anne Hathaway. To take either stance, at the expense of not offering the possibility of an opposite reading, seems irresponsible and deliberately manipulative.

Death and burial

Anne Hathaway died in August of 1623 and is buried in Stratford's Holy Trinity Church, just to the left of her husband. The Shakespeare family occupies five gravesites near the altar of the church; burial in Holy Trinity was 'prestigious but by no means exclusive', and depended on one's ability to pay for the burial space (Horsler 2010, p. 114). Dugdale records the engravings of all of the family graves in 1656, so unless they were moved sometime between 1649 and 1656, their present place was their original place.

Anne's is one of the three family graves with a Latin epitaph (along with John Hall and Thomas Nash, cf. Edmondson and Wells and McKinnon in this volume, p. 333 and p. 79), but it is the only grave in the Shakespeare family plot with a brass plaque. The plaque dates from at least 1730, but the epitaph itself can be dated as early as 1634, since Dugdale reproduces it in his manuscript notes from that year (Robert Bearman, personal communication). The epitaph reads: 'Here lyeth interred the body of Anne wife of William Shakespeare, who departed this life the 6 day of August 1623 being of the age of 67 yeares', followed by six Latin verse lines, beginning, 'Mother, you gave me the breast, you gave me milk and life; / Woe is me, that for so great a gift my return will be but a tomb' (cf. McKinnon in this volume, p. 79).

The most frequently suggested authors for the epitaph are John Hall (written on behalf of his wife), or Susanna herself, since the epitaph is written from a child to a mother, during Susanna's lifetime. A third option is Thomas Greene, who, according to one scholar, next to Shakespeare and John Hall, was 'the ablest man in the town' and was 'something of a poet who wrote Latin verses in his diary' (Fripp 1928, pp. 59–60). The epitaph provides the only source of Anne Hathaway's age, and is a substantial piece of evidence about her as a mother figure, as well as about her maternal practices, particularly breastfeeding. Marylynn Salmon notes that 'a nursing mother represented selfless devotion to early modern men and women', and for Puritans in particular, 'breastfeeding represented God's gift of grace' (1994, pp. 251, 253). The use of breastfeeding as a particularly Puritan image may suggest another likely author of Anne's epitaph, Puritan vicar Thomas Wilson, who was a close associate of John Hall, and who probably had both the Oxford education and the motivation to compose an epitaph for the mother-in-law of one of his ardent supporters. Wilson was 'said to be a very good Scholar, and was the son of a very grave conformable doctor of divinity' (Hughes 1994, p. 69). In fact, Stopes argues that Wilson 'is almost sure to have officiated at the funeral of Mrs. Anne Shakespeare' and probably studied at Oxford (1907, p. 238). Before his stint as vicar in Stratford, Wilson lived in Evesham, and 'would have been well-known to several of the aldermen and burgesses' in Stratford (Hughes 1994, p. 61). It is even possible that Wilson was the visiting clergyman entertained at New Place in 1614, and later composed the epitaph for his hostess on behalf of her daughter and son-in-law.

The uneven history of this epitaph offers a window into the complex web of knowledge about Anne that has both existed and has been ignored. Throughout the seventeenth and eighteenth centuries, Holy Trinity was the top destination for tourists in Stratford. While several visitors in the seventeenth century copied Shakespeare's epitaph, no visitors to Holy Trinity, other than William Dugdale in 1656, remark on Anne's grave. As late as the 1690s, both John Dowdall in 1693 and William Hall in 1694 copied Shakespeare's epitaph, but make no mention of Anne Hathaway's grave. Further, both Dowdall and Hall comment on Shakespeare's monument, and they would have had to stand on Anne's grave in order to see it from the best angle, given that the altar rail was behind the Shakespeare family graves at the time (Chambers 1930, pp. ii, 242–3, 250–1).

Further, actor Thomas Betterton visited Holy Trinity Church and presumably looked at parish documents around 1708 to gather data for Nicholas Rowe's 1709 biography, but Rowe's biography does not contain any reference to information that Betterton could have gleaned from Anne's grave. Nearly thirty years later, when George Vertue visited Holy Trinity in 1737, he sketched Shakespeare's monument and grave, and he includes a figure standing on Anne's grave to get the best view of the monument. In the margin of the illustration, Vertue copied the death date of Anne but ignored the epitaph (Simpson 1952, Plate II). Given the relative neglect of the most reliable piece of evidence about Anne, few have remembered Anne as the devoted mother and wife of Shakespeare captured in the engraved verses on her epitaph.

Many have lamented the absence of details that might offer a window into the relationship between William Shakespeare and Anne Hathaway. The surviving historical documents about Anne Hathaway have been stitched together to create a narrative and construct a wife for Shakespeare, but often without acknowledging what is missing, or what other narratives may be possible. The material objects that remain, both legitimate and forged – love letters, a bed, remains of a house, an epitaph, a carved casket – have been made to stand in for the haunting sense of absence in the archives about this enigmatic woman who occupied the first ring of the Shakespeare circle.

WORKS CITED

Bearman, Robert 1994. *Shakespeare in the Stratford Records*. Trowbridge, Wiltshire. Alan Sutton

   2012. 'Shakespeare's Purchase of New Place', *Shakespeare Quarterly* 63.4: 465–86

Bowsher, Julian and Miller, Pat 2009. *The Rose and the Globe – Playhouses of Shakespeare's Bankside, Southwark, Excavations 1988–91*. London. Museum of London Archaeology

Chambers, E. K. 1930. *William Shakespeare: A Study of Facts and Problems*. Oxford. Clarendon Press

Dugdale, William 1656. *The Antiquities of Warwickshire Illustrated*. London. Thomas Rarren

Eccles, Mark 1961. *Shakespeare in Warwickshire*. Madison. University of Wisconsin Press

Edmondson, Paul 2013. 'A Renaissance for New Place in Shakespearean Biography?', *Critical Survey* 25.1: 90–8

Fripp, Edgar I. 1928. *Shakespeare's Stratford*. Oxford University Press

Greenblatt, Stephen 2004. *Will in the World*. New York. W.W. Norton

Greer, Germaine 2007. *Shakespeare's Wife*. London. Bloomsbury

Halliwell-Phillipps, James Orchard 1864. *An Historical Account of the New Place, Stratford-Upon-Avon*. London. J.E. Adlard

   1887. *Outlines of the Life of Shakespeare*. London. Longmans

Horsler, Val 2010. *Shakespeare's Church: A Parish for the World*. London. Third Millennium Publishing

Hughes, Ann 1994. 'Religion and Society in Stratford Upon Avon, 1619–1638', *Midland History* 19: 58–85

Ireland, Samuel 1795. *Picturesque Views on the Upper, or Warwickshire Avon*. London. R. Faulder and T. Egerton

Lane, Joan 1996. *John Hall and his Patients: The Medical Practice of Shakespeare's Son-in-Law*. Stratford-upon-Avon. Shakespeare Birthplace Trust

Lewis, B. Roland 1940. *The Shakespeare Documents*. 2 vols. Stanford University Press

Mitchell, William and Colls, Kevin 2011. *'Dig for Shakespeare': New Place, Season 2.* Birmingham Archaeology

2012. *'Dig for Shakespeare': New Place, Season 3.* Birmingham Archaeology

Pogue, Kate Emery 2008. *Shakespeare's Family.* Westport, CT. Praeger

Rogers, Joyce 1993. *The Second Best Bed: Shakespeare's Will in a New Light.* Westport, CT. Greenwood Press

Rowe, Nicholas 1709. *The Works of Mr. William Shakespear.* London. Jacob Tonson

Salmon, Marylynn 1994. 'The Cultural Significance of Breastfeeding and Infant Care in Early Modern England and America', *Journal of Social History* 28.2: 247–69

Schoenbaum, S. 1975. *William Shakespeare: A Documentary Life.* Oxford University Press

Simpson, Frank 1952. 'New Place: The Only Reproduction of Shakespeare's House, from an Unpublished Manuscript', *Shakespeare Survey 5.* Allardyce Nicholl (ed.). Cambridge University Press, pp. 55–7

Sisson, C. J. 1959. 'Shakespeare's Friends: Hathaways and Burmans at Shottery', *Shakespeare Survey 12.* Allardyce Nicholl (ed.). Cambridge University Press, pp. 95–106

Stopes, Charlotte Carmichael 1901. *Shakespeare's Family.* London. Elliot Stock

1907. *Shakespeare's Warwickshire Contemporaries.* Stratford-upon-Avon. Shakespeare Head Press

Styles, Philip 1946. *The Borough of Stratford-Upon-Avon and the Parish of Alveston.* London. Oxford University Press

Whitfield, Christopher 1964. 'Four Town Clerks of Stratford on Avon, 1603–1625', *Notes and Queries* 11: 251–61

6

His daughter Susanna Hall

LACHLAN MACKINNON

❧

William Shakespeare's monument in Holy Trinity Church will have caused quite a stir in Stratford when installed, sometime between 1616 and 1623. Such 'aedificated' (partly resembling a house), wall-mounted memorials became increasingly fashionable during the seventeenth century; Shakespeare's was thus reasonably early, and has been described as one of the best (Curl 2002, p. 118). Its novelty points to its having been wholly designed in London or by Londoners, though its placement clearly required an influential Stratford voice. Whose idea it was, we cannot know. Its uniqueness lies in its claims for its subject.

> IVDICIO PYLIUM, GENIO SOCRATEM, ARTE MARONEM,
> TERRA TEGIT, POPULUS MÆRET, OLYMPUS HABET
>
> STAY PASSENGER, WHY GOEST THOV BY SO FAST?
> READ IF THOV CANST, WHOM ENVIOVS DEATH HATH PLAST
> WITH IN THIS MONVMENT SHAKSPEARE: WITH WHOME,
> QVICK NATVRE DIDE: WHOSE NAME, DOTH DECK YS TOMBE,
> FAR MORE, THEN COST: SIEH ALL, YT HE HATH WRITT,
> LEAVES LIVING ART, BVT PAGE, TO SERVE HIS WITT.

The Latin lines tell us that Olympus now owns one whom earth buries and the people mourn, who was as wise as Nestor, as intelligent as Socrates, and whose art was level with Virgil's.

'Stay passenger'; we are passers-by, in space but also, in context, in time. 'Read if thou canst': what if we can't? Jokes about notices announcing classes for illiterates spring to mind. Maybe by 'read' we should understand 'understand'. Presumably someone will read the words to us. 'Whom' may seem at first to refer to 'thou', opening a disconcerting abyss at the line's

71

end. We ourselves die for a moment. The poem's iambic pentameters run smoothly until we hit 'Shakespeare', a meaningfully disruptive inversion of stress, a trochee where an iamb is due. 'Quick' means 'pregnant'; 'dide' irreverently proposes an erotic sense of 'did' as well as dying, itself a frequent metaphor for orgasm. 'A pun was his fatal Cleopatra', wrote Dr Johnson; here, it is somebody else's.

That somebody else, a competent versifier, rhymes efficiently and unobtrusively. The lurch after the second line may be deliberate, but it unfortunately deflects us from the verse's main purpose; if intended, it pursues a local effect distracting from the whole, the kind of ambitious mistake a young poet might well make. The stressing of 'Shakspeare', though, is accomplished. Possibly it was all composed in London: as Stanley Wells points out, Shakespeare is in a grave not a 'tomb' (Wells 2002, p. 48). Neither is he 'within' the monument. Wells surmises that some larger structure was originally intended. Perhaps only 'cost' prevented it. Maybe, though, it makes a deliberate appeal to our imaginations. We are to figure something almost inconceivably grand, to suit the claims made in Latin, rather as the Chorus in *Henry V* asks of us in the theatre. 'Cost' could have achieved nothing. This reading would push us to conclude that the lines were composed in Stratford. The author knows the true state of affairs, and deliberately draws our attention to the very plain words on the very plain grave itself.

> Good frend for Iesus sake forbeare
> To digg the dust encloased heare.
> Bles[t]e be ye man yt spares thes stones,
> And curst be he yt moves my bones.

These lines begin by greeting us openly. 'For Jesus' sake': as Christ loved us, so should we love our neighbours. The lines may joke grimly that, if resurrection is to happen, the Almighty should be given at least a sporting chance by preserving the skeleton intact (fears about the fate of jumbled bones are ancient). 'Dig' and 'dust' alliterate, as 'friend' and 'forbear' did, suggesting an earlier, less sophisticated poetry than that of Shakespeare's time; 'enclosèd' declares the fine privacy of the grave, with a possible intimation of entrapment.

In the second couplet, 'bones' and 'blessed' alliterate, emphasising the former thought but also perhaps hoping these bones themselves will be blessed. 'Blessed be the man' runs lightly off the tongue, but the second half of the line is trickier. The pile-up of 'th' with both voiced and unvoiced 's' sounds makes it much harder to say; the separation the two sounds force between 'these' and 'stones' makes the latter terribly heavy. By the time the 'friend' appears, the stones may be ancient.

'My bones': the skeleton may be unoccupied, but it remains ineluctably Shakespeare's. The voice remains, though, just as Shakespeare had promised that the Sonnets would survive time's depredations. This tiny poem contains the promise of its own immortality. The word 'I', never used, is in the end powerfully present. This is, indeed, a much subtler piece of writing than we find on the monument. Pretending to be primitive, it reminds us of the dissolution into the commonplace or proverbial so frequent at the close of individual sonnets and plays, a return to virtually pre-literate ways of thinking and modes of expression.

Similar scepticism about writing is evident on the monument, where 'living art' is now, we are told, 'but page, to serve his wit'. Overtly, this seems to mean that later, living art can only reproduce and declare Shakespeare's intelligence or creative faculty. 'Page' is an interesting word in a writer's epitaph, though. Paraphrased, the lines can mean that Shakespeare's writing itself leaves behind a 'living art', but that the work's created liveliness is only, 'but', a 'page', both leaf and servant, to put his intelligence before us.

That the work is lesser than the 'wit' is uniquely the Stratford poet's perception. The memorial poem reveals an author more bright than experienced, but one with a strong sense of Shakespeare as a person.

This reading is supported by the reference in the Latin to Socrates, who famously wrote nothing. His teaching largely consisted of asking tricky questions. It was the writer Plato who produced the 'page, to serve his wit'. As we saw earlier, the use of 'read' suggests that understanding is more important than literacy – and, of course, the theatre audience for which Shakespeare wrote neither was nor needed to be entirely literate. Many of its members probably weren't. Even those who could not 'read' the epitaph might know his name, certainly if they had come to see this particular grave.

Indeed, I suspect that the monument was commissioned as part of a publicity drive for Shakespeare which included the First Folio. His most illustrious contemporary, Edmund Spenser, was buried in Westminster Abbey, near Chaucer, in 1599. Francis Beaumont, poet, dramatist and collaborator with Shakespeare, was buried there in 1616. Poets' Corner was in the making. By 1622 at the latest, William Basse had proposed that Shakespeare join them there.

> Renownèd Spenser, lie a thought more nigh
> To learnèd Chaucer, and rare Beaumont, lie
> A little nearer Spenser, to make room
> For Shakespeare in your threefold, fourfold tomb.
>   (Oxford Shakespeare, p. lxx)

Ben Jonson replied

> My Shakespeare, rise. I will not lodge thee by
> Chaucer or Spenser, or bid Beaumont lie
> A little further to make thee a room.
> Thou art a monument without a tomb,
> And art alive still while thy book doth live
> And we have wits to read and praise to give.
>   (Oxford Shakespeare, p. lxxi)

Shakespeare is the 'Swan of Avon' (Oxford Shakespeare, p. lxxi) and, implicitly, Stratford is where his body belongs. 'Without a tomb' suggests an exact knowledge of the Holy Trinity set-up.

If Holy Trinity was to vie with Westminster Abbey, the First Folio had its rivalrous predecessors too. Jonson's First Folio appeared in 1616, but, at least as challengingly, the Spenser First Folio had appeared in 1611. The Sidney First Folio was published in 1598, and Samuel Daniel's in 1601 (Galbraith 2010, pp. 49, 53). I cannot imagine that Shakespeare's was produced without some involvement at the Stratford end, some rummaging among the dead poet's papers to see what might be left. The necessary contact would have been the inheritor of those papers, Shakespeare's daughter Susanna. She has always seemed the duller of Shakespeare's daughters, the virtuous older sister who married well, inherited the bulk of her father's estate and was principally responsible for her mother's care in old age. I shall sketch a rather different picture.

She was baptised on 26 May 1583, six months after her parents' marriage. Although forms of trial marriage were not unusual, I doubt whether the earliness of this birth could have entirely escaped notice. Her name, meaning 'purity', may constitute a promise to do better.

She was almost certainly educated. During the trial in 1598 of Elizabeth Evans, a Stratford-born prostitute, a London court heard from a witness,

Joice Cowden. Cowden stated that 'she was born on Stratford-upon-Avon and further ... that she ... went to school with the said Elizabeth Evans'. Her testimony was confirmed by George Pinder, also Stratford-born, and the court record accepts that the two women were at 'school together at Stratford-upon-Avon'.

Even if this only meant a petty school, one for young children, it shows there was some form of education for girls in Stratford. Duncan Salkeld describes Evans's signature as 'impressive, graceful, and even fine'. The clear implication is that she was well taught, beyond petty school expectations – perhaps unusually well for her profession. Her father was a cutler, according to her (Salkeld 2012, pp. 2–3) – that is, a middle-class professional not far removed from a glover. Or, indeed, a poet and dramatist.

Susanna presumably went to the same school. This would have made her at least literate. Learning to read was common for middle-class women. Their reading was often literary. Louis B. Wright points out that by 1631, Thomas Powell wrote 'instead of reading Sir Philip Sidney's *Arcadia*, let them read the grounds of good huswifery'. Wright goes on to argue that 'the implication is that even women in the lower social orders were laying claims to more abstract culture and greater familiarity with idle romance than Powell approved' (Wright 1935, p. 111). As early as 1581, Richard Mulcaster noted that 'We see young maidens be taught to read and write, and can do both passing well; we know that they learn the best, and finest of our learned languages, to the admiration of all men'. Indeed, 'To learn to read is very common' (Wright 1935, 104). Her mother's evident ability to run the Stratford end of the Shakespeare business in her husband's absence shows that Shakespeare was not averse to capable women. After her younger sibling Hamnet died in 1596, Susanna may well have become a surrogate son (not unusually). She was noticeably intelligent, as her epitaph quoted at the end of this chapter shows; the impressive firmness of her one surviving signature might indicate that she was copying, but why in that case not simply make a mark?

An intelligent daughter would naturally be interested in what her father did. Like Stanley Wells, I see Shakespeare as a literary commuter (Wells 2002, pp. 37–8). The books and papers in the house would have introduced the girl to the idea of verse, and it is highly probable that her father instructed her in the rudiments. We should remember that one of the best attested of John Aubrey's gleanings about Shakespeare is that he had for a time been a schoolmaster. Children enjoy verse; Julia Kristeva helpfully argues that poets may be those nearest a child's relation to language (Kristeva 1980a, 29–30; 1980b, 133–4, 137, 143).

Women wrote a great deal of verse in the period (Greer *et al.* 1988, pp. 5–6). Again, Powell in 1631 writes 'I like not a female poetess at any hand' (Wright 1935, 111). Nonetheless, such existed. The quantity of work they left, and Powell's insistence that 'knowledge in languages' is only appropriate for 'greater personages' than 'a private gentleman's daughter' (Wright 1935, p. 111), indicate that writing poems was familiar across a range of social levels.

If the school at Stratford was more than a petty school, Susanna could well have learned some Latin there. Equally, her father might have taught it to her. So might her uncle Edmund, who was only three years her senior, almost certainly part of the same household and presumably being educated at the grammar school. Or this bright girl might have picked it up piecemeal, by imitating, talking, listening, reading.

The Merry Wives of Windsor portrays a small-town English life probably much like Stratford's. Linguistic terms are available even to an uneducated character like the Host, who jokes about 'proverbs and no-verbs' (3.2.96). More striking is Mistress Page having Sir Hugh Evans ask her son William 'some questions in his accidence' (4.1.15). 'Accidence' is a strikingly technical word. Her husband has said that William 'profits nothing in the world at his book' (4.1.13–140), but the lesson shows that he has learned a little by rote – not that he seems to understand it.

Mistress Page hushes Mistress Quickly's indecent interjections, wanting to hear the test out (ll. 51, 67). 'He is a better scholar than I thought he was', she concludes (ll. 74–5). William can, indeed, answer some questions. Her judgement of William is not completely out, and we may wonder whether she has acquired a little Latin by osmosis. Mistress Quickly's efforts show the porousness of language, and Shakespeare's awareness of its deliquescent instability. Latin is a tongue like others, heard with others, commingling with others. Its transmission need not be wholly formal.

'Sweet lord, you play me false', Miranda says as she and Ferdinand are discovered 'playing at chess' (*The Tempest* 5. 1. SD and 174). The flirtatious implications almost eclipse the obvious. She knows the rules of chess, and she must have learned them from her father. The mental intimacy the game breeds here clearly sublimates the erotic, but chess is also a game in which well-matched players learn from each other. There is, then, a potentially didactic element in the scene.

Ferdinand avers that he would never make an illegal move, but the couple's thoughts are now clearly more on love than on their game. 'Lord', though, Ferdinand remains dominant. The scene has a terrible purity, informed, I strongly suspect, by personal observation. That Shakespeare was close at least to Susanna is, I think, shown in the importance he gives recognition scenes between fathers and daughters, for which a probable template is his own returns to Stratford after long absences, and his wondering vision of his daughter's, or daughters', growing into womanhood.

When the physician John Hall settled in Stratford in the early seventeenth century, he arrived as an armigerous middle-class professional with a rising career. The Shakespeares were well established in New Place. Nothing more natural than that they should meet, and that Shakespeare should have found the younger man interesting enough to have 'oft invited' him. However close Shakespeare's other Stratford friendships, they seem unlikely to have involved as much knowledge of a wider world or the intellectual engagements Hall, both as medical man with a wide practice and as Puritan, brought.

Susanna must have found him interesting too. And perhaps he enjoyed helping with her Latin – maybe she playfully noted the odd false construction. He was well placed to teach her and, in the process, fall in love with her.

However, Hall was a Puritan. Susanna had Roman Catholic sympathies. Early in May 1606, when she was twenty-two, she was one of twenty-one Stratfordians charged with not having taken communion on 20 April, Easter Sunday. E. R. C. Brinkworth says the number charged suggests a 'campaign' of religious enforcement. It was less than six months since the Gunpowder Plot. A campaign implies prior slackness, so this may not have been Susanna's first refusal. She may have been a 'church papist', one who was willing to attend church, but 'drew the line at receiving the Holy Communion' (Brinkworth 1972, pp. 44–5).

She failed to answer the first summons. The case is then recorded as 'dismissed', which 'probably means that she made a later appearance and satisfied the court by receiving the communion or by promising to do so' (Brinkworth 1972, pp. 45–6). Protestantism enabled women to discuss the

Bible with men (Jardine 1983, pp. 49–50); theological sparring may have formed another part of Hall's wooing.

Hall and Susanna were married at Holy Trinity on 5 June 1607. Their only child, Elizabeth, was born on 21 February, 1608, two-and-a-half weeks short of nine months later. This suggests that they may, like her parents, have anticipated the wedding, though by considerably less. The marriage may not have been entirely happy. There were no further children; Hall's notes on her illnesses are disturbingly emotionless (Lane 1996, pp. 24, 236). I suspect that she was fixated on her father, a fixation Hall could never break.

We believe that the couple moved into Hall's Croft when it was built in 1613. Hall conducted some of his practice within the house, perhaps with Susanna's involvement. After Shakespeare's death they lived in New Place, the scene of Susanna's later childhood. Her parents moved there from Henley Street in 1598, when she was fifteen.

Susanna's married social world was now presumably one of merry wives. Not that merry. On 15 July 1613, the Halls sued one John Lane in the Worcester Consistory Court for a slander committed in June. Lane had alleged that Susanna had committed adultery with a haberdasher, Ralph Smith, who had given her gonorrhoea (Pogue 2006, pp. 71–3). He did not defend the action. Lane belonged to a group opposing the vicar, Thomas Wilson; John Hall was one of Wilson's supporters, so may have been the real target of the defamation.

Elizabeth was sixteen when her mother took her on a trip to London in April 1625. We don't know why. Elizabeth may effectively have been a chaperone, Susanna may have wanted her to see London, or they simply went shopping. Likeliest is that Susanna wanted Elizabeth to see places associated with her grandfather. We only know of the trip because Elizabeth 'took cold' while away. I doubt whether it was Susanna's first visit; I think Shakespeare's posthumous literary business must have taken her there before, and may well have done now.

Holy Trinity was increasingly Puritan during most of Susanna's lifetime. By turns sidesman, churchwarden and vicar's warden (Lane 1996, p. xxv), Hall was involved with three successive vicars, who achieved an increasing plainness of worship at Holy Trinity (Brinkworth 1972, p. 21; Hughes 1987, pp. 82–4). Indeed, comparing Shakespeare to Virgil rather than Ovid (a comparison made as early as 1598) on his memorial reflects, perhaps deliberately, a Puritan change of literary emphasis. When

Elizabeth married, though, at the young age of nineteen, she chose an enthusiastic Royalist, Thomas Nash. He was thirty-two (the propensity of the Shakespeares for unconventional marriages is remarkable). They were married on 22 April 1626, and lived in Nash's house, next door to the Halls.

Anne Shakespeare died on 6 August 1623. Tantalisingly, she might just have seen an early copy of the First Folio. Unless illness intervened, she almost certainly saw the monument. Touchingly, she was buried in the space north of Shakespeare's, a space left empty at his interment. From our perspective, he appears to shelter her from even the chancel. This muffles a joke possibly contained in the lines on Shakespeare's grave about his bones' perilous proximity to the ossuary just outside. However, if we assume that standard practice was followed, the couple lie with their heads to the west. Come the resurrection, they will rise to face the altar with Anne properly on her husband's left. This seems unlikely to have been accidental. At any rate, that is what is signified, although there is good reason to believe that the remains do not actually lie directly below the stones.

Her epitaph is in Latin: it translates as

> Mother, you gave me the breast, you gave me milk and life;
> Woe is me, that for so great a gift my return will be but a tomb.
> Would that the good angel would roll away the stone from its mouth!
> And that your form, like the body of Christ, would come forth!
> Yet my prayers are of no avail; come quickly, Christ
> That my mother, though shut in the tomb, may rise again and seek the stars

Only two people could have used these words. Anne is remembered with intense affection, but only as a mother. In the second line, 'tomb' translates 'saxa'. In the last line, 'tomb' renders a form of 'tumulus', an earthen mound. (The word entered English in 1398, but was slow to catch on.) Rather than the more literal 'sepulcrum', which would have better suited the Christianity of the verse, the writer uses words emphasising the weight and soil of the grave, its clammy intimacy. Anne is 'clausa', sealed in, echoing the sense of entrapment ('enclosèd') found in the lines on Shakespeare's grave.

On 25 November 1635 John Hall died. His non-cupative (oral) will and the state of his affairs suggest death came suddenly. His epitaph, like Anne's, is in Latin. A translation reads

> Here is buried [John] Hall, most celebrated in the medical arts
> In the hope of joyous happiness in the Lord God.
> He was worthy of honour, who might have vanquished Nestor in years
> But the unyielding day takes all men.
> Lest in the tomb he might want, his most faithful wife is now here
> And he now has in death the companion of his life

'Tumulo' recurs from Anne's epitaph, Nestor from Shakespeare's monument.

In *Troilus and Cressida*, Nestor's opening speech contains a clotted pile-up of classical allusions; three different Greek myths and a Roman one flash past in eight lines, suggesting that Nestor could happily expand on them. This comic excess would have amused an Inns of Court audience. Nestor has some weighty speeches, but often serves as an observer.

Troilus and Cressida was entered in the Stationers' Register on 7 February 1603. As the Oxford editors say, it was probably written during the previous eighteen months. John Shakespeare died in September 1601, which required Shakespeare's presence in Stratford. He was not there continuously, but the play could largely have been written in Stratford, when Susanna was at the end of her teens. It could, indeed, have been the first play they discussed. Perhaps she found a comic resemblance to her father in the elderly, learned, loquacious (when permitted) and lethally observant Greek.

The really interesting thing about Hall's epitaph, though, is that to make sense at least the last two lines must have been added after Susanna's death. Hall's putative need of her again suggests planning for the long haul. The emphasis on Susanna's being 'most faithful', 'fidissima', defies all calumny.

Susanna was now sole mistress of New Place. She may have continued Hall's work as a 'wise woman'. Many medical men's widows did. The reference in her epitaph to 'comforts cordial', where 'cordial' has medicinal implications, suggests that she did.

Susanna received two notable visitors in 1643. One was a surgeon, James Cooke, then in his mid-twenties. He bought Hall's casebooks, parts of which he later edited and published, but only after a fractious scene in which, Cooke claimed, Susanna said she couldn't tell Hall's hand from another (Honan 1998, pp. 398–9). Some think this proves her illiterate. I rather think that she couldn't be bothered with someone fossicking after her husband's papers who showed no sign of knowing who her father or she were. An ordinance of the same year began the official closing of the theatres, and Shakespeare's future prospects will have looked pretty bleak. The last thing she needed was a pesky ignoramus.

More interestingly, in July, Queen Henrietta Maria stayed in Stratford, almost certainly at New Place. Hall's death and Nash's enthusiasm will have allowed Susanna to be much more overtly royalist than before. Charles I was one of Shakespeare's shrewdest early readers, but the Queen had her own enormous appetite for theatre. Courtly theatre was important in her background (Gough 2005, 195–204). Both actor and producer herself, she was central to transplanting French traditions of women acting at Court. She and Charles once acted together, performing the masque *Salmacida Spolia* in January 1640 (Britland 2006, pp. 176–7). Its author, Sir William Davenant, claimed to be Shakespeare's illegitimate child. The Queen may have wanted to check for family resemblance, but above all she will have wanted to learn about Shakespeare.

After the visit, Susanna sent the Queen a book (hard to imagine of an illiterate), now kept at the Shakespeare Birthplace Trust (Anon. 1575). An English translation of a French original (Anon. 1995), it is a tirade against Cathérine de Medici, queen and regent, for her political involvement after the St Bartholomew Day's Massacre. It claims to have been published at Heidelberg in 1575, but was actually printed by Henry Bellingham in London (Anon. 1995, p. 72). Its provenance is unknown. It could have been John Hall's. More likely, it was Shakespeare's. He lodged with Huguenots between 1602/3 and c. 1606 (Nicholl 2007, pp. 17, 18) and might have picked it up there. Equally, he will have known Christopher Marlowe's *The Massacre at Paris* (c. 1593) and may have been interested by the subject or its dramatic possibilities. It would be pleasing to believe the book was once Marlowe's own, but, sadly, fantastical.

Importantly, the book's modern editor tells us that its first edition takes no very clear religious position (Anon. 1995, p. 34). When it remarks, almost in passing, of the de Medicis that 'in most filthy and beastly whoredoms and lechery they do excel' (Anon. 1575, p. 9), the point is moral, not sectarian; the call on all estates of the realm to rebel (Anon. 1575, pp. 193–6) is similarly impartial. It uses the story of the Frankish queen Brunhilda ('Brunehault') (c. 543–613) to reflect that of Cathérine and Henri III.

It's an odd gift, a book calumniating a foreign queen accused of meddling, as the Italian Cathérine was in France, to send to another foreign queen accused of meddling, and doubly odd because Cathérine was Henrietta Maria's grandmother. Holding up a cautionary mirror to history like this implies that remarkable trust and intimacy had sprung up between the two women. Susanna clearly inherited her father's gift for getting on with all conditions of people, but used it largely in unrecorded, impenetrable privacy.

Thomas Nash died on 4 August 1647. His epitaph, again in Latin, tells us that

> Death awaits all men; a black day has stolen away
> One who was not lacking in virtue or riches.
> It has stolen him; the final light will bring him back.
> Stay, traveller; if you live for the moment, you die in misery.

The Fates, 'Fata' (here 'Death') are classically grim, set against the 'lux ultima', God's final (and highest) light. Neither the spiritual nor the mundane saves man. The verse is brief, but the Latin of the last line has a delightful patterning of consonants and vowels: 'Si peritura paras, per male parta peris', the 'viator', another passer-by, is warned.

Royalist hopes ended with the execution of Charles I on 30 January 1649. This didn't stop Elizabeth marrying another keen Royalist, John Barnard, on 5 June. Five weeks later, on 11 July, Susanna died. The wedding had gone ahead, indicating that she suffered no long illness.

Her epitaph is in English:

> Witty above her sex, but that's not all
> Wise to salvation was good Mistris Hall
> Something of Shakespeare was in that, but this
> Wholey of him with whom she's now in blisse
> Then, passenger, has't ne'er a teare
> To weepe with her that wept with all
> That wept, yet set herself to chere
> Them up with comforts cordiall
> Her love shall live, her mercy spread
> When thou has't ne'er a teare to shed

'That's not all' may express a limiting judgement on intelligence, or prepare us for the even greater attainment of wisdom. The play between 'Witty' and 'Wise' is striking. The 'that ... this' (former and latter) construction tautens the quatrain almost to epigram. 'Then' enacts a turn, what in a sonnet would be the '*volta*' between octave and sestet. The indented octosyllabics of the sestet make this look like a sonnet lacking a quatrain. 'Passenger': the same peregrine figure as addressed by Shakespeare's monument.

And, signally, the name: 'Shakespeare'. Already he needs no forename. 'Something' and 'wholly' overtly contrast Shakespeare and Hall, but 'him' could grammatically be Shakespeare rather than Hall, particularly if one hears a caesura after 'him'. Covertly, the epitaph suggests that Susanna's death brings reunion with her father, ahead of the other kin who must lie waiting. Indeed, if 'him' is Hall, Susanna's epitaph either contradicts Hall's or declares that coupledom trumps heaven, depending on our reading of 'blisse'.

Susanna's intelligence fitted her for men's intellectual companionship as much as women's. Her sympathies were blent with realism – she wept not 'with all' but 'with all / That wept'. She probably learned from her father that absolutely anyone is interesting, which may have reconciled her to provincial life. She did not share his creative drive except, I believe, where his memory was concerned.

The connections between the epitaphs suggest that one hand made them. I believe that that hand, in English and Latin, was Susanna's. I very much doubt whether there was a wide range of skilled English and Latin versifiers, otherwise unknown, conveniently on call (Ockham's razor is relevant). From the south end of the family run of graves, her epitaph echoes her father's monument by the north (poor Anne is rather over-looked). 'Shakespeare' reflects 'SHAKSPEARE'. The monument and Shakespeare's epitaph are themselves in vibrant relation. Above all, English speaks to English. Holy Trinity reveals a fascinatingly charged circuit of imaginative and loving energies, even though, as René Weis notes (Chapter 10), Susanna's bones were removed to the charnel in 1707. Through Susanna's verses (not his) she and her father survive together. And her work is signed. As Falstaff is 'Jack Falstaff with my familiars, John with my brothers and sisters, and Sir John with all Europe' (*Henry IV Part II*, 2.2.123–5), so is she 'good Mistris Hall' with Stratford and, impli-citly, 'Susanna Shakespeare' with all the world.

WORKS CITED

Alexander, Peter 1964. *Shakespeare*. Oxford University Press

Anon. 1575. *A merveylovs discourse vpon the lyfe, deedes, and behaviours of Katherine de Medicis, Queene mother: wherin are displayed the meanes which she hath practised to atteyne vnto the vsurping of the Kingedome of France, and to the bringing of the estate of the same vnto vtter ruine and destruction*

Anon. 1995. *Discours merveilleux de la vie, actions et deportements de Catherine de Médicis, Reyne-mère*, Nicole Cazauron (ed.) et Centre V. L. Saulnier. Geneva. Librairie Droz

Brinkworth, E. R. C. 1972. *Shakespeare and the Bawdy Court of Stratford*. London. Phillimore

Britland, Karen 2006. *Drama at the Court of Queen Henrietta Maria*. Cambridge University Press

Curl, James Stevens 2002. *Death and Architecture: An Introduction to the Funerary and Commemorative Buildings in the Western European Tradition, with Some Consideration of Their Settings*. Thrupp. Sutton Publishing

Galbraith, Steven K. 2010. 'English Literary Folios 1593–1623: Studying shifts in format' in John N. King (ed.), *Tudor Books and Readers: Materiality and the Construction of Meaning*. Cambridge University Press

Gough, Melinda J. 2005. 'Courtly Comédiantes: Henrietta Maria and amateur women's stage plays in England and France' in Pamela Allen Brown and Peter Parolin (eds.), *Women Players in England, 1500–1660: Beyond the All-Male Stage*. Aldershot. Ashgate

Greer, Germaine, Medoff, Jeslyn, Sansone, Miranda and Hastings, Susan (eds.) 1988. *Kissing the Rod: An Anthology of Seventeenth-Century Women's Verse*. London. Virago

Honan, Park 1998. *Shakespeare: A Life*. Oxford University Press

Hughes, Ann 1987. *Politics, Society and Civil War in Warwickshire, 1620–1660*. Cambridge University Press

Jardine, Lisa 1983. *Still Harping on Daughters: Women and Drama in the Age of Shakespeare*. Hemel Hempstead. Harvester Wheatsheaf

Kristeva, Julia 1980a. 'The Ethics of Linguistics' in Leon S. Roudiez, Thomas Gora and Alice Jardine (eds.), *Desire in Language: A Semiotic Approach to Literature and Art*. Oxford. Basil Blackwell, pp. 23–35

1980b. 'From one identity to an other' in Leon S. Roudiez, Thomas Gora and Alice Jardine (eds.), *Desire in Language: A Semiotic Approach to Literature and Art*. Oxford. Basil Blackwell, pp. 124–47

Lane, Joan 1996. *John Hall and His Patients: The Medical Practice of Shakespeare's Son-in-law*. Stratford-upon-Avon. Shakespeare Birthplace Trust

Nicholl, Charles 2007. *The Lodger: Shakespeare on Silver Street.* London. Allen Lane

Pogue, Kate Emery 2006. *Shakespeare's Friends.* Westport, CT. Praeger

Salkeld, Duncan 2012. *Shakespeare among the Courtesans: Prostitution, Literature, and Drama, 1500–1650.* Aldershot. Ashgate

Wells, Stanley 2002. *Shakespeare for All Time.* Basingstoke. Macmillan

Wright, Louis B. 1935. *Middle-Class Culture in Elizabethan England.* Chapel Hill, NC. University of North Carolina Press

7

His son-in-law John Hall

GREG WELLS

❧

John Hall, William Shakespeare's son-in-law, is seldom considered in his own right, and when he is the results are often contradictory. He may have been a highly qualified physician, or an unqualified empiric; a radical Paracelsian, or a conservative Galenist in education and practice, or ahead of his time; a Puritan with no sympathy for the theatre, or a good friend as well as son-in-law to Shakespeare. I shall try to integrate these differing views, without attempting documentary exhaustiveness.

His father was William Hall of Carlton, Bedfordshire; his mother is unknown. There are no baptismal records in Carlton for 1575, when John was born (Gray 1936, p. 344). John studied at Queens' College, Cambridge, receiving his BA in 1593/4 and MA in 1597. We have no other records of his life before he moved to Stratford-upon-Avon in 1607, but he must have gained sufficient experience in that time to be able to set up his own practice.

He never obtained, or claimed to have, the degree of Doctor of Medicine. His qualifications in fact put him in the mainstream of physicians at his time. Of 814 physicians practising outside London between 1603 and 1643, 78 per cent had formally matriculated (enrolled) at a university (Raach 1962, p. 250). Forty per cent held BAs, 34 per cent MAs and 30 per cent MDs. An MD was required for licensing by the College of Physicians of London or to teach at a university, but not otherwise. An academic doctorate was no more necessary as a medical qualification then than it is now. Hall never used the title of Doctor, nor was he addressed so by his contemporaries, though he has frequently and confusingly been granted it *post mortem*. He may, like many English students, have travelled around the Continent and studied for a few weeks or months at one or more universities. If such short-term unregistered students paid their bills and stayed out of trouble, they commonly left no record behind them.

Outside London, physicians were supposed to be licensed by the local Bishop but this was not in practice essential, and the records are patchy. Physicians often applied for a licence only when a dispute arose with a patient or colleague, for the extra status it gave. There are no records of licences in the Worcester Diocese before 1661, so either they have been lost or none were granted. John was recognised as 'professor of medicine' (that is, practising medicine as a profession) by Stratford's Church Court in 1622 (Brinkworth 1972, p. 148). This was a 'Peculiar' Court, sharing some responsibilities with the Bishop but independent of him in two years out of three, so the recognition might technically be held equivalent to an Episcopal licence.

John would have studied medical textbooks as part of his MA, but in addition 'often a young physician would acquire practical bedside knowledge by working with an established physician' (Wear 2000, p. 122). William Hall's will offers some suggestions as to who this might be. John was named his father's executor, and in return was to receive everything apart from minor bequests. If he refused this duty, he was still to receive 'all my books of physic' (Marcham 1931, p. 25). This may indicate that William was also a physician but is not definitive. Medical books were commonly owned by householders, who, with their wives, would provide the first line of medical care for their households. William might have left such books to his son, the newly established physician, without necessarily being a physician himself.

William Hall bequeathed books of astronomy, astrology and alchemy to his servant Matthew Morrys, on condition that Matthew should instruct John in these arts, if he wished to learn them (it appears he did not). These are less likely to have formed part of a standard household library, and perhaps indicate William's main interest. Morrys moved to Stratford-upon-Avon at some time, and maintained friendly contact with the Halls. He named two of his children Susanna and John, after them. Two years after Shakespeare's death John made him trustee with John Greene, of the Gate House in Blackfriars (Schoenbaum 1987, p. 275).

A more likely candidate is William Sheppard, John's brother-in-law. He gained his MA at King's College, Cambridge in 1590, and his MD in 1597, and moved to Leicester in 1599 after marrying John's sister Sara. Perhaps she met William in Cambridge through her brother, as no other connection is known. If William Sheppard invited John to accompany him to

Leicester as assistant, he would then have had time for four or five years of practice, and a visit to the Continent, before setting up on his own.

The reasons behind John's move to Stratford-upon-Avon are unknown. Stratford was prosperous and had no resident physician, but that applied to other small towns as well. The only identified link is through Abraham Sturley, estate agent to the Lucy family at Hampton Lucy. The Lucys had estates near Carlton, so there might have been contact between Sturley and the Hall family there (Mitchell 1947, p. 10). There is no way of knowing whether John had met the Shakespeare family before his move, but there is a tantalising indirect connection. John's BA in 1593 was signed by William Covell, who in 1595 made one of the first printed references to 'sweet Shakespeare'. Thus the Shakespeare name at least was probably familiar to John from university times (Joseph 1993, p. viii; Eccles 1966, p. 433; Covell 1595, sig.r2v).

John and Susanna Shakespeare married on 5 June 1607, their only daughter Elizabeth being christened on 21 February the following year. There are no records of where they lived before inheriting New Place on Shakespeare's death, and they may have been tenants there before that. Hall's Croft is often suggested, and Wheler in 1814 is quoted as having seen 'in some old paper relating to the town, that Dr Hall resided in that part of Old Town which is in the parish of Old Stratford' (Halliwell-Phillipps 1886, p. 321). It cannot have been their first home in Stratford though, because dendrochronological evidence shows that the oldest part of Hall's Croft, facing onto the road, was built in the summer of 1613 (Anon 1990). If they lived there it is likely that they rented it, as there is no record of its sale, nor is it mentioned in Hall's will with his other properties. Hall did own a 'close on Evesham Way', for which he paid a charge to the Stratford Corporation from 1612 to 1616 (*Stratford-upon-Avon Corporation 1585–1619*, pp. 228, 245, 263, 276). He probably bought the close from Abraham Sturley, perhaps as a meadow and stabling for his horse.

References to contacts between John Hall and his father-in-law are sparse. In 1611 their names appeared (with sixty-nine others) on what is thought to be a subscription list raising money to support a bill in Parliament for repairs to the highways (Bearman 1994, p. 44). They shared an interest in 107 acres of land purchased by Shakespeare in 1602. He may have intended this as a marriage settlement for one or other of his daughters, though it is listed in his will as if still in his ownership in 1616.

This land was affected by the proposed enclosure at Welcombe in 1614. Thomas Greene's diary records a meeting in London on 17 November 1614, commonly assumed to have been with both Shakespeare and Hall, but Greene did not unequivocally write that. He visited 'my cousin Shakespeare', 'to see him how he did'. In the conversation that followed, 'He [Shakespeare] told me that they assured him they meant to enclose no further than to Gospel Bush ... and he and Mr Hall say they think there will be nothing done at all' (Ingleby 1885, p. iii). Shakespeare was probably reporting Hall's views based on prior discussions in Stratford, to emphasise their agreement on the issue.

Shakespeare named Hall as his executor and main legatee with Susanna in his will in 1616. He was the obvious choice, being an older and more respectable son-in-law than Judith's husband Thomas Quiney. Hall proved the will on 22 June 1616 and seems to have discharged his duties satisfactorily (Schoenbaum 1987, p. 306).

The relationship between the two men becomes important when considering whether Hall influenced Shakespeare's portrayal of physicians in his plays, a debate that started in 1860 and has continued ever since (Bucknill 1860, p. 36). The occasionally disputed consensus is, firstly, that medical matters occur more frequently and are dealt with more seriously in the later plays, and secondly, that Hall's influence is needed to explain this. Two considerations rarely mentioned in this respect are that Shakespeare's subjects and style changed over time; and that his characters are on stage for dramatic purposes, wider issues being subordinated to the immediate pressures of plot and situation.

One does not need to invoke Hall's influence to see that a physician like Dr Caius (*The Merry Wives of Windsor*, 1597–98) would be inappropriate in the later tragedies. Dr Pinch (*The Comedy of Errors*, 1594) is a schoolmaster, therefore a cleric not a physician. The scenes with a doctor in *The Two Noble Kinsmen* (1613–14) are by Fletcher, not Shakespeare. Helen's circumstances in *All's Well That Ends Well* (1604–5) were uncommon but not unknown. Wives or daughters did sometimes inherit a practice and, with conditions, continue to practise physic (Pelling and Webster 1979, p. 183). In the medical marketplace of London or Norwich, about a quarter of unlicensed practitioners (excluding nurses and midwives), or one eighth of all, were women.

The dialogue between the doctor and Cordelia in *King Lear* (1605–6) serves to slow down the action and build up tension before Lear's wakening. The advice given to Cordelia as her father regains consciousness is general enough to be given by a doctor in the 1608 quarto, but by a gentleman in the First Folio. The Scottish Doctor in *Macbeth* (1606) has been criticised for political and medical fearfulness and for avoiding any positive medical action in the sleep-walking scene. That, however, is not his dramatic function. He provides half a dialogue without which the sleep-walking scene would be a dumb show. A brisk statement that he would be back in the morning with a purge, a cupping glass and a remedy for melancholy might sound better professionally, but hardly fits the plot.

Pericles has attracted most attention, having been written in the year of John and Susanna's wedding. In a play in which the astonishing and the everyday are juxtaposed, Cerimon the physician is remarkably down to earth. He enters with the most practical medical exchanges that Shakespeare wrote. He says to a servant, 'Your master will be dead ere you return. / There's nothing can be ministered to nature / That can recover him'; and to a poor man, 'Give this to th' pothecary / And tell me how it works' (*Pericles*, 12, 6–9). Cerimon here performs the two key functions of a physician: to pronounce a prognosis, and, if possible, prescribe treatment.

Cerimon's speech about his practice has been read as a description of an ideal physician, and perhaps as praise of Shakespeare's new son-in-law:

> I ever
> Have studied physic, through which secret art,
> By turning o'er authorities, I have,
> Together with my practice, made familiar
> To me and to my aid the blest infusions
> That dwells in vegetives, in metals, stones
> (*Pericles*, 12, 28–33)

The 'secret art' should not be heard too literally. Supposedly secret remedies are a commonplace in the medical literature of the time. Hall quoted the *Thresor des remedes secrets pour les maladies des femmes* in his *Little Book* (Liébaut 1585). The reference to metals and stones has been taken as indicating a Paracelsian influence, but the parallel with Friar Laurence in *Romeo and Juliet* (1595): 'O mickle is the powerful grace that lies / In plants, herbs, stones, and their true qualities' (*Romeo and Juliet*.2.2.15–16), shows that this cannot be attributed to Hall.

It is pleasant to think that the character of Cerimon was a wedding tribute to Hall, but the combination of 'authorities' and 'practice' may be more significant. Cerimon claims to have both a traditional book-based university education, and practical proof from his own experience that his treatments work. Hall based the title of his manuscript, *A Little Book of cures, proved in practice and taken from authorities, tried and tested in certain places and on noted people*, on that of his favourite author, Martin Ruland the Younger (this and other translations are my own unless otherwise stated). The pairing of practice with authority was still relatively new and Ruland felt the need to explain it: 'I call those cures empiric, not because they are based on experience only as the empiric sect declares, but those which combine simultaneously rational teaching with practice, and are managed by method' (Ruland 1628, Sig.a3v). This is the most likely, perhaps only, point at which we see can Hall's influence on Shakespeare's writing.

Between 1616 and his death, Hall is mentioned in various records relating to his civic life. He was elected to the Corporation in 1617 and 1623, but was excused from taking up the position on both occasions. In 1625 he sold most of his share of the tithes to the Corporation (Eccles 1963, p. 105). The following year he refused a knighthood, paying a £10 fine instead. In 1628 he was elected churchwarden, and in 1629 presented a new pulpit to the church (Lane 1996, p. xxv). In the same year, trouble over his brother Dive's will meant that Hall agreed that he had given up executorship of their father's will because it would be 'a hindrance . . . in his practice being a physician' (Eccles 1963, p. 112).

Hall is usually described as a Puritan, a contested word that meant something very different in the early seventeenth century to the circumstances of the post-war Commonwealth Period. Hall would more likely have described himself as one of the 'Godly', an evangelical strand of the Church of England tending to Calvinism, emphasising preaching of the word, and consciously aiming to improve society as well as personal morality. Detractors used 'Puritan' to label behaviour that they saw as hypocritical self-serving and prurient prying into other people's affairs (Marshall 2012, p. 146). Alternatively, 'Puritanism did not involve particular, exclusive positions, but rather the holding of conventional Protestant positions in an especially zealous and committed form' (Hughes 1994, p. 62). Hall was certainly committed to the Episcopal Church of England,

and showed no sympathy for Presbyterianism or non-conformism. If Susanna's absence from Easter communion in 1606 was due to Puritan rather than Catholic leanings, she may have been the more radical of the two (Greer 2007, p. 239).

From around 1625 onwards, Hall was increasingly caught in a conflict between the Town Corporation and the vicar of Holy Trinity (Hughes 1994, pp. 69–74). If his behaviour was difficult, even intemperate, he was not alone. He and other leading citizens faced a set of insoluble problems within a confusion of overlapping responsibilities and jurisdictions. The Town Corporation was responsible for the vicar's and schoolmaster's salaries, but the Lord of the Manor held the presentation to the living. The Puritan-dominated Corporation took advantage of confusion over the Lordship in 1619 to appoint a new, learned vicar. Opponents of Thomas Wilson's appointment (including John Lane, who had accused Susanna of adultery in 1613) disrupted his installation by rioting around and in Holy Trinity, and publishing libels which led to a Star Chamber suit.

At first the Corporation supported the Vicar, increasing his stipend from £20 to £60 (a very considerable sum) in recognition of his preaching. They supported each other against the Bishop of Worcester's complaint that Wilson was taking more powers to the Church Court than he should. Relationships must have started to sour before 1629, when Wilson's stipend was cut and another preacher appointed following a dispute about the profits of the churchyard. Hall sided with Wilson, claiming that his sale of the tithes in 1625 had been intended to enhance the stipends of the vicar and schoolmaster. He finally agreed to election onto the Corporation in July 1632, but in October 1633 was displaced for breach of orders and non-attendance. The same year he was briefly and irregularly re-appointed churchwarden, and was associated with Wilson's Chancery suit against the Corporation for restoration of his stipend. Hall's relationships with the Corporation soured to the point that in 1634 the members met to discuss and deny Hall's charge that they were 'foresworn villains' (Hughes 1994, p. 68).

The animosities spilled over into an unseemly personal row about the allocation of pews in Holy Trinity, which had to be resolved by Bishop Thornborough of Worcester. Wilson had granted Hall and his family a pew which it was claimed had always been used by the burgesses' wives. Hall was only one of the people involved, but he had the advantage of having successfully treated Thornborough in February 1633. The Bishop supported Hall's case, addressing his letter on the subject to 'Mr John Hall practitioner of physic' – not a licence, but clear Episcopal recognition of his status (Thornborough 1635).

The growing antagonism may be behind the odd timing of Hall's agreement to join the Corporation in 1632, when relationships were already soured. It might have suited the Vicar to have an ally there, while at the same time the Burgesses could feel that Hall had at last recognised their importance. If it was an attempt to manage the problem it failed, as did all other attempts. The bitter quarrel continued until Wilson's death in 1638. The underlying causes may have been tensions within Puritanism itself, and a growing gap between clerical and lay understandings of their roles (Hughes 1994, p. 71). Stratford was not unique in experiencing such tensions and the change of church policies under Charles I and Archbishop Laud may have created other hidden tensions (Marshall 2012, p. 149). Whatever the reason, when Hall was forced to make a choice he was more committed to his Church than to his civic responsibilities.

Throughout this time, Hall continued to practise medicine. He would be a significant figure in the history of medicine even without the Shakespeare connection, for physicians' records from the early seventeenth century are rare. Hall's *Little Book* is in many respects unique, being a detailed record of the practice of a provincial physician, associated with neither the Court nor the London College (Hall 1635). He composed it in Latin, mostly between 1630 and his death in 1635. Hall's choice of Latin is curious. If he planned to publish, it suggests a desire to emulate Continental writers rather than add to the by-then growing number of English-language medical texts.

The small notebook, now in the British Library, contains 178 case reports of varying length, dated between 1611 and 1635, in roughly chronological order. Hall must have gone through his original notes, looking for and copying out cases of interest. Most were cases with successful outcomes, as was customary in the current medical literature, but he included some which puzzled him, including unexpected deaths. James Cooke, a Warwick surgeon, obtained the manuscript from Susanna around 1642, translated it and eventually published it in 1657, and a second edition followed (Cooke 1679). Cooke was eager to play down Hall's indebtedness to tradition and to emphasise his originality, so he left out material that contradicted this view, including several of Hall's references to his sources. Cooke's second edition has been reproduced twice in facsimile (Joseph 1993; Lane 1996). Joan Lane's commentary is particularly useful for her detailed social studies of Hall's patients. These editions have made Hall's notes relatively access-ible, and useful to historians of medicine (Beier 1987; Nagy 1988; Wear 2000). The vividness of his clinical descriptions has also made him a popular source for medical writers with an interest in history (Moschowitz 1918; Betts and Betts 1998; Pearce 2006; Fernandez-Florez 2010).

The *Little Book* refers to several members of Shakespeare's circle. Within the family Hall treated himself, his wife Susanna and daughter Elizabeth, Elizabeth's mother-in-law Mary Nash, and George Quiney (Judith Shakespeare's brother-in-law). He also treated Richard Tyler, Thomas Russell's daughter and son-in-law, Francis Collins's daughter Alice and Thomas Green's daughter Anne, several members of the Rainsford family at Clifford Chambers, their friend the poet Michael Drayton, and William Combe's mother-in-law, wife and daughter. It is likely that he also treated his father-in-law, but the clinical details did not strike him as worth recording.

Hall's cases in the *Little Book* are mostly drawn from the middling well-to-do tradesmen and more educated citizens of Stratford (teachers, clergy and lawyers), and the gentry (including some Roman Catholics) in the surrounding countryside. Among the nobility he treated the families of the Earls of Northampton and Shrewsbury, and of Lord Saye and Seal near Banbury. Naming important patients was commonplace in medical literature at the time, as a way of providing evidence for a physician's success. Payment is only rarely mentioned. The Countess of Shrewsbury gave him 'great thanks, with a large payment' for successfully treating her son, and Lady Puckering rewarded him 'so that I might help others' (Hall 1635, pp. 54, 91). He also treated Mr Nash's serving maid and a poor man named Hudson, along with many others who cannot be identified. We should not assume that the patients he recorded are typical of his practice as a whole.

Hall's references to physiology and pathology follow the traditional Galenic and Hippocratic model of four humours, blood, phlegm, yellow and black bile, which had to be balanced individually for good health. Imbalances might be due to incorrect diet, improper digestion, or blockage of excretion via the digestive system, urine, menstruation or through the skin. Corrupted humours were thought to accumulate beneath the skin until they broke out, as in smallpox or measles.

Hall's therapies, though, were taken from both Galenic and chemical texts. In the terms of his period, he was neither a Galeno-Hippocratic Dogmatist nor a Paracelsian, but a Chymiatrist, drawing on both (Moran 2005, p. 82). Galenic and chemical remedies were both derived from minerals as well as animals and vegetables, but more important than the ingredients was the method of preparation. The chemical system favoured distillation to produce essences from raw materials, while traditional methods relied more on extraction with water or oil (Moran 2005, p. 12).

Physicians were trained in the use of simples prepared from a single ingredient, as well as of compounds containing perhaps dozens of simples. Hall used traditional European simples and newer ones from the Americas and Far East such as guaiacum and sarsaparilla. The *Pharmacopoeia Londinensis* in 1618 listed 680 simples, 47 of which are metals. About 80 per cent of Hall's compound remedies are listed in the *Pharmacopoeia*. He also used several chemical pharmacopoeias, such as *Basilica Chymica* (Croll 1609).

Hall composed his manuscript in an unusual way, perhaps because his Latin was limited outside of professional study. Over a third of his text is made up of phrases, sentences or whole paragraphs borrowed from his medical textbooks and rearranged to suit the circumstances of his own patients. He used this method to describe patients, illnesses and outcomes, as well as for details of remedies. Usually he gave no reference, and it is only the existence of searchable on-line databases that has enabled his sources to be identified. The cases of his daughter and wife are good examples of his methods of composition and practice.

Elizabeth suffered from *tortura oris* (spasm of one side of the mouth) in January 1624. Hall gives a reference for the signs, then started her treatment with a purge and an ointment (Valesco 1560, pp. 88–90; Platter 1602, p. 387). Elizabeth recovered after further purging, anointing and treatment for absence of menstruation. The condition recurred in April, and Hall referred to chapters on the disease and its treatment in several texts (Houllier 1611, pp. 96–99; Platter 1602, p. 375; Rondelet 1574, ff 101v–102v; Amatus Lusitanus 1556, pp. 394–6). Treatment continued with ointments and purgatives and was eventually successful. Cooke's bald translation that 'she eat [*sic*] nutmegs often' has been taken as Elizabeth's personal quirk, but he omitted Hall's statement that this was 'as Platter strongly recommends', as well as all the other references (Cooke 1679, p. 33; Hall 1635, p. 36). The case report concludes 'all her symptoms diminished, and daily over a few days she reached complete health, freed from death and deadly illness' (Ruland 1628, p. 217; Hall 1635, p. 37).

Hall regarded himself as a specialist in the treatment of scurvy, relying mainly on two standard textbooks (Eugalenus 1604; Sennert 1624). Scurvy was at that time thought to be a severe disease of the spleen due to excess of black bile (melancholy). It had been described in travellers' accounts and medical texts from the early sixteenth century onwards, and treatment with antiscorbutic herbs such as scurvy-grass, watercress and brooklime was standard by the 1590s. There was nothing particularly advanced in Hall's treatments, though Cooke made much of them. Rather, Hall prided himself on his ability to diagnose a notoriously tricky disease that often mimicked other conditions. In his report on Bishop Thornborough's scorbutic arthritis, he borrowed a sentence from Eugalenus: 'The false appearance of the arthritis deceived and made sport of his physicians' – even though Hall regarded them as 'experienced and learned in traditional medicine' (Eugalenus 1604, p. 97; Hall 1635, p. 161).

Susanna suffered from 'lower backache, convulsions, diseased gums, foul-smelling breath, wind, melancholy, heartburn, spontaneous tiredness, difficulty in breathing, fear of choking, tightness and torment of the abdomen', all of which together pointed to scurvy (Hall 1635, p. 115). Hall applied plasters and liniments to her abdomen and lower back, and prescribed an antiscorbutic electuary (Sennert 1624, p. 674). The cure was completed with steeled wine (wine boiled with steel filings) mixed with a large number of antiscorbutic herbs, the recipe of a leading French chemical physician (Du Chesne 1607, p. 74).

A few independent witnesses indicate how Hall was regarded by his patients. Lady Tyrrell wrote an undated letter to her friend Lady Temple sympathising with her husband's mischance, and praising his intention to consult Hall: 'I know by experience that he is most excellent'; Sidrick Davenport wrote to Hall on 5 July 1632 complaining of his tardiness, and requesting an urgent visit: 'it is very strange to me, and unheard of that a physician should be incorporated of any Town or made a member of any corporation, not only to interrupt his studies but also endanger the life of his patient for want of his presence' (Joseph 1993, pp. xi, 27–8). Patients some-times refused to follow his advice, and several in particular refused to be bled.

Hall was neither greatly advanced nor conservative in his practice. He saw himself as a specialist in scurvy, more knowledgeable about diagnosis than his colleagues. He bled fewer of his patients than most of his textbooks recommended, but purged almost everyone who was not elderly, pregnant or a child, before starting specific treatments. He relied on uroscopy (visual examination of the urine) a great deal, though this was already becoming old-fashioned. He went on buying new medical books all his life.

John Hall's ledger-stone in Holy Trinity Church, Stratford-upon-Avon, records that he died on 25 November 1635, aged 60. His death was presumably unexpected, as he made a nuncupative will (orally in front of witnesses) the same day. His wife and daughter inherited everything except his 'study of books' which went to his son-in-law Thomas Nash 'to dispose of them as you see good' (Marcham 1931, p. 25). His manuscripts would have gone to one Mr Boles 'if he had been here' but as he was not 'you may son Nash burn them or do with them what you please'. Hall's will was dictated too hastily for the usual preamble expressing his faith, but the introduction to his own illness in the *Little Book* used texts from the Vulgate Old Testament and the physicians François Valleriola and Ruland to the same purpose (Hall 1635, p. 150):

Thou Lord, 'hast power of life and death; thou leadest to the gates of hell, and bringest up again' (Wisdom 16:13). I confess 'neither by human work, nor help from the art, nor advice, but only by your goodness and mercy you made me whole, and recovered me beyond all hope and expectation from the most severe and deadliest signs of a lethal fever, as if rescued from the jaws of hell and restored to perfect health' (Valleriola 1573, 1). Therefore 'I give thanks to you, most merciful God and Father of our Lord Jesus Christ, who through your fatherly mercy has made me whole. Give me grace, that I may recognise and remember your blessings with a grateful mind' (Ruland 1628, p. 231).

The combination of texts stressing divine rather than human works, and the thanks for God's mercy, reflect the evangelical element in Hall's beliefs. In other cases, too, he frequently attributed cures to divine grace, even when treating his Catholic patients.

We have little direct evidence for the relationship between Hall and his father-in-law. Shakespeare was forty-three years old, and Hall thirty-two, when Hall married Susanna in 1607. At that time Shakespeare was still much involved with the theatre in London and Hall was establishing his practice in Stratford. Any closeness between them would likely have developed later, in the two or three years before Shakespeare's death in 1616, when he was spending more time at home. They were certainly business partners, and there is no evidence that they ever seriously fell out. Susanna and Elizabeth must have created a bond between them, while Judith and Thomas Quiney's marriage problems would have made Hall seem all the more dependable by contrast. I suggest that their relationship started as one of mutual respect, and developed through shared business and family interests into a close friendship.

WORKS CITED

Amatus Lusitanus 1556. *Curationum medicinalium centuriae quatuor*. Basel. Froben

Anon. 1990. *Dendrochronological Results for Hall's Croft*. Shakespeare Birthplace Trust

Bearman, R. 1994. *Shakespeare in the Stratford Records*. Stroud. Alan Sutton

Beier, L. M. 1987. *Sufferers and Healers: The Experience of Illness in Seventeenth-century England*. London. Routledge and Kegan Paul

Betts, T. and Betts, H. 1998. 'John Hall and his Epileptic Patients – epilepsy management in early 17th century England', *Seizure* 7: 411–14

Brinkworth, E. R. C. 1972. *Shakespeare and the Bawdy Court of Stratford*. London. Phillimore

Bucknill, J. C. 1860. *The Medical Knowledge of Shakespeare*. London. Longman

Cooke, J. 1679. *Select Observations on English Bodies of Eminent Persons in Desperate Diseases: First Written in Latin by Mr John Hall, Physician*. London. Benjamin Shirley

Covell, William 1595. *Polimanteia, or, the meanes lawfull and unlawful, to judge of the fall of a commonwealth*. London

Croll, O. 1609. *Basilica Chymica*. Frankfurt. Claudius Marnius

Du Chesne, J. 1607. *Tractatus duo quorum prior inscribitur diaeteticon poly-historicum, alter vero pharmacopoea dogmaticorum restituta*. Frankfurt. Schoenwetter

Eccles, M. 1963. *Shakespeare in Warwickshire*. University of Wisconsin

    1966. 'Review: Shakespeare's Son-in-law John Hall: man and physician, by Harriet Joseph', *Shakespeare Quarterly* 17: 432–3

Eugalenus, S. 1604. *De Scorbuto morbo liber*. Leipzig. Lantzenberger

Fernandez-Florez, A. 2010. 'On the Practice of John Hall in the Field of Dermatology in the 17th Century', *Clinics in Dermatology* 28: 356–63

Gray, I. 1936. 'Shakespeare's Son-in-law: The antecedents of Doctor John Hall', *Genealogist's Magazine* 7: 344–54

Greer, Germaine. 2007. *Shakespeare's Wife*. London. Bloomsbury

Hall, J. 1635. '*Curationum Historicarum et Empiricarum, in certis locis et notis personis expertarum et robatarum, libellus'*. Egerton MS 2065, British Library

Halliwell-Phillipps, J. O. 1886. *Outlines of the Life of Shakespeare*, 6th edn, 2 vols. London. Longmans Green

Houllier, J. 1611. *De morbis internis libe.* Paris. Perier

Hughes, A. 1994. 'Religion and Society in Stratford upon Avon, 1619–1638', *Midlands History* 19: 58–84

Ingleby, C. M. 1885. *Shakespeare and the enclosure of common fields at Welcombe, being a fragment of the private diary of Thomas Greene, town clerk of Stratford upon Avon, 1614–1617*. Birmingham. Robert Birbeck

Joseph, H. 1993. *Shakespeare's Son-in-law John Hall: Man and Physician.* Hamden, CT. Archon

Lane, J. 1996. *John Hall and his Patients: The Medical Practice of Shakespeare's Son-in-law.* Stratford-upon-Avon. Sutton

Liébaut 1585. *Thresor des remedes secrets pour les maladies des femmes.* Paris. du Puy

Marcham, F. 1931. *William Shakespeare and his Daughter Susannah.* London. Grafton

Marshall, P. 2012. *Reformation England 1480–1642*, 2nd edn. London. Bloomsbury

Mitchell, C. M. 1947. *The Shakespeare Circle: A Life of Dr John Hall.* Birmingham. Cornish

Moran, B. T. 2005. *Distilling Knowledge: Alchemy, Chemistry and the Scientific Revolution.* Cambridge, MA. Harvard University Press

Moschowitz, E. 1918. 'Dr John Hall: Shakespeare's Son-in-law', *Bulletin of the Johns Hopkins Hospital* 19: 148–52

Nagy, D. E. 1988. *Popular Medicine in Seventeenth-century England.* Ohio. Bowling Green State University Popular Press

Pearce, J. M. S. 2006. 'Dr John Hall (1575–1635) and Shakespeare's Medicine', *Journal of Medical Biography* 14: 187–91

Pelling, M. and Webster, C. 1979. 'Medical practitioners' in C. Webster, *Health, Medicine and Mortality in the Sixteenth Century.* Cambridge University Press

Platter, F. 1602. *Praxeos seu de cognoscendis, praedicendis, praecavendis, curandisque affectibus homini incommodantibus tractatus: de functionum laesionibus.* Basel. Waldkirch

Raach, J. H. 1962. *A Directory of English Country Physicians 1603–1643*. London. Dawson

Rondelet, G. 1574. *Methodus curandorum omnium morborum corporis humanis in tres libros distinct*. Paris. Macé

Ruland, M. 1628. *Curationum empyricarum et historicarum, in certis locis et notis personis optime expertarum et rite probatarum, centuriae decem*. Lyons. Pierre Ravaud

Schoenbaum, S. 1987. *William Shakespeare: A Compact Life*, rev. edn. Oxford University Press

Sennert, D. 1624. *De Scorbuto tractatus*. Wittenberg. Schuerer

Stratford-upon-Avon Corporation Chamberlain's Accounts 1585–1619, BRU4/1, Stratford-upon-Avon. Shakespeare Birthplace Trust

Thornborough, J. 1635. *Grant by John Thornborough, Bishop of Worcester, April 1635*. ER78/7, Stratford-upon-Avon. Shakespeare Birthplace Trust

Valesco de Taranta 1560. *Epitome operis perquam utilis morbis curandis Valesci de Taranta in septem congesta libros*. Lyons. Tornæsius and Gazeius

Valleriola, F. 1573. *Observationum medicinalium libri sex*. Lyons. Gryphius

Wear, A. 2000. *Knowledge and Practice in English Medicine 1550–1695*. Cambridge University Press

8

His son Hamnet Shakespeare

GRAHAM HOLDERNESS

෪

1

Everything we know about Hamnet Shakespeare is that he was baptised 2 February 1585, Stratford-upon-Avon, one of a pair of twins; and buried, 11 August 1596. He was eleven years old. He was born; he lived; he died. And one more thing: he happened to be the only son of the most famous writer in history.

2

There is also a body of circumstantial evidence that surrounds the life of Hamnet, is contingent upon it, and may or may not allow us to infer something about him. We know a lot, of course, about his family, especially his father. His twin Judith lived to the age of seventy-seven, and we know a fair bit about her. The names of both twins replicate the names of a Stratford couple, friends and neighbours of the Shakespeares, Hamnet and Judith Sadler, who were Catholic recusants; surely more than a coincidence. Hamnet Sadler is remembered in Shakespeare's will, where his name is spelt, interestingly, 'Hamlett'.

Certain documented events surround the date of Hamnet's death. When Hamnet died, the Lord Chamberlain's Men were touring in Kent: on 11 August they played the market hall in Faversham. Shakespeare may have been with them.

A few months after the boy's death, Shakespeare re-submitted to the College of Heralds an application for a grant of arms to the Shakespeare family; and in the following year, 1597, he bought a large house, New Place in Stratford.

Most of the Hamnet Shakespeare story is a fabric woven around the pegs of these direct and circumstantial historical data. Some biographers have also brought to bear information from a broader spectrum of facts. Evidence of mortality rates from the Stratford burial records, to account for Hamnet's demise. Evidence about schooling, to flesh out for him an appropriate education. Evidence about housing, family life, employment, the economy, to sketch out for him an illuminating social milieu. All these data can be corroborated, authenticated, endorsed as genuine historical context and assumed as Hamnet Shakespeare's background. But none of it can be connected with him in any definitive way, since the only traces the boy left are those cold, impersonal words telling us that he was born, and that he died.

And lastly there is of course an even more indirect discursive field in which Hamnet's story might be written, and that is in Shakespeare's own works. Here we find at once the most intimate, yet the most remote of contingencies; the most irresistible, but the most inconclusive of connections. Like the child in T. S. Eliot's beautiful poem 'Marina', in the poetry of Shakespeare's plays the lost boy's story is 'more distant than stars, and nearer than the eye' (Eliot 1961, p. 115).

3

We could conclude that there is no Hamnet Shakespeare story beyond those scraps of historical record, details that could be crammed onto a very small gravestone (though he doesn't seem to have had one). However, a glance at a few mainstream Shakespeare biographies will show that the Hamnet Shakespeare biography has been fully and comprehensively written, over and over again, and in at least two principal versions.

Hamnet Shakespeare: a life

Hamnet was born a normal and healthy boy, else he would not have survived at all. One-third of children died before the age of ten. He attended school in Stratford, since that is what children of his rank did. His father returned to Stratford for prolonged visits at least once a year, so he would have spent time with the boy. Hamnet was Shakespeare's putative male heir, and the vessel of his father's dynastic hopes. Although those aspirations were disappointed, they did not die with the boy, as the coat-of-arms and the purchase of New Place confirm. In his will Shakespeare, leaving his estate to his direct female issue, took care to provide for an eventual male heir. Hamnet died from a common infection, plague or typhus. Shakespeare hastened home from Kent for the funeral. His grief was real, but not immoderate, since the deaths of children were commonplace. While other poets such as Ben Jonson left elegies for lost children, Shakespeare kept his silence. His bereavement did not initially interrupt the cheerful flow of the comedies he was writing; but in due course his work took a more serious turn towards tragedy. It may be that the grief he must have felt for Hamnet emerged here in his mature work. He bought New Place partly to safeguard the remainder of the family during his necessary absences. Traces of Shakespeare's personal emotions may be found at a number of points in the plays: in the grief of Constance in *King John*; in the apparent loss of a twin brother in *Twelfth Night*; in the death of Rutland in *3 Henry VI*.

Hamnet Shakespeare: a biography

Hamnet was born the weaker of the two twins. He died at the age of eleven, his sister lived to the age of seventy-seven. He probably suffered from some congenital disability, or a condition such as cerebral palsy. He was a great disappointment to his father, who regarded his disability as a 'foul deformity', and as proof positive of his mother's infidelity. He never went to school, and was virtually abandoned by his father, who rarely returned to Stratford. Hamnet was cared for by his mother and his grandparents. Hamnet died young as a consequence of his crippling birth defects. Shakespeare himself, on tour in remote Kent, did not come back for the boy's final illness, or attend the funeral. There is no evidence that Hamnet's death significantly influenced Shakespeare's work. Other poets such as Ben Jonson left elegies on the deaths of their children. Shakespeare kept his silence. After Hamnet's death, Shakespeare continued to pursue his family ambitions – the coat of arms, the purchase of New Place – despite the loss of his only male heir. He may have hoped to have another son, if not by Anne Hathaway, then, like King Henry VIII, with another wife. Traces of Shakespeare's personal emotions may be found in *King John*, not in the grief of Constance, but in the scene where the little Arthur leaps to his death, while the audience, *in loco parentis*, gazes helplessly on; and in the death of Mamillius in *The Winter's Tale*, as a direct consequence of his father's conduct.

4

Neither of these narrratives is implausible, or manifestly incorrect. The story is made to fit the few facts. But there is clearly a problem, when two diametrically opposed interpretations of the same data can co-exist without any recourse to definitive proof or conclusive argument. Most biographers acknowledge that their work is partly speculative, and admit that they cannot finally prove their assertions. For instance, it is almost a formula, when discussing the death of Hamnet, to observe that Shakespeare does not seem to have written any poems on the death of his child, while other poets such as Ben Jonson did. Indeed Jonson wrote poems on the deaths of his son Benjamin and his daughter Mary. Biographers freely admit that the absence of any public expression of grief could mean either of two things: that Shakespeare did not feel any; or that his grief was too deep to put into words. Frequently both interpretations are left to lie side by side, for the reader to adjudicate.

But once (if only by implication) Ben Jonson's elegy 'My First Son' (Jonson 1985, pp. 236–7) is brought into the frame, it becomes, in a paradoxical way, part of the story of Shakespeare's own bereavement. Biographers are not merely content to state that Shakespeare wrote nothing; they go further than this, and point to the Jonson poem as an exemplification of what it was he did not write. Thus Jonson's poem becomes an unwritten poem by Shakespeare, or a proxy for the emotion Shakespeare must have felt, but chose not to express (or at least not to publish). The poem defines the grief of parental bereavement as arising from an excess of hope, from investing too much paternal aspiration in one who did not live to fulfil it. Hope is therefore disappointed. But the 'sin' is entirely that of the father, who has to understand that the child was only lent for a temporary period, not given absolutely. The pain of his loss is such that he would rather not be a father at all, would prefer if possible to 'lose all father now'. He will not make the same mistake again; he will never love another human being to the same degree, never again expose himself to such anguish and disappointment.

The poem describes the father's grief in an eloquent and touching way. But there is one line that complicates the issue, and throws the elegiac act itself into question:

> Rest in soft peace, and, asked, say, here doth lie
> Ben Jonson his best piece of poetry.

By referring to the child as a poem, the poet-father's supreme achievement, the poem virtually invalidates itself, cancels itself out. If no poem can ever equal in value the worth of a human being, then surely no poem, however accomplished, on such a theme is worth writing.

In this way Jonson's poem can be seen to function as a perfect proxy for Shakespeare's silence. If we accept the poem as the kind of poem Shakespeare did not write, then it can account for either of the two biographical speculations that offer to explain that silence: he felt too little, or he felt too much. If he felt too little, he would not have thought a poem worth writing. If he felt too much, no poem he could write would ever have done justice to the subject. Either way, Jonson's poem functions as a surrogate for the personal experience of Shakespeare. It is the norm of parental and poetic feeling by which the poet-parent Shakespeare is measured and found either adequate, or deficient. The poem has become part of the Shakespeare biography, a supplement to that baffling silence. It is what he felt, or should have felt; it is what he might have written, or avoided writing; it is what he must have either experienced, or denied, suffered or repressed.

5

Let me now approach that most intractable of problems, which is the relationship, if any, between Hamnet's death and Shakespeare's work, specifically *Hamlet*. The play is not, of course, about the death of a son, but the death of a father. The poet's personal anguish is said to be displaced in the play, sublimated and projected onto the ghost of the dead father. These are Freudian terms, and Freud did indeed suggest such an explanation (Freud 1955, p. 283). Stephen Greenblatt, in his biography *Will in the World*, also offers to trace *Hamlet* back to a personal experience of grief (Greenblatt 2004) by juxtaposing a historical interpretation of Shakespeare's life with a psychological reading of his work. *Hamlet* represents both an expression of the poet's personal anguish and the culmination of a 'long term aesthetic strategy' aimed at developing methods of representing 'inwardness'. This hypothesis explains why we find from Shakespeare no immediate personal expression of grief (like Ben Jonson's poem). Shakespeare 'brooded inwardly and obsessively' for several years, nursing a private pain that was then released, perhaps by the impending death of his father John, and certainly by the coincidence of names between his own Hamnet, and the hero of the old Danish saga he chose to re-adapt for the theatre (Freud 1955, p. 311).

On the other hand Laurie Maguire and Emma Smith treat the coincidence of names between Hamnet and Hamlet as one of the *30 Great Shakespeare Myths* that need to be exploded (Maguire and Smith 2012). They offer to demonstrate that no definite link can be assumed between Hamnet's life and death, and the play of *Hamlet*. They argue that the names are different, and could not easily be confused (they ignore the fact that Hamnet Sadler's name appears in Shakespeare's will as 'Hamlett'); that Shakespeare wrote movingly of the deaths of children, before ever losing one of his own; and that 'death and grief were never far away from anyone in Elizabethan England' (Maguire and Smith 2012, p. 82). It was not difficult, therefore, for Shakespeare to imagine the pain of bereavement without the need to experience, or draw upon, his own (Maguire and Smith 2012, p. 83). The name of the hero of Hamlet derives from the play's sources, not from the name of Shakespeare's son.

6

'Through the ghost of the unquiet father the image of the unliving son looks forth' (Joyce 1922, p. 241). Biographers frequently allude to the 'Scylla and Charybdis' section of James Joyce's *Ulysses* as brilliant and seminal, but tend not to discuss it in detail. When we come to examine them, some of the reasons for this omission quickly emerge.

Stephen Daedalus is arguing about Shakespeare with a group of intellectuals in the National Library in Dublin. If we follow the logic of Stephen's thesis, we can see why it is of questionable use to anyone interested in Shakespeare and the problem of biography. Stephen argues for a highly simplistic biographical reading of Shakespeare's plays, especially *Hamlet*, in which the emotions dramatised are traced to the poet's own personal experience, and to his immediate family relationships. Using evidence from the Shakespeare biography – the tradition that Shakespeare played the part of the Ghost in his own Hamlet, and evidence pointing to a lack of feeling for his wife – Joyce suggests that old King Hamlet's accusations of adultery against Gertrude replicated Shakespeare's own experience (Joyce 1922, p. 241).

But in these pages Joyce is also doing something else, something much more intriguing. He is devising a method for talking about the relations between a writer and his writing, a method that is different from either literary criticism, or literary biography. We can find in Stephen's discourse evidence, and exposition, and demonstration, and argument, and close reading, and reasoned speculation – all the methodologies used in literary biography, and in biographical criticism. But these are all deployed within an imaginative fiction, a medium which lies some-where between the expository methods of criticism, and the poetry of Shakespeare's plays.

Compare these three statements:

Shakespeare undoubtedly returned to Stratford in 1596 for his son's funeral. (Greenblatt 2004, p. 312)

Shakespeare was almost certainly not there. (Greer 2011, p. 199)

—The play begins. A player comes on under the shadow … the player is Shakespeare …
Hamlet, I am thy father's spirit,
To a son he speaks, the son of his soul, the prince, young Hamlet and to the son of his body, Hamnet Shakespeare, who has died in Stratford that his namesake may live for ever …

He is a ghost, a shadow now, the wind by Elsinore's rocks or what you will, the sea's voice, a voice heard only in the heart of him who is the substance of his shadow, the son consubstantial with the father. (Joyce 1922, p. 252)

The statements of Greenblatt and Greer are, empirically, either true or false. Joyce's speculations are not asking to be believed at the level of fact and documentation. They are creative explorations of the evidence pro-vided to us by the documented life-history, and the performed and published works. They take us to a place where literary criticism and historical biography can't really go; a place that is closer to Shakespeare's fiction than it is to verifiable historical reality. In the role of the Ghost, Shakespeare is both son and father, conveying through his own poetry the grief of the bereaved son, and speaking as a father to the prince who is his own son's namesake. Whether or not he attended the funeral, did he not honour his son in the abiding poetry of the play? If *Hamlet* records in some way Shakespeare's sense of loss, real or imagined, of father and of son, then Hamnet is inside the play together with his father and his father's father, consubstantial, of one substance. It is 'through the ghost of the unquiet father' that 'the image of the unliving son looks forth'. The play is Hamnet's elegy, his epitaph, his memorial. More than this, if, as Greenblatt and others propose, the key emotional drivers of the play derive from the pain of Shakespeare's bereavement, then it is true that 'Hamnet Shakespeare ... died in Stratford that his namesake may live for ever'.

Shakespeare is a ghost now, a shadow, the wind by Elsinore's rocks, the sea's voice, what you will. Shakespeare made Hamnet, congenitally and aesthetically. But perversely, now and for us, the son may be more sub-stantial than his father, in the same way that a writer's work is the living substance to his fleeing shadow. The son is of one substance with the father, by whom all things were made; but as in the Christian theology from which this formula derives, we know the Father only through the Son. None can come to the Father save through Him. Which is more real, ghost or image? Shadow, or substance? 'Through the ghost of the unquiet father, the image of the unliving son looks forth.' 'More distant than stars, and nearer than the eye'. Whom do we know best, Hamnet or William Shakespeare?

WORKS CITED

Eliot, T. S. 1961. 'Marina', in *Collected Poems 1909–1962*. London. Faber and Faber

Freud, Sigmund 1955. *The Interpretation of Dreams: The Complete and Definitive Text*. James Strachey (trans. and ed.). New York. George Allen and Unwin/ Hogarth Press

Greenblatt, Stephen 2004. *Will in the World: How Shakespeare Became Shakespeare*. London. Jonathan Cape

Greer, Germaine 2011. *Shakespeare's Wife*. London. Bloomsbury

Jonson, Ben 1985. *A Critical Edition of the Major Works*. Ian Donaldson (ed.).
    Oxford University Press
Joyce, James 1922. *Ulysses*. London. Penguin
Maguire, Laurie, and Smith, Emma 2012. *30 Great Myths About Shakespeare*.
    London. Wiley-Blackwell

9

His daughter Judith and the Quineys

GERMAINE GREER

Though very little is known about Judith Quiney, commentators do not shrink from casually disparaging her. Because at 31 years old Shakespeare's younger daughter was still unmarried, it is assumed that she was unattractive. It is all the more remarkable, then, that Judith became the wife of a scion of the most distinguished and successful family in Stratford. He, we are told, 'did not prove a satisfactory husband', and theirs was 'not a fortunate union', though it lasted for nearly fifty years (Fripp 1924, p. 205).

At some point in her childhood, Judith's father went away and ended up in London. Somehow Anne Shakespeare, and her three children, Susanna, Judith and her twin Hamnet, survived until August 1596 when Hamnet died. Summer, when virulent fevers stalked the land, was often a time of high mortality but in Stratford that August only five deaths are recorded, three of them new-borns (Holy Trinity Parish Register, 243/1). Perhaps Hamnet had always been frail; perhaps he had suffered in the womb; perhaps he was carrying a birth injury. No member of the Shakespeare family would have felt the loss of Hamnet more keenly than his womb-sister. Within a year her mother would take on the mammoth task of restoring New Place together with the training of her own female workforce.

Judith then joined the ranks of vanishing women. If we examine the records of Holy Trinity we find that of the thirty-nine girls who were christened the same year as Judith, a third were buried before they reached marriageable age. Of the other twenty-six, only three were married in Stratford, and another was buried unmarried (Holy Trinity Parish Register, 243/1). If the others ever married, an outcome by no means certain, it was in their employers' parishes rather than their own.

I have decided in default of better information that, if at the age of thirteen or thereabouts Judith Shakespeare was placed in service, she was sent no further than the house of Richard Quiney and his wife Bess in the High Street. This is how I interpret the fact that she was called upon to witness a deed of enfeoffment (transfer of land) for Bess Quiney and her son Adrian in 1611 (SBTRO, ER 27/11).

Bess Quiney was the daughter of Thomas Phillips, a mercer, who had been master of the Guild of the Holy Cross in 1536 and was one of the aldermen named in the charter of 1553. Phillips, a chief figure in what I am tempted to call the mercery mafia, held a good deal of property in Stratford both from the lord of the manor and on lease from the corporation. When he died in 1558, Bess was only two or three years old and, after her sister Mary disappeared from the record, her father's sole heir. She was married to Richard Quiney in January 1581. A daughter Elizabeth was born in November 1582, a son Adrian in August 1584, a replacement Adrian in March 1586, a son Richard in October 1587, a son Thomas in February 1589, a son William in September 1590, a daughter Anne in January 1592, a replacement William in July 1593, a replacement Anne in December 1594, a son John in June 1597, and a son George in 1600. We can infer from the burial of the first William in Alveston in October 1592 that he had been sent away to nurse; if this was the usual practice in the Quiney household, it would explain the short intervals between Bess's eleven confinements.

Richard Quiney, a mercer, son of Adrian Quiney, also a mercer, grandson of another Richard Quiney, also a mercer, was elected principal burgess in 1580, Chamberlain in 1587, and Alderman in 1588. He was regarded with deep disfavour by the lord of the manor, Sir Edward Greville of Milcote, who refused the charter when he was elected Bailiff in 1592 so that Quiney had to request his cousin Sir Fulke Greville to intervene. Quiney was a staunch puritan whose first act as Bailiff was to appoint a committee to seek out undesirable women, his second to preside over the issuing of an edict that 'no innholders, alehousekeeper nor tipplers shall suffer any poor artificer, day labourer, men's servants or prentices to sit to gaming or to drink in any of their houses by day or by night (except in the time of Christmas) upon pain of imprisonment by the space of three days and three nights of them that be the householders and never to sell any more ale or beer within this borough' (*Minutes and Accounts* (M & A), iv, p. 165). The wording of this edict should make clear that this group of tradespeople does not include vintners. Stratford seems to have had only one vintner at a time; John Smith, vintner, who was to serve as Bailiff in 1598, listed as a burgess present on this very occasion, is the only person named as supplying the Corporation with the sack and claret offered to dignitaries on ceremonial occasions.

Elizabethan maidservants came in all shapes and sizes. Some were just little orphan girls who would be placed in service by the Overseers of the Poor at the age of nine or ten (SBTRO, BRU 15/9/19, 11/14, 12/63, 67, 89, 91, 116, 13/12, 21, 22). Judith would have begun her working life assisting an older servant with simple tasks, and graduated to more complex responsibilities as she demonstrated aptitude. Eventually she could have been assisting with the day's business, buying and selling the enormous range of goods that country mercers dealt in, keeping score with wooden tallies, or working in the bakehouse or the brewery or the still-room, washing, preparing food, gardening, marketing, and keeping her mistress company when she went outside the house. We know from Judith's mark on the 1611 deed of enfeoff-ment that she was not used to wielding pen and ink, which does not mean that she could not write well enough to enter details on a slate, still less that she could not read. The good behaviour of maidservants was crucial to the quality of life; in 1601 we find Richard Quiney reminding himself in a memorandum that he had to speak 'with Mr Mathiers [*sic*] and with Bess Quiney concerning a maid' (M & A, vi, p. 135).

The Stratford inventories show that a surprising number of Stratford houses included a maids' room. This usually contained two or three bedsteads as well as assorted pillows, mattresses or flockbeds and bolsters, coverlets, twillies [woven cloths], hillings [quilts] and blankets. An unmarried woman would often sleep with her maid in bed beside her. In an affluent household a maid was likely to be adequately housed, fed and clothed, possibly better than she would have been at home. One possibility is that Judith was placed in the Quiney household to learn the country mercer's trade, which we should probably understand as simply retail. In many parts of the country, only those who had served an apprenticeship could set up as shopkeepers. Judith may have been bound to serve her employers faithfully for a specific length of time, anything up to fourteen years, in return for food, lodging, raiment, training in one or several skills, and perhaps some small cash payment.

After Stratford suffered the first of a series of disastrous fires, in 1594, Quiney was despatched with other aldermen to raise funds from neighbouring towns and shires for essential repairs. As he travelled through

Northamptonshire, Oxfordshire and Gloucestershire collecting donations, his business affairs were left in the capable hands of Bess and her staff. In 1595 there was another disastrous fire. As there was also a dearth of corn, inquiry was made into the amounts being held by citizens of Stratford. Of Quiney it was said that

Master Richard Quiney useth the trades of buying and selling of corn for great sums and making of malt, and hath in his house and in his barn unthrashed 47 quarters of barley and 32 quarters of malt and pease 11 and half quarters and of wheat 20 strikes: of Master Nashe of Welcombe 6 quarters of malt and 5 of barley. We are given to understand that he hath bought since Midsummer of Leonard Bennett of Burton-upon-Stour 100 quarters of grain, videlicet barley and peas: his barley for 3s. 4d the strike and peas at 2s. 6d. the strike, for 12 months' day of payment. But what quantity of acres he soweth this year we cannot learn by reason he is now at London. He hath in household sixteen persons. (M & A, v, pp. 48–9)

At least half the people in Quiney's household in 1595 would have been servants. When the inquiry was made Quiney was in London seeking a patent for another collection for victims of the fires; he was soon off again collecting in Banbury, Coventry and Bristol. On 20 January 1596 Sir Edward Greville was entertained at the Quineys'; the management of such banquettings was complex and expensive and involved a considerable investment of energy and expertise on the part of household staff, and we should probably assume that it was handled by stay-at-home Bess rather than her gadding husband.

   The cumulative effect of the fires, a recession in the agricultural economy and the rural landlords' unremitting efforts to fiscalise their properties was to be disaster for the people of Stratford. The winter of 1596–7 saw the highest death toll of the century. The heaviest expense in all but the greatest Elizabethan households was food, and in time of dearth food quickly became unaffordable. To reserve the little corn there was to make malt was by the edict of 1595 made a crime; as making, selling and portage of malt provided a livelihood for most of the people in Stratford the condition of the people rapidly deteriorated, until in 1598 Quiney calculated that 400 citizens were on poor relief (SBTRO ER3 678).

   The letters of Abraham Sturley that kept Quiney informed while he was absent on corporation business provide valuable insights into the conduct of his household and business. On 15 January 1598 Sturley wrote to Quiney

at his lodging at the Bell Inn in Carter Lane, 'Thine are all well, male and
female; by the care of thy father, the industry of thy wife, the labour of the
maids and the blessing of God thy affairs are almost as flourishing as we
can pray for' (Fripp's translation of Sturley's Latin). The reference to maids
rather than servants suggests that Bess's staff were all female. It is about
this stage, by my calculation, that thirteen-year-old Judith Shakespeare
entered Bess Quiney's service.

On 27 October 1598 Sturley delivered Bess a letter from her husband 'and
was made partaker of the contents thereof also', which phrasing suggests
that he did not read the letter to her but was told the gist of it by her. Sitting
at her table acting as her amanuensis, he communicated her wishes to her
husband in terms that suggest that she had a degree of authority over
her husband as well as vice versa: 'My sister is cheerful, and the Lord hath
been merciful and comfortable to her in her labours and, so that you be
well employed, giveth you leave to follow your occasions for one week or
fortnight longer.'

During this time Bess was also managing the sale of malt, 'having in
house 14 quarters of her own and 7 of Sir John Hubaud'. Sturley reports
that she was rather dismayed to find that 'Lady Greville had run in
arrearages'. She visited Lady Greville at Milcote but could have 'no money'
probably because that lady, co-heiress of Lord Chancellor Bromley, had
been stripped by her rapacious husband of everything she inherited.
On such a journey Bess would have been accompanied by a maid who
would carry anything that needed to be carried, and would if necessary
be able to confirm that she had been with her mistress the whole time and
had witnessed nothing in the way of unseemly behaviour.

In 1602 a catastrophe befell the Quiney household. Quiney had been
elected as Bailiff for the second time and once again Greville refused to
ratify his appointment, which was ratified notwithstanding. Quiney spent
the third of May at the Stratford fair supervising the sale and exchange of
horses and entering each transaction in the toll book. As he was making his
nightly round of the town he came upon some of Greville's men who,
having been drinking all day, had begun brawling 'and drew their daggers
upon their host. [It being] fair time the Bailiff was late abroad to see the
town in order and coming by in that hurley burley came into the house and
commanded the peace to be kept' and 'in his endeavour to stifle the brawl
had his head grievously broken'. The injury was not one that could have

been treated; Quiney lingered for more than three weeks, probably never fully conscious, for as far as we can tell he made no will written or oral, and appointed no executor or guardian for his children. He was buried in Holy Trinity churchyard on 31 May.

Judith may have been particularly concerned for Bess's son Thomas, who was thirteen when his father died, at that age probably the most traumatised member of the family. His widowed mother would have had much ado to organise her affairs given her husband's failure to make a will, and Thomas's needs would not have been her first concern. His eldest brother Adrian seems to have been frail; his elder brother Richard was a high achiever who mastered his Latin at the grammar school and left home in 1606 to become a very successful businessman in London. After John Smythe's clamorous expulsion from the Corporation in 1601 and his death soon after, it seems that Bess Quiney was granted a vintner's licence at the borough sessions of 1603 in the right of her grandfather Thomas Dixon alias Waterman, who died that year (M & A, vi, p. 222). Selling wine was not like selling anything else, and Bess was soon in trouble. In May that year she was presented at the quarter sessions for selling wine 'at excessive price' and by 'unsealed measures' and duly fined (M & A, vi, p. 240). In the accounts for 1605 she appears as having been paid for two pounds of gunpowder, 'a pound of match' and wine for the Borough Surveyor; more wine was provided for the aldermen at a meeting in Bess's house (M & A, vi, pp. 366–7). In a list of licensed traders compiled for the borough sessions of 8 January 1606, however, though Bess was still trading in wine, no vintner was listed; her name appears as one of the mercers (M & A, vi, p. 349). Within weeks she was fined again for selling wine contrary to the statute (M & A, vi, p. 382), and she was fined again in 1607 (M & A, vi, p. 415).

If Thomas was sent away to study the mystery of vintnership, he may have gone to the Vintry in London, or to the Vintners' Company in Coventry, where the mercers were doing their utmost to absorb trading in wine into their field of operations, or to the Guild of Vintners and Butchers in Worcester (Berger 1993, p. 103). The notion that Thomas trained as a vintner is supported by the fact that he learnt French, otherwise an odd accomplishment for a man of his class. He was back in Stratford by about 1610, when he reached his majority.

The next great event in Judith's life was her sister's wedding in 1607. She is unlikely to have had a sight of the settlement that her father's agents had negotiated with the friends of John Hall that made her elder sister Shakespeare's sole heir, but she probably knew the gist of it. Abandoned to their fate, younger daughters were vulnerable; in service they were more likely to be seduced than courted. Since pregnant Ann Hathaway had made her way to the altar, the rules had changed. Strenuous preaching against premarital sex as fornication had had an effect. In 1600 we see few if any christenings in the registers within nine months of solemnisation and far more illegitimacy. Though the Hathaways believed it their duty to find good husbands for all their girls rather than a rich husband for one of them, in January 1602 orphaned Rose Hathaway, the youngest child of Thomas Hathaway, sister of the little girls who were left a sheep each in Richard Hathaway's will, bore and buried illegitimate twin daughters. Nothing is known of what became of Rose, but her story is unlikely to have had a happy ending. Judith's behaviour was beyond reproach. She was never cited in the Vicar's court, never accused of immorality or of failing to attend church as her sister was.

It is in December 1611 that we find Judith acting as a witness for the deed by which Bess and Adrian Quiney sold a messuage to William Mountford for the handsome sum of £131. The other witnesses to the deed were Thomas Greene and his wife, who were Anne Shakespeare's star boarders at New Place, which may suggest that they brought Judith with them from her mother's house. I have assumed that Greene had the deed drawn up and then went with his wife Lettice on 4 December to Bess's house for the signing, where Judith was on hand to serve as the third witness.

Meanwhile the schemes by which landholders around Stratford hoped to improve the profitability of their land-holdings were becoming more desperate. A consortium led by William Combe was formed to buy up the remaining open arable fields in Milcote, Welcombe and Old Stratford with the aim of engrossing and enclosing them and selling them on at a profit (SBTRO, BRU 15/7/10).

The poor husbandmen of Stratford, who needed to pasture their few beasts on the common to survive, would have faced starvation. The Corporation, faced with the responsibility of providing poor relief, feared the consequences if the townspeople were to lose their ancient right to the use of the stubble fields after harvest. On 9 July 1614 a third fire in Stratford destroyed fifty-four dwelling-houses, 'besides barns, stables and other houses of office' (Eccles 1961, p. 135).

In the midst of dealing with this new emergency, Greene, as town clerk, had to advise the aldermen about the kinds of action they might lawfully take if Combe's men began enclosing the land. They decided that as the ground was frozen, there was no need to do anything. The frost broke on 19 December and Combe's men moved at once, digging a trench 275 yards long in preparation for the hedging and ditching. As soon as the holidays were over the Corporation made its counter move. Acting on Greene's advice, two of the aldermen, Masters Chandler and Walford (son-in-law and stepson of Bess Quiney respectively), managed to secure a lease at Welcombe giving them rights of common (SBTRO, BRU 15/5/18, 15/13/13; BRU 2/1–5, B. 274–9, B. 281–4, B. 307, 310, 323–4, 358, 367, 369, 380).

On the evening of Saturday 7 January William Combe let it be known that he had heard that 'some of the better sort would go to throw down the ditch' (SBTRO, BRU 15/5/162). Master Chandler was told by Master Bayliss that Combe ground his teeth and snarled 'O would they durst!' in 'great passion and anger'. The following Monday Master Chandler went to see Combe for himself and told Greene on his return that Combe called them all 'factious knaves', 'puritan knaves' and 'underlings in their colour', threatening to do them 'all the mischief he can'. Undeterred, Chandler and Walford sent spades to be hidden at the worksite so that they could go in person and 'throw down some of the ditch'. When the two aldermen turned up they were outnumbered by Combe's workmen, who knocked them to the ground and beat them. The next day Greene sought assistance from a justice of the peace in swearing out an injunction to prevent a breach of the peace. It was agreed that to prevent public disorder the names of the members of the consortium would not be divulged to the public. By evening the Corporation had arrived at an accommodation with the consortium, but they had been pre-empted.

Greene's side note simply remarks:

While this was doing as it stands, the ditches by women and children of Bishopton and Stratford were filled up again. (SBTRO, BRU 15/5/ 156)

The women must have taken this action entirely on their own initiative. On one of the coldest nights of the year they had shouldered spades and mattocks, and led their children out of the town to the meadow of Welcombe, where they knocked down the hedge mound and back-filled the ditch. When the 300 yards of mound and ditch were levelled, the women marched their troops back to Stratford and Bishopton and so to bed.

The action itself was not all that unusual but it usually resulted in prison either for the women perpetrators or for their menfolk. When Alderman Chandler arrived home after his drubbing, his wife, Bess Quiney's eldest daughter Elizabeth, must have been among the first to hear of the outrage perpetrated by Combe. It looks very much as if, as the Corporation tried to come to some agreement with their powerful opposition, the widow Quiney sent her maidservants to knock on doors in Stratford and Bishopton. The power of the mercers' network can be guessed from the fact that the women who destroyed Combe's earthworks that night were never arraigned on any charge.

In the summer of 1615 twenty-six-year-old Thomas Quiney managed to get himself entangled with a young woman called Margaret Wheeler. She had evidently named Thomas as the father of the infant she was carrying and it looks very much as if Thomas had confessed that he had knowledge of her. Bess decided on a pre-emptive move. She may have known for years that Judith was in love with Thomas, but with no marriage portion and no property she dared not hope ever to marry him. Judith probably could have forced the issue, but she was true to her bond and the family and simply suffered in silence. Now Thomas's own indiscretion gave Judith a chance. I imagine that Bess simply asked Judith to put Thomas out of Wheeler's reach by marrying him. On 12 February 1616 Judith Shakespeare and Thomas Quiney were married in Holy Trinity Church Stratford. Licence was given, the ceremony performed and the register signed by the assistant vicar, Richard Watts. He would eventually become another of Bess's sons-in-law.

The marriage took place in Lent with a licence issued not by the Consistory Court of the See of Worcester but by the Court of the Peculiar of Stratford-upon-Avon. The fact was reported to the consistory court by an apparitor called Walter Nixon. Thomas was then excommunicated. Less than a month after the wedding, Margaret Wheeler was brought to bed. She and her baby both died and were buried in Holy Trinity churchyard on 15 March. Thomas was then denounced and summoned to appear before the Vicar's Court. He there confessed that he had indeed had carnal copulation with the said Wheeler. Thomas found himself sentenced to perform penance clad in a white sheet before the congregation on three successive Sundays. The sentence was remitted; Thomas was allowed to expiate his guilt by appearing in his own clothing before the vicar of Bishopton on a single occasion and giving 5 shillings for the use of the poor. Someone must have persuaded the authorities that Thomas was more sinned against than sinning.

While all this was going on Judith's father was dying. How much he knew of what was transpiring we cannot know. Judith had no need to seek his consent to her marriage. She had been at her own disposal for ten years. Shakespeare's confused attempts to harvest some sort of legacy for her with the equally befuddled assistance of Francis Collins ran the risk of infringing the terms of her elder sister's marriage settlement.

Item I give and bequeath unto my daughter Judith one hundred and fifty pounds of lawful English money to be paid unto her in manner and form following, that is to say one hundred pounds in discharge of her marriage portion within one year after my decease with consideration after the rate of two shillings in the pound for so long time as the same shall be unpaid unto her after my decease and the fifty pounds residue thereof upon her surrendering of or giving of such sufficient security as the overseers of this my will shall like of to surrender or grant all her estate and right that shall descend or come unto her after my decease or that she now hath of in or to one copyhold tenement with the appurtenances lying and being in Stratford-upon-Avon aforesaid . . . being parcel or holden of the manor of Rowington unto my daughter Susanna Hall and her heirs for ever.

It is this stipulation that strengthens the supposition that Susanna's marriage settlement required her being made sole heir, for she cannot be said to have needed the cottage in Chapel Lane for her own use. The Rowington Manor records show that Susanna did take over payment of the yearly fine or ground-rent and became the official tenant.

Item I give and bequeath unto my said daughter Judith one hundred and fifty pounds more if she or any issue of her body living at the end of three years next ensuing the day of the date of this my will during which time my executors to pay her consideration from my decease according to the rate aforesaid . . . But if my said daughter Judith be living at th'end the said three years or any issue of her body then my will is and so I devise and bequeath the said hundred and fifty pounds to be set out by my executors and overseers for the best benefit of her and her issue and the stock not to be paid unto her so long as she shall be married & covert

baron [married] but my will is that she shall have the consideration yearly
paid unto her during her life and after her decease the said stock and consideration
to be paid to her children if she have any & if not to her executors or assigns she
living the said term after my decease provided that if such husband as she shall
at th'end of the said three years be married unto or at any after do sufficiently
assure unto her and th'issue of her body lands answerable to the portion given
unto her. (Modernised from Schoenbaum 1975, p. 243)

This strikes a curiously callous note: if Judith 'or any issue of her body' is
still living three years after Shakespeare's death, a further £150 is to be
made available in the form of a trust, meaning that she and/or her child or
children could enjoy the interest on it at the usual rate of 10 per cent. Her
husband could claim the principal only if he settled on her lands to the
same value. This, *pace* some commentators, he was under no obligation to
do. The only other thing Judith had to remember her father by was his
'broad silver-gilt bowl'.

Thomas may have been unreliable and impractical, but he might also
have been fun. Judith's seems to have been a real marriage, in a way that
her sister's was not. It was consummated in short order; her first child,
christened 'Shakespeare', was born on 23 November. He was buried less
than six months later with a tolling of the great bell that had remained
silent through the whole gamut of the Shakespeare family's obsequies. By
that time Judith was pregnant again, which probably means that little
Shakespeare had been put out to nurse. She did not make the same mistake
again but nursed her second-born herself for she did not fall pregnant
again until Richard was weaned. Richard's little brother Thomas was
christened on 23 January 1620, two weeks short of the two-year interval
that is usual among births to women of the people in Stratford.

Thomas had been living in and conducting his business from a house
called Atwoods next door to his mother's on the High Street. His mother,
meanwhile, was running the mercery in partnership with her son-in-law
William Chandler from rather more commodious premises called the Cage
on the corner of the High Street and Bridge Street. When Chandler's wife
died in May 1615 Chandler swiftly remarried and negotiated a new lease,
but in a matter of weeks Thomas managed to swap Atwoods for the Cage
where he kept his warehouse for more than thirty years. Though much is
made of his occasional brushes with the law, Quiney was in trouble with
the authorities rather less often his mother was.

In late 1638 the pestilence that had been raging for months reached Stratford; by the time it retreated both of Judith and Thomas's sons, aged twenty-one and nineteen, were dead (Shrewsbury 2005, p. 398). The turbulent years that followed yield little by way of information, as the Civil Wars took a heavy toll on the town and its resources. A vintner could hardly have continued his business in the circumstances, but Thomas would certainly have been expected to supply the claret and sack for the Queen and her retinue during their three-day stay at New Place in 1643, probably at his own expense. Judith and Thomas were still together when Richard Quiney took over the lease of the Cage in 1652 and probably used it thereafter himself. When Richard died three years later he left £12 a year for his brother's maintenance and £5 for his burial, which was nearly enough to enable him to live a life of leisure. At about this time Thomas seems to have begun claiming the title of 'Gentleman'. On 9 February 1662 Judith was buried as 'Judith, uxor Thomas Quiney, Gent.', phrasing that suggests that Thomas was still alive. The curious folk who had for years been coming to Stratford in search of Shakespeare never guessed that an old lady who sat every Sunday in the Quiney pew at Holy Trinity could have answered many of their questions – if she chose.

WORKS CITED

Berger, Ronald M. 1993. *The Most Necessary Luxuries: The Mercers' Company of Coventry, 1550–1680*. Philadelphia, PA. Pennsylvania State University Press

Dyer, Alan D. 1973. *The City of Worcester in the Sixteenth Century*. Leicester University Press

Eccles, Mark 1961. *Shakespeare in Warwickshire*. Madison. University of Wisconsin Press

Fripp, E. I. 1924. *Master Richard Quyny*. Oxford University Press

Holy Trinity Parish Register, SBTRO Dr 243/1

Minutes and Accounts of the Corporation of Stratford-upon-Avon 1553–1598. 1921–2011. 6 vols. Stratford-upon-Avon. The Dugdale Society

Schoenbaum, S. 1975. *William Shakespeare: A Documentary Life*. Oxford University Press

Shrewsbury, J. F. D. 2005. *A History of the Bubonic Plague in the British Isles*. Cambridge University Press

10

His granddaughter Lady Elizabeth Barnard

RENÉ WEIS

§

In a deed poll of 1653, appointing trustees for property in and around Stratford-upon-Avon, a forty-five-year-old woman referred to her 'grandfather'. What lifts this mundane business transaction above the ordinary is the fact that the woman was Shakespeare's granddaughter Elizabeth Barnard, née Hall. As quoted in Halliwell's 1848 *The Life of William Shakespeare*, she refers to properties and land 'which were sometimes the inheritance of William Shakespeare, gent., my grandfather' (Halliwell 1848, p. 318). To posterity there is something disarming about the fact that someone once called Shakespeare 'grandfather', even if we have known all along that the Shakespeares were domestically no different from any other family in the Midlands of the time.

When Elizabeth Hall was sick, her father, a highly esteemed physician, recorded details of her illness and his cure for her, just as he had done earlier for her mother Susanna, 'Mrs Hall of Stratford, my wife', when Susanna was 'miserably tormented by the colic' ('Observation XIX'). Hall's detailed account of his daughter's sickness is of considerable intrinsic interest, not least for including an intriguing date that has rightly exercised the attention of biographers (Lane 1996, p. 34). He records that in early January 1625 (1624 Old-Style, until 1752, when the year ended on Lady Day, 25 March), 'Elizabeth Hall, my only daughter, was vexed with *Tortura Oris*, or the convulsion of the mouth'. Elizabeth was then sixteen years old. Her father cured her by administering laxative pills: 'She took five the first day, which gave her seven stools; the next day with the other five she had five stools and was happily cured.' At the same time, perhaps related to her facial inflammation, she suffered from an eye infection ('For an ophthalmia of which she laboured I used our ophthalmic water') and her periods ('courses') were stemmed. Hall dealt with these further afflictions in the same brisk manner so that at the start of April 1625 Elizabeth was well enough to travel to London.

There could be any number of reasons for her wanting to go to London just then, but the death of the King at the end of March 1625 and the accession of Charles I are the most obvious public events to have triggered such a visit. In her father's words, 'in the beginning of April she went to London and returning homewards, the 22 of the said month, she took cold and fell into the said distemper on the contrary side of the face'. Whereas previously her left side was affected, this time it was her right, and again her eye too needed tending. She took sixteen days to recover. The symptoms of facial paralysis in conjunction with eye trouble – probably an inability to close the eyelids – point to Bell's palsy (John Taplin, private communication). Patients usually recover from this condition even without treatment, but the affected eye needs to be protected and watered, as Hall did in this case. Three weeks after her recovery – in his notes Hall records 24 May as the specific date – Elizabeth became 'afflicted with an erratic fever: sometime she was hot and by and by sweating; again cold, all in the space of half an hour, and thus she was vexed often in a day'. The treatment of Elizabeth, which included rubbing her spine and the administering of intensive laxatives, finally cured her. As her concerned father put it, 'Thus was she delivered from death and deadly diseases.'

From this it appears that Elizabeth suffered bouts of serious illness between January and June 1625 when she was seventeen years old. Her father seems to have suspected that her recurring facial convulsions were at least partly connected to puberty, but her 'fever' was a different matter, enough for him to think of 'deadly diseases' such as, probably, typhus: the 'spotted fever' raged throughout the Midlands in 1624–5 and the epidemic's devastating impact was compounded by a new outbreak of plague, whence the exceptionally high mortality figures for Stratford during this period (Lane 1996, pp. xxii–xxiii). In the event Elizabeth survived for forty-five more years after these months of illness. Writing up his notes years later, Dr Hall ends his case history of his daughter's illness on a note of relief, that after this latest bout of illness she 'was well for many years. To God be praise.'

In 1625 Elizabeth and her parents were in all probability living in New Place, her grandfather's mansion house on the corner of Chapel Street and Dead (or Chapel) Lane. The Halls may have moved to

New Place when William Shakespeare became seriously ill, perhaps towards the end of 1615 or in early 1616. Elizabeth was eight years old when her famous grandfather died. He remembered her in his will, leaving her 'all my plate except my broad silver and gilt bowl', which he bequeathed to Judith. Earlier in the will Shakespeare expressed the wish that his 'niece [*sic*] Elizabeth Hall' should inherit part of the £150 due to her aunt Judith: if Judith and her children were to die within three years of the will, then her £150 would be divided up between Elizabeth (£100) and Shakespeare's sister Joan (£50) and her heirs. Little Elizabeth was very much in her grandfather's mind as he made his will in spite of the fact that, as the Halls' only daughter, she was a rich heiress.

Elizabeth Hall was born in February 1608 and baptised in Holy Trinity on 21 February that year. Her mother Susanna (née Shakespeare) and her father John Hall had married in the same church on Friday 5 June 1607. If mathematics and biology serve, she was conceived during the first few days of the Halls' marriage. Susanna and her husband had, it seems, eschewed her father's predicament: the daughter of the good doctor would be as legitimate as she could be. The name the parents chose for their newborn, 'Elizabeth', was probably the most popular girl's name in the country at the time. By calling their little girl 'Elizabeth' the Halls would seem to be making a conventional gesture of loyalty and affection.

Nothing is known for certain about the birth of Elizabeth, but one may wonder whether the tragic childbed scene in *Pericles*, which was written at just the time of Elizabeth's birth, does not bear the 'hallmark' of her arrival into this world. The play, a collaboration between Shakespeare and one George Wilkins, who wrote Acts 1 and 2, was entered on the Stationers' Register on 20 May 1608. It must have been written, therefore, at some point in the months before, and it is likely that Shakespeare would have used the period of Lent for his part, Acts 3–5, while the theatres closed. In 1608, therefore, the six weeks between Ash Wednesday (10 February) and Easter Sunday (27 March) marked the period when players and playwrights, particularly provincial ones like Shakespeare and John Heminges, returned to their families.

An added incentive for Shakespeare to be home during Lent of 1608 would have been the imminent birth of the Halls' first child. Shakespeare may have been more mindful than ever of the precariousness of human life just then, as he had only a few weeks earlier, on 31 December

1607, buried his younger brother Edmund in St Saviour's on Bankside. That Edmund Shakespeare may haunt *Pericles* is suggested by the presence in it of the poet John Gower, who only appears in this play. At the time Gower's canopied tomb stood in the chapel of St John the Evangelist where, probably, Shakespeare's brother's funeral took place. The latest Arden editor of *Pericles*, Suzanne Gossett, specifically ties the tribulations of this time in Shakespeare's life into the story of *Pericles*, 'pouring his grief over the deaths of Edmund and his infant son [Hamnet], his fears for Susanna and his delight at his granddaughter's birth into the scenes of birth and apparent deaths in the third and fourth acts. By March 1608 Shakespeare was writing the father-daughter reunion scene of the fifth act' (Gossett 2004, p. 61).

Shakespeare's first use of the word 'child-bed' occurs in *Pericles* – it is found three times altogether in the works – and may provide a further pointer to what was foremost in the dramatist's mind at this time. The line occurs in scene 11 (l. 28) when Pericles addresses Marina ('a more blust'rous birth had never babe') and then his 'dead' wife: 'A terrible childbed hast thou had, my dear, / No light, no fire' (11.55–6). We may be confident that Susanna Hall, the daughter of a rich man, the wife, moreover, of a successful doctor, enjoyed every comfort that money could buy in Stratford. Nevertheless, and even though *Pericles* is hardly a trustworthy source for information about the real lives of the Shakespeare family, the depth of anxiety in the play surrounding the birth of Marina, the fate of her mother Thaisa, and the final welling up of relief may suggest that Elizabeth's arrival into the world was a more than usually complicated one.

Elizabeth's father may well be the reason why physicians suddenly play such important roles in the two Shakespeare plays that coincide with his surmised arrival in Stratford-upon-Avon, *Macbeth* (written sometime after May 1606) and particularly *Pericles*, which features the renowned physician Cerimon who saves Thaisa, the mother of Marina. He has 'made familiar / To me and to my aid the blest infusions / That dwells in vegetives' (*Pericles* 12.31–3); all his delight lies in making the sick better. The tone of Hall's notes on his patients, including the accounts of his treatments of his wife ('Observation XIX') and daughter, point to a calm, generous and professional man who in the treatment of his patients rose above the sectarian divide of the period, as witnessed by 'Observation XXXIII', which refers to the cure by Hall of 'Brown, a Romish Priest' (Lane 1996, pp. 60–3). It is tempting to see in this wise and dedicated doctor the real life inspiration for Cerimon. Can it really be a coincidence that in *Pericles* a mother gives birth to a daughter and is saved by a famous doctor while the author's daughter, Susanna Hall, the wife of a physician, has just borne a daughter? Perhaps, but the odds favour a connection between the play and life in the Halls' household at just this time, so that the birth of Elizabeth Hall, in all its aspects, may resonate beneath the surface of *Pericles*.

Elizabeth was probably not born in the house known as Hall's Croft, because tree-ring dating (dendrochronology) carried out by the Oxford Tree-Ring Laboratory for the Shakespeare Birthplace Trust (http://dendro chronology.net/warwickshire.asp) placed the construction of the main house around 1612/13, some four years after her birth. Hall's Croft may well have been built for the increasingly prosperous Halls, in which case Elizabeth would have spent some time between the ages of four and twelve here, because by 1616, the year Shakespeare died, the family had probably moved permanently into New Place which Susanna had inherited in his will.

It is likely that Elizabeth attended petty school in Stratford; there is evidence in the Stratford-upon-Avon corporation records that opportunities for the education of very young girls existed at this time. Here Elizabeth, like other girls such as Joyce Cowden and Elizabeth Evans, the only two women who are *known* to have attended Stratford's ABC school, would have learnt to write alongside boys. Evans was eventually tried in London for prostitution in 1598 and signed her name 'Elis evens' 'in a neat italic hand' (Wells 2010, pp. 21–3). Her use of an italic hand is of particular interest to us because Elizabeth Hall in turn used an elegant italic hand in a striking signature (*Eliza: Nash*) alongside her mother's secretary hand 'Susannah[all]' on a 1647 document, which is among the most prized possessions of the Shakespeare Birthplace Trust. It seems that Elizabeth Hall may have used an italic hand because that is what was taught in petty school in Stratford rather than this being a longhand she picked up from her father (he used a distinctive form of italic), who may have been partly educated in Europe where italic was almost universal, unlike England where secretary still prevailed, as her mother's signature demonstrates.

Not long after recovering from her fever and exactly a year after her return from London, Elizabeth Hall married Thomas Nash, whose house still stands at 22 Chapel Street, although Nash probably never lived in it (the list of occupiers of the house, from 1545 to 1659, does not include him

(Taplin, unpublished 'Note on Nash's house'; see further Nash's will in Taplin 2013, II, pp. 6–12)). Nash had trained as a lawyer at Lincoln's Inn and was thirty-two at the time of the marriage, while she had turned eighteen two months earlier. The marriage was celebrated on 22 April 1626. This date is one of the possible dates of Shakespeare's birth. Nicholas Rowe and the monument in the chancel of Holy Trinity in Stratford-upon-Avon both note that Shakespeare, who was baptised on 26 April 1564, died in his 53rd year. If on 23 April 1616 Shakespeare was indeed in his 53rd year, then he must have been born on any of 21, 22, 23 April, of which the 23 April may, if only statistically, be the least likely. While it would be fitting for the national poet to be born on St George's Day, particularly because he died on that day, 22 April 1564 may have a superior claim. There are two circumstantial reasons for this and both relate to Elizabeth Hall: the prominent reference to 22 April in John Hall's 'Observation' about his daughter's return to Stratford, on that day or *for* that day, and the fact that Elizabeth Hall chose to marry her first husband on 22 April 1626. This fell on a Saturday in 1626 just as it did in 1564 when, I would argue, William Shakespeare was born (the importance of this particular 22 April to Shakespeare's surmised birthday was first noted by Thomas de Quincey: Schoenbaum 1970, p. 324). Like her grandfather, Elizabeth Hall too was eighteen when she married and, like him, she wed someone who was her senior, in her case by almost fifteen years.

Elizabeth lost her father John Hall, aged sixty, in 1635 when she was twenty-seven. At the time of his death there were unpaid debts. The claimant was a future mayor of Stratford, one Baldwin Brooks, who in 1637 organised a raid on New Place to recover goods to the value of the debt. Elizabeth must have been present during this violation of her home, which resulted in broken doors and the theft of valuable property from the 'study' of New Place, including 'divers books, boxes, desks, monies, bonds, bills'. On 12 May 1637 Susanna and her son-in-law sued and seem to have won, at least as far as the return of the books to New Place was concerned, because they would be mentioned again at a later stage.

How much did the Nashes and Susanna see of Elizabeth's aunt Judith in the Cage at the far corner of High Street and Fore Bridge Street, or indeed of Judith's surviving sons, Elizabeth Hall's cousins, Richard and Thomas Quiney-Shakespeare? Judith's sons both died in 1639, the same year when Elizabeth's uncle William, the son of Joan Hart-Shakespeare (and therefore

Shakespeare's nephew), also died aged 39. The families were bound to gather at these funerals, and Stratford was a small town where relatives ran into one another on market days and on most other days too, whether they liked it or not. For all we know, Susanna and her sister Judith as well as their children got along very well. Suspicions about the sisters' relationship linger only because of the complex nature of Shakespeare's will and its revisions, which seem intent on safeguarding the estate from Judith's feckless husband Quiney. In the end, Judith and her niece Elizabeth survived most of their relatives in Stratford-upon-Avon – apart from the Harts of Henley Street – by many years, well into the second half of the seventeenth century.

By 1642 England was plunged into a Civil War. What evidence there is suggests that the sympathies of the Nash–Hall house inclined towards the Crown: Thomas Nash was the largest contributor of funds to the Crown's cause in Stratford, parting with £100 to it (according to a minute of 24 September 1642: Lewis 1940, p. 584), rather more than Shakespeare had officially paid for New Place forty-six years earlier. When the Queen sojourned in Stratford from 11 to 13 July 1643 (Lewis 1940, p. 584) – Elizabeth Nash was thirty-five at the time – she appears to have held court at New Place in which Elizabeth and her husband Nash lived with her widowed mother Susanna. The Queen may of course have stayed in New Place simply because the former Clopton mansion was the largest, best-appointed house in the centre of town. During the Civil War period (in 1643) a friend of Dr Hall's brought round an army surgeon by the name of James Cook, who desired 'to see the books left by Master Hall'. Elizabeth probably witnessed this visit, although Cook does not mention her or her husband Nash, only Susanna. It is to Cook that we owe Hall's medical notes including the account of Elizabeth's sickness and cure. Her mother was prepared to sell her father's medical diary because the family probably needed the money to keep their estates going. Trying to fill the family coffers further, Thomas Nash sought compensation for the loss, among others, of his wife Elizabeth's 'scarlet petticoat and lacework' after troops had been billeted in Stratford. The thought of the daughter of the Protestant John Hall indulging in a scarlet petticoat is intriguing and oddly satisfying. On the other hand Mary Queen of Scots wore a scarlet petticoat at her execution, to align her fate with that of Catholic martyrs, so that Elizabeth's undergarment might echo with a rather different resonance.

In November 1646 Shakespeare's sister Joan Hart of Henley Street, the last survivor of William's siblings, died at the age of seventy-seven, followed some six months later, on 4 April 1647, by Thomas Nash. Nash's will bequeathed a major problem to his widow and mother-in-law. In Hall's testament Nash had been left Shakespeare's 'study of books', which would have been a major asset. The rest had been left to Susanna ('my house in London'), Elizabeth ('my house in Acton'), and his widow and daughter equally ('my goods and monies' which included New Place and everything pertaining to it). But Nash took it upon himself to leave New Place and its appurtenances to his cousin Edward Nash, thereby making a bequest that vastly transcended anything to which he was entitled. The house, barns and orchards all belonged to Susanna and Elizabeth. Consequently they contested the will and succeeded in preventing New Place from passing to the Nash family, at least during Elizabeth's lifetime. There may have been just enough of a loophole in the law for Nash to have tried to do this. Why, though, we will never know. Did he think that Elizabeth might marry again and have children after all and thereby erase him from her history? She was thirty-nine when she was widowed and it is unlikely that she could have started a family at that stage. Had she and Nash fallen out and was this why he desired to transfer the estate to his family, on the grounds that for the past fourteen years he had been the chief provider and the male head of New Place?

In 1647 Elizabeth Nash was a rich widow, sharing the largest private dwelling in Stratford with her widowed mother Susanna. By the summer of 1649 the sixty-six-year-old Susanna seems to have been failing; she died on 11 July. Did Elizabeth compose the famous epitaph for her mother, as 'witty above her sex' and 'wise to salvation', as Charlotte Stopes surmised (Stopes 1901, p. 104)? That Susanna's passing was not due to a sudden cause, such as a stroke or heart attack, is suggested by her daughter's re-marriage in Billesley chapel five weeks earlier, on 5 June 1649. It is unlikely that Elizabeth's marriage and Susanna's death are unrelated. Rather, Elizabeth Nash probably married her second husband in time for her mother to witness the wedding. The date and place of Elizabeth Hall's marriage to Barnard are first mentioned by Malone in his posthumously published life of Shakespeare (1831). Malone's was a 'patient, minute investigation' and involved research 'in the parish registers not only of Stratford, but also of the neighbouring villages' (Schoenbaum 1970, p. 243).

Whatever Malone's source was for 5 June 1649 in Billesley, he would not have reproduced either date or place without being certain that they were authoritative. Crucially, 5 June was the wedding anniversary of Elizabeth's parents, who had married on that very day forty-two years earlier. This consolidates the idea that Elizabeth intended both her marriages to chime with important family dates: 22 April 1626 with her grandfather's birthday (probably) and 5 June 1649 with her parents' wedding anniversary. Moreover, and given Elizabeth's apparent record of synchronising her marriages with the Shakespeare family calendar, Billesley may have been chosen because Shakespeare and Anne Hathaway had married there. Malone suspected as much: 'The ancient register of Billesley is also lost. It is observable that our poet's granddaughter was married to her second husband in the church of Billesley ... perhaps in consequence of her grandfather's having been married there' (Malone 1821, p. 118 note).

The man Elizabeth married was a wealthy widower by the name of Sir John Barnard (or Bernard) from the manor of Abington in Northampton-shire. Nothing is known about how Elizabeth Nash met Barnard. Lady Elizabeth Barnard, now aged forty-one, joined her husband and his family in Abington Manor. She left behind her two Stratford homes, New Place and Nash House, and her properties in Henley Street, which were looked after by her Hart cousins and the landlords of the Maidenhead. In 1742 the then owner of the rebuilt New Place, Hugh Clopton, told the actor Charles Macklin that when Elizabeth left New Place for her second husband's estate in Abington there was 'an old tradition that she had carried away with her from Stratford many of her grandfather's papers' (Malone 1821, p. 623). Four years after her death, Elizabeth's second husband singled out 'plate' valued at £29 which was kept in the 'study' at the Barnard mansion in Abington and sat there, it seems, alongside 'all the books' which in turn were valued at £29.11 (Fripp 1928, p. 79). One may well wonder whether or not the plate and books did not come from New Place, the former the same 'plate' that had been bequeathed to Elizabeth by her grandfather in 1616.

Scholars have long suspected that the so-called 'study' at New Place was well stocked with books, because of Shakespeare's writing spells during Lent and his evident depth of reading. Also, it stands to reason that Elizabeth Barnard would have moved important family papers such as copies of deeds and conveyances and the grant of the coat-of-arms to John Shakespeare. While Shakespeare's library probably contained copies of

Ovid, Virgil, Plautus, Terence, Plutarch and Holinshed, it is likely that he also owned copies of his plays and poems in quarto. Above all, his family must have numbered among their possessions a 1623 First Folio of the works. All these precious papers would have found their way into a library or 'study' in Abington. None of them are mentioned in Elizabeth's will, perhaps because she knew that her husband would not only need those papers if she predeceased him, but would also dispose of them in suitable fashion in due course. In fact, he left no will but, as Taplin notes, 'an administration bond was drawn up for his goods, dated 14 May 1674. Administration was granted to his daughters Mary Higgs, widow, and Mrs Eleanor Cotton, and to Henry Gilbert his son-in-law. Bernard is described in the administration as of the parish of All Saints, Northampton, and his burial is recorded in the All Saints register as having taken place at Abington on 5 March 1673-4' (Taplin 2011, p. 127, n. 23).

Elizabeth's failure to mention any New Place papers and books led Malone and Halliwell-Phillipps to the quixotic idea of looking for them behind the panelling in the Great Hall or Oak Room, which survives from the Barnards' days here. The impulse to search for genuine Shakespeare materials from New Place among the descendants of the Barnards must be right. Schoenbaum notes that '[p]erhaps the manuscripts [Shakespeare's papers] had been inherited and passed down by Lady Bernard, who appointed Edward Bagley of London her executor; or perhaps some of the papers had come into the hands of the daughters ... of Sir John Bernard ... maybe others were among the effects of a descendant of Heminges' (Schoenbaum 1970, p. 200). Higgins records that portraits of Lady Elizabeth and Sir John Barnard migrated from the Barnards' home to Kingsthorpe before its virtual demolition by its new owner and that she was allowed to see them (Higgins 1903, p. 70, n.3). Unfortunately Higgins did not leave a detailed description of what she saw. John Taplin, formerly of the Shakespeare Birthplace Trust, has extensively investigated the mysterious Bagley who features prominently in the will of Elizabeth Hall as 'my kinsman Edward Bagley' (Taplin 2011, pp. 123-40).

Elizabeth Barnard's will left monies to the daughters of her 'kinsman' Thomas Hathaway of Stratford, undoubtedly a relative through her grandmother Anne Hathaway of Shottery, and the Harts of Henley Street, who now at last came into possession of the entire Birthplace, including the eastern wing with the Maidenhead. Thanks to Elizabeth, the Harts continued to live in Henley Street until the end of the eighteenth century. Elizabeth also honoured a 'promise formerly made' to Edward Nash, referring undoubtedly to the dispute over Thomas Nash's will over twenty years earlier: after her husband John Barnard's demise, Nash would have first option on buying New Place and the monies from the sale would be divided among a number of different heirs.

When she died in 1670 at the age of sixty-two, the parish register noted her passing with a sober 'Madam Elizabeth Bernard, wife of Sir John Bernard, Knight, was buried 17th February 1669' (Higgins 1903, p. 67). Lady Elizabeth Barnard was laid to rest in the adjacent church of St Peter and St Paul. She might have been expected to join the rest of her family in the chancel of Holy Trinity, but this was not to be. She had spent the last twenty-one years of her life in Abington and, after Judith's death in 1662 at the age of seventy-seven, the same age as her aunt Joan, her immediate family were now all dead. There was no-one left in Stratford-upon-Avon and Elizabeth may have felt that the departed in Holy Trinity would miss her less than her grieving husband who would shortly be widowed for a second time. With the death of Elizabeth the direct line of William Shakespeare had ceased. Four years later she was joined by her second husband John, at which point the Shakespeares' grand home in Stratford-upon-Avon, New Place, was sold to Sir Edward Walker, whose daughter's marriage to John Clopton returned the house back to the Clopton family (Chambers 1930, 2, pp. 98–9).

But that was not quite the end of the story of Elizabeth Hall, because 311 years later her remains were almost certainly disturbed when, on 28 June 1981, the Barnard vault in the Lady Chapel of the church of St Peter and St Paul was opened. (I am grateful to John Taplin for drawing my attention to this important event and for providing me with a transcript of Arthur Marlow's report on the opening of the vault.) Among the seven adults' coffins in the vault, three had been separately stacked. They belonged to a woman in her sixties (bottom), a woman around thirty (middle), and an elderly man (top) who was identified by the crest on his coffin as Sir John Barnard. These were, therefore, almost certainly, John Barnard and his two wives. Shakespeare's granddaughter was at the bottom, while the coffin of Barnard's first wife, another Elizabeth, who died relatively young, the daughter of Sir Clement Edmondes of Preston Deanery in Northampton-shire, sat on top of it supporting her husband's; the skull and hair of

Barnard's first wife were remarkably well preserved. Barnard's first wife Elizabeth Edmondes was buried on 30 March 1642 (Higgins 1903, p. 54).

The arranging of the three coffins has been taken to suggest that they were moved at some point. The proper chronological stacking order would have followed the deaths, with the first wife (died 1642) at the bottom, then the second wife (1670), and finally Barnard (1674); unless Barnard had expressed a wish to be closer to his first wife. Also, as it was Barnard's surviving children by his first wife who buried him, they may well have wanted their mother and father to rest together as closely as possible. The presence of four infant coffins in the same vault points to the four dead Barnard children who preceded their parents to the grave (four others survived). The report about the opening of the vault in 1981 notes that, according to the pathologist who examined the remains of the older woman, 'it is a 99 per cent certainty that here lies the missing Lady Bernard, her husband, Sir John, and his first wife, also an Elizabeth.' Moreover, the 'woman in her sixties ... had, said the doctor, suffered an arthritic complaint.' If DNA sampling had been available at the time, Elizabeth Hall's remains would have provided us with an important route to Shakespeare's. At least Elizabeth's bones did not suffer the indignity of her mother's, which were dug up in 1707 and unceremoniously decanted into the charnel house of Holy Trinity, the very fate Shakespeare had wanted to pre-empt by urging posterity not to desecrate his tomb (Lewis 1940, p. 607).

WORKS CITED

Chambers, E. K. 1930. *William Shakespeare, A Study of Facts and Problems,* 2 vols. Oxford University Press

Fripp, E. I. 1928. *Shakespeare's Stratford.* Oxford University Press

Gossett, Suzanne (ed.) 2004. *Pericles.* London. Arden

Halliwell, James Orchard 1848. *The Life of William Shakespeare.* London. John Russell Smith

Higgins, Sophia Elizabeth 1903. *The Bernards of Abington and Nether Winchendon: A Family History.* Vol. 1. London. Longmans, Green & Co.

Lane, Joan 1996. *John Hall and his Patients.* Stratford-upon-Avon. Shakespeare Birthplace Trust

Lewis, Roland B. 1940. *The Shakespeare Documents.* Stanford University Press

Malone, Edmond 1821. *The Plays and Poems of William Shakespeare*. Vol. 2. London. F. C. and J. Rivington, and others

Rowe, Nicholas 1709. *Some Account of the Life of Mr. William Shakespeare*. London. Jacob Tonson

Schoenbaum, S. 1970. *Shakespeare's Lives*. Oxford University Press

Stopes, Charlotte 1901. *Shakespeare's Family*. London. Elliot Stock

Taplin, John 2011. *Shakespeare's Country Families*. Warwick. Claridges

 2013. *Shakespeare's Country Families: Appendices*. Vol. 2. Warwick. Claridges

Wells, Stanley 2010. *Shakespeare, Sex, and Love*. Oxford University Press

11

His 'cousin': Thomas Greene

TARA HAMLING

ᔕ

Thomas Greene's claim to be considered an intimate member of the Shakespeare circle rests on two pieces of evidence, both in his own hand. The first is an explicit claim to kinship; in notes kept between November 1614 and January 1615 relating to the enclosure of land at Welcombe, Greene refers three times to William Shakespeare as his 'cousin' and details some exchanges between them (SBT BRU 15/13/27–29). The second claim rests on a passing and indirect reference to a practical relationship; in correspondence dated 9 September 1609 about the activities of a tenant in his house called St Mary's, Greene mentions he is in no hurry to take possession 'because I perceived I might stay another year at New Place' (BRU 15/12/103). This brief and enigmatic comment suggests that Greene shared accommodation with Shakespeare, presumably as a paying lodger, at his town house in Stratford-upon-Avon. How long Greene lived there is not known but this tantalising glimpse into his domestic arrangements indicates not only physical proximity to the Shakespeare family but also, potentially, an active interest in their household affairs. What might it have meant to Shakespeare to have a self-styled 'cousin' at the margins of kinship occupy the physical and metaphorical body of the household, the fundamental unit of early modern society and an environment through which wider circles of influence operated?

*

Thomas Greene cannot claim an entry in the *Oxford Dictionary of National Biography* but the details of his life and career are provided by Robert Bearman, who points out that 'more evidence exists to document Shakespeare's dealings with Greene than with any other of his contemporaries' (Bearman 2012, p. 304). Bearman describes his subject as a 'representative of a minor town gentry family, who for fifteen years was town clerk, or steward, of Stratford-upon-Avon'. After training in law it appears Greene worked on an *ad hoc* basis for the Corporation before being appointed town steward in August 1603. He married Lettice, daughter of Henry Tutt, a gentleman of Hampshire, some time after his call to the bar in 1602 and their first child, Anne, was baptised in Stratford the following March. This places the Greenes in Stratford from 1602/3 and some authors suggest Greene was Shakespeare's lodger as early as 1601 (Fripp 1938, p. 543; Ackroyd 2005, p. 474). The Greenes must have been at New Place by 1608 as the reference in September 1609 to staying *another* year suggests the arrangement had been in place for some time.

Cousin

Greene describes Shakespeare as his 'cousin' in notes kept over 1614 to 1615 concerning the proposed enclosure of lands in Welcombe. As tithe-holders Shakespeare and Greene stood to lose on their investment if the enclosure went ahead, but received assurances they would be fully compensated. This was an awkward matter for Greene because his personal interest conflicted with the interests of the Corporation as his employer. Greene has been a focus of interest merely as a source of information about Shakespeare's business dealings, with some sustained effort to verify Greene's claim to kinship for what it might reveal about Shakespeare's family connections (Taylor 1945; Whitfield 1964). There is no conclusive evidence of a direct familial connection between Greene and Shakespeare and assertions that the Shakespeares served as godparents to Greene's children – Anne (b. 1603) and William (b. 1608) – are unverified.

Historians have pointed towards the lack of precision in the use of language to describe kin in pre-industrial England and the term 'cousin' could be used to refer to a wide circle of distantly related kin (Coster 2001). Greene's use of the term may reflect remote kinship but could also indicate a sense of affinity derived through some sort of practical relationship. His notes recording developments in the enclosure affair suggest growing anxiety about his conflicted position. Though described as a 'private diary' (Taylor 1945, p. 81), this sort of note-taking involved self-fashioning (Smyth 2010). It seems likely given Greene's nervous scrutiny of proceedings that his referring to a fellow investor as 'cousin' might have helped to strengthen a sense of shared business concerns.

It is possible that Greene came to lodge at New Place by drawing on the resource that kinship offered in furthering economic, political and social ambitions. Any familial connection with Shakespeare might have strengthened Greene's credentials with the town corporation. Another possibility is that Greene's references to his 'cousin Shakespeare' depend at least in part on his previous relationship as a lodger, involving close physical proximity and collaboration in domestic affairs.

Lodger

In his account of Shakespeare as lodger in the Mountjoy household in London, Charles Nicholl observes that in facilitating the marriage of the daughter of the house and an apprentice: 'his status as the lodger, in a sort of provisional intimacy with the family, seems intrinsic to the part he plays' (Nicholl 2007, pp. 17–18). The facts suggest a parallel timeframe for Greene lodging at New Place and Shakespeare lodging with the Mountjoys. Shakespeare put his own lodging there from around 1602/3. Shakespeare's involvement with the marriage of the young Mountjoy couple in 1604, as recorded in later court proceedings, might prompt us to wonder about Susanna's marriage to John Hall in 1607. Might Greene have played a role in negotiations? Coster points out that distant 'kin as a group could have a stake in the crucial business of forming households' (Coster 2001, p. 44). Shakespeare was probably living full-time in Stratford from 1611, just as Greene vacated New Place to take up residence in his own house.

Lodging was far more common in early modern England than conventional models of the household allow. One building might accommodate more than one household with the patriarch of each family unit presiding over their own domestic duties in separate chambers. As Lena Cowen Orlin points out, domestic property was often subdivided in wills to allocate specific spaces to individuals, such as widows. In these cases special care was taken to ensure access to facilities for the provisioning and functioning of that household *within* a household, such as spaces and equipment for baking, brewing, heating as well as routes through the house and grounds to fetch supplies (Orlin 2016). The same provision must have been made for lodging households, but the need to share amenities could put pressure on domestic arrangements and relationships.

The realities of lodging are exposed in the journal kept by Adam Eyre, a yeoman on the margins of gentility in Sheffield, between 1647 and 1649. Andrew Hopper explains that in order to alleviate his financial problems Eyre took a lodger, one Edward Mitchell, who came with his wife to live in Eyre's farmhouse. The two couples shared this residence but disputes between landlord and tenant soon broke out. The journal records how Mitchell locked the Eyres out of the house on two occasions. The second time Eyre broke down the door and moved all the furniture in the 'house, kitchen, and buttery, into the over parlour' so that Eyre resided upstairs with Mitchell dwelling separately in the rooms beneath (Hopper 2013, p. 33). Their differences were eventually settled by the arbitration of two neighbours. Several aspects of this case resonate in relation to the Shakespeare/Greene arrangement: first, Eyre's lodger was of similar, though slightly lesser, status, which is also the case with Shakespeare and Greene. Second, the arrangement was born of financial necessity, which raises questions about whether Shakespeare rented out space at New Place as part of his long-term investment plan in buying the property or because he over-stretched himself in doing so. Thirdly, the acrimonious quarrel between Eyre and his lodger raises the question of what the co-habitation of two families meant in physical and practical terms. This requires an understanding of the layout of New Place.

New Place

New Place was built in the 1480s as a town mansion for Sir Hugh Clopton, a younger son from a local landed family with a great manor, Clopton House. When Shakespeare bought New Place in 1597 it was a long-established landmark with a symbolic patina of ancient pedigree. There is little information about the form and appearance of the house in Shakespeare's time, as it was extensively rebuilt in a neo-classical manner around 1702, then demolished in 1759. The most detailed record of its earlier appearance is contained in a notebook kept by George Vertue, a Londoner, during a visit to Stratford in 1737. Vertue notes at the top of one page: 'This something by memory and the description of Shakespeare's house which was in Stratford-on-Avon where he lived and died and his wife after him 1623.' Underneath is a drawing of the front façade of a five-gabled building. The text underneath explains that this sketch shows:

the outward appearance towards the street. The gate and entrance (at the corner of Chapel Lane) besides this front or outward gate there was before the house itself (that Shakespeare lived in) within a little courtyard. Grass growing there – before the real dwelling house. This outside being only a long gallery, etc. and for servants.

A crude floorplan is at the bottom of the page. Possibly Vertue's notes depend on the memory of Shakespeare Hart, the poet's great-great-nephew, then about seventy years of age (Simpson 1952).

The description of the floorplan corresponds with the recollections of one Richard Grimmitt recorded by the Reverend Joseph Green in 1767. Grimmitt, born in 1683, claimed that in his boyhood he was friend to Edward Clopton 'and had been often with him in the great house near the chapel in Stratford called New Place; that to the best of his remembrance there was a brick wall next the street, with a kind of porch at that end of it next the Chapel, when they crossed a small kind of green court before they entered the house' (Schoenbaum 1975, fig. 138).

According to both Vertue and Grimmitt, the 'real dwelling house' was set back beyond a courtyard, so that Vertue's sketch shows only the 'front or outward gate'. The inner part of the house probably contained a large 'hall', synonymous with 'house' in early modern terminology, which might explain why this part of the property was later considered the 'real' house. An archaeological excavation of the New Place site from 2010 to 2012 established the footprint of the street frontage as 60 feet long and 17 feet wide with a courtyard and structures to the rear, which support the existence of an inner building. It seems likely that the architectural layout of New Place resembled the merchant's house known as 'Greyfriars' in Worcester, also built c. 1480 as a street range with a courtyard and two connecting rear wings. It almost certainly had an open hall set back behind the main range of buildings and orientated at a right angle to the street, following the general pattern in Worcester (Hughes 1990, p. 140). Greyfriars was improved in the early seventeenth century with an extended north wing, new windows and a broad staircase, and it is likely that the fifteenth-century buildings at New Place had been similarly upgraded by the time Shakespeare bought it or, perhaps, *while* he owned it.

The 'great rebuilding' of the period c. 1570 – c. 1640 was of particular importance among the gentry and wealthier middling sort (Hoskins 1953; Heal and Holmes 1994, p. 297). Vertue's sketch shows regularly spaced windows and a centralised doorway, a mid sixteenth-century fashion reflecting concern with symmetry in classical architecture. Multiple gables were a development of the Elizabethan and Jacobean periods (Summerson 1993). Indeed, Vertue's sketch looks remarkably similar to the building further along Chapel Street, now 'The Shakespeare Hotel', also with five gables but built c. 1600. The Tudor House in Long Itchington, 18 miles from Stratford, shows how earlier buildings were brought up to standard.

An original long, rectangular, two-storey building of the mid 1500s was extended, probably in the first half of the seventeenth century, with a timber-framed addition to the front of the length of the house finished with a series of five continuous gables to attics. This extension created a wide corridor running along the frontage of the property, providing access to the chambers on the first floor. The arrangement recalls Vertue's

FIGURE 2:   A contemporary parallel to the frontage of New Place: The Tudor House, Long Itchington, Warwickshire.

description of the frontage of New Place as containing 'only a long gallery etc., and for servants'. The term 'long gallery' is associated with Vertue's time rather than Shakespeare's; it suggests a space similar to that created at Long Itchington. Another comparison is the first floor of Blakesley Hall in Yardley, built in the 1590s. A corridor far wider than necessary allows direct access to several chambers; this was a novelty and convenience, given that most houses still had connecting chambers with accommodation reached through other rooms. There is a strange incongruity in Vertue's association of a long gallery (a grand space for stately display) with accommodation 'for servants'. But if a long, wide corridor provided direct access to a series of chambers along the street range of New Place, then this would seem ideally suited to rent out as lodgings.

Greene's family might have occupied recently renovated accommodation in the street range of a larger property, with the Shakespeare family occupying an inner range beyond the courtyard. In 1598, the corporation paid Shakespeare ten pence for a load of stone, which is generally understood as the surplus from remedial work to New Place. Yet owners or tenants at this social level commonly stamped their mark on a building with extensive renovations, including extended space. In the years around 1597 many other townsmen were rebuilding or renovating houses after the devastating fires in 1594 and 1595. 'Harvard House' on the High Street has a richly decorated frontage incorporating the initials of its owner, Thomas Rogers, and the date 1596. It also contains the remains of decorative wall painting, a *trompe l'oeil* imitation of panelling, in the chamber on the second floor facing the street.

It is highly likely that Shakespeare would have commissioned artisans to 'beautify' the interior of his house, an essential and expected element in the expression of status and identity (Cooper 1999). Decoration improved living conditions (by insulating and ornamenting the interior) while demonstrating wealth, social position and religious commitment (Ayres 2003; Hamling 2010). Most houses of size in Shakespeare's lifetime were adorned with wall paintings, hangings and plasterwork. Around the corner from New Place, in Wood Street, Abraham Sturley erected a large house of twelve bays some time after the fire of 1594, which was adorned with an ornate plaster ceiling and frieze with the initials JR either side of a crown, presumably to celebrate the coronation of King James in 1603. The remains of wall painting and plasterwork in houses in the town and region provide a strong indication of how the interior of New Place would have been decorated during the period Greene lived there. It also brings us closer to the domestic environment that Shakespeare would have known and, quite probably, designed.

*

By June 1611 Greene had established his own dwelling house in Stratford called St Mary's, which he described as 'a pretty, neat, gentlemanlike house'. This compares with John Leland's earlier description of New Place as a 'pretty house of brick and timber'. St Mary's, like New Place, was an older property with an air of antiquity and adjacent to a church. Was Greene's choice informed by the character of New Place, or simply what was available as a suitable property? It is tempting to see his choice as in emulation, or even in competition, with New Place.

The Greenes are not mentioned in Shakespeare's will. He may have previously given them remembrances, or overlooked them in his business-like will. The omission could be taken as a rejection of any close kinship or affinity. And yet, for a time at least, Thomas and William returned home by crossing the same threshold, they occupied the same space, shared the same facilities, and retired to bed in chambers close by. Such physical proximity and domestic divisions could engender intimacy, but also acrimony, as the example of Adam Eyre demonstrates. So Thomas Greene's place in the Shakespeare circle remains elusive.

WORKS CITED

Ackroyd, Peter 2005. *Shakespeare: The Biography*. London. Chatto and Windus

Ayres, James 2003. *Domestic Interiors, the British tradition, 1500–1850*. New Haven and London. Yale University Press

Bearman, Robert 2012. 'Thomas Greene: Stratford-upon-Avon's Town Clerk and Shakespeare's Lodger', *Shakespeare Survey 65*. Peter Holland (ed.). Cambridge University Press

Cooper, Nicholas 1999. *Houses of the Gentry, 1480–1680*. New Haven and London. Yale University Press

Coster, Will 2001. *Family and Kinship in England 1450–1800*. London. Pearson Education Limited

Fripp, Edgar I. 1938. *Shakespeare: Man and Artist*. Vol. 2. Oxford University Press

Halliwell-Phillipps, J. O. 1883. *Outlines of the Life of Shakespeare*. London. Longmans, Green and Co.

Hamling, Tara 2010. *Decorating the Godly Household: Religious Art in Post-Reformation Britain*. New Haven and London. Yale University Press

Heal, Felicity and Holmes, Clive 1994. *The Gentry in England and Wales, 1500–1700*. Stanford University Press

Hopper, Andrew 2013. 'Social Mobility during the English Revolution: the case of Adam Eyre', *Social History* 38.1 26–45

Hoskins, W. G. 1953. 'The Rebuilding of Rural England, 1570–1640', *Past & Present* 4: 44–59

Hughes, Patricia Marjorie, 1990. 'Buildings and the Building Trade in Worcester 1540–1650'. Unpublished PhD thesis, University of Birmingham

Nicholl, Charles 2007. *The Lodger: Shakespeare on Silver Street*. London. Penguin

Orlin, Lena Cowen 2016 (forthcoming). 'Rights of Privacy in Early Modern English Households' in David Gaimster, Tara Hamling and Catherine Richardson (eds.), *The Ashgate Research Companion to Material Culture in Early Modern Europe*. Aldershot. Ashgate Publishing

Schoenbaum, S. 1975. *William Shakespeare: A Documentary Life*. Oxford University Press

Simpson, Frank 1952. 'New Place: The Only Representation of Shakespeare's House from an Unpublished Manuscript', *Shakespeare Survey 5*. Allardyce Nicoll (ed.). Cambridge University Press

Smyth, Adam 2010. *Autobiography in Early Modern England*. Cambridge University Press

Summerson, John 1993. *Architecture in Britain 1530–1830*. New Haven and London. Yale University Press

Taylor, Rupert 1945. 'Shakespeare's Cousin, Thomas Greene and his Kin: Possible light on the Shakespeare family background', *PMLA* 60.11: 81–94

Whitfield, Christopher 1964. 'Thomas Greene, Shakespeare's Cousin: A biographical sketch', *Notes and Queries*, December: 442–55

PART II

§

Friends and neighbours

In distinguishing people whom we should count among Shakespeare's friends and neighbours, rather than specifically either relatives or professional colleagues, we looked for striking and undeniable evidence of personal connections such as neighbourliness, beneficiaries through legacies (either to or from Shakespeare) and close creative appreciation and engagement.

The Combe family of Stratford-upon-Avon, prominent also in the county affairs of Warwickshire, were close neighbours. Many links are recorded between several family members and Shakespeare at different stages of his life, for example the purchase of land in 1602 and the disputes about the Welcombe enclosures in 1614–15. They lived in the largest house in Stratford, which had originally been established as 'The College' for the training of priests close to Holy Trinity Church. Shakespeare's prestigious New Place was second only to The College in terms of size, and only a four-minute walk away. John Combe (whose epitaph has been attributed to Shakespeare) left him £5 in July 1614; Shakespeare bequeathed his sword to the twenty-seven-year-old Thomas Combe, a significant bequest that would surely have gone to Shakespeare's son Hamnet, who would by then have been thirty-one years old had he lived.

A link that takes us from Stratford to London is with Richard Field. He was two-and-a-half years older than Shakespeare and made a career as a distinguished publisher as well as a printer of books in several different languages, reflecting his grammar-school education. Carol Rutter suggestively imagines Shakespeare as 'Proteus to Field's Valentine' (p. 163), Shakespeare staying in Stratford to complete his education after his school fellow had left for London. It was Field whom Shakespeare sought out as a printer for his narrative poems, famous for the high quality of their printing, which suggests that Shakespeare himself closely liaised with Field and may even have proof read them in the printing house. Visits to his printing house – a kind of library in its own right – would have enabled Shakespeare to use a number of Field's books when researching his plays. It is worth remembering that, as Chris Laoutoris has explored in his fascinating book *Shakespeare and The Countess* (2014), Field's printing shop was close to the Blackfriars playhouse in which Shakespeare owned shares and where the King's Men performed from 1609. Indeed, Field was among those who protested against the former monastery becoming a boisterous playhouse. He represents just one among the complex network of printers, publishers and booksellers who kept stalls in St Paul's Churchyard, across the Thames from the Rose and the Globe Theatres, and close to The Bell Inn on Carter Lane, a favourite haunt of Stratford commuters.

Field was apprenticed to the Huguenot printer Thomas Vautrollier and married his widow, Jacqueline. David Kathman suggests that it might have been through Field that Shakespeare came to lodge with another Huguenot family, the Mountjoys, on Silver Street in the north-west part of the city. It is easy to imagine, as Kathman does, Shakespeare and his colleagues John Heminges and Henry Condell walking across London Bridge or taking a wherry to cross the Thames to their place of work. Like Shakespeare, the Mountjoys had connections with the Court and with the theatre. Marie Mountjoy made head-tires for wealthy women. One such client was none other than Queen Anne (or Anna) herself, the wife of King James I. The court case involving the Mountjoys in 1612 shows Shakespeare taking a benevolent interest in the family affairs.

We hope that Ben Jonson would be delighted to find himself among Shakespeare's friends. He was certainly a competitor. Theirs was clearly not an always easy relationship, one of professional rivalry and creative tensions, but, we have every reason to suppose, one also of mutual affection and admiration. Chatting to William Drummond of Hawthornden over the Christmas of 1618–19, Jonson said of Shakespeare 'I loved the man', quickly adding the qualification 'this side idolatry'. David Riggs reminds us of Jonson's aggressive desire for originality, pointing out a Latin motto on the title-page of *Every Man Out of His Humour* (1600), 'I don't walk in other people's footsteps'. Shakespeare, however, seems at times to have followed at least a little in Jonson's, 'the subplot of *Twelfth Night*', for example, 'amounts to a qualified endorsement of Jonson's comic method' (p. 190). He is also remembered for his critical remarks on Shakespeare's stagecraft. Referring to the Prologue in the 1616 Folio version of *Every Man In His Humour*, Riggs comments that Shakespeare was the 'perfect foil' for Jonson, whilst at the same time suggesting this apparent critique amounts to little more than caricature (p. 196).

Andrew Hadfield reminds us that during the 1590s Shakespeare tended to be seen as a comparatively light-weight poet. Richard Barnfield, after praising Edmund Spenser, Samuel Daniel and Michael Drayton, concludes his poem 'A Remembrance of Some English Poets' of 1598 by referring to Shakespeare, perhaps, as Hadfield notes, 'the fourth most important English poet of his generation' (p. 201). Although we have the benefit of evaluating Barnfield's remarks within the context of Shakespeare's whole poetic and dramatic output, he is one of several early commentators who noticed that Shakespeare had found an individual poetic tone of voice, naming it as 'sweet' and even 'honey-tongued'. The sound of the Shakespearian voice described in the 1590s would stay with him. *Antony and Cleopatra* and *The Winter's Tale* are every bit as 'honey-tongued' as *Venus and Adonis* and *Romeo and Juliet*. And, by contrast, *Coriolanus* is every bit as flinty as the 'graver labour' of *Lucrece* (1594).

In gathering together a diverse group of neighbours and beneficiaries, Susan Brock presents us with the kinds of people whom we can assume to have been present in Holy Trinity Church for Shakespeare's funeral on 25 April 1616. As they walked out of the church on that spring day, exchanging memories of their old friend, their conversations and reminiscences had their own intimate place in the beginning of his posthumous reputation.

WORKS CITED

Laoutoris, Chris 2014. *Shakespeare and The Countess*. London: Penguin Fig Tree

12

A close family connection: the Combes

STANLEY WELLS

§

Shakespeare had direct and well-documented points of contact with three generations of the Combes, a prominent Warwickshire family of wealthy Protestant landowners closely associated with Stratford-upon-Avon throughout his lifetime and beyond. He must have been aware of various members of the family, and in varying degrees of intimacy, during all his adult life; some of them became close friends. Forenames, especially William, John and Thomas, tended to recur from one generation to another in different branches of the family. This has made them notoriously difficult to sort out; confusion is both easy and common, but the first Combe with whom Shakespeare had a documented association was a lawyer named William – I shall call him William Senior – whose career centred on Warwick but who had close links with Stratford where his father, John, lived.

William, a posthumous son, was born in June 1551. According to his entry in the *History of Parliament* he was 'set to school and brought up in learning by some loving benefactors'. They did their job well: like several of Shakespeare's direct associates, such as Abraham Sturley and Richard Quiney, like Holofernes and Sir Nathaniel in *Love's Labour's Lost* – and, it may well be, like Shakespeare himself – he was as fluent in Latin as in English. A copy of *A Profitable Book of the Laws of England*, by John Perkins, a long-popular treatise on land law first printed in 1527, inscribed 'Cest le liver de Gulihelme Combes' – the equivalent of 'William Combe, his book' – along with the date of his admission to the Middle Temple in 1571, at the age of twenty, is in the collections of the Shakespeare Birthplace Trust. Written in Law French and printed in black letter, it is copiously annotated in a minute secretary hand in both French and Latin (but not, so far as I have observed, in English), suggesting that he was a learned and

149

extremely diligent student. He was called to the bar on 9 February 1578 and became a Member of Parliament for Droitwich in 1589, for the town of Warwick soon afterwards, and for Warwickshire in 1597. (At this time Parliament met only sporadically.) He was chosen reader at the Middle Temple in 1595 and served as legal adviser to the Stratford Corporation from 1597 until his death in 1610, and as an ecclesiastical commissioner from 1601 to 1608. He married Alice Hanbury, daughter of a London goldsmith; she died in 1606, and in the same year he took as his second wife Jane, Lady Puckering, widow of Sir John, lord keeper of the great seal (Lord Chancellor), who had died ten years previously, and went to live with her at The Priory, Warwick, a grand house with extensive parkland built in 1566 on the site of a priory demolished at the Reformation. The Queen had visited it in 1572 on her way back from Kenilworth. The town's Bailiff described William in 1605 as 'an honest gentleman their neighbour well respected' (Fripp 1938, p. 732).

William's high standing in Stratford is witnessed by the fact that the Corporation paid 20 pence for 'a quart of sack and a quart of claret wine' given to him for an unspecified reason some time in 1602 (Bearman 2011, p. 182), although he was not living in the town at the time. It was on 1 May of this year that Shakespeare paid this William and his nephew John £320 for about 107 acres of land in Old Stratford which William Combe had bought in 1593 (Schoenbaum, 1975, pp. 188–9). This was farming country in the northern part of the borough, around the Welcombe Hills and Bishopton. The land 'would have been made up of strips in the furlongs into which the four open fields of Old Stratford were divided, each landowner having his strips scattered through the fields to ensure a fair distribution of good and bad land' (MacDonald, 1994, p. 876). This purchase 'not only placed the dramatist among the local landed gentry and thus gave him social and financial prestige, but also placed him in the position of landlord to many tenant farmers ... He was now in such a position that many rendered him consideration and did him reverence' (Lewis, 1940, pp. 335–6). Shakespeare, described as 'William Shakespeare of Stratford-upon-Avon, gentleman', was represented in the sale by his brother Gilbert, no doubt because he was out of town. A detailed survey made around 1625 suggests that he may have given the land to his elder daughter Susanna as a marriage settlement in 1607; nevertheless he still regarded it as his to bequeath to her in his will, of 1616. Presumably he had retained, or thought he had retained, a lifetime interest in it. Or was this a security measure in case the settlement was questioned?

The fact that Shakespeare was affluent enough to spend so large a sum may be explained in part by the death only a few months earlier of his father, John, who was buried on 8 September 1601; no will survives. Shakespeare inherited from him his Henley Street house – the Birthplace – and perhaps money as well as other property. It may also be relevant that 'the unanimous tradition of this neighbourhood is, that by the uncommon bounty of the Earl of Southampton, he was enabled to purchase houses and land at Stratford' (Wheler 1806, p. 73). This statement resembles, but was not necessarily influenced by, Nicholas Rowe's report that, according to the poet and playwright William Davenant (1606–68), Southampton gave Shakespeare £1000 'to enable him to go through with a purchase which he heard he had a mind to' (Chambers 1930, 2, pp. 266–7). These two puffs of smoke, illumined by the warmth of the dedication to *The Rape of Lucrece* in 1594, surely suggest the existence of at least a small fire.

The civic authorities continued to butter William Combe up. A few months later, in January 1603, the town paid 4 shillings 'for two quarts of sack and two quarts of Rhenish wine' given by the Bailiff to Mr Verney and to Mr William Combes when the rogues were taken at Clifford Barn' (Bearman 2011, p. 217). 'Verney' was Sir Richard Verney, of Compton Verney, also a magistrate, married to Sir Fulke Greville's sister. This appears to acknowledge Combe's part in punishing criminals who had been apprehended in the village of Clifford Chambers close to Stratford. A colourful and well-documented brawl initiated by servants of Sir Richard Greville, of Milcote, had resulted in the wounding and eventual death of the Bailiff, Shakespeare's friend, the dedicated and long-serving Stratfordian Richard Quiney (Eccles 1961, pp. 97–9).

The Council also paid 3s 4d on an unspecified date in 1604 'for wine that was given to M[aste]r William Combes and [his wife] the Lady Puckering when the[y] were at the College' – indicating that they were guests at The College of their relative Thomas Combe (Bearman, 2011, p. 406). This may have been in celebration of their marriage. Then on 18 October 1604 William Combe was associated with a cringingly expressed petition made by the Corporation to the Chancellor of the diocese of Warwick on behalf of Thomas Parker who 'employed himself to the teaching of little children, chiefly such as his wife one time of the day doth practise in needle work, whereby our young youth is well furthered in reading and the free school [the grammar school] greatly eased of that tedious trouble' (Bearman 2011, p. 306). This provides valuable and little-known evidence that educational opportunities were available in Stratford for both girls and boys, who may have included Shakespeare's son and daughters, at a pre-grammar school in what was known as a petty school stage. Parker is mentioned by Fripp (Fripp 1938, p. 805), who calls him 'the preparatory Schoolmaster', as a freeholder of the land up for enclosure in 1614.

William Combe Senior's continuing high status in the town is witnessed by other items of documentary evidence. He served as High Sheriff of Warwickshire – an annually appointed office – in 1607, and on 18 December – a week before Christmas – the Corporation of Stratford voted to buy and to bestow upon him a keg – a small barrel – of sturgeon (Bearman 2011, p. 428).

Since the reign of Edward II (1284–1327) sturgeon had been (as it still is) a royal fish, highly valued and officially the property when caught of the sovereign. Presumably these fish were caught in the Avon – a fisherman called Robert Ingram lived in the borough (Bearman 2011, p. 244) – though they are now exceedingly rare in British waters. They would have been preserved, probably in salt, and no doubt were given as a corporate compliment, a kind of sweetener in recognition of Combe's services to the town – a modern equivalent might be a side or two of smoked salmon. William Combe Senior died childless in 1611 leaving a vast estate including houses, meadows and watermills. Most of his property went to his widow and to another William (II), his step-brother's grandson. He left £20 to the poor of Warwick, and £10 each to the poor of Alvechurch, Stratford and Broadway. In the light of this, Shakespeare's identical bequest of £10 to the poor of Stratford may seem less stingy than is sometimes suggested.

William Combe Senior's nephew John Combe (John Junior) forms another link with Shakespeare. Born before 1561, he was a wealthy and litigious money-broker or usurer who brought many suits against default-ing clients of Stratford (Lewis 1940, p. 328). In 1611 Shakespeare seems to have acquired from John and his uncle William an additional 20 acres of pasturage (Lewis, pp. 412–15; not mentioned in Schoenbaum.) John lived at Welcombe and died unmarried in 1614, leaving £5 to Shakespeare – not a great sum, but enough to bear witness to real friendship. His will dated January 1613 is a detailed and charitable document with curious and imaginative bequests such as 'unto Sir Francis Smith knight £5 to buy him a hawk, and to the Lady Anne his wife £40 ... to buy her a basin and ewer' – presumably made of a precious metal; £10 to Francis Collins of Warwick – the lawyer who drew up Shakespeare's will – and £100 to be lent 'unto 15 poor or young tradesmen ... 20 nobles apiece for 3 years, paying 3s. 4.' He died on 10 July 1613, on the day following the town's third great fire within twenty years, which destroyed fifty-four houses and much other property. A report by the William Combe (Junior) born in 1586 who was to be involved in the enclosure dispute (see below) and other justices declared that the force of 'this sudden and terrible fire' 'was so great (the wind sitting full upon the town) that it dispersed into so many places thereof whereby the whole town was in very great danger to have been utterly consumed' (Eccles 1961, p. 135). The Council ordered more fire-fighting equipment and petitioned the Lord Chief Justice to forbid the building of thatched houses (Eccles, pp. 135–6). New Place escaped damage, but this was a bad year for Shakespeare and fire: the Globe had burnt down eleven days previously, on 29 June, to be replaced by a tiled structure.

John Junior was buried in the chancel of Holy Trinity on 12 July 1614. It is reasonable to suppose that Shakespeare attended his funeral. John left £60 for a tomb in Holy Trinity Church, which survives and may be seen there. Elaborately adorned and, originally, colourfully painted (though now whitewashed), it bears a full-length recumbent effigy of him wearing a gown. The sculptor is believed to have been Geerhart Janssen (otherwise known as Gerard Johnson), who also carved Shakespeare's monument. If £60 fully covered the cost we might conjecture that Shakespeare's somewhat smaller monument, for which his will makes no provision, cost something in the region of £20 to £30.

John Combe's monument is said to have originally borne a jokey epitaph that has often been attributed to Shakespeare, though it was first printed anonymously in 1619 (Wells and Taylor 1987, pp. 458–9). In this version it reads:

> Ten in the hundred must lie in his grave,
> But a hundred to ten whether God will him have.
> Who then must be interred in this tomb?
> 'O', quoth the Devil, 'My John a-Combe'.

The writer, John Brathwaite, says the epitaph was 'fastened upon a tomb that he had caused to be built in his lifetime'. The best authenticated version seems to be the one transcribed by a visitor to Stratford, John Dobyns, in 1673 as (in original spelling)

> Tenn in the hundred here lyeth engraued
> A hundred to ten his Soule is new [now?] saued.
> If anny one ask: who lyeth in this Tomb,
> Oh ho quoth the Diuell tis my John a Combe

'Ten in the hundred' refers to a current rate of interest; Shakespeare himself writes playfully about this in Sonnet 6, where, advising a young man to marry and beget a child – or, better still, ten children – he declares

> That use is not forbidden usury
> Which happies those that pay the willing loan:
> That's for thyself to breed another thee,
> Or ten times happier, be it ten for one;
> Ten times thyself were happier than thou art,
> If ten of thine ten times refigured thee.

Dobyns added (in modern spelling) 'Since my being at Stratford the heirs of Master Combe have caused these verses to be razed so that now they are not legible.' The implication is that the heirs found it objectionable.

A legend that Shakespeare had written the epitaph as a joke at Combe's request and during his lifetime had developed and circulated soon after John Combe died. In 1634 a Lieutenant Hammond wrote after visiting Stratford that Shakespeare 'had written some witty and facetious verses' upon 'Mr Combe', but didn't transcribe them. Around 1650 one Nicholas Burgh quoted the last line and a half in a manuscript preserved in the Bodleian Library under the title 'On John Combe, a covetous rich man Mr William Shakespeare writ this at his request while he was yet living for his epitaph.' In 1681 the diarist John Aubrey also recorded a version of the lines as 'this extemporary epitaph' by Shakespeare on Combe, saying that they were improvised at a tavern in Stratford, and Nicholas Rowe, in 1709, says that the epitaph was written at Combe's invitation 'in a laughing manner'. The word 'engraved' in the first line puns in a not-unShakespearian fashion on the senses 'enclosed in a grave' and 'inscribed'. The epitaph resembles other known examples, including one which reads

Ten in the hundred lies under this stone,
And a hundred to ten to the devil he's gone.

This had appeared as early as 1608, six years before Combe died, so if Shakespeare really wrote the one on Combe he was adapting an existing trope – which is not impossible. If he did, and in Combe's lifetime, Combe must have forgiven him, or enjoyed the joke, since he left money to Shakespeare. It is not easy to believe that the vicar would have permitted such an epitaph to be inscribed on a tomb in Holy Trinity Church, though Dobyns implies that this was so. The question of whether Shakespeare had anything to do with the epitaph remains uncertain, though other epitaphs have also been ascribed to him (Wells and Taylor 1987, pp. 457–9).

This John had a brother, Thomas, who predeceased him, dying in 1609; he was joint owner with Shakespeare of the tithes that Shakespeare had bought for £440 in 1605 – his most substantial financial investment. In 1596 Thomas had bought the mansion known as The College, the biggest house in Stratford – the second was Shakespeare's New Place – and the only one to be built entirely of stone. The College had been built in 1351 by Ralph de Stratford as a house for the five priests assigned to chant masses for the souls of John, 'his family, the Kings of England, and the Bishops of Worcester' (Schoenbaum 1975, p. 10). It stood close to Holy Trinity on land currently occupied in part by the Methodist Church and bounded on two sides by College Lane and College Street. Shakespeare, owner of the only other house of comparable grandeur in the town, must have been a frequent visitor. It was demolished late in the eighteenth century. Soon afterwards the following description appeared in Wheler's *History and Antiquities of Stratford-upon-Avon* (1806):

The building itself, which was surrounded by extensive gardens and pleasure grounds, was capacious, handsome, and strong; being wholly constructed of hewn free-stone: the east entrance was under a large doorway . . . into a spacious hall, extending the whole length of the front, and vaulted to the roof; the concave ceiling was elegantly adorned with stucco work; and at each angle, was a rude representation of the emblematical symbols of the four Evangelists; the north wing was occupied by apartments, originally destined for the warden and officiating priests, and since converted into a modern dining room, drawing room, and library; in the opposite wing was the kitchen, with its offices, stables, coach-houses, &c, &c. (Wheler 1806, p. 91)

FIGURE 3: The College, where Shakespeare's friends the Combes lived. It was
the largest house in Stratford-upon-Avon and the only one to be built of stone.
This engraving shows it standing in extensive grounds just before its demolition in 1799
(forty years after the demolition of New Place).

Some idea of its grandeur can be gleaned from the fact that in 1670, when
records of the number of hearths in individual houses were made for tax
purposes, it had fifteen, more than any other dwelling in Stratford;
New Place came second, with ten. Clearly the building had undergone
considerable alteration since it was first built, but there is no reason to
suspect that its overall plan, of which Wheler prints a diagram, had
changed. Probably the 'rude representation of the evangelists' survived
from the days before it was converted to secular use. Here surely
Shakespeare and his family must often have been entertained, recipro-
cating with meals at New Place served on the gold and silver plate that he
eventually bequeathed – presumably as a kind of wedding dowry – to his
nine-year-old granddaughter, Elizabeth Hall, who was to become Lady
Bernard.

This Thomas's will (PROB 11/113/130), dated 22 December 1608, is of
special interest in relation to Shakespeare's in its bequest to Thomas's wife
of 'the use and occupation of all tables, bedsteads and other standards [basic
pieces of furniture] now remaining in and about the said house during her

widowhood except the best bedstead which I will, give and bequeath unto my said son William, with the best bed and furniture thereunto belonging, to have to his own use.' Clearly the bequest of bedsteads, including the second-best, to his wife is made entirely without acrimony.

It was within months of the great fire of 1614 that proposals were made to enclose large areas of arable land including the property that Shakespeare had bought from the Combes in 1602 to the north of the town, converting it into sheep pasturage. This would have added to the hardship brought by the fire, reducing income and employment and increasing the price of grain, vital to many of the townspeople. The twenty-eight-year-old William Combe (II), nephew of William I, was a prime mover. The Town Council, fearing riots as well as serious loss of income, appealed to Shakespeare among other landowners not to enclose; one of their number was later to tell young William Combe that 'All three fires' – there had been similar disasters in 1594 and 1595 – 'were not so great a loss to the town as the enclosures would be.' The two men who would have been most seriously affected financially if enclosures had gone ahead were the tithe-owners Shakespeare and Thomas Greene, the Town Clerk. By 28 October Shakespeare had entered into an agreement for compensation. From November Greene, lawyer and aspiring poet, happily kept a detailed diary of events which enables a remarkably full reconstruction of what happened. He refers to Shakespeare as his cousin. But the editor of the diary, noting that Greene uses this term of several other men to whom he is not known to have been related, remarks 'It is probable that the term "Cosen" was very loosely used by the diarist' (Ingleby 1885, p. iii; other quotations from Greene are from pp. 1–6 of this edition).

Visiting London to present a petition against enclosure on behalf of the Corporation, Greene called at some unknown location – the Second Globe was operating by now – on Shakespeare who, with his son-in-law John Hall, had arrived in the capital from Stratford on the previous day: 'my cousin Shakespeare coming yesterday to town I went to see him how he did'. The set of notes that Greene scribbled about his meeting, preserved in the Shakespeare Birthplace Trust's collections, is, except perhaps for those relating to the Mountjoy case, the one in which we come closest to Shakespeare. He knew all about the plans, and tried to reassure Greene, saying that he and Hall thought 'there will be nothing done at all'. The principal proponents of enclosure were the brothers Thomas and William

Combe, who appear to have pressed their case with arrogant high-handedness. On 9 December Greene was part of a delegation to William Combe entreating him not to go ahead, but Combe declared that when the frost broke 'the ditching would go presently [immediately] forward'. On 12 December Greene recorded that Thomas Combe had said that 'they' – presumably those who opposed enclosure – 'were all curs' – Coriolanus comes to mind. After a Council meeting on 23 December, Greene wrote to Shakespeare both personally and on behalf of the Council inviting support. His letter is lost, but in a letter to someone else Greene referred to 'the manifold miseries this borough has sustained' and to the 'above 700 poor which receive alms, whose curses and clamours will be daily poured out to God against the enterpriser of such a thing'.

On 7 January William Combe, having heard that 'some of the better sort would go to throw down the ditch', said '"Ay, O, would they durst" in a threatening manner with very great passion and anger'; on the same day he said 'they were a company of factious knaves' and that he would 'do them all the mischief he can'; he also called them 'Puritan knaves and underlings in their colour'. A couple of days later Greene heard that two of his townsmen 'had privately sent their spades before, and that by and by they would go throw down some of the ditch'. Greene, compassionately acting against his own financial interests, prudently advised them to 'go in such private manner as that none might see them go lest others might perhaps follow in company and so make a riot or mutiny'. Combe's men started to enclose the land by digging a long trench; at the very moment that an agreement was being concluded that 'there shall be no throwing down of ditches already set up ... until after 25 March', women and children of Bishopton and Stratford 'filled them up again'. William Combe punished his tenants in the village of Welcombe, virtually depopulating it. The case dragged on until, around the time that Shakespeare died, a letter from the chief justice told Combe that he 'should neither enclose nor lay down any arable nor plough any ancient greensward'. Even this did not deter him; but the land was not finally enclosed until well into the eighteenth century.

Greene's diary also includes a touching set of Latin verses in which he expresses anxiety about his wife's pregnancy, then in an advanced stage. (Happily it came to a successful conclusion.) Greene emerges from the enclosure dispute as a humane and conscientious servant of the town who was doing his duty by the inhabitants even against his best personal interests. Shakespeare seems to have been less deeply committed to the townspeople's cause, willing to remain on the sidelines rather than to take risks.

It is the Thomas Combe who had called the enclosing townspeople 'curs' to whom in 1616 Shakespeare bequeathed his sword, which would have had sentimental and commemorative as well as financial value. Shakespeare knew about swords, both on stage and off. The word occurs hundreds of times in his plays; Othello owns one that is 'of the ice-brook's temper' (*Othello*, 5.2.260), and swords are worn by civilians, such as the disguised Viola and Sir Andrew Aguecheek in *Twelfth Night*, as well as by soldiers. In real life their length and use were regulated by sumptuary laws, which, however, were often disregarded. The weapon was especially associated with gentlemen entitled to bear arms, but in 1603 a Stratford yeoman – the rank below gentleman – Lewis Cawdrey, 'drew his sword' on the town's two constables when they tried to arrest him and then ran away (Bearman 2011, p. 241). 'The nine [Stratford] men who owned either a sword or a rapier, usually coupled with a dagger, came from all walks of life, and five of them did not aspire to the status of "gentleman". One of the four who did, however, was William Shakespeare' (Jones 1996, p. 64). He would have worn it when dressed in his best 'wearing apparel' (which he left to his sister) on official occasions as a member of the King's Men, at Court or on State occasions such as King James's coronation, rather than in Stratford. It would have been of value only to a man, and to one whose social status allowed him to use it. If Hamnet had lived, he would no doubt have inherited it. The bequest of it to the twenty-seven-year-old Thomas Combe rather than to John Hall, on the surface a more likely recipient, suggests genuine affection, even that Shakespeare may have regarded Thomas as a kind of surrogate son. Baptised on 9 February 1589, he was brought up at The College but later lived at Welcombe; he was six years younger than Shakespeare's daughter Susanna and four years younger than Judith and Hamnet, with whom he may well have played as a boy. He had entered the Middle Temple when he was twenty, succeeding along with his elder brother William, who had studied at Oxford, to the chamber of his uncle, and was twenty-seven years old when Shakespeare died. Fripp, calling William Combe 'the blustering young *dominus* of the College and High Sheriff', suggests (Fripp 1938, p. 823) that 'the gift of the sword to his pugnacious younger brother [Thomas] had a touch of irony in it – 'for all that take the sword shall perish with the sword' [Matthew xxvi.52] and interestingly notes that Shakespeare left nothing to Thomas's no less arrogant brother William. Thomas appears to have mellowed in later life; on his death in 1657 he 'left land for gowns for the poor, two sermons a year, and a yearly feast for the corporation' (Eccles 1961, p. 121). Like his uncle John – and like Shakespeare's brothers Richard, Gilbert and Edmund (who, however, died young and had a child) – the eligible Thomas Combe never married, a fact worthy of note at a time when, as Jeanne Jones notes, 'Bachelors aged more than thirty were rare' (Jones 1996, p. 86). Whether he prized his legacy, history does not record. Like the silver-gilt bowl that Shakespeare left to his granddaughter, it may have been inscribed with his initials and could survive still, unrecognised and undervalued.

WORKS CITED

Bearman, Robert (ed.) 2011. *Minutes and Accounts of the Stratford-upon-Avon Corporation, Vol. VI, 1599–1609*. Stratford-upon-Avon. The Dugdale Society

Chambers, E. K. 1930. *William Shakespeare: A Study of Facts and Problems*, 2 vols. Oxford University Press

Eccles, Mark 1961. *Shakespeare in Warwickshire*. Madison. University of Wisconsin Press

Fripp, Edgar I. 1938. *Shakespeare Man and Artist*. 2 vols. Oxford University Press

Ingleby, C. M. (ed.) 1885. *Shakespeare and the Enclosure of Common Fields at Welcombe*, privately published, Birmingham

Jones, Jeanne 1996. *Family Life in Shakespeare's England: Stratford-upon-Avon, 1570–1630*. Stroud. Shakespeare Birthplace Trust

Lewis, B. Roland 1940. *The Shakespeare Documents*. 2 vols. Stanford University Press

MacDonald, Mairi 1994. 'A New Discovery about Shakespeare's Estate in Old Stratford', *Shakespeare Quarterly* 45.1: 87–9

Schoenbaum, S. 1975. *William Shakespeare: A Documentary Life*. Oxford. Clarendon Press

Wells, Stanley, and Taylor, Gary 1987. *William Shakespeare: A Textual Companion*. Oxford University Press

Wheler, R. B. 1806. *History and Antiquities of Stratford-upon-Avon*. London J. Ward

13

Schoolfriend, publisher and printer Richard Field

CAROL CHILLINGTON RUTTER

1

Near the beginning of *The Two Gentlemen of Verona*, a couple of elders
consider a son's future. It's recently been observed that 'Home-keeping
youth have ever homely wits' (1.1.2). Now, having heard 'sad talk' from
Antonio's brother on the subject of his nephew, Proteus, the servant
Panthino reports to this master what he's heard:

> He wondered that your lordship
> Would suffer [Proteus] to spend his youth at home
> While other men, of slender reputation,
> Put forth their sons to seek preferment out –
> Some to the wars to try their fortune there;
> Some to discover islands far away;
> Some to the studious universities;
> For any or for all these exercises
> He said that Proteus your son was meet.
>
> (1.3.4–12)

The uncle's complaint is that 'living dully ... at home' doesn't just
'sluggardize' (1.1.7) a young man's 'wits'; it stores up 'great impeachment
to his age / In having known no travel in his youth' (1.3.15–16).

This conversation, or a version of it, must have been the constant chatter
up and down England in Shakespeare's youth, as fathers, not only 'elites'
(like Antonio) but tradesmen, like John Shakespeare, aimed to secure
employment for their sons to set them up for life. Given his evident
ambitions for his son, it was surely a conversation Henry Field, a man
of very 'slender reputation', had, and perhaps with John Shakespeare.

161

They were near enough neighbours in the market town of Stratford-upon-Avon, the Shakespeares living at the Rother Market end of Henley Street, the Fields, down towards the river along Bridge Street; their houses three minutes walk from each other. They worked in parallel trades, Field a tanner, employed in the heavy leather industry that dealt in cattle hides, an insalubrious process that required hides to be soaked in an infusion of bird droppings and dog dung or stale beer and urine then layered and steeped in a pit for a year in an oak bark solution, while Shakespeare was employed at the lighter end of the trade, a whittawer. Tawing sheep and goat hides with alum and oil, he was preparing skins for use in his main business, the highly skilled craft of glove making (Cherry 1991, p. 295). The two were hardly equals in terms of local reputation: Shakespeare, visibly prosperous, served Stratford-upon-Avon first as alderman then bailiff, the highest municipal office on the town council; Field held no public appointment and was worth only £14 14s in inventoried goods at his death in 1592 (Kirwood 1931, p. 2). But they were alike in fathering considerable broods over the same years: Field bringing ten children to the font; Shakespeare, eight (of whom five survived infancy). The tanner's second son, Richard, baptised according to the parish register ('1561 16 November Richardus filius Henrici ffeild') arrived some two-and-a-half years ahead of the glover's eldest surviving child, William, baptised on 26 April 1564.

Years later, if Henry consulted John about whether to 'put forth' his son, it's likely to have been because he was trying to decide whether to send him up to London, just short of his eighteenth birthday, to be apprenticed for the statutory seven years to one George Bishop, a master printer, to learn the craft of printing. How quixotic a decision was that? What did a tanner, or his son, or a glover, or anyone in Stratford (or for that matter, any of the fathers in York, Wiltshire, Lincoln, Salop, Surrey, Flint; fullers, chandlers, husbandmen, labourers, 'preacher[s] of God's word', painters, butchers who sent their sons 'abroad' to London to be apprenticed to printers (Arber 1875, II, p. 165)) know about printing, an entirely metropolitan trade, restricted (except for the university printers) to London, and in London to only twenty-two printing houses? Did they have any idea how many apprentices, bound to booksellers or bookbinders, never learned the craft of printing? Or how many others, though bound to stationers, found themselves ultimately employed in different occupations? Did they have any inkling how uncertain a future young Richard would face even when he'd served his time and, free of the Stationers' Company, at liberty to publish books, would not be licensed actually to print them, not, that is, until a vacancy came up that he might sue to be appointed to among the twenty-two Master Printers, which rare occurrence no one could predict or count on? (Arber 1894, V, p. xxix).

Whatever advice the townsmen exchanged, did John cast his mind back over it ruefully three years later when reports from London told of Richard thriving 'abroad' in the world while his own now eighteen-year-old son – Proteus to Field's Valentine – looked destined to a life 'dully sluggardized at home', choosing, like Proteus, to 'hunt [. . .] after love' not 'honour', to 'set the world at naught', 'metamorphosed' by one Anne Hathaway into husband, then, six months later, father? Did John Shakespeare catch himself enviously comparing sons and wishing, as Will's future King Henry would, 'it could be proved / That some night-tripping fairy had exchanged / In cradle clothes our children where they lay' (1 Henry IV, 1.1.85–7)?

As it happened, John's perhaps 'unthought-of' Will would, in the not too distant future, cut free of youth-wasting home-life to 'try' his 'fortune' in 'the wars', 'discover islands far away', visit the 'studious universities' – if all, only in fictions. He and Richard, unlikely lad and likely, met again. And when they did (the one unlikely still, unhoused, making up the numbers in a 'cry of players', the other, more likely than ever, well and truly housed, master of his own printing house) what they shared was books – and 'words, words, words' (Hamlet, 2.2.195).

2

That sharing started in childhood. Growing up in a bustling but compact market town (population: 1,500) they were as likely as their parents to have known each other. Were they friends? Probably not like the gentlemen of Verona. Year in, year out Holy Trinity, the parish church, saw eighty baptisms (or thereabouts), most years pretty evenly matched between boys and girls. In Richard Field's birth year, 1561, forty-one boys were baptised; the following year, forty-five; the following year, thirty-eight. Not all of these survived infancy, but even so, Richard had dozens of lads near his age to lark about with and start school with, multiple Richards, Williams, Henrys, Edwards, Roberts and a couple of Rogers born to the Hathaways, Braynes, Sadlers, Whatelys, and to Welsh families named 'Ap price', 'Ap Williams', 'Ap roberts' and 'Davyes'. By contrast, the year Will Shakespeare was born, the demographic took a dive, probably on account of plague striking the town (the burial register noting against an entry for 11 July, 'hic incepit pestis'). Only thirty-nine baptisms were recorded in 1564, twenty-three of them, boys; nor did the birth rate recover for another three years. Will's potential circle, then, was much narrower than Richard's, he perhaps needing the older boys more than they needed him. Will was in petticoats (aged four) when Richard (breeched) started at the local King's New School – 'the grammar' – and began, aged seven, to acquire, in addition to his 'mother tongue', a second language, the trans-European language of learning, of humanism, connecting the literate in an early modern version of today's internet: Latin. When Will followed him to the grammar three years later, Richard was long past his accidence, ready to proceed to the upper form, perhaps patronising of the 'lowers', or worse, set by to monitor their rote repetitions.

Still, both boys had entered a select, shared space that separated them from the rest of the lads on the street, receiving an education that, focused on close analysis of text, imitation and memorisation, furnished their minds with the same stock of books and authors: Aesop's Fables, *Cato's Distichs*, Ovid's *Metamorphoses* and *Heroides*, Cicero's *Epistles*, Caesar's histories, Terence's comedies, Virgil's *Aeneid*. But it also trained them in the art of rhetoric, 'a science of persuasion', 'of public activity' (Hunter 1994, p. 103). Or more simply: what they could do with words, and to what ends. Becoming bi-lingual, both boys acquired habits of thinking, reading and writing in Latin that affected their use of English, not least an 'extraordinary sensitivity to language, especially its sound', which tuned their ears to verbal conceits, wit and wordplay (Miola 2000, p. 2). This was an education that made them acutely responsive to argument, activity a playwright would put into characters' mouths (Valentine v. Proteus; Silvia v. 'Sebastian') or a printer would arrange on a page, setting author's copy as dialogue, colloquy, catechism, debate.

Most obviously, school put into their grasp what they probably handled nowhere else as children: books. As adults, they'd have books in common. After Richard left home, the next time the two aspirational 'gentlemen of Stratford' definitely met, they met over a book.

3

Although apprenticed to George Bishop from Michaelmas (29 September, a significant contractual date, the beginning of the fiscal year) 1579, Richard Field was actually placed for 'the first six years' of his service 'to learn the art of printing' in the house of Thomas and Jacqueline Vautrollier (Arber 1875, II, pp. 93, 30). Committed Protestants and early refugees from anti-Huguenot persecution in France that culminated in the St Bartholomew's Day massacre in Paris in August 1572 (a terror Philip Sidney witnessed and accounts of which Vautrollier circulated in print in England), the Vautrolliers were living in London from about 1560. A printer, Vautrollier was granted a formal letter of denization on 9 March 1562, giving him, in modern terms, right to remain, own land and property, and operate a business. Two years later, he was admitted 'Brother' (this being the limited entry accorded to 'strangers') to the Stationers' Company. His premises were in the Blackfriars, the site of the extinct monastery, where his neighbours included numbers of French and Dutch immigrants, the redoubtable Elizabeth Cooke Russell, self-styled 'Dowager Countess', and George Hunsdon (who would later patronise Shakespeare's company as Lord Chamberlain), alongside a crew of local tradesmen: a blacksmith, shoemaker, two feather dressers, a milliner, tailor, brush-maker, painter, 'letter caster for printers', goldsmith, and bookseller from Venice (Laoutaris 2014, p. 125). If Chris Laoutoris is right to identify 'the exact location of Vautrollier's London print shop' in the 'Timber House' at the north-western corner of the Blackfriars site, the premises were up a flight of stairs in a room 28' x 28' square – premises Field would one day inherit (Laoutaris 2014, p. 128). There, Vautrollier was licensed to operate two printing presses and to employ, along with a single apprentice, 'six work-men, Frenchmen or Dutchmen, or such like'. He was hardly, as A. E. M. Kirwood points out, 'your run of the mill jobbing printer'. His earliest books in London were Orlando di Lasso's madrigals and Baildon and Chesne's *Book containing divers sorts of hands* or 'alphabet of Copies for the secretary hand' (Kirwood 1931, p. 4). More than 140 books followed, including books in French, Italian and Latin (among them, school text books); Mulcaster's *Elementary*, Ovid, Cicero, Calvin, Luther; editions of the Bible. When, as a result of having printed works by Giordano Bruno deemed heretical, Vautrollier 'had to fly to Scotland' in 1584 (Arber 1894,

V, p. xxxi), Jacqueline took 'in hand' the London end of the business, seeing Cicero's *Epistles* through the press while Thomas in Edinburgh went to work for King James, printing his *Essays of a prentice in the divine art of poesie.*

Entering the Vautrolliers' house in September 1579, Richard Field arrived just as his master had in press Sir Thomas North's translation of Plutarch's *Lives of the Noble Greeks and Romans.* The crowded scene of industry he walked into must have been bewildering. In one corner was a lad rolling ink on to pads; overhead, printed copy hanging on lines to dry (not the ink; the paper, wetted so it would take the pressing). Under a window that let in best light over his left shoulder, a compositor (or two) stood in front of his case (or cases), his type (face reversed) arranged alphabetically in some 152 compartments with 'upper case' letters above, 'lower case' below, his composing stick in his left hand, eyes moving from what he was setting, the author's copy pinned up in front of him, to his type, which he'd pick up letter by letter to set in his stick, reading left to right but composing lines of type right to left, until he had several full lines that he'd transfer to a galley then impose into locked-down full-sheet formes ready for printing. The pressman (called the 'bear') and his partner (who inked the forme with the pads the lad handed him) presided over the stout wooden-framed press that stood opposite the windows, stage left, so to speak, working the bar that turned the screw that pressed each sheet of paper in turn onto the type. The corrector (sometimes, perhaps, the author) sat hunched up somewhere reading 'proof' copy as it came off the press. The distributor was smack in the middle of things, taking the formes, as each full print run of individual sheets was finished, unlocking them, and breaking up the type, replacing each piece of type back in its case, making it available for setting the next pages. (A compositor's full case contained, it's estimated, sufficient type to print just over two pages of Shakespeare's *First Folio*). Finally, the warehouseman rolled in with supplies of fresh paper then collated from stacks of dried pages the finished book that he folded once and tied into bundles to go to the booksellers (who finished the folding and put a stitch in the seam to hold the signatures together, books being sold unbound).

Joseph Moxon, in his descriptive 'how to' guide, *Mechanick Exercises on the whole Art of Printing* (1683), instructs the Master Printer, whom he terms 'the soul of printing' who governs his 'work-men as members of the body', to ensure that his printing house allowed 'for each press about seven foot square upon the floor, and for every frame of cases ... five foot and a half in length and four foot and a half in breadth' so that 'room will be left to pass freely between the two frames' (Moxon 1958, pp. 12, 16). If Vautrollier laid out his 28' x 28' premises along Moxon's lines, accommodating two presses, four compositor's cases, the 'correcting-stone', lye- and rinsing-troughs, distributing frame, benches, tables, six journeymen ('Frenchmen or Dutchmen, or such like'), his apprentice and a couple of boys as printer's 'devils', there would hardly have been room to swing a composing stick never mind give place to casual drop-ins, an aspiring playwright, for instance, eager to read what was fresh off the press.

Along with well-appointed space, quality materials were crucial to this business and the quality of its production: sets of premium-cast type in both roman and italic; paper (that had to be imported, there being no domestic papermaking industry at this time, at a cost of 7 shillings per A3-sized ream in 1587, making the cost of the paper more than the cost of printing on it) (Gaskell 1972, p. 177); and ink (the manufacture of which, Moxon wrote, 'our English master-printers do generally discharge themselves of' because the process was 'laborious to the body', 'noysom and ungrateful to the sence', and liable to 'accidents dangerous', like explosions during the boiling stage) (Moxon 1958, pp. 82–3). The blackest and sharpest of printer's ink was imported from Venice, made of 1lb varnish (consisting of juniper gum and linseed oil) to 1oz lampblack, reduced by boiling over a slow fire, while the inferior English imitation stinted on the oils and under-boiled the mixture, producing a substance that 'furs and chokes up a form' and 'hinders the ink from drying' making it 'dull, smeary and unpleasant to the eye' (Bloy 1967, p. 101).

As Vautrollier's apprentice, Field studied all the 'mysteries', material and mechanick, of his new trade. Starting in the printing house just as Plutarch's *Lives* was in press, he saw quality printing at its most excellent – and the exacting standards his master set for publications bearing his device, a ship's anchor grasped by a (divine) hand reaching down from a cloud, its cartouche framed with a legend, 'anchora spei' (a logo Field later adopted as his own). As he worked out his seven years, Field clearly picked up 'habits learned in Vautrollier's workroom' that he demonstrated in his future life as a master printer, modelling 'himself closely upon Vautrollier', uncompromisingly painstaking, showing, in the majority of his first editions, a 'family likeness' with his master's books, and, when he printed new editions of books first printed by his master (Plutarch's *Lives* (1579; reprinted 1595, expanded, 1603)); Geoffrey Fenton's translation of Guicciardini's *History of Italy* (1579, reprinted 1593), quoting him, using 'the same ornaments, compartments and initials in the same or corresponding places' (Kirwood 1931, pp. 17–19).

Vautrollier gave Field an excellent training. He taught printing as an 'art', not just a 'mere mechanical method of reproduction' (Kirwood 1931, p. 23). But practically the greatest benefit he showed him was to die: obligingly, within months of Richard finishing his apprenticeship and entering the Stationers' Company as Freeman on 6 February 1587. (That last year, as his indentures stipulated, with George Bishop, was spent co-publishing an expanded edition of Holinshed's *Chronicles* (Arber 1875, II, p. 699).) Widow Jacqueline carried on the business (including printing Field's first effort as a publisher, a piece of anti-Spanish propaganda titled *The copy of a letter sent out of England to Don Bernadin Mendoza*, purportedly by some seminary priest, but actually the work of William Cecil, Lord Burghley, Elizabeth's most powerful Privy Councillor) until March 1588 when the Stationers' Court restrained her from printing 'any manner of book or books whatsoever', later modified: 'provided always that she meddle not with the printing of any thing else until she procure herself to be chosen and allowed to print according to the decrees of the Star Chamber' (Kirwood 1931, p. 5). But that provision was overridden. Jacqueline 'procure[d] herself to be chosen' elsewhere. On 12 January 1589, in St Anne's Church in the Blackfriars, she married Richard Field – who came thereby into possession not just of his master's wife but his master's printing house and business. He was twenty-seven years old. His bride (who'd arrived in London c. 1560, around the time of Richard's birth) was almost twice his age. Within a year, they had a boy of their own to add to Jacqueline's two already grown sons, the only child of a marriage that lasted until March 1611, when the burial of 'Mr Fields wife' was recorded in St Anne's.

4

As Master, Field could now license apprentices, which he did, binding first Launcelot Leaf, son of a York fuller, in November 1589, then in February

1592, his little brother, Jasper (Arber 1875, II, pp. 165, 179). He was now licensed not just to publish books but to print them, eight that first year, including two books in Latin for the publisher John Harrison (whom he'd have important dealings with in 1594) and Puttenham's seminal *Art of English Poesie*, dedicated significantly to Burghley, by 'a printer' who styled himself 'always ready and desirous to be at your honourable command-ment' (Sig. AB3v). Books in Italian (a 'grammar') and French ('an alpha-bet'), Spanish and Welsh followed, along with sermons and theological disputations requiring Greek and Hebrew, and a book of geometry ('the carpenter's square that is a table serving for the measuring of board, glass, stone and such like, plane and solids' (Arber 1876, III, p. 544)). If Vautrollier's publisher's catalogue was dominated with sober titles indicat-ing serious-minded writing, perhaps registering his serious-minded Prot-estantism (always excepting that early book of madrigals), Field's was much more mixed, the popular, the scandalous, alongside the political and worthy. For example, a pair of entries in the Stationers' Register has him entering, back-to-back, 'A pleasant fancy or merry conceit called "The passionate morris danced by a crew of eight couple of w[h]ores, all mere enemies to love"' followed by 'a brief discourse of man's transgression and of his redemption by Christ with a particular survey of Romish religion and Rome itself' (Arber 1875, II, p. 626).

Field's poetry list was, to modern eyes, simply stunning: Ovid's *Metamorphoses* (1589); the first full editions of Spenser's *Faerie Queene* (1596) and Sidney's *Arcadia* (1598); Chapman's 'In Noctem' and 'In Cynthiam' (1594) and his Homer (1611–14). Field was evidently the printer of choice for Thomas Campion, who acknowledged his careful printing of his Latin poetry by sending *Ad Librum* on its way with verses he Englished:

> Go now, little book, long condemned to darkness,
> yield to Field's press whatever thou hast that is foolish,
> lest any one more foolish may profane it ill understood:
> so that thence thou shalt be elegantly enough printed,
> not lacking new lustre
>
> (Fripp 1938, p. 247)

Fixing in press what was 'foolish', Field anticipated Moxon's notes 'On Compositors' who, setting type, theoretically needed to be 'no more than an English scholar, or indeed scarce so much', certainly not a 'man whose education' has 'adorned him with Latin, Greek, Hebrew, and other languages', for 'by the laws of printing, a compositor is strictly to follow his copy: viz., to observe and do just so much and no more than his copy will bear him out for; so that his copy is to be his rule and authority'. That said, 'the carelessness of some good authors, and the ignorance of other authors' had 'forced printers to introduce a custom, which among them is looked upon as a task and duty incumbent on the compositor, viz. to discern and amend bad spelling and pointing of his copy' (Moxon 1958, p. 191–2). This sort of fixing (intervention to regularise his erratic spelling), and more, almost collaboration, was what John Harington expected, entrusting his translation of Ariosto's *Orlando Furioso* to Field in 1591. Detailed instructions from the author to the printer about this ambitious project survive on marked-up manuscripts, and again, on Harington's 1596 *The Metamorphosis of Ajax* (where he tells Field 'this that follows must come in at this mark' and 'here comes in the picture of the chimney') (Donno 1962, p. 44). Both books were illustrated, Harington commenting of *Orlando*'s illustrations, 'I have not seen any made in England better' (Kirwood 1931, p. 21). And both demonstrated the quality that Field's printing showed generally, his eye-pleasing use of ornaments and initials and choice and arrangement of type, particularly on title-pages and dedications, and his obvious attention to how pages would look in print.

5

Was it Field's reputation as a printer, or Shakespeare's longing to hear a Warwickshire accent that sent the player to the Blackfriars in search of his townsman about the time Field was inheriting his kingdom? Or a little later, was Field among those who crossed the Thames to crowd Henslowe's Rose in March 1592 to see the play the world was talking about, *Henry VI* – and stunned to hear Shakespeare wrote it? Certainly, Field's premises would have beckoned a novice playwright needing material. Printers were allowed a 'copy book' of each publication. Field owned, from Vautrollier's time in printing and his own, a substantial library, titles at the top of Shakespeare's reading list: Ovid, Virgil, Plutarch, Holinshed. Where did Field keep those books? Did he give Shakespeare access to them?

What is certain is that they were in contact during the plague year 1593 when the playhouses were closed for months and the players were either on tour or out of work. Shakespeare was writing – not for the stage this time. A poem titled *Venus and Adonis*. It would be his first printed work. And Field would print it: two quarto editions in 1593 and 1594 of a book that, astonishingly, would run through twelve editions in Field's lifetime. It was clearly a best-seller.

So why in June 1594 did Field relinquish his rights in *Venus and Adonis* to John Harrison, a stationer known of old who was selling the book in his shop 'at the sign of the white greyhound in Paul's Churchyard' and who, as publisher, would secure the rights to Shakespeare's *The Rape of Lucrece* (1594), employing Field to print *Lucrece* along with the next three editions of *Venus* (Arber 1875, II, pp. 630, 655)? Germaine Greer wonders what Shakespeare's wife, in Stratford, made of his deliciously erotic poem, written in the demotic, and so available to be 'passed hand to hand' and read by 'excited housewives'. Did she enjoy its 'lightness of touch' even as 'she shrank from its rampant sensuality' (Greer 2008, p. 190), perhaps not appreciating its farcical sexual comedy, Venus's first encounter an undignified rugby tackle of both Adonis and his horse, throwing 'Over one arm, the lusty courser's rein; / Under her other … the tender boy' (*Venus and Adonis*, 31–2)? And if Anne didn't get the joke, what about Jacqueline Vautrollier Field? Was her sober (and now deeply matronly) Huguenot blood incensed against Shakespeare's 'toy'? Was it she who insisted Shakespeare's poems be assigned to another publisher (printed 'by' Richard Field but '*for*' John Harrison)?

There is no record of Shakespeare and Field ever meeting again. Their paths might have crossed when Shakespeare resided with the Mountjoys in Silver Street, from 1604, or when, in 1613, he leased the gatehouse in Blackfriars' Ireland Yard, just before Field moved his printshop to The Splayed Eagle in Great Wood Street. Then again, they may have stayed clear of each other, animosity festering between them. Two years on from *Venus*'s reassignment, November 1596, Field was among thirty-one residents of the Blackfriars (along with Elizabeth Russell and George Hunsdon) who signed a petition protesting against plans by Shakespeare's company, the Chamberlain's Men, to convert space in the precinct into a theatre. Was this, in a role reversal, Field's Proteus-style betrayal of Shakespeare? Or, given that Hunsdon signed against the interests of his own company, were the petitioners simply early modern 'nimbys', householders annoyed at the prospect of 'coaches … clog[ging] up Ludgate' with the 'daily resort of people' coming to a playhouse (as they'd complain in another petition in 1619)?

If there was a rift over *Venus and Adonis* or the Blackfriars, maybe the playwright, late in his career, patched it with a fleeting homage to the lad remembered from childhood who'd perhaps met him, the 'whining' younger 'schoolboy' with his 'satchel' and 'morning face', on the corner of Bridge Street, and walked him, 'creeping like snail', 'to school'. In *Cymbeline* (1610) when Innogen-as-Fidele is asked the name of the decapitated corpse she says was her 'master', she answers 'Richard du Champ' (4.2.379), that is, Field, the French version of the signature Field used printing books in Spanish: 'de Campo'.

Field outlived Shakespeare by eight years, marrying a second wife in his fifties and having with her five children, baptised in St Michael, Wood Street, between 1614 and 1624. In a career lasting thirty-six years he produced some 295 books, 183 printed for other publishers (Kirwood 1931, p. 13). Of the books he published himself, Philip Barrough's household manual, *The Method of Physick Containing the Causes, Signs, and Cures of Inward Diseases in Man's Body, from the Head to the Foot* was the most reprinted, in six editions, the first, 1590, dedicated to Lord Burghley. A well-thumbed, beautifully illustrated copy of the fifth (1617) edition printed on sturdy paper with no ink bleed-through and no furring of type-face – quality materials, quality printing – survives in the collection of the Shakespeare Birthplace Trust, bound in a weathered leather cover, its clasp fallen off, its pages interleaved with little pin-pricked paper squares drawn with floral patterns, probably embroidery stencils (kept there for safety?). If (and it's a big 'if') Greer is right that Shakespeare, in his last years, was ill with 'the disease called Morbus Gallicus', syphilis, he might have consulted Field's Barrough. Barrough details this 'grievous sickness' that, 'borrowed' from 'the Indians' 'by Columbus' and 'brought . . . home instead of their gold', was a 'curse' to 'all Christendom'. Its terrible cure, 'with quicksilver', makes grim reading: teeth drop out, palates rot, bones are 'eaten', so that 'if it healeth not, it driveth the whole channel of vicious humours into the head' (Sig. Bb6v). The disease not only metamorphosed a man quite. It made him mad.

How ironic to think of this best-seller as Field's answer (and antidote) to Shakespeare's best-seller, reframing love's conceits as medical diagnosis: Venus returned as venereal disease, valentines exchanged effecting protean changes on lovers literally maddened by love. A couple of grammar-school boys might have appreciated such turns of wit. But if Field's Barrough speaks to Shakespeare's ending, perhaps Shakespeare's *The Two Gentlemen of Verona* (probably his first play, perhaps a tribute to home) remembers their beginning. Maybe Richard Field is, after all, 'set down' by William Shakespeare – who, with his fellow printers (we can thank) 'set down' Shakespeare to us.

WORKS CITED

Arber, Edward (ed.) 1875, 1876, 1894. *A Transcript of the Registers of the Company of Stationers of London 1554–1640*. Vols. *i, ii, iii, iv, v*. Privately printed. Birmingham

Bloy, C. H. 1967. *A History of Printing Ink Balls and Rollers 1440–1850*. London. E. Adams and Mackay Ltd

Cherry, John 1991. 'Leather' in John Blair and Nigel Ramsay (eds.), *English Medieval Industries*. London. A. & C. Black

Donno, Elizabeth Story (ed.) 1962. *Sir John Harington's A New Discourse of a Stale Subject called the Metamorphosis of Ajax*. London. Routledge and Kegan Paul

Fripp, Edgar I. 1938. *Shakespeare Man and Artist*. 2 vols. Oxford University Press

Gaskell, Philip 1972. *A New Introduction to Bibliography*. Oxford University Press

Greer, Germaine 2008. *Shakespeare's Wife*. London. Bloomsbury

Hunter, G. K. 1994. 'Rhetoric in Use' in Peter Mack (ed.), *Renaissance Rhetoric*. Basingstoke. Macmillan

Kirwood, A. E. M. 1931. 'Richard Field, Printer, 1589–1624', *The Library* Fourth Series, 12.1: 1–39

Laoutaris, Chris 2014. *Shakespeare and the Countess: The Battle That Gave Birth to the Globe*. London. Fig Tree

Miola, Robert 2000. *Shakespeare's Reading*. Oxford University Press

Moxon, Joseph 1958. *Mechanick Exercises on the whole Art of Printing*. Herbert Davis and Harry Carter (eds.). London. Oxford University Press

14

Living with the Mountjoys

DAVID KATHMAN

§

William Shakespeare made his fortune in London during more than two decades as an actor, poet and playwright, but he never kept his primary residence there, as far as we can tell. The few traces of his London residences in the historical record suggest that he moved every few years, presumably renting rooms along the way. Nearly a century after the fact, John Aubrey recorded that Shakespeare had lived in the northern suburb of Shoreditch, location of the Theatre and Curtain playhouses. There is no contemporary record of this, but Aubrey's source was William Beeston, whose father Christopher had performed with Shakespeare in the Lord Chamberlain's Men (Honan 1998, p. 122). Shakespeare appears in the London subsidy rolls as a resident of St Helen's Bishopsgate parish in October 1597 and November 1598. St Helen's was in the north-east part of the city, convenient for walking to the Shoreditch playhouses. Further subsidy records in October 1599 and October 1600 show that Shakespeare had moved across the river to the Liberty of the Clink in Southwark, the location of the newly built Globe playhouse, though he does not appear in the records of the Globe's parish, St Saviour's Southwark (Schoenbaum 1975, pp. 161–3).

We do not know exactly where or with whom Shakespeare lived in St Helen's or in Southwark, but we know quite a bit about one of his next London residences, thanks to a lawsuit discovered in 1909 by Charles William Wallace and his wife Hulda. Probably by 1602, and certainly by 1604, Shakespeare had moved to the parish of St Olave Silver Street, in the northern part of the city inside Cripplegate; specifically, he rented a room in the house of Christopher and Marie Mountjoy, French Huguenot immigrants, on the corner of Monkwell and Silver Streets. We know this because of a lawsuit in the Court of Requests in which William

Shakespeare gave a deposition on 11 May 1612. This deposition is of great interest for including the earliest of the six known surviving signatures of William Shakespeare, but it, and the lawsuit of which it is a part, are also very interesting for the details they give us about Shakespeare's life in London in the first decade of the seventeenth century.

Shakespeare's landlord, Christopher Mountjoy, was a Huguenot (French Protestant) tire-maker, or maker of ornamental headdresses for wealthy ladies. He was born in Crécy in north-west France, probably around 1560, and at some point in his youth he emigrated to England as one of the many refugees from the French Wars of Religion. He was living in London by 1582, when he appears in the subsidy rolls as one of four servants of John Dewman, a Dutch immigrant tailor living in the parish of St Anne and St Agnes, in the north-west part of the city just inside Aldersgate. By that time Mountjoy was newly married to his wife Marie, who was only fifteen or sixteen at the time, and it must have been soon afterwards that their daughter Mary was born (Nicholl 2008, pp. 96–103). By about 1594 the Mountjoys had settled in St Olave Silver Street, a short walk north-east of St Anne and St Agnes, and 'Mrs Monjoyes childe' [*sic*] was buried there on 27 February 1596. The form of this entry in the parish register is unusual in only mentioning the mother, and Charles Nicholl has speculated that it may mean the child was illegitimate (Nelson 2006, pp. 63–4; Nicholl 2008, p. 110). Whether or not that was so, the following year Marie Mountjoy was apparently having an affair with Henry Wood, a merchant living in nearby Swan Alley, and she went to the physician-astrologer Simon Forman in December 1597 because she feared that she might be pregnant. Marie had previously consulted Forman in an effort to find some lost jewellery, and would consult him again the following March to ask whether her husband would get sick. Christopher Mountjoy also went to Forman in March 1598 to ask about an apprentice who had fled (Schoenbaum 1981, p. 22).

By the turn of the century, a couple of years before Shakespeare met them, the Mountjoys were respectably middle class. In both the 1599 and 1600 subsidy rolls, Christopher Mountjoy had to pay 26s 8d of tax on a nominal £5 of goods; compare this to 1582, when the Mountjoys were still part of John Dewman's household and only had to pay fourpence apiece (Nicholl 2008, p. 130; Lang 1993, p. 125). They achieved this rise in status through Christopher's trade of tiremaking, a family business to which

Marie and Mary also made major contributions. Mountjoy has sometimes been described as a wigmaker or even a hairdresser, but these terms are misleading; while tire-makers dealt with hair and could make wigs if necessary, their main product was 'head tires' for wealthy ladies, consisting of hair intertwined with silver or gold wire, embroidered with silk, lace, gauze, and gold thread, and inlaid with jewels or pearls (Hotson 1949, pp. 174–84). This was a very specialised trade, one that, by its nature, brought high-end tire-makers like the Mountjoys in contact with wealthy and powerful clients. The most eminent such client for the Mountjoys was Queen Anna, wife of King James I, whose accounts show her paying a total of £59 in 1604 and 1605 to 'Marie Mountjoy, tirewoman' (The National Archives (TNA) SC 6/JASI/1646, fol. 28r (original) or 29r (new); Hotson 1949, p. 182). This was during the time when William Shakespeare was rooming with the Mountjoys, and when King James had recently become the patron of Shakespeare's company.

Shakespeare would have seen such elaborate head-tires on aristocratic ladies in his company's many visits to perform at Court, and they would also have been part of the inventory of costumes and stage properties owned by the Chamberlain's/King's Men. Surviving costume lists for the rival Admiral's Men include head-tires, and the 'Diary' of Philip Henslowe lists two payments of 12 shillings apiece to a Mrs Gosson for head-tires in 1601–2 (Foakes 2002, pp. 185, 198, 293, 318). No business records of this type survive for Shakespeare's company, but Ben Jonson's *Volpone*, performed by the King's Men in 1605, includes a scene where Lady Would-Be fusses over her hair and asks her waiting-women, '. . . I pray you, view / This tire, forsooth: are all things apt, or no?' (3.4.17–18) (Jonson 1999, p. 178). Presumably the boy playing Lady Would-Be would have worn a real tire for this scene.

Shakespeare mentions head-tires in several of his plays, most notably in three written in the 1590s. In *The Two Gentlemen of Verona*, Julia looks at a portrait of the noble Silvia and says, '. . . I think / If I had such a tire this face of mine / Were full as lovely as this face of hers' (4.4.181–3). In *The Merry Wives of Windsor*, Falstaff tries to woo Mistress Ford by telling her, 'Thou hast the right arched beauty of the brow that becomes the ship-tire, the tire-valiant, or any tire of Venetian admittance' (3.3.50–3). In *Much Ado About Nothing*, as Hero is being dressed for her wedding, her maidservant Margaret remarks, 'I like this new tire within excellently, if the hair were a thought browner' (3.4.12–13); here, as in *Volpone*, there was presumably an actual head-tire on stage. These plays were all written before Shakespeare personally knew the Mountjoys, but metaphors drawn from the tire-maker's art begin popping up regularly in his later plays: 'Thou immaterial skein of sleave-silk' (*Troilus and Cressida* 5.1.27–8); 'Sleep that knits up the ravelled sleave of care' (*Macbeth* 2.2.35); 'Here lay Duncan, / His silver skin laced with his golden blood' (*Macbeth* 2.3.111–12); 'Be't when she weaved the sleided silk / With fingers long, small, white as milk' (*Pericles* 15.21–2); 'Breaking his oath and resolution like / A twist of rotten silk' (*Coriolanus* 5.6.97–8); 'Any silk, any thread, any toys for your head' (*The Winter's Tale* 4.4.316–17) (Hotson 1949, pp. 180–1). It is interesting that all of these plays were written after Shakespeare began lodging with the Mountjoys in about 1602, suggesting that he may have absorbed some terminology and imagery from his landlord's workshop.

We can only speculate as to exactly how and why Shakespeare ended up as the Mountjoys' lodger, but one possibility is that he met them through his Stratford-upon-Avon contemporary Richard Field. Field was born in Stratford two-and-a-half years before Shakespeare and came from similarly modest origins; his father, a tanner, certainly knew Shakespeare's father, a glover, and the two boys had most likely attended school together back in Stratford. Field went to London to be apprenticed as a printer, spending most of his apprenticeship under the Huguenot printer Thomas Vautrollier. When Vautrollier died five months after the apprenticeship ended, Field married his widow Jacqueline and took over the business, thus becoming London's leading printer of French and other foreign-language books. In 1593 Field was both the printer and the publisher of Shakespeare's first published work, *Venus and Adonis*, and he was involved with the printing or publishing of many of the major sources for Shakespeare's plays, suggesting that Shakespeare may have had access to his townsman's shop (Kathman 2004). Though we have no direct evidence that the Fields knew the Mountjoys, Jacqueline Field was a fellow Huguenot immigrant, so it seems likely that they were at least acquainted within the London Huguenot community. S. Schoenbaum claims that Jacqueline would have known the Mountjoys through the Huguenot church in London; this is not impossible, but no evidence connects the Fields to any church besides St Anne Blackfriars, where they were married in 1589 and where Jacqueline was buried in 1611. Schoenbaum also says that the Fields moved to

Wood Street, near the Mountjoys, around 1600, but they actually lived in Blackfriars until Jacqueline's death in 1611 (Schoenbaum 1981, p. 22).

Regardless of how he ended up there, Shakespeare met the Mountjoys around 1602, according to his own later testimony, and probably became their boarder then, as he certainly was two years later. In the deposition he gave on 11 May 1612, Shakespeare testified that he had known Christopher Mountjoy 'for the space of ten years or thereabouts'. They lived in the parish of St Olave Silver Street, located in the north-west part of London, between Cripplegate to the north-east and Aldersgate to the south-west, in the square area where the fort of Roman London had been. This was not a particularly convenient location for somebody who worked in Southwark, as Shakespeare did in 1602–4, but his acting colleagues John Heminges and Henry Condell lived in St Mary Aldermanbury, a short walk to the east, and it is not difficult to imagine the three friends walking to work together. In order to get to the Globe, they would have had to walk south to Cheapside, most likely via Wood Street, then make their way further south to the Thames, perhaps via Bread Street; once they reached the waterfront, near Queenhithe, they would have hired a wherry to take them across the Thames to Bankside. Walking across London Bridge was another option, but that would have required going far out of their way to the east. On the other hand, walking straight down to the Thames from Silver Street via Bread Street would have taken Shakespeare past the Mermaid Tavern of literary fame, which was between Bread Street and Friday Street south of Cheapside, near Old Fish Street (Rogers 1928, pp. 6–36). Shakespeare certainly knew the proprietor of the Mermaid, William Johnson, who was a trustee for Shakespeare's 1613 purchase of the Blackfriars Gatehouse (Hotson 1949, pp. 76–88; Rogers 1928, pp. 24–5).

The Mountjoys' house was on the north-east corner of Monkwell (aka Muggle) Street, which ran north, and Silver Street, which ran east. St Olave's parish church was on the south side of Silver Street opposite the Mountjoys' house, and opposite the house on the west side of Monkwell Street was Barbers' Hall, where members of the Barber-Surgeons' Company dissected cadavers. South of that, where the westernmost bit of Silver Street turned south and became Noble Street, was the neighbourhood's largest house: Windsor House, formerly known as Neville's Inn, which John Stow in his 1598 *Survey of London* described as 'a great house builded of stone and timber'. Stow had little to say about Silver Street, speculating that the name comes 'of silversmiths dwelling there' and noting that the street has 'divers fair houses' (Stow 1908, 1, pp. 299, 315).

But the monetary associations of Silver Street's name proved irresistible to poet Samuel Rowlands, who in *The Melancholic Knight* (1615) says of his wealthy friends, 'For they and I, I know shall never meet / In Golding Lane, nor yet in Silver Street.' Similarly, in *The Staple of News* (1625), Ben Jonson has one of his characters refer to 'Silver Street, the region of money, a good seat for a usurer' (3.Int.3). But in his *Epicoene* (1609), written not long after Shakespeare's known time on Silver Street, Jonson makes another allusion that may refer to the Mountjoys. The character Otter says of his wife: 'All her teeth were made in the Blackfriars, both her eyebrows i'th' Strand, and her hair in Silver Street' (4.2.81–3) (Chalfant 1978, p. 162; Jonson 1988; Jonson 2004). In one sense, these place-names are humorously descriptive of Mistress Otter (her teeth are black, her eyebrows are strands, her hair is silver), but it is tempting to think that Jonson was also making an allusion to his friend Shakespeare's landlords and their hair-related business.

With all this as background, we can turn to *Bellott v. Mountjoy*, the lawsuit in which William Shakespeare was a key witness. Although the lawsuit was filed in 1612, and it mainly concerns events that took place in 1604, the story really begins a decade earlier that that, in 1594. In or around that year, an English trumpeter of Welsh ancestry named Humphrey Fludd married a French widow and brought her to London along with her teenage son, Stephen Bellott. Soon afterward, Fludd placed his stepson in the household of Christopher Mountjoy, where the boy was eventually bound as an apprentice to learn the art of tire-making. Fludd describes himself in his deposition as 'one of his Ma[jesty's] trumpeters', but he had only been appointed a royal trumpeter three years earlier on 13 March 1609. Between 1608 and 1618 he was paid numerous times for carrying official letters to and from France, and he died in 1625 (Ashbee and Lasocki 1998, 1, pp. 433–4).

By all accounts, master and apprentice had a good relationship during this period. Bellott later said that he 'did obtain the good will and affection' of Mountjoy during his apprenticeship, and Joan Johnson, who was a maid in the house at the time, testified that Mountjoy 'seemed to bear great good will and affection towards the plaintiff when he served him, giving him report to be a very good servant'. (The quotations are from the bill of complaint of Stephen Bellott and the deposition of Joan Johnson. Like all subsequent quotations from the lawsuit documents, TNA REQ 4/1/4/1, they are taken from the transcriptions in Nicholl 2008, pp. 279–301.)

After his apprenticeship term ended in 1604, Bellott travelled to Spain for a few months before returning to Silver Street. He had reason to return, because he was in love with Christopher Mountjoy's daughter Mary, with whom he had worked on a daily basis during the six years of his apprenticeship. Mary wanted to get married, and her mother and father were all for the match, but Stephen Bellott was reluctant to take that step. The Mountjoys went to their lodger William Shakespeare, who was apparently well respected by everybody, and asked him to persuade Bellott to go through with the marriage. Shakespeare did so, and in fact one witness, Daniel Nicholas, says that Bellott and Mary Mountjoy were 'made sure' by Shakespeare, 'giving each other's hand to the hand', meaning that he formally betrothed them in a troth-plight or 'handfasting' ceremony, which was considered a binding contract. Bellott later claimed that Christopher Mountjoy had promised the couple a dowry or marriage portion of £60 to be paid after the wedding, plus an inheritance of £200 to be paid after Mountjoy's death, and this became the focus of the subsequent lawsuit. In any case, the couple was married in St Olave's parish church on 19 November 1604 and set up shop with Christopher Mountjoy.

But Mountjoy and his former apprentice did not get along as colleagues, and after about six months Stephen and Marie left Silver Street to set up their own rival tire-making shop. They rented a chamber in the house of George Wilkins (Chapter 22) in St Giles Cripplegate, a bit to the north of St Olave's, the parish where Bellott's stepfather Humphrey Fludd lived. Wilkins described himself in his 1612 deposition as a victualler, meaning that he kept a tavern, but other evidence from the Middlesex Sessions Rolls and elsewhere suggest that his establishment was also a brothel, and that Wilkins himself was (in modern parlance) a pimp. In any case, Wilkins had regular dealings with seedy underworld types and was repeatedly accused of violent acts, including once kicking a pregnant woman in the belly (Prior 1972). Interestingly, Wilkins also had a brief career as a writer, beginning shortly after the Bellotts came to live with him. His play *The Miseries of Enforced Marriage* was performed by the King's Men in 1607, and a variety of evidence indicates that he collaborated with Shakespeare on *Pericles* around the same time, writing most of the first two acts (Jackson 2003). It is tempting to think that Shakespeare may have met Wilkins through the Bellotts, though this is nothing more than speculation, and it is just as likely that the Bellotts met Wilkins through Shakespeare.

After the Bellotts had been away for more than a year, Mary's mother Marie Mountjoy died, and was buried in St Olave's on 30 October 1606. The Bellotts then moved back to Silver Street to help Christopher Mountjoy run the business, but the master and his former apprentice did not get along any better than before. Once again, the Bellotts stayed for only six months before leaving; after several years of further disputes, the relationship was poisoned beyond repair, and Stephen Bellott filed suit against Christopher Mountjoy in the Court of Requests on 28 January 1612. Bellott's bill of complaint accused Mountjoy of refusing to pay the allegedly agreed-upon £60 marriage portion, as well as 40 shillings that Bellott had loaned to him, and of going back on his promise to leave the couple £200 at his death. In his answer, filed six days later, Mountjoy denied all this. He claimed instead that he had agreed to pay £50 to Bellott if he and Mary stayed and worked in Mountjoy's shop for two years, which they had not done. He claimed to have given them £20 worth of 'household stuff' and £10 in cash when they left the first time, and claimed to have more than repaid the 40-shilling debt by paying a £3 debt that Bellott owed to a brewer, and by paying for silver wire and other tiring materials that Bellott used. On 5 May, Bellott filed a replication that reiterated his initial claims and responded to Mountjoy's new assertions, and Mountjoy immediately filed a rejoinder reiterating his claims. (Transcriptions of these documents are in Nicholl 2008, pp. 279–86.)

As was typical in filings of this type, Bellott and Mountjoy each depicted himself as struggling to scrape by, trying to do the right thing with limited resources, and his opponent as a hard-hearted villain. Mountjoy claimed that Bellott had reneged on a promise to furnish his own 'apparel' during his apprenticeship, forcing Mountjoy to pay for all of Bellott's clothing and other needs for six years; he also claimed to have given Bellott six pounds' worth of 'money and other necessaries for the journey' when the latter travelled to Spain. Bellott denied both of these allegations in his replication, and other evidence tends to support him. Bellott's stepfather Humphrey Fludd subsequently testified that he had given Bellott two cloaks and three suits of apparel during his apprenticeship, and that Mountjoy had been so 'strict' (i.e. stingy) with young Stephen that Fludd and Stephen's mother often had to give him money and 'pay the barber for cutting the hair of his head'. Another witness, Daniel Nicholas, confirmed Fludd's account, and even Christopher Mountjoy's brother Noel was forced to admit under oath that Bellott's friends 'might send him sometimes a cloak or pair of stockings or such a thing'. In general, evidence from a variety of other sources suggests that, at the very least, Christopher Mountjoy was a cranky and not particularly charitable man (Nicholl 2008, pp. 11–12, 134–5).

On 11 May 1612 the first set of witnesses was examined in court, answering questions (interrogatories) provided by Bellott's lawyer. The first was Joan Johnson, who had been a servant in the Mountjoy household at the time of the marriage. She testified that Marie Mountjoy 'did give countenance unto and think well of' the marriage of Stephen Bellott and Mary Mountjoy, and that Christopher 'did send and persuade one Mr Shakespeare that lay in the house' to persuade Bellott to marry; Johnson also said that 'it was reported in the house' that Bellott was to get £50, but she knew nothing of the terms. Family friend Daniel Nicholas testified that 'he heard one Wm: Shakespeare say' that Christopher Mountjoy had a good opinion of Stephen Bellott, and that Shakespeare had told him that the marriage 'was effected and solemnized upon promise of a portion with her'. Nicholas also said that when he had later asked Shakespeare about the promised portion at Bellott's request, Shakespeare had said that Mountjoy had promised £50 and household stuff.

However, when Shakespeare gave his own deposition, he could not or would not give a definite answer to the key question. After confirming that Stephen Bellott had been 'a very good and industrious servant', Shakespeare confirmed that Marie Mountjoy 'did solicit and entreat' him to persuade Bellott to marry, and that he 'did move and persuade the complainant [Bellott] thereunto'. He also said that Christopher Mountjoy had promised a marriage portion, 'but what certain portion he remembereth not, nor when to be paid'. Either Shakespeare genuinely did not remember the amount, or he was being extra cautious, unwilling to commit himself to a number under oath. In any case, it is interesting to note that Shakespeare's role in the marriage of Stephen Bellott and Mary Mountjoy is echoed in two of the plays that he was writing around this time: *Measure for Measure*, in which pre-marriage troth-plights are a significant plot device, and *All's Well That Ends Well*, in which a reluctant

French groom (Bertram) is persuaded to marry by someone (the King) who then performs a handfasting ceremony on the couple.

The court was initially going to decide the Bellott–Mountjoy case based only on this first set of depositions, but a month later it postponed the hearing and gave the parties a chance to call more witnesses (Schoenbaum 1981, p. 39). A second set of depositions on behalf of Bellott was taken on 19 June, and a set of depositions on behalf of Mountjoy was taken four days later on 23 June. For this second session, Bellott's lawyer called Daniel Nicholas again, along with William Eaton (Bellott's apprentice), George Wilkins, Humphrey Fludd, Christopher Weaver (a Silver Street neighbour), and Noel Mountjoy (Christopher's brother and former apprentice). Three of the interrogatories focused on Christopher Mountjoy's wealth and his generosity (or lack thereof) towards Bellott, while the other one focused on whether Mountjoy had sent anyone to persuade Bellott to marry Mary, and what was said. This last interrogatory was obviously aimed at Shakespeare, who was originally slated to testify again but ultimately did not. Daniel Nicholas confirmed that Shakespeare had told him that Mountjoy had promised a marriage portion to the couple, and that Mountjoy had told him that if they did not marry, Mary would never get a groat from him. On 23 June, Mountjoy's lawyer called back Christopher Weaver and Noel Mountjoy plus one new witness, Thomas Flower of St Albans Wood Street. Weaver testified about how he had tried to make peace between Bellott and Mountjoy three weeks earlier; Noel Mountjoy testified that Bellott had asked him to falsely say that the £10 received by Bellott from his father-in-law had actually come from Noel; and Flower testified that Marie Mountjoy had urged her husband to give the couple more, but that he had refused because he knew not what he might need for himself. This, plus the third-hand account of Christopher Mountjoy saying that his daughter 'would not get a groat' out of him, supports the picture of Mountjoy as a crabby, tight-fisted man.

A week after this last set of depositions, the Court of Requests effectively washed its hands of the matter by referring the case to the 'Reverend and grave overseers and Elders of the French Church in London', with the consent of both parties (TNA REQ 1/26, fol. 421). This was done because Bellott and Mountjoy were both at least nominally members of the French Church, though the difficult nature of the case, based as it was on hearsay evidence, was undoubtedly also a factor. The church elders eventually decided in Bellott's favour, but it was a rather hollow victory; they only ordered Mountjoy to pay 20 nobles (£6 13s 4d), far less than Bellott was seeking, and they declared that both parties were 'debauched'. In May 1613 the church elders found that Mountjoy had still not paid the judgement, and they censured him for having two bastard children by his maidservant, and other offences. Eventually, the church excommunicated Mountjoy for his 'lewd acts and adulteries' (Nicholl 2008, pp. 302–4). After remarrying in 1615, Mountjoy moved to St Giles Cripplegate and was buried there on 29 March 1620, after making a will which could be interpreted as trying to disinherit his daughter Mary. Mary died at some point after 1621, and Stephen Bellott, after also remarrying, died in 1647. By that time William Shakespeare had been dead for thirty years, and in another twenty years the house on Silver Street where he had lodged with the Mountjoys would be consumed in the Great Fire, obliterating the physical traces of the place where he had lived in London during one of his most productive periods as a playwright.

WORKS CITED

Ashbee, Andrew, and Lasocki, David 1998. *A Biographical Dictionary of English Court Musicians 1485–1714*. Aldershot. Ashgate

Chalfant, Fran C. 1978. *Ben Jonson's London: A Jacobean Placename Dictionary*. Athens. University of Georgia Press

Foakes, R. A. (ed.) 2002. *Henslowe's Diary*, 2nd edn. Cambridge University Press

Honan, Park 1998. *Shakespeare: A Life*. Oxford University Press

Hotson, Leslie 1949. *Shakespeare's Sonnets Dated and Other Essays*. London. Rupert Hart Davies

Jackson, MacDonald P. 2003. *Defining Shakespeare: Pericles as Test Case*. Oxford University Press

Jonson, Ben 1988. *The Staple of News*. Anthony Parr (ed.) Manchester University Press

1999. *Volpone, or The Fox*. Brian Parker (ed.) Manchester University Press

2004. *Epicene, or The Silent Woman*. Richard Dutton (ed.) Manchester University Press

Kathman, David 2004. 'Field, Richard (*bap.* 1561, *d.* 1624)', *Oxford Dictionary of National Biography*. Oxford University Press

Lang, R. G. (ed.) 1993. *Two Tudor Subsidy Assessment Rolls for the City of London: 1541 and 1582*. London Record Society

Nelson, Alan H. 2006. 'Calling All Biographers', in Takashi Kozuka and J. R. Mulryne (eds.), *Shakespeare, Marlowe, Jonson: New Directions in Biography*. Aldershot. Ashgate

Nicholl, Charles 2008. *The Lodger Shakespeare: His Life on Silver Street*. New York. Penguin

Prior, Roger 1972. 'The Life of George Wilkins', *Shakespeare Survey 25*. Kenneth Muir (ed.). Cambridge University Press, pp. 137–52

Rogers, Kenneth 1928. *The Mermaid and Mitre Taverns in Old London*. London. The Homeland Association

Schoenbaum, S. 1975. *William Shakespeare: A Documentary Life*. Oxford University Press

1981. *William Shakespeare: Records and Images*. Oxford University Press

Stow, John 1908. *A Survey of London*. Charles Lethbridge Kingsford (ed.), 2 vols. Oxford University Press

15

Ben Jonson

DAVID RIGGS

§

William Shakespeare and Ben Jonson (born in 1572) had a lot in common. They both were bred in the households of humble tradesmen. Both received a first-rate classical education in grammar school, married at an early age, and left their marital households for extended periods of time. Both entered the theatrical profession as actors and reinvented themselves as playwrights. Both of them wrote plays that were, on average, considerably longer than comparable scripts written by their contemporaries. Each used the stage to improve his position in society. Shakespeare, who was eight years older and a better actor than Jonson, put his career in the theatre on a solid footing at the age of thirty. In 1594, while Jonson toiled in obscurity, Shakespeare became an actor-shareholder and attached playwright in the prestigious and profitable Lord Chamberlain's Men.

In *The Case is Altered* (1597), his earliest extant play, Jonson followed Shakespeare's lead. Shakespeare had based his innovative *The Comedy of Errors* (1594) on two farces by the Roman dramatist Plautus while incorporating a post-classical focus on romantic love and marriage. Jonson in turn based *The Case is Altered* on two Plautine comedies, augmented by scenes of wooing and ending in multiple marriages. Shakespeare's *The Two Gentlemen of Verona* would have supplied Jonson with the triangular device of the faithful lover, his disloyal friend and go-between, and his ill-used fiancée. Yet this shared plot formula brings fundamental differences between the two playwrights into sharp relief. Where Shakespeare explores the emotional resonances of the imbroglio between Valentine, Proteus and Silvia, Jonson's heroine Rachel attracts no less than six pairs of wooers and disloyal go-betweens to her house. The unanswered question here is what makes Rachel, who speaks a mere thirty-seven lines, so attractive? On a purely symbolic level, the answer would seem to lie in the heap of gold that Rachel's miserly stepfather Jaques obsessively hides under piles of dung. Over the long run, Jonson would discover how to transmute the raw materials of sex, money and knavery into a 'centre attractive' that draws fools into its vortex (Donaldson 2011, pp. 110–11). Over the short run, Jonson's scatological pun on Jaques/jakes, privy, which was inescapable in the wake of Sir John Harington's *The Metamorphosis of Ajax* (1596), would come back to haunt him.

Shakespeare and Jonson had a more direct encounter in 1598, when the Lord Chamberlain's Men, including Shakespeare, performed Jonson's *Every Man In His Humour*. At this juncture, Shakespeare would have seen Jonson as a fellow innovator in a vernacular renaissance of classical comedy. In *The Comedy of Errors* the older playwright had orchestrated the movement through folly and misrule to clarification and harmony that is intrinsic to the structure of Shakespeare's festive comedies. *Everyman In His Humour* offers an anatomy of eccentricities structured along similar lines. Prompted by a pair of witty gallants, an assortment of fools act out their humours (cowardly bragging, hysterical jealousy, affected oaths, bad poetry) until things get out of hand; a merry magistrate restores a measure of sanity and invites (most of) them home to supper. Jonson incorporated reminiscences of Shakespeare's Falstaff into his portrayal of the braggart soldier Bobadilla. Shakespeare, in turn, would incorporate the comic routines of Jonson's gulls Stephano and Matheo into the subplot of *Twelfth Night, or What You Will*, and would refashion Jonson's jealous husband Thorello in his tragedy of *Othello*. The two playwrights were learning from one another.

The earliest performances of Jonson's plays coincided with the emergence of Shakespeare as a published playwright. In 1597, the Lord Chamberlain's Men began selling scripts of Shakespeare's plays to publishers, probably in the hope that the added publicity would boost attendance at the playhouse. In 1598, the publishers put Shakespeare's name on the title-pages of his plays for the first time. During that same year, the literary critic Francis Meres compared Shakespeare to Plautus and Terence among the ancients, and ranked him alongside the contemporary playwrights Christopher Marlowe, George Chapman and Ben Jonson. Shakespeare was being invested with the mantle of a literary author, and he noticed. MacD. Jackson has shown that Shakespeare wrote or revised one or two of his 'rival poet' sonnets and composed sonnet 55 ('Not marble nor the gilded monuments / Of princes, shall outlive this powerful rhyme') in response to Meres's treatise. Shakespeare's admiring allusions to Marlowe in *As You Like It* likewise bear the marks of Meres's influence. The interrelated issues of publication, authorship and rivalry clamoured for the attention of the reading public (Jackson 2005, pp. 233–43).

The Lord Chamberlain's Men, absent Shakespeare, performed Jonson's *Every Man Out of His Humour* in 1599. Jonson, who prepared the quarto text that appeared in 1600, appealed directly to the new marketplace for literary drama. The quarto title-page emphasised the superiority of the printed work '*As it was first composed* by the author B.J. *containing more than hath been publicly spoken or acted*' (title-page modernised from Jonson 2012, I, p. 249 – all quotations and citations from Jonson refer to this edition). Jonson's uncut text features an elaborate critical apparatus that often seems un-actable. His presenter Asper ('an ingenious and free spirit, eager and constant in reproof, without fear controlling the world's abuses' ('The Characters of the Persons' 2–3)) is a thinly veiled surrogate for Jonson. 'The author's friend' Cordatus expounds the theory and practice of Jonson's 'comical satire' to the conventionally minded Mitis over a series of eleven critical choruses. In theory, Jonson's 'comical satire' (title-page) derives from the definition of comedy traditionally attributed to Cicero: '*imitatio vitae, speculum consuetudinis, imago veritatis* [an imitation of life, a mirror of custom, a representation of truth], a thing throughout pleasant and ridiculous and accommodated to the correction of manners' (3.1.415–17). In practice, *Every Man Out Of His Humour* assembles a motley crew of social deviants – an envious scholar, a vainglorious knight, a profane jester, an uxorious merchant, his coquettish wife, and a foppish courtier – and subjects them to ridicule, exposure and abject humiliation. In conclusion, Jonson dramatised his sense of entitlement by introducing the character of Queen Elizabeth, who magically transforms Macilente the envious scholar into Asper, the Queen's corrector of manners.

The critical choruses of Jonson's first comical satire launch several gibes in Shakespeare's direction. These include glancing allusions to a bit of hyperbolic language in *Julius Caesar* (3.1.150–1 and n.) and to romantic plot formulas that would soon be on display in Shakespeare's *Twelfth Night, Or What You Will* (3.1.407–11 and n.). Asper's last words invite the audience to 'make lean Macilente as fat as Sir John Falstaff' (5.6.134–5).

These references distinguish Jonson's comical satire from the Elizabethan popular tradition exemplified by Shakespeare's comedies and histories. They bear no trace of personal animosity on Jonson's part. Nevertheless, his initiative did prompt a response from his newly designated rival.

Shakespeare's pastoral comedy *As You Like It* (1599–1600) glances at the rhetoric and objectives of Jonson's comical satire through the figure of 'the melancholy Jaques' (another pun on jakes, privy; see 3.4.60). A chance encounter with the fool Touchstone in the forest of Arden prompts Jaques to deliver Shakespeare's first speech in praise of folly (2.7.12–43). But when Jaques imagines what he would do if he *were* a fool (2.7.47–61; 70–87), he sounds just like Asper, Jonson's comical satirist:

> I must have liberty
> Withal, as large a charter as the wind,
> To blow on whom I please, for so fools have ...
> (47–9)

> Give me leave
> To speak my mind, and I will through and through
> Cleanse the foul body of th'infected world ...
> (58–60)

Within the comic universe of *As You Like It*, Jaques's project leads nowhere. Duke Senior immediately reminds him that he lacks the moral probity that would entitle him to sit in judgement over others. In his conversations with William Drummond of Hawthornden, Jonson said that he himself, like Shakespeare, 'was given to venery' in his youth (*Informations* 219–25). Moreover, Shakespeare's multi-layered plot continuously champions the folly of yielding to one's natural inclinations over the wisdom of continence and self-control. The love-struck Orlando 'would not be cured' (3.2.380), while the fool Touchstone wisely observes that 'the truest poetry is the most feigning' (3.3.15–16). Although Shakespeare is notoriously reticent about the premises of his dramaturgy, *As You Like It*, apparently in response to Jonson's innovation, endorses a poetics of irony, indirection and paradox.

Cynthia's Revels, or The Fountain of Self-Love (1600), the second of Jonson's comical satires, is a mythologised allegory of self-love. On the one hand, self-infatuation is the reigning vice that afflicts the horde of 'mimics, jesters, panders, parasites' (3.4.20) who loiter in the precincts of Cynthia's court. On the other, 'allowable self-love' (5.2.22) is the just prerogative of Criticus, 'A creature of a most perfect and divine temper' (2.3.93) who embodies Jonson's self-image as a poet-scholar. *Cynthia's Revels* dramatises Criticus's rise to the office of Cynthia's masque-writer, and thus looks forward to the brilliant court masques that Jonson would prepare for King James I. Criticus's masque has a keen satirical edge: the pseudo-courtiers who perform it are diametrically opposed to the virtues they ostensibly personify. The playwrights John Marston and Thomas Dekker subsequently claimed (with some justification) that Jonson had singled them out for ridicule. They would soon retaliate in Marston's *What You Will* (1600) and in Dekker and Marston's *Satiromastix* (1601). The Poets' Quarrel, which engaged the attention of Elizabethan theatre-goers from 1599 to 1601, was underway!

Shakespeare's *Twelfth Night, or What You Will* (1600), responds, both directly and obliquely, to Jonson's *Every Man In His Humour*, *Every Man Out Of His Humour* and *Cynthia's Revels, or The Fountain of Self Love*. The subplot of *Twelfth Night, or What You Will* amounts to a qualified endorsement of Jonson's comic method. Having acted in *Every Man In His Humour*, Shakespeare had an intimate grasp of the relationship between Jonson's gulls and the wits that exploit them. The interplay between Stephano, Jonson's 'country gull', and his cousin Young Lorenzo provided the model for Shakespeare's Sir Andrew Aguecheek and Sir Toby Belch in *Twelfth Night, or What You Will*. When – to give just one example – Shakespeare wrote the passage where Sir Toby urges Sir Andrew to expose his follies to the world – 'Wherefore are these things hid? Wherefore have these gifts a curtain before'em? Are they like to take dust, like Mistress Mall's picture?' (1.3.105–7), he was recalling Young Lorenzo's exhortation to Stephano: 'And will you now with nice modesty hide such real ornaments as these, and shadow their glory as a milliner's wife doth her wrought stomacher with a smoky lawn or a black cypress?' (1.2.83–5) (Musechke and Fleisher 1933, p. 732).

The subplot involving Malvolio put Shakespeare in a more complicated relationship to Jonson: here, he adopts the methods of Jonson's comical satire but contests its central premise of 'allowable self-love'. Early in *Twelfth Night, or What You Will* the Countess Olivia diagnoses her steward's malady: 'O you are sick of self-love, Malvolio' (1.5.77). Shortly thereafter, her waiting-woman Maria devises the jest that will bring

Malvolio out of his humour: 'it is his grounds of faith that all that look on him love him; and on that vice in him will my revenge find notable cause to work' (2.3.134–6). The 'physic' of Maria's forged love letter winds Malvolio up to a ridiculous extreme of self-infatuation, which, in turn, leads to his punishment, exposure and abject humiliation. Shakespeare's indebtedness to the comic method of *Everyman Out Of His Humour* leaps to attention here; but his endorsement of Jonson's project has a double edge. As Malvolio fortifies his self-infatuation with expressions of contempt for his supposed inferiors ('You are all idle, shallow things, I am not of your element' (3.4.111–12)), he gravitates into the orbit of Criticus, Jonson's exemplar of 'allowable self-love'. The triumph of Feste, the Fool, over Malvolio, the self-proclaimed exponent of reason ('I do not now fool myself ... for every reason excites me to this, that my lady loves me' (2.5.143–4)), reconfirms Shakespeare's praise of folly in *As You Like It*. Like his predecessor Touchstone, Feste conceives of folly as the universal condition of human experience: it 'does walk around the orb like the sun, it shines everywhere' (3.1.33–4).

The romantic intrigue in *Twelfth Night, or What You Will* deploys the romantic plot formulas that Jonson had ridiculed in *Every Man Out Of His Humour* (3.1.407–11 and n.) to mount an oblique assault on the whole notion of 'allowable self-love'. In pointed contrast to Malvolio's fatuous self-regard, *Twelfth Night* celebrates the irrational love that impels Viola to advance Orsino's suit to Olivia, unites Sebastian and Olivia, and moves Antonio to attend Sebastian at his own peril. Like Orlando, these lovers 'would not be cured'.

The publication of Robert Chester's *Love's Martyr ... Allegorically Shadowing the truth of Love in the Constant Fate of the Phoenix and Turtle* (1601) transferred Shakespeare's evolving rivalry with Jonson into the realm of lyric poetry. The main attraction of *Love's Martyr* lay in the eight 'Poetical Essays on the former Subject ... by the best and chiefest of our modern writers', namely Shakespeare, Marston, George Chapman and Jonson. This collaborative venture challenged Shakespeare, whose non-dramatic poetry up until now had consisted of erotic narratives and mellifluous sonnets, to write the kind of austere, philosophical lyric that Chapman and Jonson already excelled at. Jonson's 'Epos' (after-song), his main contribution to the 'Poetical Essays', argues that true love only comes into being when passion, or 'blind desire' (37), is chastened by reason.

Shakespeare's counterstatement to Jonson's argument is his remarkable 'anthem' to the Phoenix and Turtle, whose love paradoxically preserves and effaces the distinction between self and other: 'So they loved as love in twain / Had the essence but in one, / Two distincts division none' (25–7). As in *Twelfth Night, or What You Will*, true love defies rational understanding: 'Reason in itself confounded, / Saw division grow together' (41–2) so that 'it cried … / Love hath reason, reason none' (45, 47–8). Taken in tandem, Jonson's 'Epos', which he re-titled 'Epode', and Shakespeare's 'The Phoenix and Turtle' foreshadowed the polished clarity of the cavalier lyric and the logical compression of metaphysical wit (Bednarz 2012, pp. 14–18, 103–39, 163–97).

While Shakespeare and Jonson matched wits over the topic of true love, the quarrel between Jonson and his attackers grew increasingly hostile. During the earlier half of 1601, Jonson heard that the Lord Chamberlain's Men had hired the playwright Thomas Dekker to write a play lampooning him. Thus forewarned, Jonson lampooned Dekker, Marston and the actors in *Poetaster, or The Arraignment*, which the Children of Queen Elizabeth's Chapel performed by 14 September 1601. By and large, Jonson's last comical satire restates positions that he had adopted in *Every Man Out Of His Humour* and *Cynthia's Revels or The Fountain of Self-Love*. But *Poetaster* broke new ground in targeting Shakespeare's company, the Lord Chamberlain's Men, for ridicule. Midway through the play, the actor Histrio explains that his company (the Lord Chamberlain's Men) has hired Demetrius (Dekker) 'to abuse Horace [Jonson] and bring him in a play' (3.4.262). Jonson's *Apologetical Dialogue* subsequently conceded that he had singled out individual players as specific objects of ridicule: 'Now for the players: it is true I taxed 'em, / And yet but some, and those so sparingly / As all the rest might have sat still' (128–3). In fact, Jonson's full-throated attack on the players was anything but sparing. He portrays them as child-abusers and government spies who supply the censorious Tribune Lupus with false accusations of libel. Their business manager Aesop, whom scholars have consistently identified with the actor John Heminges, 'smells ranker than sixteen dunghills and is seventeen times more rotten' (3.4.241–3).

At the conclusion of his remarks on 'the players' Jonson adds that he is only 'sorry for / Some better natures, by the rest so drawn / To run in that vile line' (137–9). Commentators have irresistibly conjectured that these lines refer to Shakespeare, and the inference is plausible enough given Jonson's later assertions that Shakespeare was 'honest' and that he 'loved the man' (Jonson 2012, *Discoveries*, pp. 473–4). That being the case, what did Jonson mean by the phrase 'run in that vile line'? On the face of it, he meant that Shakespeare, along with other 'better natures' in the company, had performed in Dekker's *Satiromastix*, the play against which Jonson launched his pre-emptive strike. But the Cambridge student who wrote the second part of *The Return from Parnassus* (1601–2) gave the character 'Kemp' (i.e., the actor Will Kemp, recently of the Lord Chamberlain's Men) a speech alleging that 'our fellow Shakespeare puts them all down, ay and Ben Jonson too . . . our fellow Shakespeare hath given him a purge that made him bewray his credit' (Anon. 1949, lines 1769–73). Kemp's claim gains credibility in light of Shakespeare's close ties to his fellow actors. In his will he left 'my fellows John Heminges, Richard Burbage, and Henry Condell' 26 shillings 'apiece to buy them rings'. Shakespeare had a motive to retaliate on his 'fellows'' behalf.

Where did Shakespeare administer the purge that made Jonson 'bewray [befoul, beshit] his credit'? Scholars have focused on the character Ajax (yet another pun on a jakes) in *Troilus and Cressida*. The rogue Thersites seizes upon the scatological aspect of the character's name when he wryly observes that 'Ajax goes up and down the field, as asking for himself' (3.3.237–8). Cressida's servant Alexander describes Ajax in a speech (1.2.18–27) that sounds suspiciously like a parody of Mercury's praise of Criticus in *Cynthia's Revels* (2.3.93–109) (Bednarz 2001, pp. 19–52). But these references are sufficiently veiled as to have escaped the attention of *Troilus*' modern editors. Shakespeare taxes Jonson so sparingly that it is hard to see what 'Kemp' was so excited about. Or did the actor playing Ajax give a scathing impersonation of Jonson?

The 'Apologetical Dialogue' that Jonson appended to *Poetaster* brought the earlier phase of Jonson's rivalry with Shakespeare to a close. Moving forward, Jonson de-emphasised the claim that that stage comedy was 'accommodated to the correction of manners'. In the comic masterpieces he wrote between 1606 and 1614, Jonson created a ribald universe where unscrupulous wits prey on incorrigible fools with gleeful abandon. Meanwhile, Shakespeare, having assimilated the techniques of comical satire, now embarked on the series of great tragedies that would secure his literary reputation once and for all.

But Shakespeare abruptly changed course in the final phase of his career. Beginning in 1607–8, he returned to the genre of comedy in a succession of late romances that flew in the face of Jonson's neoclassical dramaturgy. Where Jonson still adhered to the Ciceronian definition of comic realism as 'the imitation of life, the mirror of custom, the image of truth', Shakespeare's *Pericles* (1607–8), *Cymbeline* (1609–10), *The Winter's Tale* (1609–11) and *The Tempest* (1611) depict miraculous events in fabulous settings and ornate, grandiloquent language. Where Jonson confines the action of his comedies within the limits of a single day and a fixed location, Shakespeare's late romances (apart from *The Tempest*) unfold across huge expanses of space and time.

In *The Winter's Tale* Shakespeare ruminates about the premises of a radically vernacular, as opposed to a neoclassical, dramaturgy. King Polixenes' assertion to Perdita that nature encompasses art because

> nature is made better by no mean
> But nature makes that mean. So over that art
> Which you say adds to nature is an art
> That nature makes
>
> (4.4.89–92)

struck Jonson as tantamount to saying that nature becomes artful all by itself, irrespective of classical traditions. Jonson's rejoinder appears in his prefatory address 'To the Reader' of *The Alchemist* (pub. 1612), where he asks 'But how out of purpose and place do I name art? When the professors are grown so obstinate contemners of it and presumers on their own naturals, as they are deriders of all diligence that way' (6–8). Jonson borrowed his characterisation of 'presumers on their own naturals' from Quintilian, leaving readers to decide for themselves whether or not it applied to Shakespeare. Jonson apparently thought that it did. The same passage crops up in his *Discoveries* (1622–36) in the midst of an extended section covering 'Judgements on Poets', 'Our Shakespeare' and 'Discrimination between kinds of wit' (Jonson 2012, *Discoveries*, pp. 539–42 and n; 424–578) (Honigmann 1982, pp. 96–100, 118–19).

Jonson's *The Alchemist* prompted Shakespeare to re-frame the differences between Jonsonian comedy and Shakespearian romance. As Harry Levin observes, *The Alchemist* and *The Tempest* form a sequence of 'magian' comedies that present reverse images of one another. Jonson's protagonist Subtle is a fraudulent magician who deludes the fools that seek his aid. Shakespeare's hero Prospero is a priestly magician who uses illusion to improve the lives of shipwrecked castaways (Levin 1969). Although both plays observe the unities of time and place, the similarity highlights the differences between them. The setting of *The Alchemist* is virtually identical with the theatre in the Blackfriars district where it was performed; *The Tempest* takes place on a magic island peopled by an airy spirit and the 'monster' Caliban. Jonson's comedy marks the passage of time by the succession of knocks on Lovewit's door; each visitation confronts Subtle and his accomplices with a new contingency in a perpetual race against the clock. Conversely the timeframe of Shakespeare's romance unfolds in the out of doors, where it is synchronised with the natural rhythms of the sun, the air and the sea. Finally, both plays draw on a common fund of alchemical metaphors involving projection, sublimation and miraculous prosperity contingent on moral purity. Where *The Alchemist* deploys this symbolic apparatus to structure a ludicrous confidence game, *The Tempest* conceives of it as an effective programme of spiritual transformation.

Two years later, the Induction to Jonson's *Bartholomew Fair* (1614) offered a succinct critique of *The Winter's Tale* and *The Tempest* from the standpoint of a classically trained humanist and masque-writer:

If there be never a servant-monster i' the Fair, who can help it? He says – nor a nest of antics? He is loath to make nature afraid in his plays, like those that beget *Tales, Tempests,* and such like drolleries, to mix his head with other men's heels – let the concupiscence of jigs and dances reign as strong as it will amongst you. (95–9)

Jonson maintains that Shakespeare's 'servant-monster' (Caliban) and 'nest of antics' (the twelve satyrs who dance in *The Winter's Tale*) cater to the sub-literary taste of a popular audience in thrall to 'the concupiscence of jigs and dances'. In staging these spectacles Shakespeare confuses the offices of the dramatist and the choreographer 'mix[ing] his head with other men's heels'. Shakespeare's servant-monster belongs in one of the grotesque anti-masques that precede the formal dances in the masques that Jonson prepared for the Jacobean Court. And in fact, a trio of Shakespeare's twelve satyrs is said to have 'danced before the King' (4.4.323–4), presumably in the 'antic dance' of satyrs who appeared in Jonson's masque of *Oberon* earlier in 1613.

The second round of exchanges between Shakespeare and Jonson culminated in the Prologue to the anglicised version of *Every Man In His Humour* in the 1616 Folio of Jonson's *Works*. Jonson here defines himself in opposition to a tribe of needy poets who cater to the 'ill customs of the age' (4). Although Jonson indicts an entire class of popular writers, Shakespeare stands out as the conspicuous repeat offender. He is the playwright whose characters in the Lancastrian tetralogy 'with three rusty swords, / And help of some few foot-and-half-foot words, / Fight over York and Lancaster's long jars, / And in the tiring-house bring wounds to scars' (9–12). His work is the perfect foil to Jonson's,

> Where neither Chorus wafts you o'er the seas,
> [as in *Henry V*]
> Nor creaking throne comes down, the boys to please,
> [as in *Cymbeline* and *The Tempest*]
> Nor nimble squib is seen, to make afeared
> The gentlewomen, nor rolled bullet heard
> To say it thunders, nor tempestuous drum
> Rumbles, to tell you that the storm doth come
> [as in *King Lear*]
>
> (15–20)

These references insist upon the superiority of Jonson's neoclassical realism, which depicts 'deeds and language such as men do use, / And persons such as Comedy would choose / When she would show an image of the times' (21–3). But Jonson's caricature of Shakespeare's dramaturgy is a straw man, for it does not reckon with Shakespeare's deeply coherent imitation of a natural order that was still legible in the early modern universe.

The appearance of *Mr. William Shakespeare's Comedies, Histories, and Tragedies* (1623) seven years after the author's death gave Jonson a unique opportunity to express admiration and affection for his long-time friend and rival. Jonson's prefatory tribute 'To the Memory of My Beloved, The Author Master William Shakespeare And What He Hath Left Us' hails Shakespeare as a kindred spirit who has created a body of vernacular drama that challenges comparison with 'all that insolent Greece or haughty Rome / Sent forth' (39–40). When Jonson remarks that

> though thou hadst small Latin and less Greek,
> From thence to honour thee I would not seek
> For names, but call forth thundering Aeschylus,
> Euripides and Sophocles to us
>
> (31–4)

he does not disparage Shakespeare's lack of learning, but rather employs a familiar strategy of praising oratory. Even though Shakespeare had a limited knowledge of classical literature, his achievement rivalled that of the great authors whom he had never studied. In retrospect, Jonson's tribute to 'My beloved . . . Shakespeare' was a remarkable act of critical recognition. At a moment when vernacular plays were just beginning to acquire the status of literature, Jonson rightly foresaw that his friend and rival was 'not of an age, but for all time' (43).

Jonson's last words 'Concerning our Shakespeare' appear in his *Discoveries* (pub. 1641), where he writes that 'I loved the man, and do honour his memory (on this side idolatry) as much as any' (473–4). Jonson offers his appraisal at the end of an extended passage on 'running judgements upon poetry and poets' (424–67). In this context Shakespeare provides the consummate example of a major poet (he 'had an excellent fantasy, brave notions, and gentle expressions' (475)), who is praised for the wrong reasons. Harking back to John Heminges's and Henry Condell's preface to Shakespeare's 1623 Folio, Jonson recalled that 'the players have often mentioned it as an honour to Shakespeare, that in his writing, whatsoever he penned, he never blotted out line. My answer hath been, "Would he had blotted a thousand"' (468–70).

This bit of remembered dialogue contains a salutary reminder that Jonson lived in an era when writers and critics could still look at Shakespeare 'on this side idolatry', as a great playwright who could occasionally sound long-winded. Actors and directors, who think nothing of cutting a thousand lines from *Henry VI, Part II* or *Cymbeline*, exercise this kind of critical judgement whenever they prepare a script for production. Ben Jonson had the inestimable good fortune to encounter Shakespeare before his name became a byword for literary greatness. Jonson's critical distance from his mighty rival enabled him to explore roads that Shakespeare did not take. Over the course of that journey, Jonson's genius flourished even as Shakespeare enlarged his own repertoire.

WORKS CITED

Anon. 1949. *The Three Parnassus Plays (1598–1601)*. J. B. Leishman (ed.). London. Ivor Nicholson & Watson

Bednarz, J. 2001. *Shakespeare and the Poets' War*. New York. Columbia University Press

2012. *Shakespeare and the Truth of Love: the Mystery of 'The Phoenix and Turtle'*. New York. Palgrave Macmillan

Donaldson, I. 2011. *Ben Jonson: A Life*. Oxford University Press

Honigmann, E. A. J. 1982. *Shakespeare's Impact on His Contemporaries*. London. Macmillan

Jackson, MacD. P. 2005. 'Francis Meres and the Cultural Context of Shakespeare's Rival Poet Sonnets', *Review of English Studies* 56: 224–46

Jonson, B. 2012. *The Cambridge Edition of the Works of Ben Jonson*. D. Bevington, M. Butler and I. Donaldson (eds.). 7 vols. Cambridge University Press

Levin, H. 1969. 'Two Magian Comedies: The Tempest and The Alchemist', *Shakespeare Survey* 22. Kenneth Muir (ed.). Cambridge University Press, pp. 47–58

Musechke, P. and Fleisher, J. 1933. 'Jonsonian Elements in the Comic Underplot of *Twelfth Night*', *Publications of the Modern Language Association* 48: 722–40

16

Richard Barnfield, John Weever, William Basse and other encomiasts

ANDREW HADFIELD

Shakespeare was certainly well known to his contemporaries as an author, even if he was not uncritically celebrated. The three Parnassus plays, satirical works performed at St John's College, Cambridge, around the end of the sixteenth century, have a clear understanding of Shakespeare as a poet and playwright. The plays reflect on the progress of two aspiring poets, Philomusus and Studioso, eager to learn their craft so that they can spend their lives in contemplation and composition on the celebrated hill of Parnassus, home of the Muses. Much of the action in *The Pilgrimage to Parnassus, The Return to Parnassus* and *The Return from Parnassus: The Scourge of Simony* (the only one of the plays to be published in 1606) satirises poor writing and the vices that lead to such writing. Hence there are characters called Stupido, who, as his name suggests, lacks the intelligence necessary to write good poetry; Amoretto, who is rather too taken up by the charms of the ladies to write well; and Luxurioso, who is excessively concerned with physical pleasure. There is also Gullio, rather impressionable and addicted to the latest fashion, who is determined to 'worship sweet Mr. Shakespeare' (Anon. 1949, p. 192). Gullio refers to Shakespeare as 'sweet' throughout the plays, a sign that Shakespeare is considered to be adept at producing mellifluous Ovidian verse but that, in the author's opinion, he lacks the true seriousness of a major poet such as Edmund Spenser, who is praised throughout as the best English poet since Chaucer. In the most extended discussion of contemporary poetry near the start of the third play, the sensible Judicio makes explicit what has been implicit in Gullio's penchant for

Shakespearian verse: viz., that the author thinks of Shakespeare as a talented crowd pleaser who has not yet made his mark as a major writer:

> Who loves not Adon's love or Lucrece's rape?
> His sweeter verse contains heart-throbbing line,
> Could but a graver subject him content,
> Without love's foolish languishment
>
> (Anon. 1949, p. 244)

Judged against the very highest standards Shakespeare is a skilful light-weight who has the capacity to do rather better.

The author knows that Shakespeare is also a playwright: Gullio quotes a passage from Act 2 of *Romeo and Juliet*. Towards the end of the final play Will Kemp and Richard Burbage appear. Burbage praises Philomusus as a potentially fine actor: 'I like your face, and the proportion of your body for Richard the Third', and he requests Philomusus to recite some dramatic verse. He is rewarded with the opening lines of the play: 'Now is the winter of our discontent / Made glorious summer by the son of York' (Anon. 1949, p. 343).

The references to Shakespeare throughout the three plays show that he was known to this writer as an important, somewhat underachieving, poet, his work being always impressive but dictated too much by the prevailing cultural norms. Perhaps the author is suggesting that Shakespeare should not write for the common stage if he wishes to write proper poetry – a speculation that is supported by the harsh comments made about Ben Jonson as an equally limited writer, 'The wittiest fellow of a bricklayer in England', 'a mere empiric, one that gets what he hath by observation' (Anon. 1949, p. 244). The author clearly has a detailed knowledge of the stage as well as poetry and the publishing world – John Danter the printer appears in the following scene – which should make him a reliable source about the contemporary literary scene, and his comment that Shakespeare had given Jonson a purge has been frequently analysed as an insight into the relationship between the two rival playwrights (Bednarz 2001, ch. 1). It is, of course, possible that the author was involved in some form of conspiracy to hide the true identity of Shakespeare, but the comments made about Shakespeare throughout the Parnassus plays indicate that he was well known to those interested in literature as an important author of both poetry and plays. The anonymous author finds it easy to identify actors who worked with Shakespeare and other poets and playwrights he would have known, situating Shakespeare within a familiar literary world that we can recognise.

Furthermore, his judgement of Shakespeare's abilities and achievements suggests the scorn of the highly educated for those with less obvious intellectual training. The author makes it clear that more application is required from 'sweet Mr. Shakespeare' if he wishes to earn his full respect, further confirmation (albeit indirect) that Shakespeare was not thought to be a graduate or an aristocrat by this contemporary witness. Significantly, the evaluation of the Parnassus plays was shared by other writers. Richard Barnfield (c. 1574–1620), in his last collection, *Poems in Diverse Humours* (1598), published a poem, 'A Remembrance of Some English Poets', which is remarkably similar in its judgements to those in the Parnassus plays. Barnfield begins with Spenser, seeing him as the most important living poet who should be poet laureate: 'Crowned mayst thou be, unto thy more renown, / (As King of Poets) with a Laurel Crown' ('A Remembrance of Some English Poets', lines 3–4 in Barnfield 1990, p. 182). There follows praise of Samuel Daniel and Michael Drayton and the poem concludes with a celebration of Shakespeare as the fourth most important English poet of his generation:

> And Shakespeare thou, whose honey-flowing vein,
> (Pleasing the world) thy praises doth obtain.
> Whose *Venus*, and whose *Lucrece* (sweet, and chaste)
> Thy name in fame's immortal book have placed.
> Live ever you, at least in fame live ever:
> Well may the body die, but fame dies never.
>
> (lines 13–18)

The lines endorse Shakespeare in an equivocal manner, representing his achievements in the same ways as the Parnassus plays. Shakespeare's poetry is again characterised as enjoyable and easy on the ear, his honeyed words popular with the masses who read literature. He rightly deserves fame, but posthumous celebrity is not necessarily the same as the judgement of fellow poets. Barnfield and the author of the Parnassus plays understand Spenser and Shakespeare in identical ways: the former is the true poet, the latter the fashionable darling of modern readers.

Barnfield refers specifically to Shakespeare's published poetry and, unlike the author of the Parnassus plays, he has no obvious interest in

Shakespeare's drama, which might suggest that he is a somewhat less valuable witness than that author. But there are interesting and suggestive links between Barnfield and Shakespeare, which seem to indicate that his opinion of Shakespeare's work is based on detailed knowledge. *Poems in Diverse Humours* was published by John Jaggard, brother of William, who was later to publish Shakespeare's First Folio. This may be coincidence and so might be the publication of two of Barnfield's poems in *The Passionate Pilgrim* (1599), published by William Jaggard, a collection of twenty poems attributed to Shakespeare. Of these, five are now known to be by Shakespeare (two sonnets and three extracts from *Love's Labour's Lost*), ten by unknown authors, one by Christopher Marlowe and Sir Walter Raleigh (a combined version of 'The Passionate Shepherd to His Love' and 'The Nymph's Reply to The Shepherd'), one by Bartholomew Griffin and one perhaps by Thomas Deloney. Barnfield is therefore the second most significant poet in the anthology, suggesting a close association between the poets in the minds of the publisher, whose brother had published Barnfield's poems in the previous year. It is implausible to think that Barnfield did not know who Shakespeare was, making him either a reliable judge of Shakespeare's poetry or someone else who must have been involved in the conspiracy to hide his true identity.

Barnfield's sonnet sequence, *Cynthia* (1595), provides yet more connections between Barnfield and Shakespeare, which suggest that the two poets kept a close eye on each other. Although *Cynthia* is yet another work of the 1590s that is in thrall to the influence of Spenser, Barnfield's sonnets are the only collection 'apart from Shakespeare's to be addressed to a man', a fact that has led some to argue that he was the rival playwright of the sonnets (Massai, 2014; Daugherty 2010). Even if we do not wish to make such a strong claim, it is still obvious that, in Paul Hammond's words, 'There are enough verbal resemblances between Barnfield's poems and Shakespeare's for us to conclude that the latter studied the two earlier collections with some interest' (Hammond 2002, p. 73). Shakespeare reworks ideas and poetic conceits from Barnfield's *The Affectionate Shepheard* (1594) in sonnet 20 when he adopts Barnfield's stanzas comparing and contrasting the love of a woman and a man for the same boy in having his speaker argue that 'Nature has thwarted him by making the boy male' (Hammond 2002, p. 75). Furthermore, sonnet 20, which opens with the lines 'A woman's face with nature's own hand painted, / Hast thou the

master-mistress of my passion', which confuse and combine gender char-
acteristics and sexual identity, can be read as a 'remaking' of Barnfield's
sonnet 10. This poem describes Ganymede, the poet's love, whose body is
made by Venus and so designed for love, but whose mind is inclined to
chastity so that 'He loves to be beloved, but not to love' (line 14). Barnfield's
poem plays on doubleness, the chaste mind in the desirable body, with the
further implication that the abstinence is really a tease, the apparent
indifference to sexuality serving – deliberately – to inflame desire. The
final twist is that the apparently serious poem about chastity and fleshly
desire, couched in Neo-Platonic language, is really about a prick-teaser,
Ganymede.

Shakespeare represents a similar creature, who, to cite Paul Hammond
again, 'is created by Nature to be a woman, and has feminine features but
male genitals', and he develops Barnfield's understanding of the contrasting natures contained within the boy 'into a challenge to the boy as to
whether his male gender really does make him unavailable': 'But since she
[Nature] pricked thee out for women's pleasure, / Mine be thy love, and
thy love's use their treasure' (Shakespeare 2002, p. 421; Hammond 2002,
p. 83). The women can enjoy the boy's sexual favours, which result in
treasure (pleasure, children), even though the poet asserts that he really
has the boy's love. Shakespeare is re-using and re-working the conceits
and contrasts of Barnfield, carefully to develop the same-sex passions that
Barnfield had established in the 1590s. Barnfield praises Shakespeare in
1598 as one of England's most significant poets for his 'honey-flowing
Vein', the same year in which Frances Meres referred to Shakespeare's
'sugared sonnets' (Meres 1598, p. 281). Perhaps all writers came to identical conclusions after reading Shakespeare's poetry; more likely his work
was known and discussed by poets who had a strong sense of who was
writing what. Shakespeare was undoubtedly reading Barnfield in the
1590s, and the 1609 edition of the sonnets contains poems written in
the 1590s, possibly reworked later, which may refer to Shakespeare's
experiences, or which may be establishing, following Barnfield, a vari-
ation on the Elizabethan sonnet and the sonnet sequence. But the crucial
point is that however we read the relationship between the surviving
poems, the two poets clearly knew who the other was and read each
other's work. Barnfield is another writer who knew the real identity of
Shakespeare.

A further witness to Shakespeare's identity is provided in the first poem published in response to his death, the elegy 'On Mr. William Shakespeare who died in April 1616', which appeared in print in 1633. The poem is evidently an attempt to have Shakespeare's recently interred remains join Chaucer's, Spenser's and Francis Beaumont's in Poet's Corner in Westminster Abbey:

> Renownèd Spenser, lie a thought more nigh
> To learnèd Chaucer, and rare Beaumont lie
> A little nearer Spenser to make room
> For Shakespeare in your threefold, fourfold tomb.
> To lodge all four in one bed make a shift
> Until Doomsday; for hardly will a fifth
> Betwixt this day and that, by fate be slain
> For whom your curtains may be drawn again.
> (William Basse, 'Elegy on Shakespeare', cited from a
> manuscript signed by Basse (c. 1626):
> Centerwall, 2006, p. 267)

It is therefore extremely likely, as Brandon S. Centerwall argues, that Ben Jonson's elegy in the First Folio satirises this poem:

> My Shakespeare, rise! I will not lodge thee by
> Chaucer or Spenser, or bid Beaumont lie
> A little further, to make thee a room;
> Thou art a monument without a tomb,
> And art alive still, while thy book doth live,
> And we have wits to read, and praise to give.
> (Ben Jonson, 'To The Memory of My Beloved,
> The Author Master William Shakespeare And What he
> Hath Left Us', lines 19–24 in Jonson 2012, V, p. 369)

There is no manuscript witness that enables us to date Basse's poem with absolute certainty, but the substance strongly indicates that it was written very soon after Shakespeare's death and was part of a campaign to have Shakespeare removed from Stratford and made part of the small pantheon of English poets in the capital. Jonson's poem shows just how well known Basse's elegy had become by the time that the First Folio was published, a further indication that poets circulated their work widely and could assume that such literature was read and understood (Centerwall 2006, pp. 282–4). Basse imagines the four poets waking up together on the Day of

Judgement, their graves re-arranged now then undisturbed until the end of time, allowing visitors to the Abbey to see the chief figures of English literature resting serenely together. As we know, this did not happen, and, given the inscription on Shakespeare's grave, was probably not something that Shakespeare's family or the citizens of Stratford were likely to have allowed:

> Good Friend For Jesus Sake Forebear
> To Digg The Dust Enclosed Hear:
> Bless Be Ye Man Y[t] Spares These Stones
> And Cursed Be He Yt Moves My Bones.
> (Centerwall 2006, p. 268; original spelling)

As the second half of Basse's elegy admits, the enterprise may have been doomed from the start. The author turns from confident celebration to an acceptance that the status quo might well remain whatever his efforts:

> If your precedency in death doth bar
> A fourth place in your sacred sepulchre
> Under this carvèd marble of thine own,
> Sleep, rare tragedian, Shakespeare sleep alone
> Thy unmolested peace, unsharèd cave
> Possess as lord, not tenant of thy grave.
> (lines 9–14)

Jonson would appear to be responding to the embarrassment of a fellow poet, as well as celebrating the achievements of Shakespeare, and, in doing so, showing how acutely he understood what had been happening in the literary world. Jonson is also validating his own achievements as well as those of Shakespeare in highlighting the significance of the book rather than the grave and so drawing attention to the folios of both writers. Neither he nor Shakespeare needs to be buried close to Chaucer or Spenser – and, needless to say, Beaumont – to obtain their rightful place in literary history.

It is not absolutely certain that Basse actually wrote the poem attributed to him. The elegy was first published in the first edition of John Donne's poetry (1633), but it was omitted from the second edition and is one of two poems from that edition that are no longer attributed to Donne. Brandon Centerwall has made a serious case that the elegy is actually by Donne, after all, and that subsequent manuscript copies which attribute the elegy to Basse are a result of the humiliation of the failed attempt to move the writer's remains to Westminster Abbey. Basse, a minor poet whose verse was competent but never inspired, rather nobly stepped forward 'on Donne's behalf to claim both the authorship of the piece as well as general responsibility for the unfortunate turn of events', revising the poem in later manuscript versions as the one in his hand demonstrates (Centerwall 2006, p. 270; Kathman 2014a). The case is intriguing and in some ways plausible, as it is odd that Basse's poem appeared in the edition of Donne and the purpose of the elegy must surely have caused some discomfort to its author. However, there is no obvious reason why Basse might have wanted to hide Donne's embarrassment – biographies of Donne find no other connection between the two writers (Bald 1970; Stubbs 2006) – and it would have been an extremely unusual sacrifice to have made.

The point that needs to be made is that whoever wrote the poem, and however we read it, the verse testifies to the existence of Shakespeare as a poet, who was well known to other poets, and who was regarded, whether through his poetry alone or the combined reputation of his poetry and drama, as one of the most significant literary figures in the history of English literature in his lifetime (Hadfield 2009; Cheney 2004). Basse and Donne would both have known who Shakespeare was, making them part of the circle of Jacobean writers in London who knew who was writing what and who would therefore have been able to identify Shakespeare the writer, just like the author of the Parnassus Plays, Richard Barnfield and Ben Jonson.

John Weever (1575/6–1632), the poet and antiquary, was the first writer to address a poem to William Shakespeare (Kathman 2014b; Honigmann 1987). Weever published a long collection of epigrams in 1599, *Epigrams in the Oldest Cut, and Newest Fashion* (1599), the title advertising the volume as one that delighted in paradox, wit and variety. Weever's aim was surely to capture the diverse nature of Martial, the acerbic and pithy Roman writer who had defined the genre when the empire was at its most successful and, also, its most morally problematic, his volume having a profound influence on the epigrams of Ben Jonson published in the first folio of Jonson's works (Jonson 2012, V, pp. 101–98). Weever's poems, arranged in groups of around twenty for a seven-week period of reading, range, like Martial's, from the light, scornful and pleasingly contained, to celebrations of major public figures, including writers. Weever is never quite as bold as Martial in recounting the sexual peccadilloes of his urban readership, but many poems take their cue from his Roman predecessor. The third epigram of the fifth week, 'In Stellam', pours scorn on the hypocritical morals of its subject, the poem ironically transforming her into a star:

> Virginity doth Stella still commend,
> That for a virgin so she may be counted;
> Virginity she might though reprehend,
> Since she with Rufus in the coach was mounted:
> For tell me Stella, virgin as thou art,
> To bear a virgin, is it a virgin's part?
>
> (Weever 1599, Sig. E8r)

Hardly a memorable poem of lyrical brilliance but one that shows that the author had a clear understanding of literary culture – the reference to Stella as a star perhaps referring to Sir Philip Sidney's *Astrophil and Stella*, especially as Sidney's Stella, Penelope Devereux, was notorious in the later 1590s for her liaison with Charles Blount, eighth Baron Mountjoy and Earl of Devonshire (Freedman 1983). The seventh epigram in the fifth week, 'In Braggadochionem', deals with a figure derived from Spenser's coinage, Braggadochio, the cowardly, deceitful and boastful false knight from the opening book of *The Faerie Queene* (1590), showing that Weever also understood the latest literary fashions:

> Did Braggadochio meet a man in field?
> 'Tis true, he did, the way he could not shun:
> And did he force great Brundon weapons yield;
> Nay there he lies. To untruss when he begun,
> He stole his weapons and away did run:
> Vain is thy vaunt, and victory unjust,
> Thou durst not stay till he his points untrussed.
>
> (Weever, 1599: Sig. F1r)

The poem relies on a quibble on 'untruss', meaning to discard and to expose oneself, showing how Braggadochio reveals his true nature in secretly stealing the weapons of his unprepared opponent, thus revealing his true nature as a coward who boasts about a victory that never took place. Weever shows that he is a good reader of Spenser and the pleasure of the poem for contemporary readers was probably in recognising a common experience of reading and understanding the most celebrated English poet rather than appreciating the brilliance of Weever's wit and moral insight.

Other poems celebrate various significant public figures, such as Richard Houghton, Weever's patron, to whom the volume was dedicated; leading aristocrats and court figures such as Roger Manners, Earl of Rutland and William Parker, fourth Baron Monteagle; contemporaries at Cambridge such as Dudley North and Nathaniel Fletcher; friends, such as Thomas Kedgewin and Richard Upcher; and writers such as Ben Jonson and William Warner. Weever includes an epigram on Spenser, whose recent death Weever mourns:

> *Epig. 23 In obitium Ed. Spenser Poetae prestantiss.*
>
> Colin's gone home, the glory of his clime,
> The Muses' mirror, and the shepherds' saint;
> Spenser is ruined, of our latter time
> The fairest ruin, faëries' foulest want:
> Then his Time-ruins did our ruin show,
> Which by his ruin we untimely know:
>   Spenser therefore thy *Ruins* were called in,
>   Too soon to sorrow lest we should begin.
> (Weever 1599, Sig. G3r)

Weever's poem reads like a check list of Spenser's great works – *The Shepheardes Calender, Colin Clouts come home againe, The Faerie Queene* and 'The Ruines of Time' from the *Complaints* volume – as well as a fitting tribute to a major writer. Yet again, Weever is showing how well-read he is and how knowledgeable about the state of contemporary English culture. In fact, Weever was well known to dramatists writing around the turn of the century – Marston, Jonson, Dekker and, probably, the author of the Parnassus Plays – who, according to E. A. J. Honigmann, satirised him in a variety of plays, just as he had satirised them in his work (Honigmann 1987, pp. 42–56). Like the author of the Parnassus Plays, Barnfield and Basse, Weever lived and worked within a group of writers who were invariably eager to make their literary conversations public, showing who they knew and how closely they were all connected.

It is important to appreciate this familiar context of public declarations of friendship and intellectual intimacy when reading Weever's epigram on

Shakespeare. 'Ad Gulielmum Shakespear' is not a random poem by someone who happened to quite like some poems he had read, but a writer
showing that he could be an arbiter of taste and part of a vibrant literary
circle because he knew who the most important people were, their work
and their significance:

> Honey-tongued Shakespeare, when I saw thine issue,
> I swore Apollo got them and none other;
> Their rosy-tainted features clothed in tissue,
> Some heaven-born goddess said to be their mother:
> Rose-cheeked Adonis with his amber tresses,
> Fair fire-hot Venus charming him to love her;
> Chaste Lucretia virgin-like her dresses,
> Proud lust-stung Tarquin seeking still to prove her:
> Romeo, Richard; more whose names I know not,
> Their sugared tongues, and power-attractive beauty
> Say they are saints although that s[ain]ts they show not
> For thousands vows to them subjective duty:
> > They burn in love; thy children, Shakespeare, het them,
> > Go, woo thy muse, more nymphish brood beget them.
> > > (Weever 1599, Sig. E6r)

Weever's is surely the most complicated, nuanced and thoughtful of the
poems discussed in this short chapter. Even so, it contains recognisable
features which show that commentators agreed about Shakespeare's
achievements at the end of the 1590s. Weever – like everyone else –
describes Shakespeare as a 'sweet' writer, his poems notable for their
'sugared tongues', mellifluous and appealing but perhaps not quite as
serious as the very best (no one would have begun a poem calling Spenser
'Honey tongued'). His use of adjectives – 'rosy-tainted', 'rose-cheeked',
'fire-hot', 'virgin-like', 'lust-stung' – is designed to capture Shakespeare's
Ovidian verse style, with its powerful combination of beauty, sex and
violence (Bate 1993; Taylor 2000).

Weever, as he does in his poem to Spenser, shows just how well he
knows Shakespeare's writing: he has read *Venus and Adonis* and *The Rape
of Lucrece*, and is able to refer to *Romeo and Juliet* and *Richard III*
(or perhaps *Richard II*). Furthermore, he has read such works carefully
and knows how Shakespeare's style works and how he is known to a wider

readership that will recognise and admire Weever's ability to understand and imitate another poet. Weever represents Shakespeare as a parent nurturing and increasing his 'Nymphish brood' of writings, establishing a pointed contrast between the lush sexuality and disturbing violence of his writing.

There may also be a sly series of references to the sonnets, assuming that Weever could have seen them in manuscript. Many of Shakespeare's sonnets concerning a young man – the sonnets may be addressed to more than one (Edmondson and Wells 2004, pp. 72–8) – explore the relationship between the possibility of generation through having children and the legacy of a poet being his poems. Sonnets 13 and 97 contain specific puns on the lack of 'issue' of a young man, implicitly contrasting his failure to reproduce to the fertile act of writing poetry, while sonnets 18 and 19 make this pointed contrast more specific, with 19 concluding with the couplet: 'Yet do thy worst, old Time: despite thy wrong / My love shall in my verse ever live young.' The comparison is frequently made in English Renaissance poetry (McFaul 2010). Even so the connection is striking, as Shakespeare made such extensive use of this particular image and the links perhaps suggest either that Weever saw Shakespeare's poems in manuscript, or that Shakespeare made use of Weever's poem – as he clearly did Barnfield's – when composing his sonnets.

All four writers make similar judgements of Shakespeare's writing, that he is a wonderful but limited poet who needs to be more ambitious, a conclusion they appear to have reached independently and which they all think makes Shakespeare's work distinctive. They also testify that the works attributed to Shakespeare in print in the 1590s – *Venus and Adonis* and *The Rape of Lucrece* – were written by the author of plays that were published anonymously in the same period: *Romeo and Juliet, Richard II* and *Richard III*. Clearly the reason for the discrepancy in naming one group and not the other concerns the history of the book and the distinction made between poetry and prose in Elizabethan England, not the identity of the author in question (Erne 2003).

Shakespeare may seem to us to be a very different author to his contemporary Elizabethan and Jacobean writers, an inspired genius whose brilliance was utterly unfathomable and incomprehensible, Coleridge's 'myriad-minded' author whose work covered all subjects with equal brio. But it is equally obvious that this was not how he was read or understood by his contemporaries. They knew who he was, what he had written, and the characteristic style he adopted. He was one of them, part of a larger group of writers in London and the surrounding provinces, who they would read and discuss and who, in turn, would read and discuss their writing with some of them. Shakespeare was one of the best, having talent and ability that few could hope to match, but he was by no stretch of the imagination perfect, indulging his penchant for Ovidian style and taste at the expense of truly serious writing. Nothing in the surviving evidence left by Richard Barnfield, William Basse (or John Donne), John Weever or the author of the Parnassus Plays indicates that they had any doubts about who Shakespeare was or that they thought that 'Shakespeare' was an unusual phenomenon that required explanation.

WORKS CITED

Anon. 1949. *The Three Parnassus Plays, 1598–1601.* J. B. Leishman (ed.). London. Nicholson and Watson

Bald, R. C. 1970. *John Donne: A Life.* Oxford. Clarendon Press

Barnfield, Richard 1990. *The Complete Poems.* George Klawitter (ed.). Selinsgrove. Susquehanna University Press

Bate, Jonathan 1993. *Shakespeare and Ovid.* Oxford. Clarendon Press

Bednarz, James P. 2001. *Shakespeare and the Poets' War.* New York. Columbia University Press

Centerwall, Brandon S. 2006. 'Who Wrote William Basse's "Elegy on Shakespeare"?: Rediscovering a Poem Lost from the Donne Canon', *Shakespeare Survey 59.* Peter Holland (ed.). Cambridge University Press, pp. 267–84

Cheney, Patrick 2004. *Shakespeare: National Poet-Playwright.* Cambridge University Press

Daugherty, Leo 2010. *William Shakespeare, Richard Barnfield, and the Sixth Earl of Derby.* Amherst. Cambria Press

Edmondson, Paul and Wells, Stanley 2004. *Shakespeare's Sonnets.* Oxford University Press

Erne, Lukas 2003. *Shakespeare as Literary Dramatist.* Cambridge University Press

Freedman, Sylvia 1983. *Poor Penelope: Lady Penelope Rich, An Elizabethan Woman.* Bourne End. Kensal Press

Greene, Thomas 1982. *The Light in Troy: Imitation and Discovery in Renaissance Poetry.* New Haven. Yale University Press

Hadfield, Andrew 2009. 'Spenser's Rosalind', *Modern Language Review* 104.4: 935–46

Hammond, Paul 2002. *Figuring Sex Between Men From Shakespeare to Rochester.* Oxford. Clarendon Press

Honigmann, E. A. J. 1987. *John Weever: a Biography of a Literary Associate of Shakespeare and Jonson, together with a photographic facsimile of Weever's Epigrammes (1599).* Manchester University Press

Jonson, Ben 2012. *The Cambridge Edition of the Works of Ben Jonson.* David Bevington, Martin Butler and Ian Donaldson (eds.). 7 vols. Cambridge University Press

Kathman, David 2014a. 'Basse, William'. *ODNB* (accessed 15.10.2014)
     2014b. 'Weever, John'. *ODNB* (accessed 15.10.2014)

McFaul, Tom 2010. *Poetry and Paternity in Renaissance England: Sidney, Spenser, Shakespeare, Donne and Jonson.* Cambridge University Press

Massai, Sonia 2014. 'Richard Barnfield', *ODNB* (accessed 15.10.2014)

Meres, Francis 1598. *Palladis Tamia: Wits Treasury Being The Second Part of Wits Commonwealth.* London

Shakespeare, William 2002. *Complete Sonnets and Poems.* Colin Burrow (ed.). Oxford University Press

Stubbs, John 2006. *Donne: The Reformed Soul.* London. Viking

Taylor, A. B. (ed.) 2000. *Shakespeare's Ovid: The Metamorphoses in the Plays and Poems.* Cambridge University Press

Weever, John 1599. *Epigrammes in the Oldest Cut, and Newest Fashion.* London

17

Last things: Shakespeare's neighbours and beneficiaries

SUSAN BROCK

Concerned most of all, it seems, with the protection of his property holdings in the face of a family scandal and a lack of male heirs, Shakespeare's will, his last legal act in the final months of his life, looks mean-minded, unsympathetic, chaotic. We see hasty revisions, likely prompted by the sexual misconduct of his new son-in-law Thomas Quiney and the anticipated death of his sister Joan's husband, and the puzzling omission and later insertion of the bequest to his wife. The same process is at work in the several lines on page two of the will, where Shakespeare, with small gifts of money and keepsakes, recompensed his Stratford friends and neighbours for services rendered and favours done, and discarded those that had offended. To Francis Collins, gent. (1573–1617), who was responsible for drawing up the will and a witness, £13 6s 8d; to Thomas Russell, esq. (1570–1634), appointed overseer with Collins, £5; to William Reynolds, gent. (1575–1633) and to Hamnet Sadler (c. 1562–1624), godfather to Shakespeare's dead son and a witness (both added as an afterthought), 26s 8d each to buy memorial rings; to brothers Anthony Nash, gent. (d. 1622), and Mr John Nash (d. 1623), 26s 8d each ('in gold' struck out); to William Walker (1608–61), Shakespeare's godson, 20s in gold. Mr Richard Tyler the elder (1566–1636) was struck out. Julyns or July or Julius Shaw (1581–1628), John Robinson (fl. 1589–1616) and Robert Whattcott (fl. 1593–1637) served as witnesses without reward.

Shakespeare's will was drafted, according to the date at the top of the first page, on Thursday 25th of January 1616 and then revised two months later on Monday 25th March, a coincidence as potentially suspect as the date of his birth and death both falling on 23 April. Perhaps advised by

Francis Collins, a burgess of Stratford from 1602 to 1608 and town clerk in 1617, who had acted for him in a number of legal transactions and had a reputation locally as a maker of wills to the great and good of Stratford, Shakespeare started working on his will three months before he died. It was a case of 'do as I say not as I do' as Collins drew up his own will only the day before his death. Shakespeare might have dictated to his lawyer the main bequests and terms of the will from his sickbed, believing death was approaching, and then made a temporary recovery. Collins, or a clerk under his supervision, incorporated his wishes in the appropriate legal form, leaving gaps to be filled in when the will was formally signed and witnessed. But within nine weeks many things had changed in Shakespeare's life and he changed his will accordingly.

Regardless of its content, Shakespeare's will is not a prime example of the scrivener's art. But it is typical of Collins. His work, for example on John Combe's will in 1613 (TNA PROB11/126/415), the minutes of Stratford Corporation (SCLA BRU2/2) and Stratford Bailiff Daniel Baker's memorandum book of 1602–3 (SCLA ER2/25), all show lack of attention to detail, omissions, interlineations, signs of haste and a surprising level of unconcern with outward forms. In his professional life Collins not unusually employed several styles of handwriting so, unfortunately, identification cannot always be certain. What is true is that attorneys normally made the rough first draft and their clerks the fair copy. We likely see Collins's hand here.

In the light of his apparent technical failings, what made Francis Collins a sought-after legal counsel and friend to Shakespeare's circle? Was he cheap? The signs are otherwise. Unlike his predecessor as town clerk, Thomas Greene, who was also involved in Shakespeare's affairs but not mentioned in his will, Collins did not progress beyond the Inns of Court, Clements in his case (Eccles 1961, p. 118). Nevertheless at his death he was rather better off than Greene, providing legacies to his family members alone of £165 (TNA PROB11/130/512), while Greene's 1640 will records in total legacies of no more than £120 and no mention of land or property (TNA PROB11/186/420). First recorded in 1598 working in the Court of Record, Stratford's small claims court (Bearman 2011, p. 14), Collins remained a jobbing attorney to the end of his life, apart from his brief spell as town clerk, earning a living from fees for official duties for the borough and private law work. Was he a personable colleague, a clubbable man? He was clearly a close friend of the Combes. John Combe left him and his son John, Combe's godson, £10 each, and Collins's wife Susan £6 13s 4d in his will of 1613 (TNA PROB11/126/415). Thomas Combe (d. 1608) had promised money to his children, of which there were three sons and four daughters under twenty-one alive at Collins's death aged forty-four in September 1617. When Greene resigned as town clerk in 1617, Collins was hastily recruited (SCLA BRU2/2, p. 330) as a safe pair of hands to block the ambitious and quarrelsome Thomas Lucas. Was his informality, a risky trait in a lawyer, attractive to those who did not want to be mired in legal detail? Collins's own business affairs were not without mishap. At his death he was caught up in an unresolved legal dispute with John Rogers, vicar of Stratford, and the said Thomas Lucas (both of whom we shall meet again later) about revenues which were to generate 20 shillings per annum for the poor of Stratford. The story is told in a statement to the Corporation in August 1617 (SCLA ER 1/1/81). As Stratford overseer of the poor 1602–8, Collins had direct experience of what that bequest could do (Whitfield 1964, p. 254).

An unusual circumstance of Collins's life was his dual location in Stratford and Warwick, the county town, as well as holding land in the manor of Henley in Arden, which he sold in October 1616 (Wellstood 1919, p. 84). His election as town clerk was on condition that he 'come and dwell amongst as [sic] so long as he continueth in the said office' (SCLA BRU2/2, p. 326). At the time of his death less than six months later he clearly had two homes: 'If I die at Stratford my body to lie in the parish church there. If at Warwick then in the Church of St Mary's there.' His burial in Stratford was recorded on 27 November 1617.

Shakespeare's was a Warwickshire will. Of the twenty-five legatees, executors, overseers and witnesses named, twenty-one connected him with his life in Stratford. The few exceptions were his theatrical colleagues and the man to whom Shakespeare entrusted the responsibility of ensuring that the instructions in his will were properly carried out, Thomas Russell. Russell is conspicuous by his absence from Stratford's history but he was a significant link between Shakespeare's London and Stratford lives. Described by his biographer Leslie Hotson as a 'right, representative Englishman' (Hotson 1937, pp. 278–9), Russell connected Shakespeare into the county gentry of Warwickshire and Worcestershire who had friends and relations among the minor nobility, in the Inns of Court and the

Universities. It is likely that Shakespeare knew Russell as the occupier of the manor of Alderminster, four miles south of Stratford on the road to Oxford, where he lived between 1598 and 1611, having inherited it from his father Sir Thomas Russell, for his mother Margaret's lifetime (TNA PROB11/57/83). Six years Shakespeare's junior, Russell was born in Strensham, Worcestershire but from the age of four, after his father's death, was brought up in Bruton, Somerset, in the house of his stepfather Sir Henry Berkeley. His principal home was at Rushock near Droitwich, where he died in 1634.

To appreciate fully the network of connections which might have bound Shakespeare and Russell, especially through his mother's second marriage to Berkeley, Leslie Hotson's work (Hotson 1937) is essential reading. He paints a bucolic but undocumented picture of a first meeting at Stratford market between Shakespeare and Russell as young men in their respective roles as buyer on behalf of John Shakespeare's wool dealings and seller of fleeces from Russell's Cotswold estates (Hotson 1937, p. 28). More persuasive are the blood and social connections between the Berkeley family and the Earl of Southampton, which might support Hotson's theory that Russell made the connection between poet and patron. Most convincing is Russell's connection to the Digges family, through his second marriage to Anne Digges, widow of Thomas Digges, mathematician and author of *Stratioticos* (the second edition of 1590 was published by Shakespeare's Stratford contemporary Richard Field). The Digges's home in Philip Lane was in the London parish of St Mary Aldermanbury, where they were neighbours of John Heminges, who lived there from 1588 until his wife's death (Edmond 2009), and William Leveson, one of the trustees for the division of the Globe shares in 1599 (Hotson 1937, pp. 160–1). Russell's younger stepson, Leonard Digges, who was brought up in Alderminster before he went up to Oxford in 1603, contributed commendatory verses for Heminges and Condell's 1623 Folio and for the 1640 edition of Shakespeare's *Sonnets*. He took his degree in 1606 (Hotson 1937, p. 237) and then disappears from view, possibly travelling in Spain until after Shakespeare's death. Edward Blount, publisher of Digges's translation of Claudian's *The Rape of Proserpine* (1617) and the 1623 Folio, may have been aware of Digges's continuing connection with Stratford and invited him to contribute the commendatory verse which alludes for the first time in print to Shakespeare's monument in Holy Trinity Church in 1623. John Davies of Quinton connected Russell (for whom he witnessed a vital document in

1603), Digges (to whom he left a silver bowl in his will of 1631) and Shakespeare (mentioned with Davies in John Combe's will of 1613) (Hotson 1937, pp. 249–50).

So why did Shakespeare choose Thomas Russell as overseer? His social status and connections gave him the authority and experience to look after Shakespeare's affairs in both Stratford and London but no more so than another Stratford neighbour, Sir Henry Rainsford of Clifford Chambers. Rainsford, knighted in 1603, was involved in every aspect of Stratford's business and political life, for example in the Commission for collecting alms after the fire of 1614, where he named Richard Tyler as one of the deputies. He was the trusted friend of many influential people in the town like Thomas Greene, his steward in 1604 (SCLA DR33/59), Thomas Combe, Rainsford's godfather, and the Reynolds family, especially William Reynolds and his mother, and was related to others, for example the Nash brothers, who were first cousins of William Barnes whose son, also William, was Rainsford's stepfather. Coincidentally Rainsford's home in Clifford Chambers had earlier been held by the Russell family (Chambers 1930, II, p. 178).

There are a few traces of the private man which might provide an explanation. As a young man Russell was wild enough to leave Queen's College, Oxford without a degree to marry at twenty (Hotson 1937, p. 42). Widowed by twenty-nine, he left his young daughter with his mother-in-law to go seafaring with seasoned navigator Sir George Gifford, a Gloucestershire neighbour (Hotson 1937, pp. 101–2). On his return he pursued a widow fifteen years his senior and lived with her for at least three years before their marriage, bringing up four stepchildren, the youngest of whom with at least one of her children he supported into adulthood. He was the sort of friend who offered a safe haven in time of plague in 1630 to the children of Endymion Porter (Bruce 1860, p. 254). He loved dogs, hunting birds, horses and country sports and wagered on them all (Hotson 1937, pp. 204–6). Perhaps Shakespeare just liked him. There is no evidence that Russell played any part in the execution of his last wishes.

One of the enduring stories about Shakespeare's death was started by John Ward, vicar of Stratford, nearly fifty years later (Ward 1839, p. 183). It appeals because it shows us Shakespeare off duty, having one drink too many with fellow-writers Ben Jonson and Michael Drayton and then suffering, not a hangover, but a fever which led to his death. Whatever the truth of this anecdote, Drayton turns up in this chapter because, like Digges, he had a life in Stratford-upon-Avon as part of a social circle which overlapped with Shakespeare's.

What brought Drayton to the village of Clifford Chambers on the River Avon a little way south of Stratford, was Anne Rainsford née Goodere, his first patron's daughter and inspiration, some argue, for his *Idea's Mirror*, and her son Sir Henry Rainsford his 'incomparable friend' (Drayton 1953, I, p. 156). He visited for some months every summer to rest and to write, he explained to William Drummond of Hawthornden in a letter of 14 July 1631 only five months before he died (Newdigate 1941, p. 187). It is inconceivable that some of the business comings and goings of the Rainsford household would not have impinged on their house guest, and while there Drayton lived as a local, being treated by Shakespeare's son-in-law John Hall for a tertian fever (Lane 1996, pp. 40–1). Of course Shakespeare and Drayton knew each other in the small world of literary London where they shared a printer in Nicholas Ling, read each other's work and saw each other's plays, but were they friends? Shakespeare merits only four lines in Drayton's review of poets and poetry, his epistle to Henry Reynolds 1627 (Drayton 1953, I, pp. 151–6) and those are 'somewhat pedestrian and lukewarm in [their] praise' (Pringle 2013, pp. 43–4), nor does Shakespeare refer to Drayton directly. The Rev. John Ward's special relationship between Drayton and Shakespeare seems for the most part to be merely circumstantial and dependent on geography.

At New Place five men witnessed Shakespeare's signature on the three pages of his will. Francis Collins was present as Shakespeare's attorney. How did the other four come to be there? A mixture of expediency and sentiment might be the answer. Hamnet Sadler was Shakespeare's friend of over thirty years. Julyns Shaw, Shakespeare's neighbour from next door but one in Chapel St., might have been called round to add gravitas. He had been elected bailiff for the second time in the autumn of 1615 but he was also an old friend of the Shakespeare family. When Shaw's father Ralph, also a wool dealer, died in 1592, Shakespeare's father had appraised the goods in his house in Henley St. (SCLA BRU15/7/142).

It is more difficult to account for John Robinson and Robert Whattcott's presence. A John Robinson is named in the will as Shakespeare's tenant at the Blackfriars Gatehouse. If it was he that was present at the making of the will, he would be the only one of Shakespeare's London circle known to be in Stratford-upon-Avon on 25 March 1616. The unlikeliness of this coincidence leads most Shakespeare biographers to reject the identification, preferring instead to suggest that he was one of Shakespeare's or the Halls' servants (Eccles 1961, p. 142), but the evidence is only circumstantial. John Robinson was not an unusual name in Stratford, occurring in the baptismal and marriage registers of Holy Trinity four times between 1579 and 1609 (the only burial being recorded in December 1614). John, son of Thomas Robinson, baptised in November 1589, might be the same John Robynson who married Margrett Frecleton in September 1609 and had the misfortune to be the victim of more than one assault for which he pursued a series of suits in Stratford's Court of Record, for example against John Perkins in summer 1608, when he was represented by Francis Collins (SCLA BRU12/7a/29). But Robinson of the Blackfriars, perhaps up in Stratford to sort out a business matter relating to his lease with the ailing Shakespeare not well enough to travel to London, seems to be as likely a candidate for witnessing the document which would affect his tenancy.

Robert Whattcott is known to have been involved with the Shakespeares three years before when Susanna Hall sued John Lane the younger for slander in July 1613 in Worcester Consistory Court. Lane had claimed some five weeks earlier that this respectable doctor's wife and mother of a daughter just past her fifth birthday had had sex with Ralph Smith at John Palmer's house and had the symptoms of a venereal disease. In the abbreviated documentation of the court, Whattcott 'fecit fidem etc.' (Lewis 1940, II, pp. 449–51). He gave his word on the side of Susanna and Lane was excommunicated. Did he provide an alibi for Susanna or Ralph? When the alleged deed was done had he been at John Palmer's, possibly the son of Adam Palmer who had lived next door to Susanna's grandmother in Wilmcote (Alcock with Bearman 2002, pp. 64–5) now living in Aston Cantlow? The plaintiff hardly needed a character reference from Whattcott, who seems to have farmed in a modest way in Tredington about ten miles south of Stratford. In 1605 he sued Richard Suche (defended by Francis Collins) for allowing his dogs to kill two of his sheep the previous Christmas Eve (SCLA BRU15/5/93). Nor was he of particularly blameless character. Robert Whattcott's sympathies may have been with Lane rather than Susanna. Valerie Swift has drawn my attention to the fact that he had in his youth been a rather lively lad, found guilty of adultery with Mistress Anne Stock of Tredington and of slander against her husband and excommunicated for some ten months in 1594 to 1595 (WAAS, Worcester Consistory Court Deposition Book, BA2012/4, fos. 335r–355v, 435v–486r passim). The same Richard Suche of nearby Darlingscott was called to give evidence in the case (fo. 362r–367r). Whattcott might also be the Robert Whatcott alias Wheatcroft of Draycott, some eight miles from Tredington in the parish of Blockley, whose will was proved in the same Bishop's Court in January 1637 (WAAS 008.7/3585/224/225).

And so to the men who benefited from Shakespeare's will. The Nash brothers became formally related to the Shakespeares on 22 April 1626 when Thomas, son of Anthony and nephew of John, married Elizabeth Hall, granddaughter of William and daughter of Susanna, cementing business connections dating back nearly twenty-five years. The Nashes were not originally from Stratford and did not move to the town until about 1577, at which time the brothers were probably both under six and would have been beneath the notice of the teenage Shakespeare. Their father Thomas Nash may have come from Bicester in Oxfordshire and both Anthony and John may have been born at Ipsley on the border of Warwickshire, where their father was the servant of Sir John Hubaud, his uncle by marriage (Whitfield 1967, p. 124). Sir John's brother Ralph sold to Shakespeare for £440 a part interest in the Stratford tithes in July 1605, witnessed by, among others, Francis Collins, who drew up the contract, and Anthony Nash (Schoenbaum 1975, pp. 192–4). Anthony and John also witnessed Shakespeare's purchase from the Combes of arable land and rights of common in Old Stratford in May 1602 (Schoenbaum 1975, pp. 188–90). In October 1614 Anthony witnessed the agreement made with William Replingham guaranteeing Shakespeare against any losses he might suffer as a result of the enclosures in Welcombe (Schoenbaum 1975, pp. 231–2). Anthony, who had lived at Welcombe as early as 1586 (Whitfield 1967, p. 126), was, like Shakespeare, ambivalent about the business. As collector of the Welcombe tithes on Shakespeare's behalf, it seems likely that he would have advised him to take action to look after his financial interests. Indeed Robert Bearman suggests that Anthony Nash may have managed all of Shakespeare's business affairs (Bearman 1994, pp. 76–7). In his will of 1622 Anthony left to his son John 'one of my rings that his brother Thomas [as executor] shall allot to him' (TNA PROB11/140/510). An attractive but ungrounded speculation is that the ring might have been the one purchased as a keepsake with Shakespeare's bequest (Whitfield 1967, p. 128).

John Nash was a very different character who lived by grace and favour of his brother, kept somewhat dubious company, and was not opposed to public disorder. His friendship with Shakespeare must have been through his brother and the wider social connections of Stratford, as their lives do not otherwise intersect. He may have lived away from Stratford but was back by August 1594 when his daughter Mary was baptised. In 1602 he married as his second wife Dorothy Bellars, recently widowed by the death in October that year of her husband Francis Bellars, landlord of the Bear Inn. Coincidentally Anthony in the same year purchased the inn at the bottom of Bridge Street and it was here that the John Nashes lived until 1619, the property being empty in 1622 when Anthony left the Bear to his son Thomas, later to be Shakespeare's son-in-law. Named as licensee of the Bear in 1619/20, we might picture John Nash pulling pints over the bar, but it seems more likely that he left the day-to-day work to his more experienced wife, presented in 1606 for keeping unlawful games, and a servant, treated by Dr Hall (Lane 1996, p. 13), possibly the Thomas Jelfes presented in 1602/3 for making malt for brewing (Eccles 1961, p. 122). Nash took a more managerial role, bringing a suit to recover a debt of £11 15s owed by a customer for victuals and horse feed in September 1613 (SCLA BRU12/8/22) and looking after his other interests, for example his tithes in Drayton near Shottery, held under a lease to Sir John Hubaud (SCLA BRU15/12/102). It was not until three years after Shakespeare's death, in the spring of 1619, that John Nash made his mark in Stratford history leading the faction, or conspiracy as some saw it, supporting the vicar John Rogers against 'all the old biting, and young sucking, Puritants of Stratford [who] are joined with their two Justasses [*sic*] a piece maliciously to displace and utterly undo their Minister, and to bring to his place as arrant a k_____ as themselves' (Fripp 1938, II, p. 843), who favoured the appointment to the living of radical young Thomas Wilson. It boiled down to a doctrinal dispute which escalated through armed riots, libels and the erection of a symbolic maypole, into a Star Chamber case (TNA STAC 8/26/10). On one side was the Puritan group in the Corporation led by Thomas Lucas the troublemaker and Alderman Daniel Baker supported by Dr John Hall, on the other followers of the old way led by John Nash and a motley crew including William Reynolds, to whom Shakespeare left a bequest, William Hathaway, half-brother of Shakespeare's wife Anne, and John Lane, the Nash brothers' nephew and Susanna Hall's defamer (Fripp 1938, II, pp. 838–45). There is no record of the judgement against Lane and his fellows, but the new Puritan vicar, Thomas Wilson, remained in his post until his death in 1624.

Unrepresented among Shakespeare's Stratford legatees, women were the social glue which bound its society together. Thomas Greene records in his diary on 3 April 1615 that his wife had been reliably informed by Margaret Reynolds that Thomas Combe the younger had paid Mistress Mary Nash, likely the wife of Antony, £30 as part payment for 'her good will to depart with her estate' in his machinations over the Welcombe enclosures (Ingleby 1885, p. 9). Though the Reynoldses were not on Greene's 1614 list of ancient freeholders in the fields of Old Stratford and Welcombe (SCLA BRU15/1/94), Margaret held property there and was not afraid to exert her rights, strong men refusing to 'meddle without their "Landlady" (meaning Mistress Reynolds)', as she recounted proudly to Mistress Greene and Francis Collins (Ingleby 1885, pp. 8–9). Shakespeare would have been well aware, as he made his own will, that the Reynolds family, especially Margaret, had benefited greatly from John Combe's will, proved only five months before. Shakespeare himself had received a small legacy. By his mother's will proved in June 1615 (TNA PROB11/125/631) William Reynolds now owned both her lands in Welcombe as well as property near The College. On 3 August 1615 Shakespeare may have been a guest at Reynolds's wedding in Clifford Chambers to Frances de Bois, a Frenchwoman of Philip Lane in London (Eccles 1961, p. 123), possibly a member of the Rainsford household (Bloom 1893, p. 41). The new Mistress Reynolds and Shakespeare would have had friends in common, as both Thomas Russell and John Heminges knew her parish well.

There seems no reason, apart from forgetfulness, that Reynolds had not been included in the first draft of the will as a man of property and as representative of a family that had long-standing ties with the Shakespeares – some of them dangerous. We can only speculate that Shakespeare might have been making a point as he revised his will in March 1616, by adding friends and neighbours with known recusant tendencies like Reynolds and Sadler (Wood 2003, p. 338). Or, perhaps, reflecting on his own mortality, he was reminded of his father's faith. With John Shakespeare, Reynolds's parents, Thomas and Margaret, were named in 1592 by Commissioners appointed by Archbishop Whitgift to identify non-churchgoers (Fripp 1929, pp. 148–9). The Reynoldses were among fifteen self-confessed Catholics who willingly paid the monthly fine levied for non-attendance, though by the autumn they had either conformed or promised to do so (Fripp 1938, I, p. 306). With Hamnet and Judith Sadler and Susanna Shakespeare, Reynolds's mother Margaret was cited for not receiving communion the previous Easter in the Church Court held in the Stratford parish church in May 1606 (Brinkworth 1972, p. 131).

It is more surprising that Shakespeare had not included Sadler in the first draft of the will than that Richard Tyler was cut out of the second. Sadler's connection to Shakespeare was personal and sentimental. Shakespeare named his twins Hamnet and Judith after Sadler and his wife in 1585 and they may have had Shakespeare in mind when they named their ninth child William in February 1598, conceived not long after they had mourned together the death of Hamnet Shakespeare in August 1596. The presence of Sadler in the room as witness may have triggered in Shakespeare a sudden change of mind.

Both Tyler and Sadler were Shakespeare's contemporaries, Tyler slightly younger and Sadler likely to be slightly older, with very similar backgrounds in Stratford's trading class. The sons and heirs of butcher, baker and glovemaker who served their time as burgesses and aldermen, the three men are likely to have been classmates at the Grammar School, Tyler entering at the same time as Gilbert Shakespeare. William Tyler the butcher, Richard's father, was appointed a burgess in September 1564 at the same time as John Shakespeare, twice serving as Bailiff in 1577–8 and 1585–6, and was Alderman until his retirement in January 1599. Richard inherited his father's house in Sheep St. and also held property in Chapel Lane (SCLA BRU8/3/7). Sadler seems to have been brought up in the household of his uncle and aunt, Roger and Margaret Sadler in Henley St., following his uncle's trade of baker. Roger Sadler, who had been a constable with John Shakespeare in 1559 and an alderman until 1578, made his 'cosin' Hamnet his chief beneficiary and executor in his will proved in January 1579 (TNA PROB11/61/33). He bequeathed to him three tenements in Church St., and, after the death of his wife, the lease of the house in which he was living. Sadler was tortoise to Tyler's hare. His highest civic office was Constable in 1593. Tyler, at least four years younger, was elected burgess in 1589 but stopped attending Corporation meetings after a few years and disappears from the Council minutes in July 1594 (Fox 1990, p. 24).

Richard the elder, as Shakespeare writes him to distinguish him from his son of the same name born in 1592, is described as gentleman in 1604

(Folger Z.e.8 p. 21). In the 1598 assessment of grainholding in the town, Tyler held more than his social and financial equals Julyns Shaw, Hamnet Sadler's brother-in-law John Smith, Alderman Henry Walker, Anthony Nash and Shakespeare (Fox 1990, pp. 135–40). He was the subject of scandal in the winter of 1588 when he married, for love and without her parents' blessing, Susanna Woodward, then around sixteen, daughter of 'wealthy Puritan' Richard Woodward of Shottery (Fripp 1924, p. 55). And Tyler was not above a street brawl. He was charged for affray in January 1607 and again in May (Bearman 2011, pp. 407–8 and 448) but his opponent was Thomas Lucas, that notoriously prickly character.

What had happened between January and March 1616? About the time that Shakespeare called in Francis Collins to change his will, he may have heard the news that Tyler had been named in a complaint from the Corporation of Stratford to the Lord Chancellor for mishandling their funds meant for the relief of victims of Stratford's third disastrous fire in twenty years (Eccles 1961, p. 136). Tyler with four others had been granted a licence to collect alms from neighbouring towns and counties for rebuilding the town (SCLA ER1/1/65) but the collection did not go smoothly, with complaints that the collectors were slow to gather in money and even slower to present their accounts. Tyler, described as 'unreasonably slack', was taken off the Commission, despite his protestations that the burgesses had shown little interest in receiving his collections (SCLA BRU15/16/14). In the winter of 1597–8 Sadler had accompanied Richard Quiney, a member of the Corporation and a school friend of Sadler's, to collect alms in Suffolk and Norfolk after the fires of 1594 and 1595, for which Quiney paid Sadler £8 3s 4d, some of which might have been reparation for fire damage (SCLA ER1/1/43). Robert Bearman notes that Quiney regularly dispensed money directly to claimants and pocketed expenses without the funds passing through the hands of the Corporation (Bearman 1994, p. 32). Twenty years later more precise accounting was expected. Tyler's reputation survived as, in September the same year, his Sheep St. neighbours approved his collecting alms from the County of Kent for his own use, presumably for his costs and his own repairs (SCLA BRU15/1/201).

Meanwhile, immediately after the death of his uncle, Sadler married; his first child John was born in September 1580. As well as his inheritance, he occupied a house on the corner of Sheep St, and High St, opposite Henry Walker, and held property from the manor of Rowington, which he surrendered in 1596 (Ryland 1896, p. 201). In 1599 he was given three years to find the money to replace the thatch he had used to reroof his fire-damaged buildings with more expensive but less flammable tile (SCLA BRU15/12/54). From the late 1590s through the 1600s he was involved in disputes with fellow townsmen over non-payment of debts mostly related to his business. Sadler's payments from Quiney for travelling with him on Corporation business stopped with Quiney's murder in 1602. In 1594 and 1603 he was presented for non-compliance with the Assize of Bread (SCLA BRU12/liii, fo. 55v, BRU15/12/71), in 1608 for having a muckhill in front of his house to the annoyance of the market traders (SCLA BRU15/12/95).

Sadler and his wife Judith had fourteen children between 1580 and 1599, of whom six died as infants. There is an authentic picture of their married life in Elizabeth Quiney's letter to her husband away in London with Sadler probably around January 1598: 'Judith Sadler waxeth very heavy for the burden of her childing and also of the want of her husband' (SCLA ER1/97 fo. 142v–143v). Judith died in March 1614, leaving her husband with three children under eighteen in his care. The lack of a mother's attention may explain or excuse the consequent behaviour of their daughter Judith. As Shakespeare redrafted his will in reaction to the scandalous behaviour of his own Judith's new husband, Sadler's twenty-year-old daughter was three months pregnant with a fatherless child, christened Robert on 21 September 1616. One suspects that Shakespeare, had he known of Sadler's scandal, would have taken the same hard line as he had towards the misdemeanours of Richard Tyler.

William Walker was only seven-and-a-half when Shakespeare left him 20s in gold. Shakespeare may have known this small boy as a playmate of his granddaughter Elizabeth, who was more or less the same age, but was likely acknowledging his friendship with his father Henry Walker, mercer and alderman of Stratford. They may been thrown together in 1608, when Shakespeare, unusually, resorted to Stratford's court of record to pursue one John Addenbrooke for a debt of £6. As bailiff that year, Walker presided over the Court. There is no evidence that Walker played more than an official role (Lewis 1940, II, pp. 393–400), nevertheless two months after the beginning of the suit, he invited Shakespeare to stand as godfather to his second child, William, on 16 October and Shakespeare, perhaps in Stratford to attend his mother's funeral on 8 September and to pursue his suit while the theatres were closed by plague in London, accepted.

How many godchildren had William Shakespeare? When Hamnet Sadler stood godfather to Hamnet Shakespeare the striking Christian name they shared made clear the links of friendship between the families. The young Williams, sons of Hamnet Sadler and Richard Tyler baptised on 5 February and 9 July 1598 respectively and young adults by 1616, might have been godchildren named for the poet but were not named by him in his will.

The Walker family connections with the Shakespeares dated back to 1558, when the will of their kinsman, Henry Walker of Snitterfield, was witnessed by Richard Shakespeare, William's grandfather. William Walker's father leased a tenement in Chapel Street from the Corporation in 1601 where the Town Hall now stands. He was one of the stalwarts of Stratford Corporation, being bailiff three times and alderman until his death in November 1644 (SCLA BRU2/3 p. 238). When he grew up William followed his father's trade of mercer, and showed the same commitment to the town, serving with him as a member of the Corporation for seven years between 1637 when he was first elected burgess (SCLA BRU2/3 p. 145) and his father's death. He was promoted to alderman in September 1648 and within a year was elected bailiff (SCLA BRU2/3 25 p. 318). William Walker was buried in Stratford on 1 March 1681. Reminiscing about his childhood, he may have shared with John Ward the story of how his last sight of his famous godfather was drinking hard with a Mr Drayton from Clifford Chambers and an old friend up from London.

The friends that Shakespeare remembered in his will were of all ages and of all classes, though many laid claim to the title gentleman or played a significant part in the civic life of Stratford-upon-Avon. Through them Shakespeare was acquainted with the gentry of Warwickshire and the surrounding counties, whose social and business connections he certainly exploited. It is not inconceivable that on a single day most of them may have passed though the Guild Hall to attend court, presiding, suing and being sued for debt and misdemeanours, breaking rules and regulations, and even grievous bodily harm, or serving as witnesses or attorneys on behalf of others. How did this group of Stratford citizens come to be the poet's special friends? Perhaps like Jonson, they responded to Shakespeare's 'open and free nature' (Jonson 2012, p. 522) and he to theirs, for almost all were mavericks in some way – only his godson and his godson's father led long and stainless lives.

WORKS CITED

Primary

Exact references are included in the text

SCLA   Shakespeare Centre Library and Archive, Shakespeare Birthplace Trust, Stratford-upon-Avon
TNA   The National Archives, London
WAAS   Worcestershire Archive and Archaeology Service

Secondary

Alcock, N. W. with Bearman, R. 2002. 'Discovering Mary Arden's House: Property and society in Wilmcot, Warwickshire', *Shakespeare Quarterly*, 53.1: 53–82

Bearman, R. 1994. *Shakespeare in the Stratford Records*. Stroud. Alan Sutton Publishing

(ed.) 2011. *Minutes and accounts of the Corporation of Stratford-upon-Avon and other Records, vol. VI 1599–1609*. Stratford-upon-Avon. Dugdale Society

(ed.) in progress. *Minutes and accounts of the Corporation of Stratford-upon-Avon and other Records, vol. VII 1610–1620*. Stratford-upon-Avon. Dugdale Society (Dr Bearman kindly allowed access to his forthcoming edition which also includes correspondence on Corporation business)

Bloom, J. H. 1893. Transcripts of the register of Clifford Chambers, unpublished MS

Brinkworth, E. R. C. 1972. *Shakespeare and the Bawdy Court of Stratford*. London. Phillimore

Bruce, J. (ed.) 1860. *Calendar of state papers: domestic series, of the reign of Charles I, 1629–1631 preserved in the State Paper Department of Her Majesty's Public Record Office*. London. Longman, Green, Longman, & Roberts

Chambers, E. K. 1930. *William Shakespeare: A Study of Facts and Problems*. 2 vols. Oxford. Clarendon Press

Drayton, M. 1953. *Poems*. J. Buxton (ed.), 2 vols. London. Routledge & Kegan Paul

Eccles, M. 1961. *Shakespeare in Warwickshire*. Madison. University of Wisconsin Press

Edmond, M. 2009. 'Heminges, John (bap. 1566, d. 1630)', in *Oxford Dictionary of National Biography*, online edn, Oxford University Press http://0-www.oxforddnb.com.pugwash.lib.warwick.ac.uk/view/article/12890, accessed 19 Oct. 2014

Fox, L. (ed.) 1990. *Minutes and Accounts of the Corporation of Stratford-upon-Avon and other records. vol. V 1593–1598*. Hertford. Stephen Austin for the Dugdale Society

Fripp, E. I. 1924. *Master Richard Quyny Bailiff of Stratford-upon-Avon and friend of William Shakespeare*. Oxford University Press

(ed.) 1929. *Minutes and accounts of the Corporation of Stratford-upon-Avon and other records. vol. IV 1586–92*. London. Oxford University Press for the Dugdale Society

1938. *Shakespeare: Man and Artist*, the 2 vols. Oxford University Press

Hotson, J. L. 1937. *I, William Shakespeare do appoint Thomas Russell, Esquire*. London. Jonathan Cape

Ingleby, C. M. (ed.) 1885. *Shakespeare and the enclosure of common fields at Welcombe : Being a fragment of the private diary of Thomas Greene, town clerk of Stratford-upon-Avon, 1614–1617*. Birmingham, printed for the editor by Robert Birbeck

Jonson, B. 2012. 'Timber: or, Discoveries: Made upon men and matter' in D. Bevington, M. Butler, I. Donaldson (eds.), *The Cambridge Edition of the Works of Ben Jonson*, 7 vols. Cambridge University Press.

Lane, J. 1996. *John Hall and his Patients*. Stratford-upon-Avon. Alan Sutton

Lewis, B. R. 1940. *The Shakespeare Documents*. 2 vols. Stanford University Press

Newdigate, B. H. 1941. *Michael Drayton and his Circle*. Oxford. Shakespeare Head Press

Prescott, A. L. 2008. 'Drayton, Michael (1563–1631)', in *Oxford Dictionary of National Biography*, online edn. Oxford University Press. http://0-www.oxforddnb.com.pugwash.lib.warwick.ac.uk/view/article/8042, accessed 19 Oct. 2014

Pringle, R. 2013. 'The muses quiet port: Clifford Chambers and Michael Drayton' in *Round the Square and up the Tower: Clifford Chambers Warwickshire*. Clifford Chambers. Hosking Houses Trust and http://hoskinghouses.co.uk/wp/place-and-setting/the-muses-quiet-port/, accessed 19 Oct. 2014

Ryland, J. W. 1896. *Records of Rowington being extracts from the deeds in the possession of the feoffees of the Rowington Charities*. Birmingham. Cooper

Schoenbaum, S. 1975. *Shakespeare: A Documentary Life*. Oxford. Clarendon Press in association with Scolar Press

Smith, G. G. (ed.) 1904. *Elizabethan Critical Essays*. 2 vols. London. Oxford University Press

Thomas, D. & Cox, J. 1985. *Shakespeare in the Public Records*. London. Public Record Office

Ward, J. 1839. *Diary of the Rev. John Ward A.M. Vicar of Stratford-upon-Avon extending from 1648 to 1679*. C. Severn (ed.). London. Henry Colburn

Wellstood, F. W. 1919. *Records of the Manor of Henley in Arden*. Stratford-upon-Avon. Shakespeare Head Press

Whitfield, C. 1961. 'The Kinship of Thomas Combe II, William Reynolds and William Shakespeare', *Notes and Queries* (vol. 206 NS 8): 364–72

1962. *Robert Dover and the Cotswold Games: Annalia Dubrensia.* London. Sotheran

1964. 'Four Town Clerks of Stratford on Avon, 1603–1625'. *Notes & Queries* (vol. 209 NS 11): 251–61

1967. 'Anthony and John Nash: Shakespeare's legatees'. *Notes and Queries* (vol. 212, NS 14): 123–30

Wood, M. 2003. *In Search of Shakespeare.* London. BBC

PART III

❧

Colleagues and patrons

Among Shakespeare's most significant colleagues are some of his closest and longest-lasting friends. We decided to place three of the most significant people in his professional life – Richard Burbage, John Heminges and Henry Condell – here because their intertwining careers seem to have been the foundation of strong friendships. Other members of the Burbage family, James the father and Cuthbert, Richard's older brother, were among Shakespeare's professional friends. Among the colleagues included here are several rivals. Playwrights who collaborated, it may be assumed, were by the nature of their profession always seeking to outshine their colleague-competitors.

Andy Kesson presents Shakespeare as a newcomer on an already well-established literary and theatrical scene, re-reading the famous remarks published in *Greene's Groatsworth of Wit* (now attributed to Henry Chettle) not as an attack from which Shakespeare needs defending, but 'as the opportunity to see the early Shakespeare from the perspective of his new colleagues in the London theatres' (p. 236). Some writers who collaborated with Shakespeare may not yet have been identified; likewise 'Shakespeare' may still be quietly present in plays in which his hand has not yet been identified. As a result of this, some of his writing may 'survive in forms which are no longer associated with his authorship' (p. 246).

Setting the scene for Shakespeare's arrival was the Burbage family of which the founding patriarch, James, was influential and innovative in the emergence of what was to become the professional theatre. His brother-in-law, John Brayne, financed the first public playhouse, The Red Lion in Stepney, 'the structural model for all the outdoor theatres that followed it' (p. 250), the first of which, The Theatre, was built by James Burbage. As John H. Astington points out, James was a member of the Earl of Leicester's Men, the most prominent company of its day. It performed in Stratford-upon-Avon in 1573 when Shakespeare was nine, and 'we may think that Shakespeare's turn to the theatre was influenced in his boyhood by Richard Burbage's father' (p. 250). The Burbages remind us of the tough-edged nature of the theatrical profession; Richard himself was referred to as 'a stubborn fellow' (p. 254). They seem to have been around at Shakespeare's initiation into the world of the theatre, and would remain there for the rest of his life and beyond.

Two other actors, the broad comedian Will Kemp and his successor in the company, the more intellectually witty and musical Robert Armin, come under the special focus of Bart van Es, who, in thinking afresh about how Shakespeare's work was formed, highlights 'the transformative effect that these individuals had on the playwright's style' (p. 262). He reminds us of the international success of English theatre at this time, exemplified by Kemp's and other company members' continental travels and reputations as singers and acrobats as well as actors. It is fascinating to think about how these men first came to know about each other and recognised how they could mutually enhance each other's creative lives.

Elizabethan and Jacobean literature flourished under patronage at a variety of social levels, including royalty, the supporting aristocracy and other members of the nobility. City playhouses were supported by the enabling fiction that the performances were dress rehearsals for Court appearances, the ever-respectable face of theatre and a useful escape route from Puritanical censure. The theatre companies that Shakespeare was associated with performed hundreds of times at Court under royal patronage during the reigns of Elizabeth I, James I and Charles I (p. 321). Alan H. Nelson regards literary rather than theatrical patronage as being of most interest for the study of Shakespeare's friendships. All of his non-dramatic works had patrons, not necessarily aristocratic. The famous 'Mr W. H.' to whom the printer Thomas Thorpe dedicated the Sonnets in 1609 is sometimes discussed as though he were a nobleman in disguise, but in 2015 Geoffrey Caveney plausibly suggested a new non-aristocratic nominee, the publishing associate, William Holme (Alberge 2015). Nelson takes the view that Shakespeare himself had no direct involvement with the publication of the Sonnets.

Three identifiable collaborators with Shakespeare are his fellow playwrights George Wilkins, Thomas Middleton and John Fletcher. It is possible that George Wilkins, as the keeper of both inns and brothels, had a unique insight into the private lives of members of the Shakespeare circle. As well as co-authoring *Pericles*, Wilkins, like Shakespeare, testified in the Belott–Mountjoy case of 1612. Duncan Salkeld, who has worked extensively in the archives of Bridewell prison (to which sexual offenders were consigned) notes that 'Belott and his wife Mary took lodging in a chamber belonging to Wilkins just after their marriage' (p. x). From the 1980s, Thomas Middleton has emerged as a significant Shakespearian collaborator, both as a co-author of *Timon of Athens* and as an adapter of the surviving texts of *Measure for Measure* and *Macbeth*. As Emma Smith points out, forms of collaboration included 'play-patching, division between plot and sub-plot or between outline and realisation, the sub-contracting of acts or specific speeches, a junior writer apprenticed to a more experienced colleague' (p. 301). John Fletcher, the son of a bishop and a graduate of Corpus Christi College, Cambridge, was fifteen years younger than Shakespeare. He was a man of learning and relatively high social status, as his portrait demonstrates, who had already gained experience in collaborating with Francis Beaumont before joining up with Shakespeare. Lucy Munro, pointing to a close relationship between the morris dance in *The Two Noble Kinsmen* and the second antimasque dance in Beaumont's *The Masque of the Inner Temple and Gray's Inn*, which gave 'spectators at the Blackfriars a glimpse of courtly entertainment', fascinatingly speculates that 'Beaumont, Fletcher and Shakespeare may have planned further collaborations' (p. 310).

This section ends with Paul Edmondson tracing a similar rise in social status between Shakespeare and the two men who were to be largely responsible for his posthumous fame, John Heminges and Henry Condell. As churchwardens and sidesmen of St Mary's Church, Aldermanbury, they were highly respected members of their communities. Shakespeare's professional relationship with them may have started as early as 1593 and they remained close friends for the rest of his life.

WORKS CITED

Alberge, Dalya 2015. 'Has the Mystery of Shakespeare's Sonnets Finally Been Solved?' *The Guardian* www.theguardian.com/culture/2015/jan/31/shakespeare-sonnets-mr-wh-dedication-mystery, accessed 12 February 2015

18

His fellow dramatists and early collaborators

ANDY KESSON

Around the time that Shakespeare was putting a dog on stage in *The Two Gentlemen of Verona*, a contemporary was accusing him of being an animal. Though Ben Jonson would later call him the 'Sweet swan of Avon' (Oxford Shakespeare, p. lxxi) in a commendatory poem published in the First Folio, the first reference to Shakespeare in print called him a crow and a tiger. Alongside these animal references, Shakespeare also found himself called a puppet, an upstart and 'an absolute Johannes fac totum' (which means something like 'jack of all trades, master of none' or 'know-it-all') (*Greene's Groatsworth* 1592, pp. 83–5). This was not only the first recorded response to Shakespeare's work, but the first appearance of Shakespeare in print. Shakespeare had clearly been writing work for the theatre and his earliest sonnets may well have already circulated in manuscript, and much of this early work would later be printed for book readers. He nevertheless first appeared in a book as the subject of discussion, rather than its author. Though he would later come to be venerated by playgoers, readers and actors, this first appearance makes clear that he could be an object of vitriol to at least one of his contemporaries, an untrustworthy beast operating beyond his powers who should be avoided by other playwrights. Why might Shakespeare appear that way to his early contemporaries?

The pamphlet attacking Shakespeare was called *Greene's Groatsworth of Wit*. It purported to be by the fiction-writer and playwright Robert Greene, but is now more generally thought to have been written by the writer and printer, Henry Chettle (Jowett, 1993). Because they have been drawn to their subject through their love of Shakespearian drama, Shakespeare scholars, and particularly biographers, have tended to assume there must be something wrong with the *Groatsworth* vision of an imperfect, parvenu Shakespeare whose work was provocative to contemporaries.

Indeed, the *Groatsworth* has been as threatening to Shakespeare scholarship as Shakespeare seems to have been for the *Groatsworth* author. Schoenbaum calls the debate generated by *Groatsworth* 'wearying' (Schoenbaum 1970, p. 51), quoting John Semple Smart's opinion that 'This passage from Greene has had such a devastating effect on Shakespearian study that we cannot but wish it had never been written or never discovered' (Smart 1928, p. 196). Park Honan, a scholar not given to rhetorical excess, describes it as 'virtually a rape of Shakespeare' (Honan 1998, p. 158). Since Shakespeare scholars almost universally approach this passage with hostility or contempt, it seems likely that Smart and Honan here articulate a position that informs many readings of this passage. As Russell Fraser notes, biographies often ignore anything 'unedifying' in their accounts of Shakespeare's life (Fraser 1988, p. 90). Greene's supposed hatred for Shakespeare has become so important for Shakespeare scholarship that it continues to be identified with Greene despite John Jowett's highly convincing demonstration that Greene was almost certainly not the writer of the attack. Germaine Greer, for example, refers to Greene twice in her book *Shakespeare's Wife* as 'Shakespeare's old enemy' (Greer 2007, pp. 204 and 302), whilst Stephen Greenblatt's biography of Shakespeare uses Greene's supposed authorship of *Groatsworth* as the foundation for an unlikely theory that Falstaff in some way represents Greene himself (Greenblatt 2004, p. 218). Unfounded assumptions about the authorship of *Groatsworth* and the kind of dissatisfaction it articulates have produced misunderstandings of Shakespeare's early and subsequent career; in addition to Greenblatt's Falstaff, for example, the highly productive connection between Shakespeare's *The Winter's Tale* and Greene's *Pandosto* has not been appreciated by scholars who see the two men's relationship as essentially antagonistic. *Groatsworth* has been treated as something to attack, or a document from which Shakespeare needs defence or exoneration, rather than as the opportunity to see the early Shakespeare from the perspective of his new colleagues in the London theatres.

Because of this fixation on the negative language of the *Groatsworth*, and the consequent need to explain it away, most accounts of Shakespeare's first appearance in print make reference only to the terms puppet, upstart, tiger, crow and *Johannes fac totum*. But in the pamphlet, these terms are followed by a sentence that helps to put them in context, but which has received rather less attention:

For other newcomers, I leave them to the mercy of these painted monsters, who (I doubt not) will drive the best minded to despise them (*Greene's Groatsworth* 1592, p. 86).

It is not entirely clear whether Shakespeare is envisaged here as part of the 'newcomers' or the 'painted monsters' (or both), but this sentence is useful for the way it characterises its own moment in terms *both* of newcomers *and* (newer, or at least upstart) monsters. This sentence has not only been overlooked by Shakespeare scholars, but its very terms have sometimes been flatly denied. Thus Ernst Honigmann, for example, insists that *Groatsworth* attacks Shakespeare as 'a social upstart, not a newcomer' (Honigmann 1988, pp. xiii and 1), and goes on to argue that 'Aged 28, Shakespeare is not a complete newcomer on the literary scene, for Robert Greene, one of the most popular writers of the previous decade, regards him as a serious threat'. These are odd assertions given that the word 'newcomer' is specifically employed as part of the *Groatsworth* attack. The pamphlet gives access to a Shakespeare who was a newcomer in the eyes of his early, more established colleagues.

Debates around Shakespearian authorship often depend on whether scholars see him as a sole author or as someone who occasionally collaborated with other writers, and a more collaborative Shakespeare has emerged from scholarly debate. But in many ways his most important collaborations were not with writers but with playhouse entrepreneurs and theatre company business men (and it is worth remembering that those who ran playhouse buildings were not always the same men who ran playing companies), along with actors, carpenters and those who organised costumes, props and stage effects. Indeed, it is Shakespeare's emergence from these collaborators into the world of writing, as an actor becoming a playwright, that seems to animate the *Groatsworth* attack. This chapter therefore tries to resituate Shakespeare the 'newcomer' by seeing him as he arrived in the world of the London playhouses, which were even newer than Shakespeare himself.

Three years after Shakespeare's birth, the first Elizabethan playhouse, the Red Lion, opened a mile outside London in 1567. The Red Lion is often left out of theatre history accounts of the period, or seen as an early but disconnected anticipation of The Theatre, which opened just over ten years later. But in fact several other public playhouses opened soon after 1567. In the following decade, four London city inns – the Bel Savage (by 1575), the Bull (by 1577), the Cross Keys and the Bell (both by 1577/8) – also set up spaces for regular theatrical performance. The choristers at St Paul's were performing in a specially built theatrical space during the same decade, and may have begun doing so much earlier. There was a playhouse in Newington Butts by 1576, which may have been in operation some time earlier. All of this means that The Theatre, often described as London's first Elizabethan playhouse, was in fact somewhere between the fourth to ninth on record when it was built in 1576. It opened in the same year as the new indoor playhouse at the Blackfriars, and the following year saw the Curtain open. Ten years later, in 1587, around the time that Shakespeare might have moved to London or become involved with drama, the Rose opened in Southwark. As Shakespeare grew up, then, an entirely new theatrical culture was also growing up around London.

None of these playhouses were older than William Shakespeare himself. If he seemed like a newcomer to the writer of *Groatsworth*, the playhouses felt new too, as is made clear by the sudden clamour against playgoing on the part of priests and anti-theatrical pamphleteers through the late 1570s and 1580s. But Shakespeare was different to the first people who worked in the new playhouses. We don't know quite when Shakespeare began working as an actor, playwright or theatre businessman, but he did so at a time that seems to have felt like a generational shift. As we have seen, purpose-built commercial playhouses first started to open in and around London from the mid-1560s, and such playhouses continued to be used as theatrical spaces until they were closed down in the early 1640s. That meant that there was a generation of theatre practitioners (working from around 1565 to 1590) for whom the playhouses were completely new, another (c. 1590–1620) who had grown up as the playhouses opened, and a third (c. 1620–42) who might well have taken these buildings for granted. This is helpful because it reminds us that Shakespeare belonged firmly to the middle generation. The *Groatsworth* attack on Shakespeare reminds us that he was an oddity to the first generation of theatre writers. Considering Shakespeare from the earlier period returns us to a time before 'Shakespeare': before his literary fame, the 1623 Folio genre division and his posthumous canonisation. It returns us to a period which did not yet recognise, but was just about to coin, the terms playwright, actor and theatre. It reminds us to see him as strange, even if we might not want to see him as an upstart puppet tiger.

The years immediately preceding the *Groatsworth* attack are often described by biographers as Shakespeare's lost years, defined by a supposed gap in the records between the christening of his twins in Stratford on 2 February 1585 and the *Groatsworth* attack that makes clear that Shakespeare had established some kind of public identity by September 1592. But David Bevington reminds readers of an often forgotten suit brought before the Queen's Bench in October 1589, in which Shakespeare was a party (Bevington 2010, p. 23). Bevington points out that Shakespeare either travelled to London to represent his family or was already living there: 'Perhaps then the so-called seven "lost" years should be reduced by half.' Even so', Bevington continues, 'the late 1580s provide an intriguing gap in the record.' Fraser, meanwhile, points to Shakespeare's suing of John Clayton for £7, lent to him in May 1592 (Fraser 1988, p. 90). These two pieces of evidence, both pointing towards a fiscally minded Shakespeare definitely located in London, have often been left out of accounts of the lost years.

Perhaps more provocatively for our sense of Shakespeare the writer, these lost years deny us the possibility of understanding both the private development and public emergence of Shakespeare the writer. The last two centuries have produced differing accounts of Shakespeare as either a so-called early or late starter, depending on whether he started in the mid-1580s or the early 1590s (see Honigmann 1988, p. 60). Scholarship is also divided between those who see Shakespeare as initially a collaborator or reviser of earlier plays, and others who see him as someone who was, from the start, the sole author of original plays. Finally, it isn't clear which, if any, theatre companies counted Shakespeare amongst their players before his membership of the Chamberlain's Men from 1594 (Honigmann 1988, pp. 59–76; Schoone-Jongen 2008).

If we wish to take seriously the use of the word 'newcomer' in *Groatsworth*, this might help us with some of these issues: the public nature of Shakespeare's authorship, at least, became obvious some time before the 1592 publication of the *Groatsworth*. Whatever Shakespeare was doing before that date, and whatever writing it involved, his authorship was not a matter of public knowledge or consumption until soon before the *Groatsworth* writer was incensed by this apparent newcomer. As David Bevington puts it, *Groatsworth* and its reception 'indicate that Shakespeare was becoming well known in London's theatrical world, and was even a controversial figure' (Bevington 2010, p. 17). But the sense of surprise in *Groatsworth*, in particular, strongly suggests that Shakespeare had only just become well known and controversial before this point, since it appears to be animated by a sense of shock as well as indignation.

Shakespeare's arrival in the second generation to work in the new commercial playhouses was marked by the silencing of most of the writers associated with the first generation. *Greene's Groatsworth of Wit* is, amongst other things, a valediction to life as well as to the stage, since whatever Greene's own contribution was to it, it records or invents his final thoughts. In the early 1590s the major voices of the early playhouses went quiet: alongside Robert Greene, Thomas Kyd, Christopher Marlowe and John Lyly. Perhaps the only early contemporary who continued to write across the length of Shakespeare's own career is Anthony Munday. But Munday's work combined a range of genres very different to those employed by Shakespeare, including political tracts, unfinished prose fiction, translations of Spanish novels and civic pageants. His work therefore serves as another reminder that the form Shakespeare's writing career would go on to take should not be taken for granted. Mary Bly has warned that 'When scholars limit themselves to Shakespeare, the oddness of Renaissance culture is unnoticed' (Bly 2012, p. 113). The opposite is also true: because he is often read in isolation, the oddness of Shakespeare easily goes unnoticed.

Indeed, it is not at all clear what the word 'Shakespearian' would have meant if Shakespeare, like so many of his early contemporaries, had stopped writing within a decade of his first public work. Munday aside, Shakespeare's writing career is significantly longer than that of his early contemporaries, and his later work and its subsequent reception present multiple challenges for understanding his career as it unfolded. Even the relatively brief careers of the writers already mentioned throw up anomalies in our images of them. *Greene's Groatsworth of Wit* is Greene's most famous text, even though he probably did not write it; Marlowe's work is often described as 'Marlovian', but the term's intimations of Machiavellian ambition do not seem to fit a highly eroticised and playful work like *Hero and Leander*; John Lyly, meanwhile, was celebrated in his own lifetime for inaugurating a model for writing which he then went on to transcend. It may therefore be difficult to pin down the idea of the 'Shakespearian' from the point of view of Shakespeare's early collaborators.

Another way to ask this question, then, is to propose a counterfactual narrative which prevents us seeing Shakespeare's early work via his later work or via his subsequent canonisation, a narrative in which, perhaps, Shakespeare died or moved on to another career during his first decade as a professional writer. What meanings would his corpus have for us if Shakespeare had stopped writing in 1595? Might it be possible to reconstruct a non-retrospective Shakespeare: a Shakespeare before 'Shakespeare'? This would give us a clearer sense of how the early Shakespeare felt to his contemporaries.

Given the modern tendency to celebrate Shakespeare's universal, timeless humanity, it is striking that when the author of *Groatsworth* thinks of Shakespeare – and wants us to think of Shakespeare – he remembers the line 'O tiger's heart wrapped in a woman's hide'. As Katherine Duncan-Jones notes, this line associates Shakespeare with his 'exceptionally ruthless and ambitious character [Queen Margaret] who posed a severe threat to the commonwealth' (Duncan-Jones 2011, p. 41). In contrast to the literature of the 1580s, which made successive moves to widen the scope of women readers and women characters in both theatre and prose fiction, violence, anger and misogyny lie at the heart of Shakespeare's early canon. Indeed, the early work is committed to war more thoroughly than that of any other early contemporary, including Marlowe. Perhaps only *The Taming of the Shrew*, *The Comedy of Errors* and *Venus and Adonis* are non-war narratives, and none of these could be described as a pacifist's dream. But the plays also exhibit an unusual wariness of women. If *The Taming of the Shrew* provides an object lesson in the social confinement of women, Tamora, Margaret and Joan of Arc might be said to provide admonitory counterexamples. Frank Hook even suggests that Peele's *Edward I* was revised 'to meet a commercial demand for terrible queens in the wake of Shakespeare's Queen Margaret' (Hook 1961, p. 212). In *The Rape of Lucrece*, *The Two Gentlemen of Verona*, *Titus Andronicus* and *Venus and Adonis* (the latter with the gender roles reversed), Shakespeare returns to the scene of threatened or actual rape. If *The Taming of the Shrew* can be read as an argument for containing women within private, domestic spaces, the lack of women in Shakespeare's other early plays (and elsewhere in his canon) is in striking contrast to the examples of Lyly, Middleton or Webster. Much of the dialogue between the two main women in *The Comedy of Errors* concerns the marginalisation of women, which suggests a playwright aware of this problem, though his work does not suggest an interest in overcoming it onstage. This may explain why the *Groatsworth* has recourse to a line about monstrous femininity when it tries to pinpoint the early Shakespearian.

However, Shakespeare's representation of female characters does permit us to trace one way in which he worked with contemporary playwriting. The ethical challenges of *Titus Andronicus* have inevitably overshadowed the play's exploration of and challenges to contemporary performance. In particular, whatever challenges are posed by the narrative experiences of a character like Lavinia through the play, the principal theatrical challenge the character poses, then and now, strikes at the heart of character itself: how to portray a person who loses the ability to speak and gesture.

In exploring this question, Shakespeare, his collaborators and his company were responding to recent innovations in the new theatres around them, and particularly those innovations associated with the best-selling literary figure of the time, John Lyly (Kesson 2014). Lavinia's mutilations and the challenges they pose to the boy who portrays her are a recapitulation in reverse of Pandora in Lyly's *The Woman in the Moon* (2006, passages described here can be found at I.i.54–90). In Lyly's play, the ultimate deity is female, and her final and most perfect act of creation is the first female human. This is a radical rewriting of the Christian creation story, but it is also an extraordinary rethink of stage possibilities, as Lyly requires a boy actor to appear onstage first as part of the set, then as a prop and finally as a person. Whatever challenges this posed on stage, in print the quarto finds it impossible to refer to this character with any consistency: it is an 'it' and an 'image' before it comes to life, and then 'she' and 'Pandora' thereafter. First the image is brought forth from 'Nature's shop' (presumably in a form of discovery space), then the body is infused with 'spirit', then it starts to move, and finally she is given the power of speech – and it is this power which inaugurates the quarto's use of a gendered pronoun and a name. Indeed, the stage direction '*Image speaks*' is immediately followed by a speech heading, '*Pandora (kneeling)*'. As the play continues, Pandora's identity is repeatedly figured not only through her speech but through a series of unusually carefully scripted gestures: '*She plays the vixen with everything about her*', '*She thrusts her hands in her pocket*'.

Lavinia undergoes this process in reverse. When Pandora thrusts her hands in her pocket or the quarto tells us '*Image speaks*', Lyly's play maps out the very gestures and words that Shakespeare takes away from his character. From a theatrical perspective, it is crucial to note that he also takes them away from his actor: indeed, it is the script's power over the boy's body which enables the illusion of the Goths' power over Lavinia's body. *Titus Andronicus* intersects with other early plays, of course, not least *The Spanish Tragedy*, and the noises of the hunt that dominate the second fifth of this play might usefully be compared with the bell that rings during the same section of *The Massacre of Paris*. But in the figure of Lavinia, Shakespeare can be seen to be responding to and transforming Lyly's recent challenge to the performance of identity and humanity. Given the *Groatsworth* association of Shakespeare with a misogynistic line, we might note that Shakespeare transforms Lyly's celebration of femininity into something much less positive. Instead of a tiger's heart wrapped in a woman's hide, Lavinia's hide becomes a barrier to her heart, her inability to sign in either word or gesture an interpretative impasse to her soul. Once again, seeing Shakespeare via his early contemporaries allows us to see a very different Shakespeare, one invested in the technical possibilities of the actor's body, a concern that works to marginalise as well as victimise the bodies of boys playing women.

Shakespeare's later embrace of the transvestite heroine, another example of Lyly's influence, has often been celebrated by feminist and queer scholars, but it could just as easily be read as another way to decentre women's bodies. In Lyly's *Gallathea*, two girls are forced to dress as boys and quickly fall in love with one another. This love continues even after both girls realise their passion is not heterosexual. Cupid, meanwhile, is bitten by the crossdressing bug, and spends much of the play dressed as a girl. This is a play that Shakespeare repeatedly returned to, from *The Two Gentlemen of Verona* to *The Tempest* (Scragg 1982), but his re-enactments of *Gallathea* tend to downplay its queerness and its exploration of female identity. Rather than a boy dressed as a girl dressed as a boy, Shakespeare may simply be giving us a boy dressed as a boy.

The play *Locrine* is a good site from which to think through early Shakespeare and the representation of different kinds of authorship. The title-page to this play names somebody called W.S. as a figure who has given an existing play some kind of new treatment: 'Newly set forth, overseen and corrected, by W. S.' As Peter Kirwan has pointed out, previous models of Shakespeare's authorship tend towards binary positions in which a play is either in or out of the canon (Kirwan 2015). The *Locrine* title-page refuses any such reading, presenting the play instead as an older text in which a more recent intervention by W.S. is deemed significant enough to be described in terms which may suggest revision, rewriting or reworking, whether for performance or publication. Kirwan puts this in the more cautious terms of translation or compiling, but the point still stands:

> W. S. is in some way responsible for the text's new form in a capacity substantive enough to elevate him to the level of a translator or compiler ... The pattern of initials, and the careful qualification of the role of W.S., certainly fits with the possibility that this could be the first, modest announcement of Shakespeare's participation in the creation of a dramatic text. (Kirwan 2015, p. 133)

Such an elevation, brought about by an intervention in other people's plays, may explain the fury at the newcomer-upstart recorded in the *Groatsworth*. Both Shakespeare's potential connection to the play and the publisher's decision to enunciate W.S.'s connection to it make provocative challenges to traditional notions of the Shakespearian, as Sonia Massai notes:

> This blind spot [an inability to recognise Shakespeare in the play] may be due to our expectation of what Shakespeare's debut in print should have looked like: 'W.S.' is not a literary dramatist self-consciously using the medium of print for the sole purpose of shaping his literary reputation; 'W.S.' is a popular dramatist whose name is for the first time deemed attractive enough to entice readers to buy the edition of an older play. (Massai 2009, p. 7)

Kirwan points out that, though scholarship has accepted a model of Shakespeare's early career as essentially collaborative, it has been less ready to accept specific claims to collaboration 'except where those contributions are distinguished *a priori* as bibliographically distinct' (i.e., *More* or *The Spanish Tragedy*). This is especially surprising since, as Kirwan notes, W.S. is given the only credit in 1595 for what had been an earlier, collaborative play. This is exactly what the *Groatsworth* author had complained about three years earlier. As Roslyn Knutson notes, 'On the whole, new plays were the most profitable members in the repertory of every company in the diary' (Knutson 1985, p. 2). But new plays also required a greater injection of capital, since they needed to be commissioned and paid for. A 'newcomer' playwright, busily revising older plays, may have seemed a threat to established writers of plays since he offered theatre companies a cheaper way to make their existing repertories work for them, rather than commissioning entirely new works.

Terence Schoone-Jongen has argued that '*Groatsworth* proves that Shakespeare, after having been an actor for some time, was a playwright of at least some note by September of 1592' (Schoone-Jongen 2008, p. 35). But is that a fair summary of the early Shakespeare as the *Groatsworth* sees him? It might be more accurate to summarise the *Groatsworth* attack as a depiction of a professional writer addressing other professional writers with regard to an actor who wants to be a playwright *but cannot quite do it*. This is not how the passage is usually understood. Eric Sams, for example, suggests that *Groatsworth* 'need not denote a Johnny-come-lately. On the contrary, the playwright thus described must surely have been already successful' (Sams 1995, p. 68). This quasi-writer is an inter-polator, someone whose work is imbricated into others' writing and who is then credited as its sole or primary creator. If this reading of *Groatsworth* has any validity, it does not quite square with Schoone-Jongen's depiction of the pamphlet as evidence of Shakespeare as 'a playwright of at least some note'. We might instead read *Groatsworth* in the opposite direction: this is a pamphlet that wants to identify Shakespeare as a non-playwright of some note. It is, in other words, a document that records changes in the playwriting culture of the new playhouses and marks out Shakespeare as the newcomer most representative of those changes.

Shakespeare, then, was an unfamiliar sort of writer to his immediate contemporaries, and the early period of his career is helpful in allowing us to see that unfamiliarity. Because of his later canonisation, we have tended to take him, his career and the playhouses he worked in for granted. The period between 1565 and 1595 witnessed a commercial, enterpreneurial, popular, creative, literary and theatrical revolution. Neil Rhodes has insisted that the epigraph to *Venus and Adonis* shows that the early Shakespeare 'signals that he will achieve literary immortality not with crowd-pleasing pap, but by drinking from the fountain of the god [Apollo] himself. In his first publication, in fact, Shakespeare presents himself as Jonson was to do: as an exclusive, high-end writer, defying Envy and hugely ambitious' (Rhodes 2013, p. 102). He is the first writer working for the new playhouses to mark himself out in this manner, at least in print.

One of the challenges of this early period is to understand what we mean by sole authorship at a time when much, perhaps all writing ought to be understood as both potentially anonymous and collaborative. Like 'non-plussed', 'unkempt' and 'nonchalant', 'anonymous' seems to be one of those English negatives for which there is no direct opposite. It may be worth considering the various ways in which Shakespeare operated as both an anonymous and a non-anonymous theatrical practitioner in the early part of his career, to think in terms of a paradoxically anonymous or partially anonymous Shakespeare: someone whose writing might not be associated with his authorship in his lifetime, someone whose writing was much more dissipated than the 1623 collection might suggest and might therefore survive in forms which are no longer associated with his author-ship. The *Groatsworth* is, in this sense, highly contradictory in its sense of a writer with no real identity yet whose house style can also be summoned with a single line. These ideas seem to inform some of the problems with the early Shakespeare and his – and our – notion of his career. As I often say to my students when they worry about future employment, the word 'career' is misleading as a noun, much more accurate as a verb. Early Shakespeare careered through multiple professional possibilities – actor, business man, playwright – and, as *Groatsworth* shows, such careering prompted clashes and collaborations in the very definition of authorship itself.

WORKS CITED

Bevington, David 2010. *Shakespeare and Biography*. Oxford University Press

Bly, Mary 2012. 'Defining the Proper Members of the Renaissance Theatrical Community', *Renaissance Drama* 40: 113–23

Duncan-Jones, Katherine 2011. *Shakespeare: Upstart Crow to Sweet Swan 1592–1623*. London. Methuen Drama

Fraser, Russell 1988. *Young Shakespeare*. New York. Columbia University Press

Greenblatt, Stephen 2004. *Will in the World: How Shakespeare Became Shakespeare*. New York. Norton

Greene 1592. *Greene's Groatsworth of Wit Bought with a Million of Repentance (1592): Attributed to Henry Chettle and Robert Greene* 1994. D. Allen Carroll (ed.). Binghamton, NY: Medieval & Renaissance Texts & Studies

Greer, Germaine 2007. *Shakespeare's Wife*. London. Bloomsbury

Honan, Park 1998. *Shakespeare: A Life*. Oxford University Press

Honigmann, E. A. J. 1988. *Shakespeare: The 'Lost Years'*. Manchester University Press

Hook, Frank 1961. *The Life and Works of George Peele*, 3 vols. Vol. 2. London. Yale University Press

Jowett, John 1993. 'Johannes factotum: Henry Chettle and *Green's Groatsworth of Wit*', *Bibliographical Society of America* 87.4: 453–86

Kesson, Andy 2014. *John Lyly and Early Modern Authorship*. Manchester University Press

Kirwan, Peter 2015. *Shakespeare and the Idea of Apocrypha: Negotiating the Boundaries of the Dramatic Canon*. Cambridge University Press

Knutson, Roslyn 1985. 'Henslowe's Diary and the Economics of Play Revision for Revival 1592–1603', *Theatre Research International* 10: 1–18

Lyly, John 2006. *The Woman in the Moon*. Leah Scragg (ed.). Manchester University Press

Massai, Sonia 2009. 'Shakespeare, Text and Paratext'. *Shakespeare Survey 62*. Peter Holland (ed.) Cambridge University Press, pp. 1–11

Rhodes, Neil 2013. 'Shakespeare's Popularity and the Origins of the Canon' in Andy Kesson and Emma Smith (eds.), *The Elizabethan Top Ten: Defining Print Popularity in Early Modern England*. Farnham. Ashgate

Sams, Eric 1995. *The Real Shakespeare: Retrieving the Early Years, 1564–1594*. London. Yale University Press

Schoenbaum, S. 1970. *Shakespeare's Lives*. Oxford. Clarendon Press

Schoone-Jongen, Terence 2008. *Shakespeare's Companies: William Shakespeare's Early Career and the Acting Companies, 1577–1594*. Farnham. Ashgate

Scragg, Leah 1982. *The Metamorphosis of 'Gallathea': A Study in Creative Adaptation*. Washington, DC. University Press of America

Smart, John Semple 1928. *Shakespeare: Truth and Tradition*. London. Edward Arnold

19

His theatre friends: the Burbages

JOHN H. ASTINGTON

§

The Burbage family dominated theatrical enterprise in London for three-quarters of a century. Shakespeare appears to have entered their larger family of colleagues and collaborators in the early 1590s, and remained a friend until his death in 1616, or for roughly a third of the Burbages' career of management and entrepreneurship, spread over three generations. The men of the family predominate in standard histories of the stage – James, the father, and his two sons Cuthbert and Richard – but women were equally significant in the family enterprise, particularly James's wife Ellen (née Brayne), who lived until 1613, and Richard's wife Winifred (née Turner), who remained a shareholder in the family's theatre properties practically until the parliamentary closing of the theatres in 1642. For more than sixty years the Burbages lived in Shoreditch, a region of the northern London suburbs with a rich theatrical culture, examined at more length in what follows.

Both James and Richard were actors, as Cuthbert never was, the younger son eclipsing the father in fame and skill, and acting until the very end of his life; Richard Burbage died, probably quite suddenly, at the age of fifty, three years after the death of his colleague and collaborator Shakespeare. His brother later wrote that he had a thirty-five-year career on the stage. It was Richard whom Shakespeare would have seen and talked to practically daily for roughly twenty years, the talented interpreter of all his major parts, from Richard III to Prospero. His face, voice, physique and gesture were familiar to many, from the monarchs Elizabeth and James to the lowliest regular playgoers at the Globe. He died in March 1619 shortly after the death of King James's wife Queen Anne, and mourning for him is said to have overshadowed that for her. If we think of him now as the first truly great English tragic actor, in the line of Betterton, Garrick and Kean, contemporary praise hailed him, as it did his great coeval Edward Alleyn, as a 'delightful Proteus', capable of considerable range and versatility. As a leading member of a repertory company Burbage would have taken larger parts in all the plays they staged, including Shakespeare's and Jonson's comedies.

The founding patriarch of the family, James Burbage, creator of two important theatre buildings, was probably born just outside London, at Bromley in Kent, about 1531, of the same generation as Shakespeare's father John, both men who grew up during the English Reformation and the religious and political turmoil of the 1550s. Apprenticed in London as a joiner, Burbage married a Londoner, Ellen Brayne, in 1559, and established a household in the centre of the city. His two sons who survived to adulthood were both christened in the parish of St Stephen Coleman Street, Cuthbert in 1565 and Richard in 1568. By completing his apprenticeship Burbage had become a London citizen and freeman, and his sons inherited his status. Although much of Shakespeare's adult life was spent in London, he was never, as the Burbages were, among its citizens. James appears to have practised his trade as joiner – a woodworker in furniture and domestic fittings, distinct from the construction and building trade of carpenter – for a year or two following his marriage, but became increasingly involved as a stage player with the troupe of the Earl of Leicester, the prominent Elizabethan aristocrat and politician, rising to lead the company by 1572. The growth of the Burbage family fortunes depended on the continued patronage of powerful figures, of whom Leicester was the first. Before the foundation of the Queen's Men in 1583, Leicester's was probably the most accomplished Elizabethan troupe of actors, and as a servant of the Earl Burbage gained both political and artistic distinction.

Before the building of permanent playhouses in London, an enterprise in which Burbage was a pioneer, theatre companies spent much of their time touring elsewhere in England. Indeed, Leicester's men seem to have had within their founding brief their patron's desire to spread his name and goodwill about the country, in areas where he had interests and allies (MacLean 2002, pp. 246–71). Though a London citizen and permanent resident, then, Burbage must have spent a good deal of his thirties and forties on the road, moving from place to place, and making do with temporary accommodation. Touring continued to be part of a player's life in subsequent years, and Richard Burbage probably visited some of the same inns and played his roles in some of the same town halls as his father had before him. From a Shakespearian perspective, one of the more intriguing touring performances by Leicester's Men was given on their visit to Stratford-upon-Avon in 1573, when the young William was nine, and might have been taken by his father to see the play, as was his contemporary Robert Willis, growing up thirty-five miles from Stratford at roughly the same time. Willis's account of seeing *The Cradle of Security*, standing between his father's legs in the Bothall in Gloucester, gives us a strong impression of touring plays and of playgoing in Shakespeare's childhood (Douglas and Greenfield 1986, pp. 362–4). Willis's memoir, made in his seventies, was intended to illustrate the depth and persistence of early experience, and we may think that Shakespeare's turn to the theatre was influenced in his boyhood by Richard Burbage's father.

Only three years later James Burbage is likely to have retired from full-time playing (Cuthbert later recalled that his father had been an actor only 'in his younger years'), as he made the decision, famous in theatrical history, to build and open a permanent playhouse, called, simply, 'the Theatre', but in its title especially recalling the prominence given to Roman theatre buildings within a civic plan. In his retrospective review of the rise of the Burbages, written in 1635, Cuthbert called his father 'the first builder of playhouses', although in fact he wasn't. The idea is likely to have been picked up from his brother-in-law John Brayne, a man of the London middle classes and a freeman of the Grocers' Company, who was evidently rather richer. In 1567 Brayne had speculated on a specially built playing arena in Stepney, at a property called the Red Lion. The building had a large platform stage and a stage house, with galleries for an audience; it was the structural model for all the outdoor theatres that followed it, including the Theatre, the Rose, the Globe and the Fortune (Wickham et al. 2000, pp. 362–4). It was probably not very successful – we hear no more about it after the year it was erected – but any losses he incurred in the venture did not cure Brayne of theatrical investment. Of the 'many hundred pounds taken up at interest' that Cuthbert Burbage stated that his father raised to fund the Theatre, John Brayne was the original godfather of a considerable part, and in the remaining ten years of his life he saw nothing but trouble as dividend on his capital.

The Burbages, by contrast, prospered. In 1576 the entire family moved to Shoreditch, outside the medieval city walls, to live in close proximity to the new playhouse, now the family business, built of timber on a plot of rented ground, and surrounded by older buildings. Foundation remains of this playhouse were uncovered between 2008 and 2011 at its site north of modern Holywell Lane, and reveal it to have been a polygonal wooden structure with an outer diameter of about 72 feet, more or less the same size and consequent capacity as the later Rose (Bowsher 2012, p. 58). Today the site of the Theatre is surrounded by rather grubby urban bustle; in 1576 it must have been fairly rural and peaceful, with the open spaces of Finsbury Fields to the west and south; it would have been across the fields that audiences approached the playhouse, from Moorgate and Bishopsgate on the northern limits of the city – John Stockwood called it the 'gorgeous playing place erected in the fields' (Wickham et al. 2000, p. 339). Burbage's land stood within the confines of the dissolved Holywell Priory of St John the Baptist, only forty years earlier one of the largest English nunneries, founded in the twelfth century. The Theatre was braced against the old Priory barn (or rather the reverse), and the surroundings must have included some fragments of 'bare ruined choirs', although most of the Priory church had been pulled down by 1576 and 'repurposed' as building stone: some of the blocks of the rediscovered foundations of Burbage's playhouse may once have been part of the conventual walls.

As well as such reminders of the old religion, the playhouse had important neighbours. Thomas Manners, first Earl of Rutland, had been granted a long crown lease on much of the Priory land, and extended his London residence there, just to the south and east of the property leased by Burbage (Edward Manners, grandson of Thomas, was third Earl of Rutland at the time of the building of the Theatre); his family held the house and land for many years, and it was Francis Manners, the sixth Earl, for whom Richard Burbage and Shakespeare were commissioned to design and execute a tournament impresa for the Accession Day tilt in March 1613, as was Burbage alone for the same event three years later (Chambers 1930, 2, p. 153; Young 1987, pp. 72–3). Perhaps some kind of acknowledgment of local connection lay behind these commands, although the literary and theatrical prominence of two royal servants would also have recommended themselves. Francis Manners was newly established in his earldom, concerned to sustain his profile at Court and to show his loyalty to the crown; he and his brother had been involved in the Essex rebellion in 1601.

Burbage's playhouse may have been intended as a London base for Leicester's company, but between 1576 and its disassembly late in 1598, to be reborn as part of the Globe the following year, it saw a variety of tenants and great performers, including the legendary Richard Tarlton; at his death in September 1588 Tarlton was buried at St Leonard Shoreditch, having been living in Holywell Street. Richard Burbage was then twenty, and had already begun his career as a player. Though we now think of him as a tragic specialist, and as the elegies at his death celebrated him, one of the strongest impressions of his young manhood must have been the remarkable charisma of Tarlton the comedian, whom he probably also knew as a neighbour.

One clear sign of the Theatre's success was its immediate emulation: in 1577 a second playhouse, the Curtain, was built on land immediately to the south in Curtain Close, part of the old Priory lands. That theatre, still being used in 1613 and owned by 'sharers' in 1624 – possibly even surviving until the Restoration – was the longest lived of the wooden Os (Wickham et al. 2000, pp. 404–18). In 2008 the remains of its foundations also were possibly located: further archaeological examination of the site, under development at the time of writing, may tell us more (Bowsher 2012, pp. 62–7). The financial success of the Theatre, at any rate, led James Burbage in 1585 into an agreement with Henry Lanman, owner of the Curtain, to share profits from the two houses. Audiences in Shoreditch could fill two theatres. In the event it was the Curtain that was to stage many of Shakespeare's hits from the mid 1590s onwards, including the popular *Romeo and Juliet*. Shakespeare and Richard Burbage were certainly playing together at the Theatre from 1594, but they may also have done so earlier, in other companies with which their names have been associated, notably Pembroke's Men, a company that came to grief in the bad plague year of 1593, but had a couple of years of prominence before that date.

Before Philip Henslowe built the Rose in 1587, Shoreditch was the theatrical centre of London, and probably remained so for another dozen years. Guessing that Shakespeare arrived in London about 1590, Shoreditch would have been the place to make professional contacts in the theatre; when the Chamberlain's Men were formed in 1594 Shoreditch was their working home. Certainly Shakespeare was living nearby in the later 1590s, just inside the north-eastern city walls, in the parish of St Helen Bishopsgate, half a mile to the south of the northern playhouses. According to John

Aubrey, compiling notes in the early 1680s towards his *Brief Lives*, Shakespeare had once lived in Shoreditch (Chambers 1930, 2, p. 252). His informant was William Beeston, himself then living at the southern end of the parish in Hog Lane, modern Worship Street. Hog Lane was historically an actors' street. Though he was then a player at the Rose in Southwark, Gabriel Spencer had been living there before he was, famously, killed in a duel with Ben Jonson, in September 1598, in Hoxton Fields, just to the north. William Beeston, in his seventies when he spoke to Aubrey, had been born in Shoreditch about 1606, and had inherited property there from his father Christopher, who had indeed known and acted with Shakespeare and Richard Burbage, as a junior member of the Chamberlain's Men in the later 1590s. Once he had graduated from his apprenticeship to the actor Augustine Phillips (by later 1602) Christopher Beeston joined Worcester's Men, and remained living on Holywell Street as a neighbour of the Burbages throughout the first decade of the new century. Before they moved themselves to the new Red Bull playhouse in Clerkenwell (1607?), Queen Anne's Men, as Worcester's troupe had become in the new reign, were performing at the Curtain. Aubrey's story, at least, has a strong pedigree, and it seems likely that Shakespeare spent his first years in London living and working within the theatrical community surrounding the Burbages.

If on the one hand the Theatre was a success, on the other Burbage's enterprise was dogged by conflict on two fronts: disagreement with the Braynes about its financing and their share in its profits, and difficulties with legal tenure. Family connections, then as now, did not necessarily guarantee harmony. James Burbage had financed his theatre with the substantial backing of his wife's brother John Brayne, but discord marked their relationship thereafter, in the course of which Ellen appears to have sided with her husband, and taken up after Brayne's death (1586) by his widow, in legal wrangling that lasted into the early 1590s, and featured one physical mêlée in the yard of the playhouse, with Richard Burbage wielding a broomstick to beat off the Brayne party (Wickham et al. 2000, pp. 358–63). Such aggressiveness he may have inherited from his father; nothing we know of him in later life suggests that it persisted. Simultaneously the landlord, Giles Allen, no friend of the theatre, wanted Burbage to close his playhouse, and hedged over renewing his lease after its initial ten-year term expired. Burbage himself seems to have been sustained partly by his own rugged character; he was tough and outspoken: William Fleetwood, the Recorder of London, called him 'a stubborn fellow' (Wickham et al. 2000, p. 346). Burbage felt he could resist civic dignitaries and legislators like Fleetwood, however, because of the power of his patrons. In 1584 he called himself 'my Lord Hunsdon's man'; he had passed from the patronage of Leicester to that of Henry Carey, Lord Hunsdon, a cousin of the Queen, who would become Lord Chamberlain in 1585 and patron of the playing company founded in 1594. Simultaneously his elder son Cuthbert, in his early twenties, became attached to the entourage of Walter Cope, a gentleman usher and secretary to the chief Elizabethan minister, Lord Burghley, and his assistant in the profitable Court of Wards; in 1589 Cuthbert Burbage was successful in using his court connections to regain control over the mortgaged lease of the Theatre.

It was at about this point in the family fortunes that William Shakespeare became an associate of the Burbage circle, possibly performing with Richard in the Earl of Pembroke's company, becoming known as a successful playwright, and hence a figure of considerable interest to the owners of playhouses, for whom theatrical hits meant profit. Undoubtedly Shakespeare acted at the Theatre, as well as the Curtain, during the middle years of the 1590s, and he must have encountered James Burbage, then in his sixties, particularly after the foundation of the Chamberlain's Men in 1594. James was to die early in 1597, but he remained active in entrepreneurship until the end of his life. Dissatisfied with his uncertain footing at the Theatre, and evidently having considerably improved his financial standing over twenty years as a playhouse owner, early in 1596 he bought the 'Parliament Chamber' at Blackfriars for £600, as outright owner, that is, rather than a lessee (Wickham et al. 2000, pp. 501–30). His plan, almost immediately put into motion, was to convert what had first been a fourteenth-century dining hall for the Dominican friars, a large stone structure with a pitched timber roof, into a covered playhouse for the use of his son's still-new company, no doubt reckoning on the support of the powerful figures at Court who had supported him in the past. Shakespeare and the other actors must have been aware of this radical project, to move their theatre both indoors and into the heart of the city: Blackfriars was and is to the immediate south-west of St Paul's Cathedral (Astington 2014, pp. 15–31). Burbage's immediate gamble failed, although it was to succeed magnificently in the longer term, until the place was sold by his grandson in 1651, when theatre was no longer a tolerated business. Immediately, late in 1596, when Burbage's intentions were plain, the neighbours, ironically including Lord Hunsdon, complained to the Privy Council, and the plan was stalled; James Burbage died shortly thereafter. To his sons he bequeathed his property and not a little of his determination. The Blackfriars playhouse was to be the culminating success of the Burbage family enterprise, after they regained direct control of it in 1608.

Cuthbert, the heir to the estate, became chief business manager of the Burbage investments, and hence financially involved in Shakespeare's company, though never as an actor. His solution to the problems with the Theatre was to demolish the building late in 1598, regarding it as the Burbages' rather than Allen's property, and to use its timbers to build a new similar playhouse on a leased site in Southwark, on the south bank of the Thames, a place where playhouses had stood since the 1570s. This new theatre was the famous Globe, opened in the summer of 1599; prior to that date Shakespeare's fellows remained in Shoreditch, playing at the Curtain. At the same time Shakespeare had moved from the north of the city to somewhere in Southwark, in anticipation of his new place of work. For a while, it seems, on playing days he made the journey, in reverse, that Richard Burbage walked for much of the last twenty years of his life: the mile and a half or so down Bishopsgate and Gracechurch Street, across London Bridge, and along Maid Lane to the Globe. Burbage remained living in familiar territory, within a community of many other actors, even when his theatre business moved south-westwards. The Blackfriars property had perhaps been willed to Richard as his responsibility; it was he who leased it in the following year of 1600 to Henry Evans, an investor in the children's players of the Chapel, who began to stage their plays there. The lease was to run for twenty-one years, and the theatre history we now know would be quite different if the Chapel venture had been more wisely managed. As it was, their plays incurred official displeasure early in 1608, and later in the year Evans surrendered his lease to Burbage, who immediately organised a consortium of his colleagues to run it as their own, second, theatre. Playing probably did not begin there until late 1609, but in the final few years of his career Shakespeare saw his plays produced at two quite distinct theatres, and the Burbage brothers, as major shareholders in the Globe and outright owners of the Blackfriars, saw their business expand and prosper, surviving the burning down of the Globe in summer 1613 and its rebuilding within the year. Shakespeare's own artistic involvement with his colleagues' Jacobean indoor playhouse was not prolonged, but he did, no doubt encouraged by his fellows, buy property in the Blackfriars complex in 1613 (Chambers 1930, 2, pp. 154–69).

The royal title bestowed on Shakespeare's and Richard Burbage's acting troupe at the start of the new reign in 1603 can only have helped consolidate the support the Burbages received from powerful patrons. Early in 1605 Richard Burbage responded to his brother's master, Sir Walter Cope (knighted by the new king), in his search for entertainments for Queen Anne and her visiting brother, the Duke of Holstein. Burbage nominated *Love's Labour's Lost* as a play 'the queen hath not seen', and likely to please her with its 'wit and mirth'; it was immediately appointed to be performed at night either at Southampton House, at Holborn and Chancery Lane, or at the residence of the chief minister Robert Cecil, Viscount Cranborne, in the Strand (Chambers 1930, 2, p. 332). The master of Southampton House was Henry Wriothesley, Earl of Southampton, the dedicatee of Shakespeare's early poetry, and friend of the young Francis Manners, future Earl of Rutland. Another rising star at Court was William Herbert, third Earl of Pembroke, aged twenty-three when King James came to the throne, patron of Ben Jonson and other literary figures, and Lord Chamberlain from 1615 to his death in 1630. He and his brother Philip were 'the most noble and incomparable pair of brethren' to whom the Shakespeare Folio was dedicated; four years earlier he had written that he could not bring himself to watch a court performance of *Pericles* by the King's Men in May 1619 'so soon after the loss of my old acquaintance Burbage', who had probably first acted the title part in that play (Nungezer 1929, p. 73).

In April 1616 Richard Burbage, then approaching the age of forty-eight, had lost *his* old acquaintance and 'fellow' Shakespeare, and later in the same year presumably received the mark in cash willed to him by his old colleague, as also to John Heminges and Henry Condell, to buy a memorial ring. Shakespeare's true legacy, we might think now, as Burbage may also have thought then, was the succession of outstanding stage parts that the leading Jacobean actor had brought to life, from Richard III onwards; he himself had rather less than a remaining three years in which to continue to play them in the theatre, while a few years later still Heminges and Condell were to bring them before the literary attention of the great variety of readers. In 1616 Burbage was still living in Shoreditch, as he had for all but the first few years of his life, no longer within the grounds of the old Priory but in a substantial house in Holywell Street – modern Shoreditch High Street, to the north of Liverpool Street Station. His probable apprentices, Nicholas Tooley and Richard Robinson, are likely to have lived as members of his household while he was their master; when Tooley died in 1623, then living in the house of Cuthbert Burbage, he left £80, a substantial sum, to provide charity for the poor of Shoreditch. In 1616 Cuthbert was living near to his brother, possibly immediately next door; both their houses had been broken into and robbed in February 1615, targeted by local thieves, no doubt, because they were among the most prosperous members of the neighbourhood (*Calendar* 1936, pp. 62, 250). Family bonds, intermarriage and local associations tied many members of the theatrical profession together: three years after Richard Burbage's death, his widow remarried to his former apprentice Richard Robinson, who henceforth became the stepfather of the surviving children of his old master. Shakespeare, already a married father when he arrived in London, did not put down the roots he otherwise might have done; his movement from one district to another within London and the suburbs, so far as we can trace it, stands in strong contrast with the settled establishment of his chief colleague and lead actor.

The immediate family of James Burbage himself seems to have been remarkably cohesive, and formed a nucleus for the larger 'family' of the Chamberlain's/King's company, in which Shakespeare had a place, and the bonds of which are apparent in the warm acknowledgments and signs of favour that we can read in the wills of the first generation of players who had worked with Richard Burbage. If the Burbages were benign colleagues, however, they were also substantial stakeholders in playhouse property, and made money from their investments. When the new actors of the 1630s appealed for a more equitable system of profit sharing there is more than a little hint of hurt in Cuthbert Burbage's written response to the Lord Chamberlain (at that date Philip Herbert, who had succeeded his brother in the post as fourth Earl of Pembroke), that Burbage goodwill was being flouted, and the family myth of success brought into disrepute. Cuthbert recalls his father in 'those first times' establishing an originary patrimony that had supported 'many of other players and their families' and had been fostered by 'the infinite costs and pains by the family of the

Burbages, and the great desert of Richard Burbage for his quality of playing' (Wickham et al. 2000, pp. 226–7).

Richard Burbage's Jacobean years in Shoreditch saw the pinnacle of his artistic and financial success, but also a history of loss which in modern terms we might read in tandem with the great roles of that period: Othello, King Lear, Macbeth, Antony, Coriolanus, Leontes and Prospero. A succession of children was born to Burbage and his wife Winifred, only to die in infancy and early childhood. The Burbages buried a son named after his father in 1607, the evocatively named daughter Juliet Burbage in 1608, and in October 1616 the three-year-old Winifred, named after her mother. Winifred the elder was in the final weeks of pregnancy when her daughter died, and when the new child was born he was christened at the parish church of St Leonard Shoreditch as William Burbage, a living memorial of the most remarkable partnership in the entire history of the theatre. A small child when his father died, he lived on until at least the early interregnum, an inheritor of his parents' theatrical and other property, and as witness to the failed attempt by the Blackfriars actors to regroup and revive playing, and then to sell his grandfather's playhouse in 1651, following the execution of the king early in 1649, before himself fading into historical obscurity. In 1641 William Burbage's name appeared with that of his stepfather, the player Richard Robinson, in support of the man who had presided at his christening, and subsequently at his father's burial, the vicar John Squire. Shoreditch was caught up in the doctrinal wars that prefaced the military conflict, and Squire was attacked as a Laudian, and ejected from his ministry; within a couple of years the Parliamentary earthworks defending London from the king's army were set up a short distance north of the church.

By the date he made the 1635 deposition to the Lord Chamberlain, in the year before his death, Cuthbert Burbage had also acquired, as had Shakespeare before him, a family coat of arms. If Ben Jonson's joke about Sogliardo's arms in *Every Man Out Of His Humour* glanced at 'Non Sanz Droict' ('Not without mustard'), so, proleptically, the scene also mocks the Burbages. Sogliardo's new arms feature 'On a chief argent, a boar's head proper' (Bevington et al. 2012, pp. 335–6). The Burbages went three times better: their shield features three boars' heads (Howard and Chester 1880, p. 121). It would be amusing to think that in their escutcheon a scene of theatrical farce was being remembered, under the noses of the College of Arms, in which Richard Burbage had perhaps first played the mocker Carlo Buffone, although the boar was also the badge of King Richard III, one of the most celebrated Burbage bravura roles. Richard had undoubtedly understood the visual language of heraldry, so close to the emblematic mode of 'devices' of the kind he had provided for the Earl of Rutland. As to what other kinds of work he practised to create his reputation as a painter, celebrated in the elegies at his death, we now have no knowledge. His work as a lead actor would have left him little time for other work in the theatre, but it may be that he occasionally helped create stage properties, like the impresa shields required in the second act of *Pericles*, for example. The similar ornamental shields he provided for Rutland's appearance at the Court tilts perhaps could be seen, after the event, and until the disturbances of the civil wars, in the Shield Gallery at Whitehall Palace (Young 1987, pp. 131–4); there is little reason to think that anything by his hand survives in the collection of paintings created by William Cartwright, and partially surviving at Dulwich. The small, worn, squarish head-and-shoulders painting of a man with a receding hairline and pointed beard in that collection (DPG 395) has a very tenuous claim to be a portrait of the actor, although it is still often so reproduced in books on Shakespeare's theatre; that it is a self-portrait is a spurious designation originating in 1890.

Burbage's first art was the evanescent creativity of the stage player, living on in the memories of those who saw and heard him, and of those who had been told of such impressions. Among the first group was the youthful Prince Charles, born in 1600 and seeing Burbage in many leading roles at his father's Court during his boyhood and teenage years. Imprisoned and awaiting his trial and execution in 1648–9, King Charles spent some of his time reading Shakespeare in the Folio edition, recalling as vivid early experience, we may think, the rhythms, colours and intonations of Burbage's voice in many of the lines he read.

WORKS CITED

Astington, J. H. 2014. 'Why the theatres changed' in A. Gurr and F. Karim-Cooper (eds.), *Moving Shakespeare Indoors*. Cambridge University Press

Bevington, D., Butler, M. and Donaldson, I. (eds.) 2012. *The Cambridge Edition of the Works of Ben Jonson*, 7 vols. Cambridge University Press

Bowsher, J. 2012. *Shakespeare's London Theatreland*. Museum of London Archaeology

Calendar to the Sessions Records, Volume II 1614–1615. 1936. British History Online

Chambers, E. K. 1930. *William Shakespeare. A Study of Facts and Problems*. 2 vols. Oxford University Press

Douglas, A. and Greenfield, P. (eds.) 1986. *Cumberland, Westmorland, Gloucestershire*. University of Toronto Press

Howard, J. J. and Chester, J. L. (eds.) 1880. *The Visitation of London, 1633*. London. Harleian Society

MacLean, S.-B. 2002. 'Tracking Leicester's Men: the patronage of a performance troupe' in P. W. White and S. R. Westfall (eds.), *Shakespeare and Theatrical Patronage in Early Modern England*. Cambridge University Press

Nungezer, E. 1929. *A Dictionary of Actors*. New Haven. Yale University Press

Wickham, G., Berry, H. and Ingram, W. (eds.) 2000. *English Professional Theatre, 1530–1660*. Cambridge University Press

Young, A. 1987. *Tudor and Jacobean Tournaments*. London. George Philip

20

His fellow actors Will Kemp, Robert Armin and other members of the Lord Chamberlain's Men and the King's Men

BART VAN ES

One afternoon in the late summer of 1599 Robert Armin (the well-known ballad writer and comic) took a walk from his home on the north side of London, crossed the Thames, and went to visit the newly completed Globe playhouse, where Shakespeare and his company had just started to perform. Armin may well have gone to see the troupe earlier when they were based at the Curtain because that playhouse was just a short ramble across the fields from his front door. Back then, he would have seen 'Will Shakespeare, Augustine Phillips, Henry Condell, Will Sly, Will Kemp, Richard Burbage, John Heminges, Thomas Pope, Christopher Beeston, and John Duke', who are listed as performing in Ben Jonson's *Every Man In His Humour* in 1598 (Jonson 1616, p. 72). Some of this company were familiar to Armin as neighbours: Augustine Phillips and his apprentice, the boy actor Christopher Beeston, for example, attended his church (Denkinger 1929). All of them were famous and Armin must at least have known them by sight. In 1599 he almost certainly saw the newish comedy *Much Ado About Nothing*. We can deduce this because Armin's *A Pill to Purge Melancholy* briefly makes mention of 'one pleasant conceit or other of Monsieur de Kemp on Monday ... at the Globe' and refers more than once to 'the Ass's burden' (A4^b). This looks like an allusion to Dogberry (who is obsessed with having been called an 'ass' (*Much Ado* 4.2.74, 76, 84; 5.1.248, 298)), a role that we know Shakespeare had written specifically for Kemp. As he looked at the stage from an 'upper room' Armin must have wondered what it would be like to work with William Shakespeare. In less than a year he would know at first hand.

The year between the late summer of 1599 and that of 1600 is a particularly rich time for which to isolate the circle of Shakespeare's fellow actors. This was the most important single moment of transition for the company. Not only would Armin take over from Kemp, the newly built Globe would also tie Shakespeare more closely to a small group of theatre owners (or 'housekeepers'), a circle even more exclusive than that of the Chamberlain's fellowship. Richard Burbage, John Heminges, Augustine Phillips and Thomas Pope, like the playwright, owned a portion of the playhouse and Armin would soon become part of that group. Outside that tight circle, competition with other groups of performers intensified. Edward Alleyn, with whom Shakespeare had worked in his earliest years as a playwright, was setting up a rival theatre (the Fortune) to the North of the city in direct imitation of the Globe. Children's troupes were also being established in the capital to compete with the adults, first at St Paul's and soon afterwards at Blackfriars. Several of these boy actors, such as Nathan Field, would eventually become sharers in Shakespeare's company. The wider circle of the players (which extends beyond even the twenty-five 'principal actors' listed in the playwright's collected works in 1623) thus comes into sharp focus if we pay attention to this changing of the guard in the first year of business on the south bank.

It would be possible to write biographies of at least half a dozen of these men of the theatre, but Armin and Kemp (who must have had many conversations with Shakespeare between 1599 and 1600 as one comic star took the place of another) constitute a special case. They were, in every imaginable way, opposites. Through that opposition they illustrate the broad spectrum of those who might be termed Shakespeare's 'fellow actors' and showcase the transformative effect that these individuals had on the playwright's style. By 1599 Armin was established as an actor, but (as I have argued is true of Shakespeare, van Es 2010) he had not started his working life in this way. Having picked up a good education in King's Lynn, Armin had come to London in 1581 to begin an apprenticeship as a goldsmith, moving from this to fame as a writer of popular ballads and pamphlets, only eventually to become a performer in the mid 1590s as part of Lord Chandos's Men. In contrast to this, the 'Monsieur de Kemp' whom Armin watched on the stage at the Globe was a seasoned professional. Founding Chamberlain's Men sharers such as

Kemp, Pope and George Bryan, were veterans of the travelling theatre whose first affiliation was to the stage rather than to print.

Kemp has, on the whole, been ill-served by biographers. It is easy to caricature him as the big, rough-faced, muscular man who gurned his way through performances of *A Midsummer Night's Dream* as Bottom – an overbearing figure whom Shakespeare would have been eager to drive from the fellowship. To really understand him, his exceptional talent and the men he brought into the Shakespeare circle, we need to go back to the 1580s. It was in that decade that the English tumblers and ballad singers defined themselves as performers and established their international fame. That word 'international' is important. Perhaps the starkest contrast between Armin (watching the stage in 1599) and Kemp was not the physical difference between a diminutive satirist and a clownish strong man but the opposition between pan-European and domestic appeal. It is sometimes asked where Shakespeare (who seems never to have left the island) would have got the knowledge of foreign travel that is evident in his plays. The question is a little silly because the possible sources for such information are nearly infinite and the detail itself is often inaccurate, but if one wanted an answer, a ready solution is available in Kemp and his circle. Unlike Burbage or Armin (whose skills were fundamentally verbal) Kemp was fluent in the language of music, mime, tumbling and dance, which transferred very easily overseas and allowed him to perform as far afield as Denmark, Germany, the Netherlands and possibly Rome.

So Armin at the Globe watching Dogberry's exchanges saw a performer with a continental reputation. We first come to hear of Kemp in the retinue of the Earl of Leicester during his campaign in the Low Countries in the years 1585–6 (Bald 1959). That retinue was notoriously opulent – so much so that descriptions of the entertainment were physically cut out of Holinshed's *Chronicles* to be replaced by a more restrained account. Kemp's own presence was part of that opulence, with several special payments being made as rewards for his feats (Bald 1943). He would have been part, for example, of the extravagant production of the *Labours of Hercules*, which impressed the citizens of Utrecht. The physical prowess of the English players had a major impact on the continental public. Already in 1586 there is record of the Earl of Leicester and the Prince Elector at Amersfoort enjoying Kemp's leaping, just as in 1600 the citizens of Norwich would leave record of his prodigious ability by marking the height of his final jump on the city's guildhall (Kemp 1600, D1[a]). When Kemp, Thomas Pope and George Bryan appear in the Danish court records it is as 'instrumentalister och springere', i.e. musicians and leapers (Baskervill 1929, p. 129). People across Europe paid handsomely for such wonders. The Mayor of Norwich gave Kemp £5 on the spot (which would be very good as the day's takings of an entire London theatre) but the European salaries were still more impressive. When Kemp and the other future Chamberlain's Men Thomas Pope and George Bryan moved to Elsinore after leaving the Low Countries in 1586 they were paid 6 thalers a month and soon received an offer from the Elector of Saxony to come to work for him for 100 thalers per annum – enough to pay for Shakespeare's house, New Place in Stratford, through a single year's work (Chambers 1923, II, p. 272). Though Kemp's departure from the Globe partnership in 1599 is always viewed as a financial miscalculation, it is quite possible that he felt the big money was to be made elsewhere, hence his projected journey over the Alps.

Men like Kemp, Thomas Pope and George Bryan, for whom Shakespeare wrote in the mid to late 1590s, were big earners, experienced European travellers, and highly talented acrobats. They were also famous for their music – so much so that more records of their jigs and ballads survive in German versions than in their native English. At times they worked with the help of a local translator, but clearly the music, dance and art of mime easily transferred from one culture to another. It was, above all, the jig that brought these skills together, uniting audiences from Denmark to Southern Germany and from the Earl of Leicester to the ordinary citizen. This international experience of travel and court performance was not something Armin or Shakespeare would ever achieve.

Armin watching Kemp in 1599 might well have been envious of this actor's status. Equally significant in terms of Shakespeare's circle, he must also have been struck by the way that the playwright was crafting parts that were specifically tailored to his skills. The original text of *Much Ado About Nothing* retains record of the casting as Armin would have seen it, with Verges marked down as 'Cowley' and Dogberry marked down as 'Kemp' (Shakespeare 1600a, G3[b]). This use of actors' names in Shakespeare's working papers is a distinctive feature of his 'company style' from 1594 onwards – where multiple speakers within a play come to be characterised through their physical distinctiveness (van Es 2013, pp. 79–98). Another example is the succession of thin men that the playwright marked out for a junior member of the ensemble, John Sinclo, which includes the Beadle who comes to arrest Doll Tearsheet in *2 Henry IV*: a 'nut hook', a 'tripe-visaged rascle', a 'thin man in a censor', and 'filthy, famished, correctioner' (Shakespeare 1600b, K3^b–K4^a). No doubt Sinclo also had his part in the original cast of *Much Ado About Nothing*, although in this case no record survives in the text itself.

The bulky, rough-faced Kemp along with Pope, Cowley and Sinclo would have been a daily element of Shakespeare's social circle as he wrote a series of comic masterpieces between the years 1594 and 1599. A unique part of the fun of seeing a new Shakespeare play at that time would have been seeing what the author had come up with for this well-known set of individuals. Sometimes they were even playing the same characters in a new situation, as when Falstaff, Bardolph and Mistress Quickly made their way from *Henry IV, Part I* to the very different world of *The Merry Wives of Windsor* around 1597. That group would suffer disruption from the intrusion of Armin, not only because Armin was physically different (a 'pixie', as one audience member described him (Chambers 1930, II, p. 341)), but also because his ideas and background were so opposed to Kemp's.

Kemp was always an embodiment of vitality, with a plain-speaking persona that resisted pretensions to eloquence. The all-singing, all-dancing acrobatic performances that established Kemp's reputation give some sense of the life force that Shakespeare would harness. A set of 1595 Stationers' Register entries gives an account of their character, listing 'Kemp's Pleasant New Jig of the Broom Man', 'Master Kemp's New Jig of the Kitchen Stuff Woman' and 'Kemp's New Jig betwixt a soldier, a miser, and Sym the clown' (Baskervill 1929, pp. 107–8). Significantly, it was worth the publisher's investment to register these publications and link them with their performer (a degree of eminence that Armin's publications did not achieve). Even the musical scores for some of these entertainments can be traced to Kemp's performance, and the last of them survives in the original English, giving a vivid picture of the clown in his element.

'Kemp's New Jig betwixt a soldier, a miser, and Sym the Clown', also known as *Singing Simpkin*, begins with the sprightly entry of a young wife and Simpkin himself:

> WIFE: Blind Cupid hath made my heart for to bleed,
>   Fa la, la, la, la, la, la, la, la.
> SIMPKIN: But I know a man can help you at need,
>   With a fa, la, la, la, la, fa, la, la, la, la, la.
>   (*Singing Simpkin* in Clegg and Skeaping 2014, ll. 1–4)

Kemp's sung exchanges with the young wife are very bawdy, featuring jokes about pregnancy and anal sex, such as the following (as she tries to hide a young rake from her returning husband):

> WIFE: I have a place behind here,
>   Which yet is known to no man.
> SIMPKIN: She has a place before too,
>   But that is all too common.
>   (*Singing Simpkin*, ll. 47–8)

These double entendres are accompanied by quick action, with Simpkin, inevitably, ending up hiding in a chest while the suspicious husband enters and begins his search. These two elements combine when the chest is opened and Kemp manages (outrageously) to persuade the cuckolded old man that his intentions were innocent. The swagger of Simpkin at this moment is fantastic: he even has the gall to send the husband out 'to fetch a quart of wine', tipping him with half a crown of his own cash. Just as inevitably, the clown overplays his hand, boasting to the wife and explicitly telling his audience that 'some forty weeks hence / you may come to a christening' (ll. 175–6). 'Christening' rhymes with the 'listening' that the aged husband is doing and the jig ends with a wild acrobatic dance in which the old man and his servant chase Kemp around the stage. We do not know if Kemp played Sir John Falstaff. One or two details in Henslowe's *Diary*, however, suggest a connection and certainly, seeing Falstaff hiding in the laundry basket in *The Merry Wives of Windsor*, an audience must have been reminded of this very famous farce (printed just two years earlier) featuring Kemp. If nothing else, it would have been the logical jig on which to conclude that play.

Athletic, self-mocking, charmingly boastful, Will Kemp would have been a defining figure amongst Shakespeare's professional associates from the mid to late 1590s. The broad humour of *Singing Simpkin* gives a taste of the festive mode that he attracted from his writers; it has something, for example, of the rhyme 'a country lass brown as a berry; / Blithe of blee in heart as merry' that Kemp commissions in *Nine Days Wonder* in 1600 (Kemp 1600, B4ᵃ). Still more so, 'Kemp's Applauded Merriments of the Men of Goteham' featured in the earlier production *A Knack to Know a Knave* match up with the self-mocking identification with the general citizenry that we find in all of the actor's work. In this anonymous play (which probably dates back to the 1580s) a set of artisans prepare to deliver a petition to King Edgar, full of awe for the royal personage they are about to encounter:

> MILLER: Now let us constult among ourselves,
> How to misbehave ourselves to the King's worship.
>
> (Anon. 1963, F1ᵃ)

The Miller is a kind of director figure, trying to keep his company in order as its various members contend with one another for the honour of taking the top role. The Smith, who has boundless ambition, is especially keen to be a performer and must be pacified through the interventions of the Miller:

> SMITH: Why, sir, there was a god of our occupation, and
> I charge you
> by virtue of his godhead, to let me deliver the
> petition ...
> My bellows, my coal trough, and my water shall
> enter arms
> with you for our trade.
> MILLER: Hear you neighbour, I pray conswade yourself and
> be not
> wilful, let the Cobbler deliver it, you shall see him
> mar all.
> SMITH: At your request I will commit myself to you, and lay
> myself
> open to you like an oyster.
>
> (Anon. 1963, F1ᵃ)

This exchange has more than a little in common with those of *A Midsummer Night's Dream*, where the weaver Nick Bottom's rather touching enthusiasm ('Let me play the lion too. I will roar that I will do any man's heart good to hear me' (1.2.66–7)) needs to be kept in check by Peter Quince. The key thing about this scene is perhaps less the casting of Kemp (who seems a perfect fit for the Smith) than the awareness of the circle of old-style travelling players who were part of his unit, the 'mad men of Gotham' who achieved such acclaim. Their clownish solecisms ('constult', 'conswade' and others) are typical of the knockabout humour that this cluster of actors excelled in: similar misspeaking is found, for example, in Costard and Dull's contributions to *Love's Labour's Lost*.

The group consisting of Kemp, Pope, Bryan and the hired man Cowley form a pretty coherent unit: dynamic, self-consciously vulgar and able to shift for themselves. Their fame had brought them a great deal of money. Pope had several houses, owned tenements and had shares in both the Curtain playhouse and the Globe. There was a swagger about them, Pope being described as 'boorish' (at least in his stage persona) and still living 'in the remembrance of many' a decade after his death (Rowlands 1600, D8[a]; Heywood 1612, E2[b]). This swagger was certainly there in Kemp, who was proud of his fame and strength and boasted of the 'general love and favour' of many thousands 'from the highest to the lowest, the richest to the poorest' (Kemp 1600, p. 23). Kemp was in every sense mobile: accompanied by one or more musicians, a boy servant, and also ready to call on a composer of ballads, he could move quickly from location to location and class to class. His retinue was effectively a small acting company in itself – one that combined easily with others (such as the group of English tumblers at the Danish Court in 1587 or 'Ned Alleyn and his company' in the original performances of *A Knack to Know a Knave*). Kemp was clearly well able to collaborate with others, but he could also break away quickly to pursue independent ventures, like the promised morris dance to Rome of 1601. This sense of making mirthful connections and moving on rapidly is a dominant motif of the *Nine Days Wonder*. One can see it too in the way that Kemp parts work in Shakespeare's drama: these roles, such as Lance in *The Two Gentlemen of Verona*, Lancelot Gobbo in *The Merchant of Venice*, or Bottom himself in *A Midsummer Night's Dream* tend to be rooted in a distinct comic sphere that exists at a distance from a more elevated circle of characters. Kemp was on easy terms with that world of everyday people and was happy to play the clown when it came to the great and the good.

Armin, looking down from his 'upper room' at the playhouse in 1599, had nothing of this cross-class camaraderie, and one can easily imagine him making disparaging remarks about Kemp as an 'ass'. He would certainly glory, in later years, about having taken the comic lead in *Much Ado About Nothing*, ostentatiously quoting Dogberry's lines. Kemp, who was normally easygoing, was riled at Armin's presumption. His complaints the following year about a 'penny poet' who is 'a little stooping in the shoulders' and has broadcast abuse 'on a public stage' (Kemp 1600, D3^b–D4^b) point clearly enough at the new arrival in Shakespeare's troupe. Armin was very much part of the group of beastly ballad makers at whom Kemp directs his ire in the *Nine Days' Wonder*: the idea of being supplanted by such a person must have hit him hard.

Armin was not merely a ballad writer, he was a self-conscious and self-promoting author (though less elevated as a stylist, one might compare his career to that of Thomas Heywood, who started out as a published poet, became a playwright, then a hired actor, before eventually becoming a sharer in Worcester's Men). By the time that Shakespeare was sizing him up as a potential new member of his company, Armin had a very large portfolio of publications and although most of these are now lost, a considerable number survive. Nashe in *Strange News* (1592) and Harvey in *Pierce's Supererogation* (1593) thought of 'Armin' as a by-word for mass print of dubious quality. As a resident of St Botolph's, Armin had placed himself equidistant from the publishers who clustered around the city's cathedral and the actors at the Theatre and Curtain (which lay no more than ten minutes' walk from his door). Scholars such as Nora Jonson and Richard Preiss have pointed to Armin's unique exploitation of this middle position – using his act as the clown of the Curtain to promote his print persona and *vice versa*. Such a position inevitably ruffled feathers, but Armin was not afraid of making enemies in the pursuit of his art: indeed he made his combative attitude, like the combination of print and performance, a key part of his appeal. These distinctive features make Armin's entry into the Shakespeare circle all the more interesting. Fellowship with Kemp may to some extent have been forced upon Shakespeare because this performer was not only already famous but also an established fixture within the Strange's Men ensemble, which made up the bulk of the new Chamberlain's Men in 1594. The situation with Armin was different because here Shakespeare would have had a decisive influence on the choice.

There is much to be gained from abandoning the old 'row with Kemp' narrative, which sees Shakespeare as the active party in driving out his company's comic star. It is often suggested that Shakespeare chose Armin because he would be easier to control than his predecessor. In this account Kemp is imagined as typical of the clowns complained of in *Hamlet* who speak 'more than is set down for them' and who 'set on some quantity of barren spectators to laugh' (3.2.38, 39–40). This is not terribly likely. For one thing, Kemp was a professional for whom Shakespeare and others had written carefully scripted exchanges; for another, it is difficult to imagine an actor less likely to be controllable than Armin, whose entire self-presentation was as a figure of chaos. Snuffe, one of several of Armin's stage characters appearing in *A Pill to Purge Melancholy* (1599), signs off as one 'that scorns thy puffy stuff' – a crazy, riddling figure who refuses to follow the rules of an orderly dialogue (A3^b). In *A Nest of Ninnies* (1608) Armin writes of his mad exploits and insists on the privilege of his motley: 'if I do offend as I make no question, my pardon is signed', he declares (A2^a). Here, as elsewhere, Armin casts himself as a force of disorder to be held in check only by threats of violence: the 'martyr' of the deity Folly who demands of his audience 'with your goad stick prick me onto the true tract' (A2^b).

It was not only Armin's self-proclaimed liberty that might have militated against his being chosen as a member of Shakespeare's company. Much of what we know about Armin is off-putting. He was, for example, happy to peddle sensationalist journalism like *A True Discourse of the Practices of Elizabeth Caldwell*, for which he supplied a promotional epistle in 1604. This pamphlet about a self-confessed poisoner is characteristically pitiless; Armin rejoices that in her execution she should 'so aptly taste the follies of vice and villainy' (Concluding Epistle, p. 1). Armin in print is frequently sadistic and judgemental. His poetry collection *Quips Upon Questions* (1600) is dominated by an agenda of condemnation: prostitutes, gluttons, drunkards and those who 'sleep too much' are sent with a kind of crazy zealotry to 'feel the whip' or suffer similar pain. The hard edge of Armin's Calvinism – which is evident everywhere from his first appearance in print as part of *A Brief Resolution of Right Religion* (1590) to his last will and testament – cannot have made him an easy man to welcome into an acting troupe.

In this light, the choice of Armin in place of the likeable and bankable Kemp looks much less of a safe option; if it tells us anything about Shakespeare, it shows his willingness to innovate and to take risks. Of all Shakespeare's actors, Armin was the most idiosyncratic. His style is unmistakable, obsessed above all by the contortion of both language and bodies. One long, almost unreadable, section of *A Pill to Purge Melancholy* encapsulates that quality: it appears to be a letter written by one of Armin's characters, Snipsnap, to a now feminised version of his own clown persona, Snuff. The author threatens to 'curb ye and knife ye, and cut ye, and wound ye and ulcer ye and hurt ye, then honour ye and hower ye and sour ye, and sip ye and sop ye, and sauce ye' ($1B^b$), starting a train of images that runs on for over seven pages of alliterative prose. *A Pill* is still sometimes listed as being anonymous, but what strongly connects it to Armin's other output (aside from the match of publisher and the use of Armin characters such as Snuff and Blue John (Sutcliffe 1996)) is this disturbing switching between violence, absurdity, and the language of comfort. The speaker will 'knife' and 'ulcer' but then 'honour' the addressee; throughout, nonce words like 'hower' sit alongside violent ones such as 'strip' and 'strap'. This is hardly comic, at least not to the modern reader, but it does give access to a stark vision that is an obvious influence on Shakespeare's work, not least his darker post-1599 creations, such as *Troilus and Cressida* and *King Lear*. In Armin publications, such as *Quips upon Questions* and *Fool upon Fool* (which, like *Pill*, are attributed to the character Snuff), the human and the animal are repeatedly conflated. The second poem in *Quips*, for example, describes a man's wit as something to be 'scraped out like a parchment' made from the skin of a dog. In *A Pill to Purge Melancholy* there is the same dominant metaphor in which the jester's action reduces his victim to something inanimate: most often a foodstuff that is 'served', 'carved', 'spiced', 'sugared', or 'spewed'. The physical and intellectual aggression of Armin's output is stunning; such a person entering Shakespeare's circle could hardly fail to have a transformative effect.

The brief scene of 'Kemp's Applauded Merriments' in *A Knack to Know a Knave* may plausibly be claimed as an influence on the rehearsals of *A Midsummer Night's Dream* and it is just possible to argue that *Singing Simpkin* is a factor shaping Falstaff's actions in *The Merry Wives of Windsor*. But that mapping of an actor's earlier work onto Shakespeare's development becomes much easier with Robert Armin. This is not only because Armin had such a distinctive mode of verbal contortion, but also because it was he who had effectively invented the dramatic character of the motley fool. Armin had described six of these figures in *Fool upon Fool* of 1600 and had consistently presented himself in this guise in his

collection of verses, *Quips upon Questions,* published the same year. He
had also played a version of this character in his own play *The Two Maids
of Moreclack,* which, like the poems, had been completed before he joined
Shakespeare's company. So dominant had this character become that
Armin actually employed it outside the world of his fiction. He published
as 'Snuff, the Clown of the Curtain' and on occasions (such as academic
festivities at Oxford) he appeared 'in motley' as a fool (Armin, *Nest,* A2[b]).

The obvious answer to the question of what attracted Shakespeare to
Armin (who cannot have been an easy colleague) was the character of the
jester. Armin – in the tradition of the courtly wise fool – was a good mimic,
could translate Italian and quote Latin, and was deeply committed to the
intellectual wordplay and absurdist logic chopping of learned wit. These
qualities are immediately in evidence in the first character that Shakespeare
wrote for him when he joined the Chamberlain's Men in 1600: Touchstone
in *As You Like It.* This very name references Armin, not just because the
touchstone was a tool of the actor's original profession of goldsmith, but
also because in *The Two Maids of Moreclack* Armin had already played a
character called Tutch. Touchstone acts as linchpin to this drama, connecting its separate spheres: he accompanies Celia and Rosalind in their
journey from court to forest; he mingles with the Arden natives (mocking
William and marrying Audrey); and he becomes a figure of fascination for
the exiled Duke's party, especially Jaques. This connectivity is important.
Kemp's 'applauded merriments' had always fitted neatly into a subplot:
the world of the rude mechanicals in *A Midsummer Night's Dream* or the
guard of *Much Ado About Nothing* intrudes very little into the sphere of
the high gentility. That was the standard pattern in English stage writing –
with clown scenes alternating neatly with the serious action, providing
light relief. This was not at all what the company would get with Armin,
who, even in this first role of Touchstone crossed into the ambit of the
courtiers to deliver a long disquisition upon the seven degrees of the lie.
That speech placed Armin in his favoured role of on-stage satirist. Like the
songs and riddles of the Fool in *King Lear,* it bears comparison with the
actor's own writing (not least the witticisms of Will Sommers in *Fool upon
Fool*). Across a series of roles in the new decade – Feste, Thersites, Lavatch,
the Fool in *King Lear,* Autolycus, and others less easy to pinpoint –
Shakespeare pushed Armin's trickster-like character to its limits, thereby
also changing the tone of his plays as a whole.

Back in 1599, as Armin watched Shakespeare and his fellows in *Much Ado About Nothing*, that coming decade of close collaboration was a distant prospect; only in retrospect would 1600 be seen as a changing of the guard. The 'wooden O' of the Globe was a circle that pulled many talented men into Shakespeare's ambit; Armin and Kemp being just the most famous and most readily traced in the plays themselves. Their biographies – and equally those of actors such as Nathan Field, Edward Alleyn or Thomas Heywood, who might easily have taken up a substantial portion of this chapter – show that the profession of 'player' in Early Modern London could encompass very different kinds of people, from descendants of the travelling minstrels to classically educated dramatists. The distance between the dancer-turned-player Kemp and the writer-turned-player Armin should make us cautious about how we use the word 'player' to characterise Shakespeare, as if actors were all alike. Armin's journey to the Globe in 1599 both literally and figuratively crossed the paths of printers, playwrights and patrons before it ever came to the world of the actors – this was a journey that Shakespeare himself had also made.

WORKS CITED

Anon. 1963–4. *A Knack to Know a Knave*, Malone Society Reprints. Oxford University Press

Bald, R. C. 1943. 'Leicester's Men in the Low Countries'. *Review of English Studies* 19: 395–97

  1959. 'Will, My Lord of Leicester's Jesting Player'. *Notes & Queries* 104: 112

Baskervill, Charles Read 1929. *The Elizabethan Jig and Related Song Drama.* University of Chicago Press

Chambers, E. K. 1923. *The Elizabethan Stage*, 4 vols. Oxford. Clarendon Press

  1930. *William Shakespeare: A Study of Facts and Problems.* Oxford University Press

Clegg, Roger and Skeaping, Lucie 2014. *Singing Simpkin and Other Bawdy Jigs: Musical Comedy on the Shakespearean Stage: Scripts, Music and Context.* University of Exeter Press

Denkinger, Emma Marshall 1929. 'Actors' Names in the Registers of St. Bodolph Aldgate', *PMLA* 41: 91–109

Heywood, Thomas 1612. *An Apology for Actors.* London. Nicholas Oakes

Johnson, Nora, 2003. *The Actor as Playwright in Early Modern Drama.* Cambridge University Press

Jonson, Ben, 1616. *Works.* London. William Stansby

Kemp, William, 1600. *Nine Days Wonder.* London. Nicholas Ling

Preiss, Richard 2014. *Clowning and Authorship in Early Modern Theatre.* Cambridge University Press

Rowlands, Samuel 1600. *The Letting of Humour's Blood.* London. William Ferbrand

Shakespeare, William, 1600a. *Much Ado About Nothing (Q1).* London. Andrew Wise and William Aspley

   1600b. *Second Part of Henry the Fourth (Q1).* London. Andrew Wise and William Aspley

Sutcliffe, Chris 1996. 'The Canon of Robert Armin's Work: an Addition', *Notes & Queries* 43: 171–5

Van Es, Bart 2010. '*Johannes fac Totum*?: Shakespeare's First Contact with the Acting Companies', *Shakespeare Quarterly* 61: 551–77

   2013. *Shakespeare in Company.* Oxford University Press

21

His literary patrons

ALAN H. NELSON

Shakespeare's many patrons included magnates who lent their names or the names of their offices to his playing company; dedicatees of literary works; and powerful individuals for whom he performed specific services. In each case the question arises: did patronage involve personal acquaintance, or even grow into friendship?

Theatrical patronage

Without a patron, early modern stage-players risked being classified as masterless men, no better than rogues and vagabonds. While knights or minor lords might patronise players in the middle of the sixteenth century, the privilege became restricted to barons and earls during the reign of Elizabeth (1558–1603), and to members of the royal family during the reign of James (1603–25) (Chambers 1923, 4, pp. 269–71).

Shakespeare's playing company was patronised by the Lord Chamberlain from about 1594, and by King James from 1603. During the years leading up to 1594 Shakespeare can be connected, with varying degrees of certainty, to a plethora of patrons. His *Titus Andronicus*, according to the title-page of its first edition (1594), was performed by the players of three earls: Derby, Pembroke, and Sussex. Philip Henslowe's contemporary 'Diary' (Foakes 2002, pp. 21–2) reports that the same play was performed by players of the Earl of Sussex, the Lord Admiral and the Lord Chamberlain.

At the very beginning of 1594 the Earl of Derby was Ferdinando Stanley (d. 16 April 1594), styled Lord Strange until his father's death on 25 September 1593. Pembroke was William Herbert (d. 1601). Sussex was Robert Radcliffe, who succeeded at the death of his father, Henry, on 4 December 1593. The Lord Admiral was Charles Howard, Baron Howard of Effingham: his patronage of the Admiral's Men extended from 1576 to 1603. The Lord Chamberlain was Henry Carey (d. 4 July 1596), 1st Baron Hunsdon; succeeded by Sir William Brooke (d. 6 March 1597), 10th Baron Cobham; and by George Carey (d. 9 September 1603), 2nd Baron Hunsdon (*ODNB* 2004; Cokayne 1910–59).

On 17 May 1603, following the death of Queen Elizabeth on 24 March, Shakespeare's company acquired a new patron in King James. The list of company servants named in the royal licence begins with Lawrence Fletcher, a relative newcomer, and continues with William Shakespeare, Richard Burbage, Augustine Phillips, John Heminges, Henry Condell, William Sly, Robert Armin and Richard Cowley. Fletcher's precedence in the list has been attributed to a career spent partly in Edinburgh, where he may have been a protégé of the Scottish King (Schoenbaum 1975, pp. 195–6).

If a survey of theatrical patronage looks like excerpts from *The Complete Peerage*, that is exactly the point: patronage was an upper-class affair. Shakespeare obviously knew who his patron was at any given time, but did his patron know him? (A cat may look at a king, but is the king cognisant of the cat?) Some degree of acquaintance was not impossible. Ben Jonson, also an actor and a playwright, was the darling of many an aristocrat; and when Richard Burbage, Shakespeare's colleague, died in 1619, William Herbert, 3rd Earl of Pembroke, lamented 'the loss of my old acquaintance Burbage' (*ODNB*).

Some interaction with theatrical patrons has been attributed to Shakespeare by his biographers. Lord Cobham, then Lord Chamberlain, was apparently offended by the braggart knight in the *Henry IV* plays, whence Sir John Oldcastle, a distant relative, metamorphosed into the entirely fictional Sir John Falstaff (Schoenbaum 1991, p. 50). In 1597 another Lord Chamberlain, George Carey, was invested as Knight of the Garter, 'and it is generally agreed that the first performance of William Shakespeare's *Merry Wives of Windsor* was held to commemorate the occasion' (Duncan-Jones 2001, p. 97). A tale from the *mythos* claims that Queen Elizabeth, patron of patrons, asked Shakespeare for a play showing 'Falstaff in love' – yet another link to *The Merry Wives of Windsor* (Schoenbaum 1975, p. 146).

Despite such reports, many of them probably fictional, magnates patronised playing companies, not individual players. Very little in the record indicates that theatrical patronage was based on or developed into personal acquaintance, let alone active friendship.

Literary patronage: Nashe, Shakespeare and Southampton

Of far greater interest than theatrical patronage for the study of Shakespeare's friendships is literary patronage. 'Between 1550 and 1650', writes Michael G. Brennan (Brennan 1988, p. 1), 'aristocratic literary patronage in England was a system invested with high hopes and golden images but, at the same time, expected to deliver practical benefits. The majority of writers who endeavoured to engage the sympathetic interest of noble patrons were seeking some form of protection, preferment or reward.'

Until recently, details of literary patronage have been comprehended only vaguely. Franklin B. Williams, Jr, compiler of the *Index of Dedications and Commendatory Verses in English Books before 1641* (1962), conceded (p. ix) that 'readers must look elsewhere for a comprehensive survey of Renaissance literary patronage, including such aspects as motives for dedicating books, the grounds for choosing patrons, and the rewards sought or received'. Brennan cites the well-documented case of Richard Robinson, who in 1603 received about twenty-five copies of his own book from the printer, for private sale (Brennan 1988, pp. 14–16).

Early modern printers and publishers elicited texts from contemporary authors either gratis, for a direct payment, or in exchange for free copies. Authors and publishers might also dedicate books to wealthy men and women in the hope of receiving a gratuity. 'It is customarily assumed', writes Williams, 'that these ... writers relied upon their modest dedication fees as much as they did upon the pittances they received from the booksellers' (William 1962, p. x).

Hard evidence is finally available in a letter noted by Duncan-Jones. Sir George Carey, brother of the Lord Chamberlain and holder of the same office four years later, wrote to his wife Elizabeth on 13 November 1593:

Nashe hath dedicated a book unto you, with promise of a better. Will Cotton [a servant] will disburse £5 or 20 nobles in your reward to him, and he shall not find my purse shut to relieve him out of prison, there presently in great misery, maliced for writing against the Londoners (Duncan-Jones 1998, p. 15).

The proposed reward of £5 or £6 13s 4d puts paid to the claim that dedication fees were necessarily 'modest', as either amount might represent half a year's salary for a university graduate. Sir George Carey and his wife, moreover, were sufficiently acquainted with Thomas Nashe to know his personal circumstances, and to care about him.

The book mentioned by Carey is Nashe's *Christ's Tears over Jerusalem. Whereunto is annexed a comparative admonition to London* (1593), dedicated 'To the most honoured, and virtuous beautified lady, the Lady Elizabeth Carey: wife to the thrice magnanimous and noble descended knight, Sir George Carey, Knight Marshal, etc.' (Thus Nashe compliments the husband as well as the wife.) Nashe twice promises a 'better' book in the future, first in the body of the letter, then in the closing sentence:

Vouchsafe it benign hospitality in your closet, with slight interview at idle hours: and more polished labours of mine ere long shall salute you. Some complete history I will shortly go through with, wherein your perfections shall be the chief argument. (sig. *2v)

Most resplendent lady, encourage me, favour me, countenance me in this, and something ere long I will aspire to, beyond the common mediocrity. (sig. *3)

Alas, Nashe neither produced a 'complete history' nor dedicated a second book to Countess Elizabeth.

Nashe couched his request for a gratuity in the general tradition of literary patronage:

Diverse well-deserving poets have consecrated their endeavours to your praise. Fame's eldest favourite, Master Spenser, in all his writings high prizeth you.

While Spenser did not in fact 'prize' (or praise) the countess in 'all his writings', he did address a compliment to her in some surviving copies of *The Faerie Queene* (1590). Another 'well-deserving poet' who had dedicated a work to Countess Elizabeth was Thomas Churchyard, in *Churchyard's Challenge* (1593). In the heat of his praises, Nashe also plays the bully:

I hate those female braggarts that contend to have all the Muses beg at their doors: and with doves, delight evermore to look themselves in the glass of vainglory, yet by their sides wear continually Barbary purses, which never ope to any but pedantical parasites.

By giving Nashe a reward, the Countess will be spared the indignity of deserving his hatred.

A more prominent dedicatee was Ferdinando Stanley, Lord Strange. By 1593 Strange had received praise from Robert Greene, Anthony Munday and (evidently) Thomas Nashe (Williams 1962; *ODNB*). In *Pierce Penilesse* (1592) Nashe praised a patron under the pseudonym 'Amintas'; three years later, in *Colin Clout's Come Home Again* (1595), Edmund Spenser addressed a eulogy to Lord Strange under the pseudonym 'Amyntas':

> He, whilst he lived, was the noblest swain
> That ever pipèd on an oaten quill:
> Both did he other, which could pipe, maintain,
> And eke could pipe himself with passing skill.

Thus Spenser praises Strange as both a patron of poets and a poet in his own right.

Nashe may have dedicated one additional work to Ferdinando Stanley: this was his scandalous 'Choice of Valentines', also known as 'Nashe's Dildo', not printed in its entirety until 1899 (Akrigg 1968, p. 38). While dedicated in some sources to a deliberately cryptic 'Lord S', the abbreviation is expanded in the lesser-known Folger copy (MS V.a.399) as 'Lord Strange'.

Given that Strange was both literary patron of the hour and likely patron of Shakespeare's playing company, Shakespeare's choice of an altogether different patron for his literary endeavours ought to surprise us. In 1593 and 1594 he dedicated two successive publications to Henry Wriothesley, Earl of Southampton: *Venus and Adonis* and *The Rape of Lucrece*. Over his lifetime Southampton was the recipient of some twenty outright dedications, eight dedicatory epistles and three 'presentations'. Before 1593, however, when he turned twenty, only one book had been dedicated exclusively to him: John Clapham's Latin *Narcissus* (1591). Barnabe Barnes's *Parthenophil and Parthenope* (1593) concludes with several dedicatory poems, including one to Southampton, but Shakespeare's *Venus and Adonis* is the first work in English openly dedicated to the earl.

Venus and Adonis and *Rape of Lucrece* are the only works with dedications unquestionably composed by Shakespeare. Both these early publications were seen through the press with great care; both were printed by Shakespeare's countryman Richard Field; both were dedicated 'To the

Right Honourable Henry Wriothesley, Earl of Southampton, and Baron Tichfield'. Shakespeare's 1593 dedication is fluent but conventional:

I know not how I shall offend in dedicating my unpolished lines to your lordship, nor how the world will censure me for choosing so strong a prop to support so weak a burden. Only if your honour seem but pleased, I account myself highly praised, and vow to take advantage of all idle hours till I have honoured you with some graver labour. But if the first heir of my invention prove deformed, I shall be sorry it had so noble a godfather, and never after ear [i.e., plough] so barren a land for fear it yield me still so bad a harvest. I leave it to your honourable survey, and your honour to your heart's content, which I wish may always answer your own wish and the world's hopeful expectation.

Though less prolix than Nashe, Shakespeare adopts a similar formula: praise for the dedicatee; deprecation of his own talents; and promise of better work in the future if this effort is approved. Shakespeare, no bully, promises no ill consequence if no reward is forthcoming.

Shakespeare's 1594 dedication is more idiosyncratic and more passionate:

The love I dedicate to your lordship is without end, whereof this pamphlet without beginning is but a superfluous moiety. The warrant I have of your honourable disposition, not the worth of my untutored lines makes it assured of acceptance. What I have done is yours, what I have to do is yours, being part in all I have, devoted yours. Were my worth greater my duty would show greater, meantime, as it is, it is bound to your lordship, to whom I wish long life still lengthened with all happiness.

The open declaration of 'love' and the 'warrant' which the poet has received 'of your honourable disposition' together suggest that *Venus and Adonis* had attracted both personal recognition and a substantial gratuity. The argument of Gary Schmidgall (1990, p. 80) that 'Shakespeare's two dedications are in every respect orthodox and impersonal' overlooks the notable differences between them.

The first edition of Nashe's *The Unfortunate Traveller*, printed in 1594, contains a dedication to Southampton, while the second, printed later the same year as 'Newly corrected and augmented', substitutes an 'Induction to the dapper Mounsieur Pages of the Court', presumably because the first edition failed to attract a reward. In contrast, Shakespeare's mild but presumably successful dedication of 1593 led to the second, more impassioned dedication of 1594; both dedications then survived unchanged in

FIGURE 4: The only person to whom Shakespeare himself dedicated any of his works was Henry Wriothesley, 3rd Earl of Southampton (1573–1624). This portrait dates from the time the narrative poems were published (1593 and 1594), and may have been painted for his coming of age in 1594. He was clearly proud of his long locks of dark auburn hair (which feature in other known portraits). For centuries the androgynous features of the sitter were thought to be those of a woman, Lady Norton. But the rich attire is male, earrings were often worn by high-ranking and artistic men, and the portrait was correctly identified in 2002.

some nine subsequent editions of *Venus and Adonis* and five of *Lucrece*, to 1616 (*STC* 23354–60b, 22346–50).

Literary patronage: supposititious dedicatees

Shakespeare is implicated in three additional literary dedications. Robert Chester's *Love's Martyr: or, Rosalins complaint* (1601) is mysterious on several counts. Chester was solely responsible for the first part of the volume, which he dedicated to Sir John Salusbury (or Salisbury). His own long and obscure poem is addressed to an unnamed female identified as the Phoenix; by inference, the turtle (or, as we would say, turtle-dove) is male. Presumably the Phoenix is Lady Salusbury, the turtle, Sir John. Chester catalogues the beauties of the Phoenix's face and body in a 'catalogue' poem which – if Lady Salusbury is the subject – is perhaps too closely observed for comfort: 'Her breasts … Her belly … "Be still my thoughts" … Her thighs … Her legs …' (pp. 3–7).

The second part of the volume has a separate title-page and an explanatory note (sig. Z1):

Hereafter follow diverse poetical essays on the former subject: viz: the Turtle and the Phoenix. Done by the best and chiefest of our modern writers, with their names subscribed to their particular works: never before extant. And now first consecrated by them all generally, to the love and merit of the true-noble Knight, Sir John Salisbury.

Shakespeare is one of four named 'modern writers' who 'consecrate' their work to Salusbury. The other three are John Marston, George Chapman and Ben Jonson.

Shakespeare's verses, commonly titled 'The Phoenix and the Turtle', are among the most cryptic which flowed from his pen. They include strange triplet stanzas:

> Death is now the phoenix' nest,
> And the turtle's loyal breast,
> To eternity doth rest.
>
> Leaving no posterity
> 'Twas not their infirmity,
> It was married chastity.
>
> . . .

To this urn let those repair
That are either true or fair.
For these dead birds sigh a prayer.

Neither the lack of posterity nor the urn fits Sir John Salusbury, whose marriage to Lady Ursula was notably fecund, issuing in seven sons and three (or four) daughters. Both husband and wife, moreover, were still living and breathing in 1601 (*ODNB* 2004, 'Salusbury family').

James P. Bednarz, attempting to extract clarity from obscurity, imagines that the four modern poets agreed that the Phoenix ought to be represented first as dead, as if by mistake; then as alive (Bednarz 2012, p. 133): 'Shakespeare's part in this planned collaboration was to detail the bird's immolation; Marston's was to illustrate its subsequent rebirth.' But this explanation is perhaps too clever to be credible. Why imagine the death of the Phoenix and Turtle at all? Why tout an unexplained 'infirmity' that resulted in some counter-factual want of 'posterity'? Why sigh a prayer for 'these dead birds' if the 'birds' are not dead after all?

A better answer might be that Shakespeare and three other 'modern poets' were asked to submit poems on the theme of the Phoenix and the Turtle, without reference to Sir John Salusbury or his wife. Asked for a poem, Shakespeare graciously submits one. This scenario, also speculative, has the advantage that it doesn't contradict everything known about Sir John Salusbury's personal life, nor does it reduce Shakespeare to a kind of idler wheel in somebody else's machine. This scenario also accords with the message of the first title-page:

To these are added some new compositions of several modern writers whose names are subscribed to their several works, upon the first subject: viz. the Phoenix and Turtle.

Shakespeare may have been chosen because he was a friend of Salusbury, or a friend of Chester, or perhaps because he was a 'modern poet' who hoped to reap a monetary award for co-operating in a literary enterprise. Bednarz writes,

We cannot be certain about how closely Shakespeare knew Salusbury or how long they had been acquainted with each other by 1601, but a prior connection is feasible because John's wife Ursula Halsall was the natural but acknowledged daughter of Henry Stanley, the fourth earl of Derby. Stanley's son, Ferdinando, Lord Strange, her half-brother, sponsored an acting company with which Shakespeare was probably involved sometime between 1592 and 1594. (Bednarz 2012, p. 77)

So here we are, back to Lord Strange. But did Marston, Chapman and Jonson have a similar tie? I prefer the scenario that Chester fancied himself a modern poet, and prevailed upon colleagues more worthy the name to piece out his own efforts with other poems on the same theme.

The next dedication occurs in *Shakespeare's Sonnets* (1609). It may be said with only small exaggeration that no two Shakespeare scholars have ever agreed on the identity of 'Mr. W.H.', the volume's apparent dedicatee. My own presumption is that the dedication was composed by Thomas Thorpe the printer, not by Shakespeare; and that Shakespeare had no part in the publication of the volume. I further believe that no contemporary would likely address an earl as 'Mr.' (or 'Master'), and consequently that the dedicatee cannot have been either William Herbert, Earl of Pembroke, or (with his initials reversed) Henry Wriothesley, Earl of Southampton. Neither am I persuaded that an 'S' was accidentally omitted so as to make 'Mr. W.SH.' into 'Mr. W.H.' (Foster 1987, pp. 42–54). Who is the dedicatee? I do not know. But since it was not (in my opinion) written by Shakespeare, the dedication has no bearing on Shakespeare's friendships.

Finally, the First Folio of 1623 was dedicated:

To the most noble and incomparable pair of brethren, William, Earl of Pembroke, etc., Lord Chamberlain to the King's most excellent Majesty; and Philip Earl of Montgomery, etc., Gentleman of his Majesty's bed-chamber; both knights of the most noble order of the Garter, and our singular good lords.

By this time Shakespeare had been dead for seven years, so the two earls were not his patrons in any conventional sense. But the authors of the dedication, John Heminges and Henry Condell, obviously expected that the first and second sons of Lady Mary Herbert née Sidney (Philip Sidney's sister) would support their enterprise. We encountered the father of the two earls as the playing-company patron named on the title-page of *Titus Andronicus* (1594); when this second Earl of Pembroke died in 1601, his eldest son succeeded as the third earl; younger brother Philip, meanwhile, became 'Earl of Montgomery' in his brother's place. (Upon William's death in 1630, Philip would become fourth Earl of Pembroke.) The 'incomparable brethren' are invoked as favourers of William Shakespeare and familiar with his plays:

your lordships have been pleased to think these trifles something heretofore; and have prosecuted both them and their author living with . . . favour (sig. A2)

For Heminges and Condell, the playwright is 'a friend and fellow'; to the 'incomparable pair of brethren' he is, when all is said and done, 'your servant Shakespeare' (sig. A2v).

Should the First Folio have been dedicated to King James instead of the two 'incomparable brethren'? The King, alas, did not attract dedications of purely literary works, no matter how significant (Williams 1962: see James I).

Miscellaneous patronage

The Master of the Revels was inevitably a kind of patron to playwrights active during his tenure. For Shakespeare this court officer was Edmund Tilney up to his death in 1610, and thereafter Sir George Buc (Chambers 1923, 1, pp. 88–105). At a visit to the site of the Revels Office in the grounds of the Order of St John of Jerusalem, Clerkenwell, I was told of the numerous meetings which must have occurred between Tilney and Shakespeare at this very location, and invited to imagine a conversation of this sort: 'Good day, Master Tilney, I've brought you a new play. Hope you'll allow it!' 'Take a chair, Will, and read it to me over a tankard of ale. Knowing you, I'm sure it will be fine!' Evidence, however, suggests that the players submitted a clean manuscript copy of a play, which would be carefully read, annotated and signed off by the Master of the Revels, or approved with conditions. The Master's signature at the end of the play manuscript, not his verbal assent or friendly approval, was the authority for public performance (Dutton 1991, pp. 194–9). No doubt Shakespeare and his fellows kept their licensed playscripts locked up in a cabinet or a trunk as protection against objections from rival court officers.

On 7 February 1601 *Richard II*, an 'old play', was performed at the behest of Robert Devereux, second Earl of Essex, in the lead-up to his fatal rebellion. Though the performance became the subject of an investigation, the Lord Chamberlain's Men suffered no ill consequences. Essex was not a patron of the company, and Augustine Phillipps, who might have taken the rap, was let off the hook. It could not have hurt to have had in reserve a copy of the play licensed for performance by the Master of the Revels (Schoenbaum 1975, pp. 158–60).

The closest we can come to an authenticated face-to-face meeting for Shakespeare is the inquiry by Sir George Buc, about this same time, into the authorship of an old play, *George a Green, Pinner of Wakefield*. Buc solicited opinions from two established actors, William Shakespeare and Edward Juby (Nelson 1998). Though Buc was not technically the patron of either man, he was Master of the Revels designate (*ODNB*). While everything in the episode bespeaks personal acquaintance, nothing hints at friendship.

Finally, on 31 March 1613 'Mr Shakespeare' was paid 44s by the steward of the sixth Earl of Rutland, Francis Manners, 'about my Lord's impresa'; Richard Burbage was paid the same amount 'for painting and making it'. This looks like a side-business conducted by Shakespeare the word-smith and Burbage the amateur painter. The *impresa* – comparable to a coat of arms – was provided as a professional service (Schoenbaum 1975, p. 220).

Henry Wriothesley, Third Earl of Southampton

Of all the patrons under review, only Henry Wriothesley stands out as a likely 'friend' of William Shakespeare. A full and generous word-portrait of Wriothesley is available in George Akrigg's 1968 monograph, *Shakespeare and the Earl of Southampton*. Southampton was a strikingly handsome and affected youth, with a feminine appearance, long hair and a come-hither look. He resisted early marriage, preferring the company of young males, as epitomised in the letter from an informer reporting his dalliance with Piers Edmonds:

[Edmonds] was Corporal General of the Horse in Ireland under the Earl of Southampton, he ate and drank at his table and lay in his tent, the Earl of Southampton gave him a horse, . . . the Earl of Southampton would coll [i.e., embrace] and hug him in his arms and play wantonly with him. (Akrigg 1968, pp. 181–2)

Did Southampton 'play wantonly' with Shakespeare? Known circumstances bespeak the possibility. In 1593 Shakespeare was twenty-nine, Southampton just twenty. Though earls may be presumed to have a preference for their own social class, many surrounded themselves with dependants of a lower social rank. Granted, both were publicly heterosexual, Shakespeare marrying early, Southampton marrying late. But Shakespeare spent most of his professional life in London separated by some 100 miles and two or three days' travel from his wife and family, begetting no more children after his twenty-third birthday. In his plays he created several characters perceived by modern critics and audiences as quietly but convincingly homosexual; note Antonio's 'desire' for Sebastian in *Twelfth Night*, or Antonio's for Bassanio in *The Merchant of Venice*. Many of the first 126 of his 154 *Sonnets* seem to have been written to or about a 'lovely boy' (or several lovely boys) and are imbued with homoerotic overtones. These are only some of many possible links between Shakespeare and Southampton (Akrigg 1968, pp. 216–64).

A homosexual relationship of an unequal sort is recorded between the Earl of Oxford, then in his late twenties, and the Italian choirboy who accompanied him on his return to London from Venice. The Earl was older, richer and socially superior, his counterpart younger, impoverished and socially inferior (Nelson 2003, pp. 155–7, 213–18). Homosexuality in this unequal mode was understood, recognised and practised.

Between Southampton and Shakespeare the relationship would have been more balanced, and thus closer to a modern sense of a companionate partnership. Yes, Southampton was above the poet in social status, and considerably younger; but Shakespeare was a rock-star modern poet capable of setting young male hearts aflutter, as we know from *Pilgrimage to Parnassus*: 'I'll worship sweet Master Shakespeare, and to honour him will lay his *Venus and Adonis* under my pillow' (Leishman 1949, p. 192). Thus each man would have brought his own gifts to the relationship. Though Shakespeare was probably far from a social butterfly, it is difficult to believe that this master word-smith was not a spell-binding companion.

Did the connection between Southampton and Shakespeare last beyond the poetically productive years 1593 and 1594? Did a personal tie lead the Earl to invite Shakespeare's company to Southampton House, London, for a performance of *Love's Labour's Lost* following the Earl's release from prison in 1604? Whether the friendship lasted but a year, or more than a decade, it was sufficiently powerful to inspire great admiration, and, particularly in *Venus and Adonis*, *Lucrece* and the Sonnets, great poetry.

WORKS CITED

Akrigg, George 1968. *Shakespeare and the Earl of Southampton*. Cambridge, MA. Harvard University Press

Bednarz, James P. 2012. *Shakespeare and the Truth of Love: The Mystery of 'The Phoenix and Turtle'*. Basingstoke. Palgrave Macmillan

Brennan, Michael 1988. *Literary Patronage in the English Renaissance: The Pembroke Family*. London and New York. Routledge

Chambers, Edmund K. 1923. *Elizabethan Drama*, 4 vols. Oxford University Press

Cokayne, G. E. 1910–1959. *The Complete Peerage*. 12 vols. in 13 parts. London. St Catherine Press

Duncan-Jones, Katherine 1998. 'Nashe in Newgate', *Times Literary Supplement* (22 March), 15

2001. *Ungentle Shakespeare: Scenes from his Life*. London: Arden Shakespeare

Dutton, Richard 1991. *Mastering the Revels: The Regulation and Censorship of English Renaissance Drama*. University of Iowa Press

Foakes, R. A. (ed.) 2002. *Henslowe's Diary*. Cambridge University Press

Foster, Donald W. 1987. 'Mr. W.H. R.I.P.', *PMLA* 102: 42–54

Leishman, J. B. (ed.) 1949. *The Three Parnassus Plays (1598–1601)*. London. Nicholson and Watson

Nelson, Alan H. 1998. 'George Buc, William Shakespeare, and the Folger *George a Greene*', *Shakespeare Quarterly* 48: 74–83

2003. *Monstrous Adversary: The Life of Edward de Vere, Seventeenth Earl of Oxford 1550–1604*. Liverpool University Press

Oxford Dictionary of National Biography 2004, 60 vols. Oxford University Press; cited as *ODNB*

Pantzer, Katharine F. (ed.) 1976–91. *A Short-title Catalogue of Books Printed in England, Scotland, and Ireland . . . 1475–1640*. 3 vols. London. Bibliographical Society; cited as *STC*

Schmidgall, Gary 1990. *Shakespeare and the Poet's Life*. Lexington, KY. Kentucky University Press

Schoenbaum, S. 1991. *Shakespeare's Lives*. Oxford. Clarendon Press

1975. *William Shakespeare: A Documentary Life*. Oxford. Clarendon Press

Williams, Franklin B. 1962. *Index of Dedications and Commendatory Verses in English Books before 1641*. London. The Bibliographical Society

22

His collaborator George Wilkins

DUNCAN SALKELD

George Wilkins is remembered today largely for two reasons – for co-writing *Pericles* with Shakespeare and for running a tavern or bawdy house. Neither activity has enhanced his reputation. By all accounts, he was an unlikeable figure, a man evidently given to violent outbursts and physical attacks against women. Critics have kept their distance from him and wished that Shakespeare might have done so too. Neither W. W. Greg's edition in collotype facsimile of *Pericles*, nor his later study of editorial questions in Shakespeare, so much as mentions Wilkins by name (Greg 1940, 1956). G. E. Bentley's *The Jacobean and Caroline Stage* ignored him as a dramatist altogether (Bentley 1956), as did Derek Traversi's short catalogue of Renaissance drama (Traversi 1980). Biographers of Shakespeare have found his association with Wilkins unfortunate. Park Honan deems Shakespeare 'not to be blamed' for this particular association (Honan 1999, p. 329). For Katherine Duncan-Jones, Wilkins was a misogynistic lout, a 'distinctly second-rate, though by no means talentless writer' (Duncan-Jones 2001, pp. 205–6). Peter Ackroyd wonders why Shakespeare 'would condescend to work with a tyro' (Ackroyd 2006, p. 434), while René Weis silently passes over any and all of Wilkins's literary contributions (Weis 2007). Charles Nicholl, who devotes three useful chapters to Wilkins, nevertheless thinks him 'a mediocre writer' (Nicholl 2008, p. 199). What we now know of Wilkins's character fits uncomfortably with what we suppose we know of 'sweet Shakespeare', 'good Will', or 'Friendly Shakespeare', terms used by contemporaries William Covell, John Davies of Hereford and Anthony Scoloker. Wilkins is something of an anomaly, a dreadful man but a writer who ought to be of considerable interest, for Wilkins clearly knew the red-light world of bawds, panders and prostitutes that also lies at the heart of the play they both produced.

Most of what we know about the life of George Wilkins has emerged through prosecutions of him that have survived in the Middlesex County Sessions records (Prior 1972 and 1976). He was an aspiring writer whose extant work seems to have emerged from the two-year period between 1606 and 1608. His father apparently died in the dreadful London plague of summer 1603: sixth in the list of burials for 19 August 1603 in the register of St Leonard's, Shoreditch, is 'George Wilkins the Poet' of Holywell Street. The address will prove significant. On 11 February 1609/10, the register of St Giles without Cripplegate gives the baptism of Thomas 'son of George Wilkens Poett [sic]'. Apart from the anomaly of the word 'poet' listed among far less elevated trades such as 'water-bearer' or 'joiner', the wording of the two entries points to a plausible family connection. Two sonnets that preface the 1595 publication of Spenser's Amoretti and Epithalamion, one headed 'G.W. Senior to the Author' and the other signed 'G.W. I' (probably 'Junior'), would appear to confirm this father–son relationship. Wilkins's major writings appeared in years framed by outbreaks of infection that closed the theatres. The registers of St Giles illustrate just how devastating the effects of plague could be in a parish: just 8 burials in March 1603, 29 in April, 46 in May, 78 in June, 590 in July, and 600 in August, among them Wilkins's father. As winter approached, the numbers gradually reduced, though sickness seems to have lingered into the spring of 1604.

Wilkins's marriage is likely to have been to Katherine Fowles at St Lawrence, Jewry in February 1601 (Prior 1972, pp. 143–4). He next surfaces in the records as one of the witnesses in the Belott–Mountjoy case of 1612, alongside William Shakespeare who testified on 11 May. Stephen Belott had taken his father-in-law Christopher Mountjoy (a French Huguenot living in Silver Street) to court for non-payment of his wife's dowry. Belott and his wife Mary took lodging in a chamber belonging to Wilkins just after their marriage. Shakespeare, it seems, had resided with the Mountjoys between 1602 and 1604 and was eventually asked to testify in the dispute. Wilkins gave himself as a 'Victualler of the age of thirty-six years or thereabouts' from the parish of St Sepulchre; Shakespeare as a 'gentleman' of Stratford-upon-Avon. Neither provided any information that might settle the contention or reveal more about their own situations. Wilkins would subsequently be named in a number of inquiries and prosecutions. On 4 April 1610, he was bound over to keep the peace towards Anne Plesington, a 'noted quean' and 'common harbourer of lewd persons'. Just over two weeks later, he provided sureties for prosecuted neighbours John Fisher and Thomas Cutts. He was charged on 3 March 1611 with 'abusing one Randall Berkes' and shockingly, 'kicking a woman on the belly which was then great with child'. Berkes was a stationer, and one of Wilkins's sureties in this case was another stationer, Henry Gosson, publisher (but not printer) of the 1609 quarto of *Pericles*. Other allegations against him included verbal and physical attacks on constables, and, notably, having 'outrageously beaten one Judith Walton and stamped upon her, so that she was carried home in [a] chair'. On 25 August 1614, Wilkins's wife Katherine sued a neighbour, Joyce Patrick, for calling her a 'bawd'. Charles Nicholl, commenting on Wilkins's dissolute world, observes, 'Two themes emerge with obsessive regularity from Wilkins's police-record: violence and prostitution, and sometimes they combine in acts of violence against women who are said or inferred to be prostitutes' (Prior 1972, pp. 144–5; Nicholl 2008, p. 204).

Wilkins lived in Cow Cross, a short lane that linked St John's Street Clerkenwell to the infamous red-light zone of Turnbull (or 'Turnmill') Street. A 1567 map of London, known as the 'Agas map', shows just a handful of houses on this lane, quietly nestling amid the gardens and fields that surround it, with no hint at all of the location's rowdy, bawdy notoriety. In the 1570s, Turnbull Street was regularly frequented by merchants, trades-men and law-students from the Inns of Court and Chancery, attracted by entertainments available at two local brothels. These establishments were part of a joint enterprise run by Gilbert East (who seems later to have become bailiff or henchman to Philip Henslowe) and Lucy Baynham, popularly known as 'Black Luce'. East and Luce hosted several itinerant prostitutes at their houses but kept a select group, including Mary Dornelly, Elizabeth Kirkman, Meg Goldsmith and Elizabeth Kelsey (who wore a pearl earring), for their wealthiest guests. Sometimes, when insufficient girls were available, East would force his wife Margaret up into a garret to serve customers. East was well connected locally. His landlord was William Breech, the Head Constable of Clerkenwell and occasional client with Mary Dornelly. According to Mary (whose surname may reflect an Irish accent), 'East and his wife are two abominable and lewd persons, none worse in the world' (Salkeld 2012, pp. 135–9). Living close by, in Cow Cross, was Henry Boyer, a painter, the pimp on whom East and Luce generally relied.

Prosecutions in the Middlesex County Sessions repeatedly involved persons associated with the area of Cow Cross, Turnmill Street, St John's Street and Clerkenwell. A case in 1607 specifies a number of Wilkins's neighbours who had their windows shattered by a 200-strong crowd armed with 'stones and clubs', among them Richard Todde, Henry Pierson, Edward Savage, Richard Bronwen and John Sharpe (Jeaffreson 1974, pp. 26). Living in the same street in 1609 were butchers Robert Mitchell, William Haydon and Robert Pittes (Jeaffreson 1974, p. 56). In March 1615, a former resident of Cow Cross was charged with having stolen a collection of twenty-six books from a local resident, John Drawater (Jeaffreson 1974, p. 109). A clutch of cases heard towards the end of the afternoon of 7 June 1578 at Bridewell report misdemeanours in 'a trumpeter's house', in 'Bowmer's house' in St John's Street, at the Rose in Turnmill Street and at Black Luce's in Turnmill Street. This thoroughly disreputable area had connections with the world of the playhouses. Christopher Beeston, Thomas Heywood, Thomas Dekker and John Weever all resided, at least for a time, in Clerkenwell. Edmund Tilney and his brother Robert lived in the parish, and St John's Gate was where Tilney held office as Master of the Revels. Intriguingly, St John's Street was also home to Matthew Shakespeare, brother-in-law it seems to George Peele, Shakespeare's collaborator on *Titus Andronicus* (Salkeld 2012, pp. 142–4).

It is perhaps hardly surprising, given his pattern of violent conduct, that Wilkins has tended to be ignored as a writer. His earliest publication seems to have been a thinly re-written Latin translation of a work originally by Arthur Golding in 1564, which he published as *The Historie of Justine* (1606). It appears that he followed it with a prose pamphlet *Three Miseries of Barbary* (c. 1606), a domestic tragi-comedy *The Miseries of Enforced Marriage* (1607), and a prose tale of *The Painful Adventures of Pericles, Prince of Tyre* (1608). He collaborated with other authors, including Thomas Dekker on *Jests to Make you Merry* (1607) and with Day and Rowley on *The Travels of the Three English Brothers* (1608). There is some possibility that he may also have had a hand in Day's *Law Tricks* (1608). All this may seem relatively small beer, but Wilkins had one astonishing, runaway success. From its earliest performances, *Pericles* was hugely popular on stage and in print ran to six editions by 1635. If we are better to understand his achievement, we ought perhaps to separate the reputation and character of the man from the works he produced. Katherine

Duncan-Jones and Charles Nicholl have termed *Three Miseries of Barbary* 'xenophobic' (Nicholl 2008, p. 199) and 'undistinguished' (Duncan-Jones 2001, p. 210), and yet this work remains useful not just as a source for imaginative perceptions of early modern black culture (Wilkins called it 'a picture of Barbary') but also as a sober reflection on the London plague that took so many, including his own father. Still further, it points to the violence and cruelty that may well have informed the lost play *Titus and Vespasian*, a popular precursor to Shakespeare's first revenge tragedy, performed repeatedly in the early 1590s at Henslowe's Rose playhouse (marked 'ne' on 11 April 1591/2).

Wilkins was something of a *Johannes fac totum*, not so much a 'hack' as a writer like Thomas Heywood eager to try his hand at different genres, including drama. Given that the King's Men performed his play *The Miseries of Enforced Marriage* in 1607, one might have expected it to have received sustained critical attention. But no scholarly edition of this work has appeared in print, apart from a Malone Society facsimile repro-duction (Blayney 1963). It has been customary to dismiss the play but in its first few scenes at least, *The Miseries* is a sprightly, verbally inventive and engaging domestic tragi-comedy that covers historical events also behind *A Yorkshire Tragedy*, a work now accepted as wholly Middleton's. *The Miseries* shows a notable interest in, and some indebtedness to, the works of Shakespeare, presenting a vividly drawn tavern scene reminiscent of *1 Henry IV* with echoes of Francis, the hapless serving-boy. The swag-gering, dissolute Ilford mulls over phrases in the manner of Polonius, 'Preferment, a good word', and his usurer Gripe resorts to anthimeria ('Word me no words'), a device Shakespeare favoured though didn't invent. The play showcases Wilkins's literary pretensions, quoting Latin, remarking on the 'Zany' of old Italian comedy, dropping hints of Cervantes, striking unusual similes ('like pullen from a pantler's chip[p]ings') and introducing rare terms like 'Epythite', 'widgen' and 'Muchacho' (words not previously used by any literary writer). The play may be rather more pedestrian in its latter half, but it is certainly not without linguistic dexterity or dramatic technique.

Doubt as to the authorship of *Pericles* has been voiced since Nicholas Rowe's edition of Shakespeare in 1709. It was Nikolaus Delius who first proposed, in 1868, that George Wilkins might be the writer of the first two acts (Vickers 2002, pp. 291–5). Delius's suggestion has since been confirmed by detailed and thorough investigations by Brian Vickers and MacD. P. Jackson, both of which build carefully on a substantial body of previous scholarship. Jackson adds that Wilkins may also have had some minor hand in the brothel scenes (Jackson 2003, pp. 212–13). Complicating this attribution is the fact that the 1609 Quarto in all probability prints a memorially reconstructed text. Yet despite a veil of reporting, traces of authorial provenance emerge. In Appendix 2 of *Defining Shakespeare*, Jackson presents phrases and collocations that each act and scene of the play shares with either Wilkins's own play *The Miseries of Enforced Marriage* or Shakespeare's *The Tempest*. The Shakespearian echoes are very low for the first two acts but rise sharply for Acts 3–5. Jackson then adds 'control tests' matching collocations from Wilkins's share in *The Travels of the Three English Brothers* and Shakespeare's late plays, *The Winter's Tale* and *Antony and Cleopatra*, against *The Miseries of Enforced Marriage* and *The Tempest* (but not with both). The results confirm that comparisons thrown up by the first method are in fact consistent and reliable when cross-checked in this way. Wilkins's authorial fingerprint is identifiable especially in the repeated placement of rhyming couplets, especially in the pattern of aabcc ('rifts') and rhymes that mark a pause between blank verse directly before and after ('speech-pause rhymes' or 'rafts') (Jackson 2003, pp. 96–7). Vickers, too, notes Wilkins's characteristic use of antithesis, and insertion of rhymed couplets as *sententiae*. He further highlights Wilkins's idiosyncratic use of 'which' to begin a line, his omission of nominative relative pronouns in the middle of a phrase, and his unpredictable reliance on rhyme (Vickers 2002, pp. 294–5, 331).

A number of suggestions have been offered as to why Shakespeare might have entered into co-authorship with Wilkins. Katherine Duncan-Jones has suggested a Huguenot connection, perhaps via Richard Field who was linked professionally (and by marriage) to the Vautrollier family. She supposes that Mountjoy and Belott dined or supped at Wilkins's tavern in Cow Cross (Duncan-Jones 2001, pp. 207–8). Nicholl suggests that Shakespeare saw in Wilkins a man who knew the seedy brothel-world of Turnbull Street and Clerkenwell from the inside, and that, solely from a professional point of view, he recognised dramatic potential in sounding that experience for the brothel scenes (Nicholl 2008, p. 220). A brothel scene was required by the tale's main source, *The Pattern of Painful Adventures* by Lawrence Twine, registered in 1576. Vickers cites Ernst

Honigmann's observation that Wilkins's familiar penchant for 'shipwrecks, incest, brothels, sudden reversals etc' together with his 'special interest in Mediterranean histories' made him the most suitable collaborator with whom to work (Vickers 2002, pp. 143–4). Jackson notes Wilkins's 'persistent interest in Mediterranean escapades' and his importance for Shakespeare: 'The rough dealer in miseries, travels, travails, and painful adventures deserves our gratitude for starting off Shakespeare's chimerical masterpiece and ushering in the late romances' (Jackson 2003, p. 189). But there may also be a further, more local and practical reason.

Wilkins seems to have had a supporter (the terms 'sponsor' or 'patron' would perhaps be too strong). Three of his works, *The History of Justine*, *The Miseries of Enforced Marriage* and *Three Miseries of Barbary*, were printed by William Jaggard from his shop in Barbican, a location just a short walk from Cow Cross. Perhaps still recovering from the effects of plague, Jaggard's business was barely operating in 1606. *Justine* was one of only three books it produced that year. Trade picked up when *The Miseries of Enforced Marriage* and *Three Miseries of Barbary* were two of the thirteen books Jaggard printed the following year. Jaggard apparently saw merit in Wilkins. He went on to print *Three Miseries of Barbary* in 1607 for Henry Gosson, publisher of the 1609 quarto of *Pericles* and provider of sureties in the case involving Wilkins and Berkes. Jaggard kept his Barbican shop just outside Smithfield but he lived in Holywell Street, half a mile away in Shoreditch where he was neighbour not only to the Burbages, but also (until mid-1603) to Wilkins's father. It seems then that Wilkins enjoyed the favour of printers and publishers who suspected that he might eventually produce a blockbuster hit. A possibility emerges that stationers may occasionally have entertained an interest in particular writers. We might note in passing that Andrew Wise and Valentine Simmes seem to have been keen to foster Shakespeare on their lists: Wise listed five Shakespeare quartos on the Stationers' Register, and Simmes saw nine of them into print, if one allows the 1603 *Hamlet*. With Shakespeare and in *Pericles*, Jaggard and Gosson achieved that hit. Gosson even issued a second quarto of the play in the same year as the first, something, incidentally, that had happened before with *Richard II* and *Troilus and Cressida*. Since history has left no trace of a personal friendship between the two dramatists, it is likely that this particular collaboration was a purely commercial venture. Wilkins might have expected the play in print to make his name, if not his fortune, and by virtue of its co-writer, to a certain extent it has. In fact, it did nothing for him. The elegantly set title-pages of both 1609 quartos, presenting to the world this 'much admired play', make no mention of him at all, and ascribe the play solely to 'William Shakespeare'.

WORKS CITED

Ackroyd, Peter 2006. *Shakespeare: The Biography*. London. Vintage
Bentley, G. E. 1956. *The Jacobean and Caroline Stage*. 7 vols. Oxford. Clarendon Press
Blayney, G. H. 1963. *The Miseries of Enforced Marriage*. Oxford. Malone Society
Duncan-Jones, Katherine 2001. *Ungentle Shakespeare: Scenes from his Life*. London. Thomson Learning
Greg, W. W. (ed.) 1940. *Pericles, The Quarto of 1609* reproduced in Collotype Facsimile. London: Sidgwick and Jackson
Greg, W. W. 1942. *The Editorial Problem in Shakespeare: A Survey of the Foundations of the Text*. Oxford. Clarendon Press
Honan, Park 1999. *Shakespeare: A Life*. Oxford University Press
Jackson, MacD. P. 2003. *Defining Shakespeare: Pericles as Test Case*. Oxford University Press
Jeaffreson, J. C. (ed.) 1974. *Middlesex County Sessions*. Vol. ii. London. Greater London Council
Nicholl, Charles 2008. *The Lodger: Shakespeare on Silver Street*. Harmondsworth. Penguin
Prior, Roger 1972. 'The Life of George Wilkins', *Shakespeare Survey 25*. Kenneth Muir (ed.). Cambridge University Press, pp. 137–52
    1976. 'George Wilkins and The Young Heir', *Shakespeare Survey 29*. Kenneth Muir (ed.). Cambridge University Press, pp. 33–9
Salkeld, Duncan 2012. *Shakespeare Among the Courtesans: Prostitution, Literature and Drama 1500–1650*. Farnham and Burlington, VT. Ashgate
Traversi, Derek (ed.) 1980. *Renaissance Drama*. London and Basingstoke. Macmillan
Vickers, Brian 2002. *Shakespeare, Co-Author*. Oxford University Press
Weis, René 2007. *Shakespeare Revealed: A Biography*. London. John Murray

23

His collaborator Thomas Middleton

EMMA SMITH

§

There's no case yet for the RSC's notepaper to be altered to read The Royal Shakespeare and Middleton and Others Company, but there must now be an argument for posters and programmes for future productions of *Macbeth, Measure for Measure, Timon of Athens* and now *All's Well That End's Well* carrying a joint credit to Shakespeare and Middleton.

Mark Lawson, 'Let's face it: Shakespeare had help',
The Guardian 1 May 2012

By the middle of the first decade of the seventeenth century, Middleton and Shakespeare must have known each other, and each other's work, pretty well. The extent and nature of that artistic relationship is, however, currently being rapidly rewritten. Scholars now agree that they collaborated on *Timon of Athens*, and a consensus is almost emerging that the texts of *Macbeth* and *Measure for Measure* in the 1623 Folio represent Middleton adaptations of Shakespeare plays. But – the recent suggestion of *All's Well That Ends Well* is a case in point – there's probably more to come (Maguire and Smith 2012a). Two contemporary critical strands converge to make it highly likely that further Middletonian collaboration or adaptation will be discovered in the Shakespeare canon: the new embrace of the collaborative energies of early modern theatre; and a quantifiable and increasingly robust understanding of the textual markers of Middleton's authorship. Currently, only the writing partnership with John Fletcher at the end of Shakespeare's career is known to have lasted beyond a single play, but Middleton may yet emerge as a more significant collaborator. In addition, Middleton's own plays show him to be a creative and responsive early reader and reviser of the older playwright's work.

Thomas Middleton was born in 1580 in Ironmonger Lane in St Lawrence parish in the city of London, just off the commercial thoroughfare of Cheapside that would be such a potent setting for many of his city plays. His father William was a wealthy bricklayer granted a coat of arms in 1568 and a crest showing a chained marmoset or ape. His mother Anne remarried in 1586 shortly after William's death. Her new husband, Thomas Harvey, was a spendthrift who had lost his own money travelling to the ill-fated Roanoke colony: it seems that Anne's inheritance must have been at least part of her attraction, since immediately after their marriage they began to quarrel over William's estate, beginning a series of protracted lawsuits that rumbled on until Middleton's majority. These proceedings saw Harvey imprisoned for debt, and an accusation by Anne that he had attempted to poison her. Friends of the couple seem to have negotiated a separation in 1595, whereupon Harvey left England, but he returned some years later to a renewed round of quarrels, legal hearings and debtors' prison. If Harvey was a ne'er-do-well, Anne was clearly also a redoubtable character, attempting to keep control of her finances, active in legal matters and identified as 'a troublesome woman' by one of her hostile tenants (Eccles 1957, p. 523). It's hard not to see in this litigious and dramatic household the seeds of Middleton's elaborate interpersonal comedies such as *A Mad World, My Masters* (1605) or *A Chaste Maid in Cheapside* (1613), and of his abidingly sceptical interest in the operations of the law (Taylor 2004).

Thomas Middleton's earliest writings were not, however, for the theatre. He must have been educated at a city grammar school, and he matriculated at Queen's College, Oxford in 1598, but seems not to have taken a degree. Instead, he began the prolific and diverse writing career catalogued at more than sixty separate published works by Gary Taylor and John Lavagnino, the editors of the landmark collected Oxford edition of 2007. From the start he was ambitious: his long *The Wisdom of Solomon Paraphrased* (1597) (Taylor and Lavagnino 2007), published when he was still in his teens, was dedicated to the Earl of Essex. Other early works ranged across fashionable genres from Ovidian epyllia (*The Ghost of Lucrece*, 1600) to satire (*Microcynicon*, 1599, burned as part of the Bishops' Ban crackdown on satire in that year), to pamphlets (*The Penniless Parliament of Thread-bare Poets*, 1601). By 1601 he had apparently settled on the theatre, and was reportedly 'daily accompanying the players'. Middleton's earliest extant play, *The Phoenix*, was written for the Children of St Paul's in 1603–4 and, like the contemporary *Measure for Measure*, addresses the change of sovereign in its disguised magistrate and succession plot: he is thus a decidedly Jacobean playwright. Middleton married Mary Magdalene Marbeck in the same year, and lived with his wife and their son in Newington Butts, a village suburb not far from Southwark.

Middleton's subsequent playwrighting career traverses the genres of comedy, history and tragedy. It encompassed a fruitful collaborative relationship with Thomas Dekker, with whom he wrote a number of plays including *The Bloody Banquet* (1608–9) and *The Roaring Girl* (1611), and another somewhat less extensive partnership with William Rowley (including *A Fair Quarrel* 1614–16 and *The Changeling* 1622). He wrote for a range of different adult and boys' troupes. With *Michaelmas Term* (1604) he consolidated the fashionable urban genre of contemporary city comedy, a genre he developed with an unsentimental eye to its deliciously cynical interactions of sex, money and commodification. He was commissioned to write civic pageants for the Lord Mayors, and collaborated on the entertainment to welcome the new king to London in 1604. With *A Game at Chesse*, his audacious satire on the religio-politics of Anglo-Spanish relations, he is responsible for the period's most runaway box-office hit, a play performed at the Globe on nine successive days in August 1624.

A Game at Chesse took much of its explosive charge from its forthright politics, and for many critics it has seemed to represent Middleton's own religious views. Although T. S. Eliot famously dismissed Middleton as a kind of journalistic reporter of events who 'has no message; he is merely a great recorder' (Eliot 1963, p. 53), more recent assessments have tended to focus on what Margot Heinemann influentially identified as his puritanism (Heinemann 1980) and what Gary Taylor has modified into 'Calvinism' (Taylor 2004). It is one of the many ways in which Middleton's world view and his authorial persona differ from the religiously opaque Shakespeare's. While publicity for the new collected edition of Middleton's works in 2007 emphasised his range and richness in the tagline 'our other Shakespeare', it is perhaps easier to see differences than similarities in their work (Taylor and Lavagnino 2007, p. 82).

Both wrote extensively across dramatic genres, but Middleton was effectively a theatre-freelancer where Shakespeare was a house dramatist. Middleton, a city boy, had strong professional ties with the city, where the provincial immigrant Shakespeare did not. Middleton's habits of satirical urban comedy were a far cry from the Italianate romantic comedy of Shakespeare, just as his knowingly appetitive tragic characters make Shakespeare's look like innocents abroad, mere amateurs of venality. Middleton's increasing interest in female protagonists, from Moll Cutpurse in *The Roaring Girl* (1611) and *A Chaste Maid in Cheapside* (1613), which has a christening scene requiring more than ten female speaking roles on stage at once, to the complicated carnality of Beatrice-Joanna in *The Changeling* and the amoral manipulation of Livia in *Women Beware Woman* (1621), draws him away from Shakespearian structures and interests. Not for Shakespeare Middletonian nominative determinism – no cuckolded Shortrods (*A Mad World My Masters*) or vengeful Vindices (*The Revenger's Tragedy*, 1606) for him; and not for Middleton the delicacies of Shakespearian psychology.

If these aesthetic and ideological differences make the occasion for their collaboration on *Timon of Athens* difficult to imagine, they also make visible that collaborative process. Much of the work to understand *Timon*, and the extent of Middleton's adaptation in *Measure for Measure* and *Macbeth*, rests on the legibility of their writing differences. Sketching out a collaborative schema which allocates to Middleton the central part of *Timon of Athens* (scenes 5–10 in particular), John Jowett notices ideational differences between the two authors. Shakespeare's Timon is a philanthrope; Middleton's a sort of prodigal (rather like Sir Bounteous Progress in his recent comedy *A Mad World My Masters* (Maguire and Smith 2012b)); 'Middleton develops a stance towards money that can be summarized in the word "debt", where Shakespeare's stance can be summarized in the world "gold"; Middleton's main character is the unnamed 'Steward', typical of his interest in functional types, whereas Shakespeare's focus is the thwarted tragic protagonist Timon (Jowett 2004, pp. 144–53).

Despite – or perhaps because of – their differences in style, experience and outlook, Shakespeare and Middleton were working together on *Timon* at some point in 1605–6. At this point, Shakespeare was a highly experienced playwright with more than twenty plays for the Chamberlain's, later King's Men, to his credit. Middleton, on the other hand, a generation younger, had just begun work for the King's Men with *A Yorkshire Tragedy* (1605) and the *Hamlet*-inspired *The Revenger's Tragedy*. Jowett describes him as a writer 'in transition, moving on from city comedy to tragedy'

(Jowett 2004, p. 9), and on this he had much to learn from the author of *Hamlet* and *Othello*. On the other hand, Middleton's own experience with city comedies, including *A Trick to Catch the Old One* (1605) and *A Mad World, My Masters*, meant he was well equipped to supply writing in the fashionable genre of urban satire in which Shakespeare had not previously worked (as will be discussed below, it may be that the apparent exception to this statement, the gritty Vienna of Shakespeare's *Measure for Measure*, itself may owe something to Middleton). The fact that Middleton's *A Yorkshire Tragedy* was attributed to Shakespeare in both the Stationers' Register entry of 2 May 1608 and in the quarto published by Thomas Pavier in the same year may suggest that the work of the two writers was more intertwined in the period than it now seems to us (Taylor and Lavagnino 2007, p. 592).

Many different models of dramatic collaboration exist during this period: play-patching, division between plot and sub-plot or between outline and realisation, the sub-contracting of acts or specific speeches, a junior writer apprenticed to a more experienced colleague. Much of the evidence about the writing of *Timon* currently suggests that Shakespeare took the lead role, probably plotting the play, writing the opening scene, and focusing on Timon's own major scenes. The play draws on Thomas North's translation of Plutarch, which Shakespeare had already used extensively for *Julius Caesar* and may well have been rereading with *Coriolanus* in mind. The tendency, that's to say, has been to see *Timon* from the point of view of the Shakespeare canon rather than from that of Middleton (Maguire and Smith 2012b, pp. 195–6). But this work on attribution has been pursued not in large-scale ideational readings or by identifying similarities of tone or attitude. Rather, attribution studies tend to be more convinced by computer-aided stylistic analysis that has placed particular weight on verbal fingerprinting. This identifies characteristic markers of a particular author not in their use of unusual words but in their patterns of deployment of apparently non-distinctive syntactical units.

Middleton's own linguistic patterns have been described and elaborated by a number of scholars, especially David J. Lake, MacDonald P. Jackson and R. V. Holdsworth, drawing on methodologies developed by Cyrus Hoy in relation to the Beaumont and Fletcher canon (Lake 1975; Jackson 1979; Holdsworth 1982). One example registers the generational and educational difference between Shakespeare and Middleton. As Jonathan Hope has explored, two variable forms of common locutions exist in early modern English: a choice between 'you' and 'thou' in the second person pronoun, and '"-th" and "-s" as an ending or the third person singular present tense of verbs (e.g. "hath" versus "has")' (Hope 1994, p. 5). Both these variants have a more modern form – 'you' and '-s' – and an older variant – 'thou' and '-th'. On both of these examples, Middleton (a Londoner born in 1580) favours the newer variant and Shakespeare (born in a Midlands market town in 1564) the older. Further, their different use of the auxiliary 'do' form is distinct. Middleton's preference is for what modern English would call the 'regulated' form of the verb, as in 'I went home'. Shakespeare's strong preference is for the unregulated, now non-standard form: 'I did go home'. Hope's work is an important reminder that the Shakespeare we credit with such linguistic inventiveness and fertility is also marked by a recognisably old-fashioned syntax, particularly by contrast with his younger collaborator Middleton (Hope 1994, p. 21)

Other Middleton markers include a high incidence of hyper-metric lines (so-called 'feminine endings') and of rhyming couplets, particularly when compared with Shakespeare's own Jacobean plays. Middleton also demonstrates a quantifiable preference for colloquial contractions such as 'on't', 'for't', 'I'd', and these are so indicative of his hand that Jowett lists them, scene by scene, in his Oxford edition of *Timon* (Jowett 2004, pp. 341–7). MacDonald P. Jackson, for instance, offers a tabular summary of rates for Middletonian contractions, in which the figure for the average Middleton play is more than five times that of a non-Middleton play (Jackson 1979, p. 80). There are other indicators, too, the spellings, mild expletives, idiosyncratically narrative stage directions, and preference for '*a* as a weakened form of *of*, summarised by Jackson as an 'identikit of features from which a picture of "Middleton" may be built up' (Jackson 2007, pp. 84–5).

It is armed with this identikit textual picture that twenty-first-century editors have looked anew at the old question of Middleton's role in *Macbeth*, a question initially cued by the two songs shared by that play and Middleton's own *The Witch*. A version of *Macbeth*, with Middleton's conjectured emendations – about 11 per cent of the whole – marked typographically was published as part of the Oxford Middleton. Middleton's intervention is mainly focused on expanding the witches' roles, with songs and the scenes introducing Hecate in 3.5 and 4.1. As Inga-Stina Ewbank observes, these additions make the play 'less focused on the moral self-destruction of Macbeth, and . . . shift the emphasis on to the witches as being in command' (Ewbank 2007, p. 1168). Middleton's interpolations had previously been seen as disruptive and unnecessary: instead, Ewbank and Taylor identify Middleton as a sensitive reader of Shakespeare's work, adumbrating the themes he found in the text the King's Men wanted him to revive for later Jacobean performance (Vickers 2010; Taylor 2014).

The other Shakespeare play now understood as a Middleton adaptation is *Measure for Measure*. Jowett suggests that the 1623 Folio text represents a reworking of a 1603–4 original in around 1621. He posits a developed role for Juliet, expanded references to urban vices in the manner of Middletonian city comedy, and a change of location for topical reasons to do with the significance of Vienna in the Thirty Years War. The result is a wide-ranging picture of adaptation, such that 'our engagement with the play is in some part Middleton's engagement with Shakespeare's play': again, Middleton is Shakespeare's first attested reader as well as his collaborator (Jowett 2007, p. 1546).

There is no mention of Middleton – or any other co-author – in the 1623 Folio. Middleton's adaptations of *Macbeth* and *Measure for Measure* must have represented the most recent form of those playscripts in the King's Men archive, and therefore the working copies which John Heminge and Henry Condell presented to the publishers. The plays were kept not as Shakespeare had written them but in their current state, updated and polished by the younger playwright. These discoveries leave open the door that other plays that were not printed close to their first performances may well exist in a revised state in the First Folio. If Middleton prepared these two plays for later revivals, his hand may well be found in other Folio texts which show signs – act divisions, for instance, or the excision of oaths – that suggest a date later than that we generally ascribe to their first performance. The vehemence of some of the defences of sole authorship betrays the radical potential of this line of enquiry. Watch this space.

WORKS CITED

Eccles, Mark 1957. 'Thomas Middleton a Poett', *Studies in Philology* 54: 516–36
Eliot, T. S. 1963. *Elizabethan Dramatists*. London. Faber

Ewbank, Inga-Stina (ed.) 2007. 'The Tragedy of Macbeth' in Gary Taylor and John Lavagnino (eds.), *Thomas Middleton: The Collected Works*. Oxford. Clarendon Press

Heinemann, Margot 1980. *Puritanism and Theatre: Thomas Middleton and Opposition Drama under the Early Stuarts*. Cambridge University Press

Holdsworth, R. V. 1982. 'Middleton and Shakespeare: The Case for Middleton's Hand in *Timon of Athens*'. Unpublished dissertation, University of Manchester

Hope, Jonathan 1994. *The Authorship of Shakespeare's Plays*. Cambridge University Press

Jackson, MacDonald P. 1979. *Studies in Attribution: Middleton and Shakespeare*. Salzburg. Institut Fur Anglistik und Amerikanistik, Universität Salzburg

2007. 'Early Modern Authorship: Canons and Chronologies' in Gary Taylor and John Lavagnino (eds.), *Thomas Middleton and Early Modern Textual Culture: A Companion to The Collected Works*. Oxford. Clarendon Press, 80–97

Jowett, John (ed.) 2004. *Timon of Athens*. Oxford University Press

(ed.) 2007. 'Measure for Measure' in Gary Taylor and John Lavagnino (eds.), *Thomas Middleton: The Collected Works*. Oxford. Clarendon Press

Lake, David J. 1975. *The Canon of Thomas Middleton's Plays*. Cambridge University Press

Maguire, Laurie and Smith, Emma 2012a. 'Many Hands – A New Shakespeare Collaboration?', *Times Literary Supplement* 19 April 2012

2012b. '"Time's comic sparks": the dramaturgy of *A Mad World, My Masters* and *Timon of Athens*' in Gary Taylor and Trish Thomas Henley (eds.), *The Oxford Handbook of Thomas Middleton*. Oxford University Press, pp. 181–96

Taylor, Gary 2004. 'Middleton, Thomas (*bap.* 1580, *d.* 1627)', in *Oxford Dictionary of National Biography*, Oxford University Press, 2004; online edn, May 2008, www.oxforddnb.com/view/article/18682, accessed 1 Sept. 2014

2014. 'Macbeth and Middleton' in Robert Miola (ed.), *Macbeth: The Norton Critical Edition*. New York. Norton, pp. 296–305

Taylor, Gary and Lavagnino, John (gen. eds.) 2007. *Thomas Middleton: The Collected Works*. Oxford. Clarendon Press

Vickers, Brian 2010. 'Disintegrated: Did Middleton adapt *Macbeth*?', *Times Literary Supplement* 20 May

24

His collaborator John Fletcher

LUCY MUNRO

In February 2008 the National Portrait Gallery, London, announced the success of a campaign to raise the money to acquire a portrait of John Fletcher, £2,700 of which was raised by a raffle at Fletcher's House Tea Rooms, in Rye, Sussex, the former vicarage where Fletcher was born (Anon. 2008). While the portrait shows the dramatist at the height of his success in the early 1620s, richly clad and resting his right hand upon a table bearing an inkstand, quill and sheet of paper, the Tea Rooms' contribution to its purchase recalls his origins. We are used to thinking of Fletcher in terms of '– and Fletcher': 'Beaumont and Fletcher'; 'Shakespeare and Fletcher'. The portrait instead reminds us of his independent status and of the distinctive qualities of his family background and upbringing, both import-ant factors if we try to comprehend fully his relationship with Shakespeare.

Fletcher was baptised on 20 December 1579, the fourth child of Richard Fletcher and Elizabeth Holland. Although his background was relatively humble, Richard's eloquence and personal charm helped him to become successively Dean of Peterborough and Bishop of Bristol, Worcester and, in 1594, London. His sons were educated at the Cathedral Grammar School in Peterborough, where John is recorded as one of twenty scholars in 1588 and 1589 (Mellors 1939, pp. xliii–iv). Sir John Harington, no friend of Richard Fletcher, describes him as 'a comely and courtly prelate', saying that he 'could preach well, and would speak boldly, and yet keep *decorum* ... The Queen, as I said, found no fault with his liberal speech' (Harington 1804: 2, pp. 41, 45). Queen Elizabeth did, however, find fault with his personal life. In 1595, three years after the death of his first wife, Richard married a widow, Mary Baker; the Queen, who disliked married clergymen, suspended him for a brief time, and he had only partially regained her favour by the time of his sudden death in June 1595.

FIGURE 5: John Fletcher (1579–1625), a known collaborator with Shakespeare on three late plays, and his successor as chief playwright to the King's Men. He is shown here looking every inch the successful and prosperous playwright.

Richard's children, and his debts, were left in the hands of his brother Giles, a diplomat with his own court connections.

Little is known of John's life between his father's death and his emergence as a playwright. He had matriculated at Corpus Christi College,

Cambridge, in 1591, and Richard's death does not seem to have prevented his graduating with his MA in 1598. Nonetheless, he may have been forced to abandon plans for a career in the church or university, the paths followed by his father and eldest brother, Nathaniel, who was already a Fellow at Queens' College, Cambridge, and later became chaplain to Sir Henry Wotton and Rector of Barking and Darmsden, Suffolk. Nathaniel and John were left 'all my books to be divided between them equally' in their father's will, drawn up in 1593 (National Archives, PROB 11/87). Another brother, Theophilus, two years John's senior and – perhaps significantly – not included in the bequest of books, left Bristol to fight with Essex in Ireland in March 1599.

There is nothing in Fletcher's background to suggest that his relatives would have thought writing plays a suitable occupation. His uncle Giles was a poet and his cousins, Phineas and Giles Junior, were to follow in his footsteps; his brother Nathaniel wrote Latin verse (Barlow 1598: I2r–v), and his 'judgement, wit and learning' were praised in John Weever's *Epigrams* (1599: F2v). But writing poems and plays were very different activities, and John's family had actually been involved with the suppression of drama in August 1597, when Giles Senior was employed by the Privy Council to examine the men imprisoned after performances of the allegedly seditious comedy *The Isle of Dogs*. Among his colleagues was the notorious government agent Richard Topcliffe, and among the prisoners was John's future friend Ben Jonson. Even though all of the prisoners had been released by early October, Jonson being the last to be set free, it seems unlikely that Giles would have approved of his nephew's future career.

Family connections could not help Fletcher; instead, probably as a consequence of his friendship with Francis Beaumont, he gained the patronage of the Earl and Countess of Huntingdon. A verse letter to the Countess, written around 1620, demonstrates the warmth of their relationship. Addressing her as 'best of your kin', Fletcher pledges to

> Write something (Madame) like those honest men
> That have no business; something that affords
> Some savour to the writer. Knights and lords,
> Pray, by your leaves, I will not treat of you –
> Ye are too tetchy – nor whether it be true
> We shall have wars with Spain (I would we might),

Nor who shall dance i'th' masque, nor who shall write
Those brave things done, nor sum up the expense,
Nor whether it be paid for ten year hence.
(quoted in McMullan 1994, p. 18)

Fletcher's expressed scepticism about court protocol and display reflects
the experience of his patrons and his family, who had their own reasons to
be suspicious of royal favour. Richard's career and early death gave him an
insight into the workings of power, on which he was to gain an additional
perspective in 1601, when his uncle Giles was drawn into the Essex rebellion and narrowly escaped trial or execution. John's plays, like his father's
sermons, tread the line between political boldness and decorum, their
'liberal speech' apparently provoking and titillating rather than calling
down the wrath of the authorities. Even a play such as *Sir John Van Olden
Barnavelt*, written with Philip Massinger in 1619 and based on current
European politics, which led the censor, Sir George Buc, to score out one
scene and write 'I like not this' against it, eventually reached the stage
though the willingness of dramatists and playing company to reach a
compromise. Nevertheless, an anecdote in which Fletcher and Beaumont
meet to 'contrive their design' for *The Maid's Tragedy* but narrowly avoid
arrest when an eavesdropper hears them plotting to kill the king suggests
the delicacy with which Fletcher's plays handle their potentially explosive
political material (Anon. 1667, p. 31).

Similarly, Fletcher's bellicose attitude towards Spain – not untypical
during the increased international tension of the early 1620s – is in line
with the politics of the Huntingdons and his own family. His grandfather
had been ordained by Nicholas Ridley and deprived of his office under
Mary Tudor, establishing a staunchly Protestant tradition for his
descendants. As Dean of Peterborough, Richard exhorted Mary, Queen
of Scots, to renounce her Catholicism before her execution, and he later
assisted Archbishop Whitgift in drawing up the Calvinist Lambeth
Articles; Phineas's vehemently anti-Catholic *The Locusts*, a poem about
continental history inspired by the Gunpowder Plot, expresses much of the
family's later religious allegiances. Yet John Fletcher never wrote anything
as purely anti-Catholic as *The Locusts*, and both his habitual use of Spanish
source texts for his plays and his friendship with Beaumont, whose brother
was a recusant Catholic, suggest that his religious and political world view
was more complex than that of his cousin.

Fletcher's early career is entwined with that of Beaumont. He may have helped to polish Beaumont's first play, *The Woman Hater*, performed by the Children of Paul's in 1606, and after writing two unsuccessful solo plays for the Children of the Queen's Revels at the Blackfriars playhouse, *The Faithful Shepherdess* and *The Knight of the Burning Pestle*, the pair teamed up to write *Cupid's Revenge* and *The Coxcomb*, both genuine hits. Beaumont and Fletcher were among the first dramatists to be commissioned when the King's Men repossessed the Blackfriars in 1608. Between 1609 and 1612 they wrote a series of successful plays for the King's Men and the Children of the Queen's Revels, *Philaster*, *The Maid's Tragedy*, *A King and No King* and *The Scornful Lady* among them, to which Fletcher added solo plays such as *The Woman's Prize or The Tamer Tamed*, *Valentinian* and *Bonduca*. Beaumont's last known work is *The Masque of the Inner Temple and Gray's Inn*, performed on 20 February 1613 as part of the celebrations of the marriage of King James's daughter, Elizabeth, to Frederick, Elector Palatine. Later that year he married an heiress, Ursula Isley, and appears to have stopped writing shortly afterwards, probably as the result of a debilitating stroke (Finkelpearl 1990, pp. 41–2).

Fletcher seems actively to have enjoyed writing with others, and commentators have been tempted to think that his collaboration with Shakespeare – struggling to find inspiration after completing *The Tempest*, viewed as his last solo play – was a result of Beaumont's retirement. Rick Thomas's play *For All Time* (2009) brings together a disillusioned Shakespeare and a Fletcher who is mourning his break-up with Beaumont. As Dominic Cavendish comments, 'it presents us with the sorry sight of the Bard on the bottle: bereft of inspiration, tired of London, and bitterly resentful of the new theatrical fashions' (Cavendish 2009). A similar picture had appeared nearly a century earlier, in Horace Howard Furness Jr's 1920 play *'The Gloss of Youth': An Imaginary Episode in the Lives of William Shakespeare and John Fletcher*, in which Shakespeare is depressed by the audience's preference for comedy and their failure to appreciate the work into which he pours his heart. Faced with Fletcher's eager critique of his first scene, he complains 'I cannot, nor I will not write at *thy* behest', and Fletcher is left to remember 'those far happier days when we together wrote turn and turn about on Henry VIII and Wolsey – Thou wert glad enough to have my praise or blame of any part' (Furness 1920, pp. 15–16).

Yet the dates do not quite fit. Shakespeare and Fletcher seem to have written three plays together: 'The History of Cardenio. By Mr Fletcher. & Shakespeare', entered in the Stationers' Register by Humphrey Moseley on 9 September 1653, which is probably the 'Cardenna' or 'Cardenno' performed at Court in the 1612–13 Christmas season and again in June 1613; *All is True* (*Henry VIII*) at a performance of which on 29 June 1613 the Globe playhouse burned down; and *The Two Noble Kinsmen*, the prologue of which refers to the King's Men's 'losses' (l. 32). *Cardenio* does not appear ever to have been printed, and is now lost, unless something of Fletcher and Shakespeare survives in Lewis Theobald's 1727 play *The Double Falsehood*, which he claimed to have adapted from a Shakespeare manuscript. All three plays involve the adaptation of other authors and materials: Cardenio is the protagonist of an episode in Cervantes's *Don Quixote*; *Henry VIII* draws heavily on the account of King Henry's reign in Raphael Holinshed's *Chronicles*, even adapting its text for use as stage directions; and *The Two Noble Kinsmen* is based on Chaucer's *The Knight's Tale*.

Although *Henry VIII* and *The Two Noble Kinsmen* post-date Beaumont's retirement, *Cardenio* does not, and it is possible that Beaumont – whose earlier play *The Knight of the Burning Pestle* demonstrates his fondness for *Don Quixote* – was also involved in its composition. Furthermore, *The Two Noble Kinsmen* incorporates a sly parody of *The Masque of the Inner Temple and Gray's Inn*. In Act 3, Scene 5, a scene for which Fletcher seems to have taken primary responsibility, the Schoolmaster ushers in the morris dance, which has precisely the same personnel as the second antimasque dance in Beaumont's masque, including a he-baboon, a she-baboon and the Jailer's Daughter in the role of the she-fool, and which probably mimicked the steps of that dance. According to the printed text of the masque, the dance had pleased the King so much that it was danced again at the end of the entertainment (see Bowers 1966: ll. 211–14); by inserting it into their play, Fletcher and Shakespeare pay tribute to Beaumont's achievement, give their spectators at the Blackfriars a glimpse of courtly entertainment, and, perhaps, tease their colleague about his contribution to court festivity. Given Shakespeare's similarly ambivalent treatment of the masque in *The Tempest*, it is not surprising that he and Fletcher may have colluded in this way. Yet this set of interactions also suggests that Beaumont, Fletcher and Shakespeare may have planned further collaborations.

Coming after the plays usually thought to be central to Shakespeare's 'late' work – *Cymbeline*, *The Tempest* and the hugely popular *The Winter's Tale* – *Henry VIII* and *The Two Noble Kinsmen* complicate our view of the end of his career and apply pressure to critical common-places. Edward Dowden's highly influential book *Shakspere: A Critical Study of his Mind and Art* (1875), traces a change in Shakespeare's outlook and perspective as he moved from writing tragedies to writing what Dowden later termed 'romances': 'he turned for relief to the pastoral loves of Prince Florizel and Perdita; and as soon as the tone of his mind was restored, gave expression to its ultimate mood of grave serenity in *The Tempest*, and so ended' (223). The collaborative plays challenge this biographically orientated reading of 'late' Shakespeare because they are in many ways unlike *Cymbeline*, *The Tempest* and *The Winter's Tale* and because they remind us that those plays are also disparate in narrative, form and technique. In addition, *Henry VIII* and *The Two Noble Kinsmen* cannot belong fully to 'late' Shakespeare if they are also comparatively 'early' Fletcher.

What is more, like *The Winter's Tale*, which is based on Robert Greene's prose romance *Pandosto*, the co-authored plays – each of which owes a clear debt to an earlier work – highlight the multiple acts of collaboration between dead and living authors on which early modern literary culture was based. The prologue to *The Two Noble Kinsmen* notoriously refers to 'Chaucer, of all admired' as the play's 'breeder', worries that the spectators' booing and hissing if it fails in performance may 'shake the bones of that good man', and anxiously declares

> This is the fear we bring,
> For to say truth, it were an endless thing
> And too ambitious to aspire to him,
> Weak as we are, and almost breathless swim
> In this deep water.
>
> (ll. 21–5)

We are not used to seeing Shakespeare – or, indeed, Fletcher – in such a position, and the prologue reminds us of both the cultural prominence of Chaucer, often viewed as the 'father' of English poetry, and the compara-tively lowly status of dramatic writing, even when a play was composed by the resident dramatist and rising star of the King's Men.

Scholars have also tended to underplay the closeness of the collaboration between Shakespeare and Fletcher. *Henry VIII* and *The Two Noble Kinsmen* must have needed careful plotting, given that both dramatists contribute to the presentation of major characters such as King Henry, Katherine of Aragon, Wolsey, Palamon, Arcite and Emilia; although Fletcher may have written all of the Jailer's Daughter's soliloquies, she first appears in Act 2, Scene 1, a scene apparently written by Shakespeare. Neither does one partner invariably write particular sections of the narrative. Shakespeare seems to have written the opening scenes of *Henry VIII* and *The Two Noble Kinsmen*, but Fletcher's hand is present early in Act 2 of both plays; Shakespeare seems to have written the final scene of *The Two Noble Kinsmen* and Fletcher that of *All is True* (*Henry VIII*). Brian Vickers provides a thorough reassessment for both plays (Vickers 2004, pp. 333–432).

Yet to focus on the co-authored plays is to overlook the extent to which the works of Shakespeare and Fletcher were already intertwined before 1612. *Philaster* and *Cymbeline* are so closely related in their subject matter, genre and uncertain tonal qualities that scholars have never been able to decide conclusively which was written first, and both also owe debts to *The Faithful Shepherdess*, *Cupid's Revenge*, and Shakespeare and Wilkins's *Pericles*. *The Tempest* similarly glances at Fletcher's pastoral tragicomedy, reworking its magically empowered enforcer, the 'faithful shepherdess' Clorin, as a more conventionally male magus, and splitting its unusually civil attending Satyr into the figures of Ariel and Caliban. Moreover, Fletcher's *Bonduca* adopts and adapts the Romano-British setting of *Cymbeline*, presenting the story of Boudicca as a sustained exploration of the danger and allure of Roman political and cultural domination. Beaumont and Fletcher also rework older plays by Shakespeare. *The Maid's Tragedy* and *Philaster* have fun with themes, motifs and narrative structures from plays such as *Hamlet*, *Othello* and *Twelfth Night*. In the most sustained example of this creative appropriation, Fletcher's *The Woman's Prize* frames itself as a mock-sequel to, or spin-off from, *The Taming of the Shrew*, envisaging a world in which Katherine has died and Petruccio married again to a young woman who is determined to tame *him*. Shakespeare and Fletcher (and Beaumont) were already working together before the composition of the plays that we traditionally consider as collaborations.

We will never know why Shakespeare ceased to write plays in 1613. Perhaps, like Beaumont, he was incapacitated by illness; perhaps writing with Fletcher failed to 'rekindle [his] imagination' (Pogue 2006, p. 108); perhaps the King's Men found his writing increasingly impenetrable and eased him out, as some scholars have mischievously suggested, having already 'required him to work with a colleague who was more in touch with the demands of the public than the ageing, increasingly self-absorbed master' (Wells 2006). Nonetheless, after Fletcher succeeded the older man as resident dramatist for the King's Men, his agile creative intelligence was to take Shakespearian forms into the 1620s, spinning off *The Tempest* in *The Sea Voyage*, *The Island Princess* and *The Double Marriage*, returning to Chaucer in *Women Pleased*, and revisiting the materials of *Antony and Cleopatra* in *The False One*. Shakespeare's multiple collaborations with Fletcher thus help us to reconsider his working practices, his final years of creativity, and his afterlife on the Jacobean stage and beyond.

WORKS CITED

Anon. 1667. *Poor Robin's Jests*. London
Anon. 2008. 'National portrait gallery acquires painting of playwright John Fletcher', *Culture 24*, 6 February, www.culture24.org.uk/history-and-heritage/literature-and-music/art54068
Barlow, William 1598. *Vita et obitus ornatissimi celeberrimíq[ue] viri Richardi Cosin*. London
Bowers, Fredson (ed.) 1966. *The Masque of the Inner Temple, in The Dramatic Works* in the *Beaumont and Fletcher Canon*, Vol. 1. Cambridge University Press
Cavendish, Dominic 2009. Review of *For All Time*, Theatre by the Lake, Keswick, *Daily Telegraph*, 10 August
Dowden, Edward 1875. *Shakspere: A Critical Study of his Mind and Art*. London. Henry S. King & Co.
Finkelpearl, Philip J. 1990. *Court and Country Politics in the Plays of Beaumont and Fletcher*. Princeton University Press
Furness, Horace Howard, Jr. 1920. *'The Gloss of Youth': An Imaginary Episode in the Lives of William Shakespeare and John Fletcher*. Philadelphia. J. B. Lippincott
Harington, John 1804. *Nugae Antiquae*. Henry Harington and Thomas Park (eds.). London
McMullan, Gordon 1994. *The Politics of Unease in the Plays of John Fletcher*. University of Massachusetts Press
(ed.) 2000. *King Henry VIII*. London. Thomson Learning

Mellors, William Thomas (ed.) 1939. *Peterborough Local Administration: Parochial Government Before the Reformation. Churchwardens' Accounts, 1467–1573, with Supplementary Documents, 1107–1488*. Northamptonshire Record Society

Pogue, Kate Emery 2006. *Shakespeare's Friends*. Westport, CT. Praeger

Vickers, Brian 2004. *Shakespeare, Co-Author: A Historical Study of Five Collaborative Plays*. Oxford University Press

Weever, John 1599. *Epigrams in the Oldest Cut, and Newest Fashion*. London

Wells, Stanley 2006. *Shakespeare and Co.: Christopher Marlowe, Thomas Dekker, Ben Jonson, Thomas Middleton, John Fletcher and the Other Players in his Story*. London. Penguin

25

His editors John Heminges and Henry Condell

PAUL EDMONDSON

Their names usually appear together as Shakespeare's friends, fellow actors and 'editors' of the 1623 Folio. But how might Shakespeare have perceived them? John Heminges (1566–1630) and Henry Condell (1576–1627) were men he trusted and liked. Along with Richard Burbage, they were added to the latest draft of his will and bequeathed 26s 8d each (one mark) to buy mourning rings. Shakespeare refers to them there as 'my fellows'; all three men had sons named William. Perhaps Shakespeare's bequests formed an informal contract for them to oversee the 1623 edition of his collected plays, though Burbage died in 1619 (Wells 2002, p. 99).

Like Shakespeare, Heminges and Condell acted, invested in businesses, and acquired real estate. They lived in the parish of St Mary's, Aldermanbury, less than ten minutes' walk away from Silver Street where, in 1604 and probably for longer, Shakespeare was lodging with his friends the Mountjoys. Both men combined civic duty with religious conviction in their local church. Condell is mentioned as a sidesman in 1606 (Lee 1887, p. 469), and in 1617 Heminges signed the register twice as second warden and three times as the first, and Condell signed it twice as second warden (Edmond 2004, 12, p. 919). They helped to organise services, noted absentees, distributed local poor relief, oversaw the upkeep of the building and maintained the goodwill of its surrounding communities. Condell met with some prejudice when he took up the office 'only in regard of his profession, he being a player'. But personal testimonies noted that he had been 'a parishioner of the parish of St Mary Aldermanbury by the space of 21 years and more, hath in that parish borne all offices up to the place of churchwarden and always held in good repute and estimation among his neighbours' (Archer 2009, p. 400). In 1619, Heminges and Condell were listed as 'feoffees' (trustees) of the parish land (Bentley 1941, p. 411). Perhaps they were emulating Shakespeare in their service to the Church. Shakespeare had purchased a share of the Stratford-upon-Avon tithes in 1605, a shrewd financial investment, but one through which he took on financial responsibility for the church's upkeep. Church-wardenship there was not viable for Shakespeare, who had to spend long stretches of time in London, but he was, like his friends, demonstrating support for the established state Church of England.

Personal backgrounds

John Heminges was baptised in St Peter's Church in Droitwich on 25 November 1566. He was introduced to business early and became an apprentice for nine years with the Grocers' Company from the age of twelve. In 1585, his master, James Collins, died, bequeathing him 40 shillings. Heminges was freed two years later, aged twenty-one.

That marked the beginning of Heminges's theatrical career, bringing the business skills of a grocer to bear on the rising professional theatre. On 13 June 1587, the Queen's Men were acting in Thame, Oxfordshire when a fight broke out between two of the actors. John Towne killed William Knell. By 1590, Heminges had married Knell's widow, Rebecca, which means he might have become involved with the troupe at any time from 1587. If (as Mark Eccles proposed in 1961) Shakespeare had joined the Queen's Men following the murder of Knell, then he and Heminges could have met as early as the summer of 1587. The problem is that we do not know whether the company performed in Stratford before or after the murder and, as Schoenbaum says, 'no evidence exists of any Elizabethan troupe ever having recruited while on the road' (Schoenbaum 1991, p. 541). Or perhaps they met in 1593, the year *Venus and Adonis* was published. By then, Heminges was a prominent member of the Lord Strange's Men (he is mentioned in their travelling patent for 1593), one of three companies to have performed Shakespeare's *Titus Andronicus* and with whom Shakespeare might have had some association.

Condell, ten years younger, was baptised on 5 September 1576 in St Peter Mancroft Church, Norwich, then the second biggest city in England. He may have first met John Heminges when Lord Strange's Men visited in 1593. Or, perhaps Condell was already living in London. His father had died in October 1591 and his uncle, Humphrey Yeomans, by profession a cutler, was working as a blacksmith in St Bride's parish, Fleet Street. David

Kathman suggests Condell went to work there to support his widowed mother (Kathman 2012, p. 115). Acting troupes regularly performed at the nearby Bell Savage Inn and his uncle owned The Queen's Head tavern close to the Inner and Middle Temples. His uncle died in May 1594, leaving the property to his widow and son and dividing up the rest between his three sisters, including Condell's mother. In 1596 Condell had the good fortune to marry the wealthy Elizabeth Smart, the only child of her late father, Henry Smart, a gentleman, from whom she had inherited several large houses on the Strand, including Helmet Court, near Somerset House, as well as leases on tenements in the Savoy parish (Eccles 1991a, p. 44).

Business dealings and social status

Heminges and Rebecca had fourteen children between 1590 and 1613. Burial records suggest that three of these died as infants (Lee 1891, p. 385), so there were always plenty of mouths for a professional grocer turned theatre practitioner to feed. Condell and Elizabeth had nine children between 1599 and 1614, three of whom survived into adulthood.

From 1594, Heminges was a co-founder and shareholder of the Lord Chamberlain's Men whose shares, like Shakespeare's, would have cost him between £50 and £80 (Gurr 2004, pp. 89 and 108). His neighbour, Nicholas Bland, inherited the plot of land a hundred yards away from the Rose Theatre on which the Lord Chamberlain's Men took a lease to build the Globe, backed by William Leveson and Thomas Savage (Wood 2003, pp. 224–5). Like Shakespeare, Heminges was a founding shareholder of the Globe from 1599, for which they would have paid around £100 (Gurr 2004, p. 115). Condell was a sharer in the company by 1603 and bought shares in the Globe around 1605. In 1608, both men invested in the Black-friars Theatre, from which time, like Shakespeare, they could expect to earn around £200 a year from their shares in the company and the theatres (Gurr 2004, p. 115). After acquiring his Globe shares, Heminges instigated an important legal procedure which meant that the shareholders could bequeath their shares rather than their being redistributed among the surviving company partners.

Heminges was living in Thomas Savage's house in Addle Street when he bought it for £90 in 1605. In 1611 he bought another house in Silver Street from Savage's son, Richard (Eccles 1991, p. 458). Heminges was one of only ten seacoal meters (who monitored all coal imported into London by the sea). They were paid around £10 a year and could keep the office for life. It was a position Heminges held until 1626 (Kathman, in press), which suggests he decided to step down from the office at sixty or became too ill or tired to continue.

Heminges's son-in-law, John Atkins, led the rebuilding of the playhouse after the fire of 1613. That same year Heminges stood as a trustee for Shakespeare's purchase of the Blackfriars Gatehouse. Both men were referred to as 'of great living, wealth and power' when they were sued by John Witter on 20 April 1620 for a one-sixth share of the Globe (Bentley 1941, 2, p. 411). An epitaph on Richard Burbage by Ben Jonson imagines him being well received in heaven 'when thy fellows are angels and old Heminges is God' (Bentley 1941, 2, p. 468). Heminges was clearly a natural leader who always got his own way. Although he is referred to as 'generosus', 'a gentleman' in his daughter Mary's marriage record in 1627, he was not granted a coat of arms until 1629. David Kathman (to whom I am indebted for having corresponded with me about his work on Heminges and Condell) suggests that Heminges's wealth and social standing allowed him to refer to himself as gentleman without the official heraldry. By buying up the shares of their deceased colleagues, Heminges and Condell eventually owned half of the Globe Theatre between them. On his death in 1630, Heminges owned a quarter of both the Globe and the Blackfriars shares (Baldwin, 1927, pp. 90–117), a position that led to legal disputes in 1635.

Condell is referred to as 'gent.' in 1603 when settling the estate of his thirteen-year-old cousin (the son of deceased Uncle Humphrey), which suggests he had already acquired a coat of arms (Kathman, in press). It looks as if he was following Shakespeare's example who had inherited his coat of arms in 1601. In 1617 Condell invested, with William Washbourne of Wichenford, Worcestershire, 'a revisionary interest in half of a 30-acre estate called Brockhampton in Snowshill, Gloucestershire' (Kathman, in press), about thirty miles from Stratford-upon-Avon. They sold it in 1619. By 1625, Condell had taken out a lease on a country manor in Fulham and was regarded as well-landed and wealthy: in the dedication to a pamphlet reply to Thomas Dekker's *A Rod for Runaways* entitled *The Runaway's Answer* (1625) he is referred to as 'our much respected and very worthy friend, Mr H. Condell, at his country house in Fulham' (Bentley 1941–68, 2, pp. 410 and 412). Dekker had attacked the actors for touring during a time of plague and had mentioned that Condell 'entertained them royally' before they left (Lee 1887, p. 469).

In 1605 Heminges was one of the overseers of colleague Augustine Phillips's estate and received a silver bowl worth £50 (Honigmann and Brock 1993, p. 74). When fellow actor and colleague Alexander Cooke died in 1614, both Heminges and Condell received the management of his estate in trust for his two children and one as yet to be born child (Honigmann and Brock 1993, pp. 94–5). They also held in trust John Underwood's estate for his five children from 1624 (for which they received 11 shillings, Honigmann and Brock 1993, pp. 142–4). Condell acted as an executor for Nicholas Tooley in 1623 and received a share of the residue of his estate once all the bequests had been paid. In 1627, Condell appointed Heminges as an overseer, referring to him as one of his 'very loving friends' and bequeathed him £5 to buy a piece of plate (Honigmann and Brock 1993, p. 158). Bequests of this kind testify to their reliability with money as well as to their trustworthiness and the respect of their friends.

Men of the theatre

In the list of the principal actors at the front of the 1623 Folio, Heminges is listed third (after Shakespeare and Burbage) and Condell eighth. According to Kathman, the order of appearance is roughly chronological and based on the time when each of the men joined the company as actors or shareholders. We do not know which roles they acted in Shakespeare's plays, but Edmond Malone said Heminges played Falstaff, though no evidence for this survives. Both men are listed as having acted, along with Shakespeare, in Ben Jonson' s *Every Man In His Humour* (1598) and *Every Man Out of His Humour* (1599). Heminges and Condell also played in Jonson's *Sejanus, Volpone, The Alchemist* and *Catiline* (from 1603 to 1611).

Heminges does not appear in any cast lists after 1611, but he and Condell might have been performing in *All is True* (*Henry VIII*) when the Globe burned down on 29 June 1613. A ballad circulating within a day of the disaster mentions:

> The reprobates though drunk on Monday,
> Prayed for the Fool and Henry Condye.

We know that Heminges stuttered because the ballad records:

Then with swoll'n eyes, like drunken Flemings,
Distressèd stood old stuttering Heminges.

(Wells 2006, p. 242)

Or perhaps he was only stuttering with shock to see the Globe on fire. He is referred to as 'old Mr. Heminges' in Jonson's *The Masque of Christmas* (presented at Court in 1616), which has led to the assumption that he specialised in elderly characters. An annotated copy of Jonson's works shows that Heminges played the old Corbaccio in a revival of Jonson's *Volpone* between 1616 and 1619.

Condell took at least one leading young man's role, Ferrex in *The Second Part of the Seven Deadly Sins* for the Lord Chamberlain's Men (1597–8, Kathman, in press). He played himself in John Webster's Induction to John Marston's *The Malcontent* (1604), appearing on stage with William Sly (whom Condell tells to put his hat back on, line 33), Richard Burbage, John Sinclo and John Lowin. He is referred to as Harry Condell and sounds humorously pedantic, heralding the play as 'neither satire nor moral, but the mean passage of a history' (lines 52–3). He goes on to explain that although the play had been thought lost, 'we found it, and play it' (line 75). He quotes Plutarch in Latin (line 90) and comes across as a slightly bossy, didactic theatrical authority (Marston 1975, pp. 8–18).

He acted in Francis Beaumont's and John Fletcher's *The Captain* (1612–13), *Bonduca* (1613–14), *Valentinian* (1613–14, Kathman, in press), and played the Cardinal in the original production of Webster's *The Duchess of Malfi* (1613–14, opposite Burbage, who played his brother Ferdinand), a role he probably played for a decade – certainly a part to be relished by a churchwarden and pillar of his community. He played Mosca in the revival of *Volpone* (for which, as Lois Potter notes, he would have had to speak some Spanish), and Surly in a revival of *The Alchemist* (1616–19), demanding roles which require verbal dexterity and charisma (Potter 2012, p. 137). The evidence suggests that Condell was the better, more attractive and versatile actor of the two.

Heminges's most important off-stage role was in the business arrangements for the Lord Chamberlain's Men, later the King's Men. He received payments for performances at Court, for example the £30 paid to him and Thomas Pope on 2 October 1599. He took over as their company manager after Augustine Phillips's decease in 1605 and is referred to as the 'presenter', rather like Peter Quince in *A Midsummer Night's Dream*, liaising with the Master of the Revels and organising rehearsals, touring and transport.

Heminges, Condell and Shakespeare are among nine King's Men listed on a receipt for scarlet cloth granted by royal patent on 17 May 1603 for liveries at James I's coronation. Over the 1604–5 Christmas season Heminges presented a play for Queen Anne in which Marie Mountjoy, Shakespeare's landlady at the time, was paid a generous £50 for work on the costumes and head-dresses. Importantly, Heminges's status as a Grocer allowed him to take boy apprentices into the theatre company where they could be trained as actors. From 1595, he bound into service at least ten boys aged between eight and twelve years old. One of them, Alexander Cooke (bound 26 January 1597) became a shareholder in the King's Men and was made a freeman and Grocer in 1609. He died in 1614 and remembered 'my master Hennings' in his will (Kathman, in press). Another apprentice, Richard Sharpe (bound 21 February 1616), played the Duchess of Malfi around 1620 and adult male roles from 1626 until his death in 1632 (Kathman 2009, p. 423).

It is worth bearing in mind the number of times that Shakespeare, Heminges and Condell appeared at Court with the rest of their acting company. Overall the Lord Chamberlain's Men performed around 170 times at Court before Elizabeth I and James I in Shakespeare's lifetime; around 290 times in Condell's, and around 320 in Heminges's lifetimes, before Elizabeth, James and Charles I (Astington 1999, pp. 234–57). All three men were used to operating and interacting at the highest possible social levels.

Editors

Heminges and Condell have become the subjects of panegyric, especially exemplified by C. Connell's well-intentioned study *They Gave Us Shakespeare* (1982), which starts by describing a memorial erected to them in 1970 on the site of St Mary's, including the words: 'to their disinterested affection the world owes all that it calls Shakespeare ... They thus merited the gratitude of mankind.'

As the last surviving members of the Lord Chamberlain's Men, they were supremely well placed to oversee the compilation of the 1623 Folio. The First Folio was only ever *the* Folio to them, an enormous labour of love by anyone's standards (they had died by the time the Second Folio appeared in 1632). They were emulating Ben Jonson's ground-breaking Folio of 1616. It is my guess that Shakespeare himself had been working on an edition of his works ever since the Globe fire of 1613: manuscripts, like theatres, could easily perish. A John Heminges is mentioned in the 1620 accounts of St Martin's, Carfax, Oxford as donating 10 shillings 'toward the Clock and chimes'. If that was our John Heminges, then Mary Edmond suggests he was visiting John and Jane Davenant in Oxford on his way to Stratford-upon-Avon to collect Shakespeare's papers and consult with John Hall (Edmond 2004, p. 279).

The Folio was just over a year at the press and eighteen of the plays had never been published before. The thousands of differences between the Folio and the earlier quarto editions signal huge editorial labour. Some of the plays were set from existing quartos heavily annotated with revisions. *Troilus and Cressida*, for example, was based on the 1609 quarto with 500 variants, 'one every two to three lines' (Edmondson and Wells 2011, p. 24). *King Lear* was based on a heavily marked-up 1619 quarto, with major revisions: 'the result, with deletions, additions, interlineations, and inter-leaved sheets, must have been a compositor's nightmare. There is no wonder that the book did not appear until seven years after Shakespeare died' (Edmondson and Wells 2011, p. 25). And little wonder that no two copies of the Folio are precisely alike as corrections were made throughout the printing process.

In their address to 'the great variety of readers' at the front of the volume, Heminges's and Condell's wish that 'the author himself had lived to have set forth [i.e. to have seen printed] and overseen his own writings [i.e. through to publication]' suggests that he may have made a start. Shakespeare left some fair copies of the plays behind him, 'cured and perfect of their limbs, and all the rest absolute in their numbers, as he conceived them' ('numbers' perhaps referring to Shakespeare's metrical accuracy), so much so that 'we have scarce received from him a blot in his papers.' E. A. J. Honigmann critiques this as little more than commonplace praise (Honigmann 1965, p. 31). But he was reacting against the biblio-graphical work of A. W. Pollard and W. W. Greg who wanted to reconstruct an 'original' text based on their theories about Shakespeare's lost manuscripts. None of this has any bearing on Heminges's and Condell's resonant claim that they had access to Shakespeare's actual papers some, all, or any of which could have been used to help mark up and revise existing quarto editions and prompt-books, or have formed the control text for new scribal copies. It seems that Shakespeare's own manuscripts were the fair copy that Heminges and Condell gave to the publisher for six Folio-only plays: *The Comedy of Errors, Julius Caesar, As You Like It, Twelfth Night, or What You Will, All's Well That Ends Well,* and *Antony and Cleopatra* (Wells and Taylor 1997, pp. 145–7).

But Heminges and Condell needed the expert assistance of writers. Ben Jonson may have commissioned Martin Droeshout to provide the frontispiece for which Jonson then provided the poem caption. Jonson, Hugh Holland, Leonard Digges and James Mabbe all produced verses in praise of Shakespeare for the volume and may have formed something like an editorial board, led by Heminges and Condell. The professional scribe, Ralph Crane, made fair copies of some of the comedies. By 1623, Crane was working on another play with which Heminges and Condell were associated, Webster's *The Duchess of Malfi*. Once we accept Middleton's role as a possible adapter of *Macbeth* (possibly even during Shakespeare's lifetime), and, later, *Measure for Measure*, as well as a collaborator with Shakespeare on *Timon of Athens*, it is likely that he himself helped to compile the Folio, even though he is not acknowledged in the volume. Crane went on to work as a scribe on Middleton's works from 1624 (Howard-Hill 1993, p. 128). Germaine Greer suggests that Shakespeare's widow, Anne, also helped in supplying papers from New Place, and with indemnity against loss for the publisher (Greer 2007, pp. 346 and 348). If Shakespeare's other collaborators had any say in which works were printed, it seems that John Fletcher, for example, gave permission for *All is True* (*Henry VIII*) to appear (and with it all the memories of the burning of the Globe ten years earlier), but not their co-authored *Cardenio* and *The Two Noble Kinsmen. Pericles,* co-written with George Wilkins, was also not included. Or perhaps the company, the King's Men, helped to make the final decision as to which plays made it into the volume.

The printer, William Jaggard, had received the Royal Commission to print the Ten Commandments for all churches in the land (Wells 2004, p. 585), so perhaps Heminges and Condell first came to know him then.

From 1615, Jaggard had the monopoly on London playbills and had been involved in Thomas Pavier's attempt to publish a multi-volume Shakespeare in 1619. William Jaggard was blind, so his son Isaac was crucial to the enterprise (Howard-Hill 1993, p. 114).

The 1623 Folio shapes and constructs Shakespeare differently from the theatrical world in which he had lived and worked. The plays are ordered by genre, mixing history plays with tragedies (*King Lear, Macbeth, Cymbeline*), tragedies with histories (*Richard II* and *Richard III*), and drawing too definite a line across Shakespeare's blending together of comedy and tragedy. The imposition of act and scene divisions encourages the reader to imagine breaks in performance, not part of professional staging until after 1608, nor a feature of the quarto texts. The pagination starts afresh for each generic section, suggesting an original intention to publish three volumes. The omission of Shakespeare's poems might have been due to problems with copyright, but looks more like a literary decision. Heminges and Condell wanted to present plays and gave pride of place to Shakespeare's apparently last single-authored drama, *The Tempest*, which, as René Weis has suggested, 'distilled above all others the quintessence of their friend's work' (Weis 2007, p. 370).

The volume is dedicated to the brother Earls of Pembroke, William and Philip, who enjoyed seeing Shakespeare performed. A fascinating early response to the 1623 Folio came from the family of Sir John Salusbury (1567–1612), for whom Shakespeare wrote 'The Phoenix and Turtle' and which Edward Blount, the publisher of the Folio, had included in *Love's Martyr* (1601). Sir Israel Gollancz found the following poem in a notebook apparently by John's son, Sir Henry, which he took to be an early response to the 1623 Folio:

> *To my good friends, Mr John Heminges and Henry Condell*
> To you that jointly with undaunted pains
> Vouchsafed to chant to us these noble strains,
> How much you merit by it is not said,
> But you have pleased the living, loved the dead,
> Raised from the womb of earth a richer mine
> Than 'Curteys Cowlde' with all his 'Castelyne
> Associattes'; they did but dig for gold,
> But you for treasure much more manifold.
> (Chambers 1930, 2, p. 234)

Salusbury had probably just received a copy of the Folio from Blount, but the terms he uses here suggest he knew something of Heminges and Condell's personalities. His poem supports the view that the two men did not stand to gain financially from what they had done.

Bequests

Neither of them bequeathed as much money as Shakespeare did in his will (around £360). Condell's largest bequest was £30 a year for his son Henry for University 'or elsewhere'. There are ten bequests of £5 (one of those to the poor of Fulham parish) and 20 shillings are left for two widows drawn from 'my houses in Aldermanbury' to be paid out on feast days. Forty shillings was left to his old servant Elizabeth Weaton 'and that place of privilege which she now exerciseth and enjoyeth in the houses of the Blackfriars London and the Globe on Bankside' (Honigmann and Brock 1993, pp. 156–60). Natasha Korda understands Weaton to have been one of the female theatre gatherers who took the money at the door, helped out as needed, sometimes taking part in the plays as attendants, mending and adapting costumes (Korda 2009, p. 470). Condell's widow, Elizabeth, was executor and inherited the most, including the theatrical shares. She died in 1635. Among her bequests are twelve houses on the Strand that she was in the process of selling for an enormous £1,450. She leaves Thomas Seaman 'all my books', which presumably included her late husband's (Honigmann and Brock 1993, pp. 184–5).

Business-like Heminges, with his large family, did not leave much money. The largest bequest is £5 for his grandson, Richard Atkins, to buy books. The surviving shareholders of the King's Men received 10 shillings each to buy mourning rings. The poor of St Mary's parish received 40 shillings. His late wife's 'costly suit' and her expensive cushions are left to his daughters. Two sons-in-law were left paintings of their wives 'set up in a frame in my house'. Everything else – including the theatrical shares – was left to his 'unmarried or unadvanced children' (Honigmann and Brock 1993, pp. 164–9).

Both men requested to be buried at night (Condell on 29 December 1627 and Heminges on 12 October 1630), a fashionable practice which had started among the aristocracy and which was adopted by the aspiring middle-classes. It certainly made for less fuss and ostentation than the costly, ceremonial funerals desired by the College of Arms. Condell died at Fulham and Heminges in St Saviour's, Southwark, but they wanted to be buried at St Mary's, Aldermanbury, where they had held their parish offices, and a funeral outside one's own parish was always more expensive.

Heminges and Condell are the full-time London equivalents of Shakespeare, inextricably important presences in the tightly knit theatrical world as he experienced it for more than twenty years. They, like Shakespeare, aspired to and attained a high level of sustainable personal, artistic, social and financial achievement, all gentleman actors, theatrical entrepreneurs and showmen, who were equally at home in both the Court and public playhouses. All of them helped to represent the rising and respectable face of the professional theatre. Heminges's and Condell's literary sensibilities and their loyalty to Shakespeare helped to shape his works and reputation. They knew how and why he wrote, how he revised his work, and how he divided his time up between Stratford-upon-Avon and London. They could a tale or two unfold.

WORKS CITED

Archer, Ian W. 2009. 'The City of London and the Theatre', in Richard Dutton (ed.), *The Oxford Handbook of Early Modern Theatre*. Oxford University Press, pp. 396–412

Astington, John 1999. *English Court Theatre: 1558–1642*. Cambridge University Press

Baldwin, T. W. 1927. *The Organization and Personnel of the Shakespeare Company*. Princeton University Press

Bentley, Gerald Eades 1941–68. *The Jacobean and Caroline Stage*, 7 vols. Oxford. Clarendon Press

Chambers, E. K. 1930. *William Shakespeare: A Study of Facts and Problems*. 2 vols. Oxford. Clarendon Press

Dutton, Richard (ed.) 2009. *The Oxford Handbook of Early Modern Theatre*. Oxford University Press

Eccles, Mark 1991a. 'Elizabethan Actors, II: A-D', *Notes and Queries* 236: 44–5
1991b. 'Elizabethan Actors, II: E-J', *Notes and Queries* 236: 457–59

Edmond, Mary 2004. 'Henry Condell', in H. C. G. Matthew and Brian Harrison (eds.), *Dictionary of National Biography*, vol. 12. Oxford University Press, pp. 918–20

Edmond, Mary 2004. 'John Heminges', in H. C. G. Matthew and Brian Harrison (eds.), *Dictionary of National Biography*, vol. 26. Oxford University Press, pp. 278–9

Edmondson, Paul and Wells, Stanley 2011. 'The Limitations of the First Folio', in Christa Jansohn, Lena Cowen Orlin and Stanley Wells (eds.), *Shakespeare Without Boundaries: Essays in Honour of Dieter Mehl*. University of Delaware Press, pp. 23–34

Greer, Germaine 2007. *Shakespeare's Wife*. London. Bloomsbury

Gurr, Andrew 2004. *The Shakespeare Company 1594–1642*. Cambridge University Press

Honigmann, E. A. J. 1965. *The Stability of Shakespeare's Text*. London. Edward Arnold

1993. *Playhouse Wills*. Manchester University Press

Howard-Hill, T. H. 1993. 'Shakespeare's Earliest Editor, Ralph Crane', *Shakespeare Survey 44*. Stanley Wells (ed.). Cambridge University Press, pp. 113–29

Kathman, David 2005. 'Citizens, Innholders, and Playhouse Builders, 1543–1622', *Research Opportunities in Medieval and Renaissance Drama* XLIV: 38–64

2009. 'Players, Livery Companies, and Apprentices', in Richard Dutton (ed.), *The Oxford Handbook of Early Modern Theatre*. Oxford University Press, pp. 413–28

2012. 'Henry Condell and His London Relatives', *Shakespeare Quarterly* 63: 108–15

in press. 'John Heminges and Henry Condell', *The Cambridge World Shakespeare Encyclopedia*

Korda, Natasha 2009. 'Women in the Theatre', in Richard Dutton (ed.), *The Oxford Handbook of Early Modern Theatre*. Oxford University Press, pp. 456–73

Lee, Sir Sidney 1887. 'Henry Condell', in Sir Leslie Stephen (ed.), *The Dictionary of National Biography*. London. Smith, Elder and Company, pp. 468–9

1891. 'John Heminges', in Sir Leslie Stephen and Sir Sidney Lee (eds.), *The Dictionary of National Biography*. London. Smith, Elder and Company, pp. 384–5

Marston, John 1975. *The Malcontent*. G. K. Hunter (ed.). London. Methuen

Matthew, H. C. G. and Harrison, Bernard (eds.) 2004. *Dictionary of National Biography*. Oxford University Press

Potter, Lois 2012. *The Life of William Shakespeare: A Critical Biography*. Chichester. Wiley-Blackwell

Schoenbaum, S. 1991. *Shakespeare's Lives*. Oxford. Clarendon Press

Stephen, Sir Leslie (ed.) 1887. *The Dictionary of National Biography*. London. Smith, Elder and Company

Stephen, Sir Leslie and Lee, Sir Sidney (eds.) 1891. *The Dictionary of National Biography*. London. Smith, Elder and Company

Weis, René. 2007. *Shakespeare Revealed*. London. John Murray

Wells, Stanley. 2002. *Shakespeare For All Time*. Basingstoke. Macmillan

     2004. 'William Jaggard', in *Dictionary of National Biography*. Oxford University Press, vol. 29, p. 585

     2006. *Shakespeare & Co*. London. Penguin

Wells, Stanley and Taylor, Gary (eds.), with John Jowett and William Montgomery 1997. *William Shakespeare: A Textual Companion*. Norton. New York

Wood, Michael 2003. *In Search of Shakespeare*. London. BBC Books

Closing remarks

PAUL EDMONDSON AND STANLEY WELLS

Imagine standing on the edge of a lake and throwing a handful of pebbles into it. You are faced with a host of concentric circles which overlap, intersect, embrace, reach out in different directions, but which hold within themselves a sense of their own boundaries. The contributions we have gathered together for *The Shakespeare Circle* remind us of many different kinds of circles that emanate from the centre of Shakespeare's life and help to shape its peripheries. There are circles of familial influence and responsibility, neighbourly and professional intentions, circles of reputation among patrons, readers, critics, printers and publishers; circles of collaboration with other playwrights, actors, theatrical entrepreneurs and business investors. They overlap like Venn diagrams, leaving ample space for mutually including as well as excluding points of view.

Looking back over the chapters in this volume we are struck by a number of recurring themes, not least the intimacy of daily life as it was lived out among the neighbourhoods Shakespeare knew in both Warwickshire and London. Members of the Hathaway family from Shottery involved themselves in the civic life of Stratford and lived close to New Place on Chapel Street. New Place itself seems to have been the nexus for various members of the Shakespeare family, of which Shakespeare himself became the patriarch and chief bread-winner from the time of his father's death in 1601. This family home was among Shakespeare's primary assets and, along with his other significant local investments, shows how he ploughed money earned in London back into his hometown. The lack of privacy within individual houses was reflected in the town's social circles in which gossip thrived. In July 1613, Susanna Hall had no choice but to sue John Lane for defamation of character when he accused her of committing adultery and having a venereal discharge (or 'running of the reins'). The rumour would have spread through the town as wildly as the fire that had destroyed the Globe a month earlier. It was difficult to keep anything a secret both in the Stratford of Shakespeare's time

329

and among the close-knit theatrical circles of actors who worked together, like a brotherhood, for many years.

Life in Stratford is too often hived off in Shakespearian biographies; but looking at the overlapping circles in which people moved reveals a much more porous reality. Did the news about John Somerville's attempt to assassinate Queen Elizabeth create especially fearful reverberations on Henley Street, if the Arden family were in any way implicated? Richard Field's and William Shakespeare's families lived about a three-minute walk away from each other in Stratford. Both men put to use their grammar school education and pursued literary careers among the intellectual and artistic elite. Their professional circles intertwined around Field's printing shop at the Blackfriars, which became an important if controversial location for the ever-evolving London theatre scene. Matthew Morrys, the servant of John Hall's father, moved to Stratford where he named his children Susanna and John. He brought with him his late master's books on alchemy, astrology and astronomy, which could have been of great use to Shakespeare, especially as he prepared to write *The Tempest*. Books also came up to the town in the two-way traffic that linked Stratford to the capital. We know that Susanna, John and Elizabeth Hall went to London; carriers such as William Greenaway regularly commuted from Stratford and brought back provisions from the capital – including wines, spices and books – food for the body and the mind. With these goods came tales of travels abroad. Theatrical and non-theatrical associates of Shakespeare travelled in Europe. Stephen Bellott went to Spain; some of the actors and musicians travelled extensively. The comic actor William Kemp, for example, visited Germany, the Netherlands and Denmark (where the musician John Dowland also lived and worked for some years). From the mid 1580s until the accession of James I in 1603, England was at war with Spain in the Netherlands and saw many ordinary townsmen being pressed into military service.

An individual's character is in part inherited from his or her parents. Shakespeare's mother and father were capable and tough-minded business people. From John Shakespeare, William experienced the wool-dealing business that linked the Midlands, London and other parts of the country. John Shakespeare was a litigious entrepreneur – money-lender, glove-maker, wool dealer and public servant – from whom his eldest son learned much (even following his example, on occasion, to evade paying his taxes).

These economic and legal realities of life are reflected in the lives of Shakespeare's highly successful theatrical colleagues. Theirs was a community in which individuals of similar social backgrounds and origins shared a sense of real opportunities which led to increased prosperity and rising social status. Strong personal as well as professional links are apparent between Shakespeare and his fellows in the naming of children. Other than William Walker, who is named in his will, we do not know how many godchildren Shakespeare had, but the fact that several families he was close to named a son William suggests at least four more: William Sadler (who had a sister named Anne), William Burbage, William Condell and William Heminges. In naming a child after a family friend (John Shakespeare seems to have named his first son after the local butcher and fellow burgess, William Tyler), parents are expressing affection and a hope for emulation. It is a tribute which binds as well as celebrates friendship. There were posthumous tributes of this kind as well. His daughter, Judith, already pregnant when her father died, named her first child by his surname, Shakespeare Quiney. Slightly further afield, in nearby Oxford, William Davenant (born in 1606), who went on to become poet laureate and an adapter of several Shakespeare plays, liked to say he too was Shakespeare's godchild, or even (as recorded by John Aubrey) his illegitimate son.

Across the chapters we have been made aware of the importance of tradition which can neither be confirmed nor denied. But it remains important. One aspect of biography is its need to negotiate between the potentially conflicting natures of tradition and historical fact as evidenced in documentary records. From the anecdote by John Manningham which we quoted at the beginning of the book through the stories that the actor Thomas Betterton collected in Stratford at the instigation of Nicholas Rowe, there has accumulated a storehouse of attractive but unverified gossip and hearsay which has helped to form the texture of Shakespearian biographical studies. Scholars such as Robert Bell Wheler and Edgar Fripp are among those who have been more receptive to such discourse. Others, for example E. K. Chambers and S. Schoenbaum, keen always to follow the hard beaten track of fact as established primarily by documentary evidence, have written dismissively of tradition as 'Shakespeare mythos'. Our contributors have approached these tensions with varying degrees of creativity. The aim of some of them is to help the reader enter imaginatively into the past and to help their subjects come plausibly to life. The alternative interpretations and possibilities which present themselves are usually limited. Biography, like history, seeks the most reasonable explanation, but it is willing to admit tradition and informed speculation in order to achieve its goals. *Venus and Adonis* was the first work in English to be dedicated to Shakespeare's young patron the Earl of Southampton; it was a rare privilege for Shakespeare – as yet unrecognised as a poet – to dedicate to the Earl a work in a non-classical language. The fact that Shakespeare describes him as the 'noble' 'godfather' of his first published poem ('the first heir of my invention') may help to support the rumour (reported by William Davenant) that the Earl gave Shakespeare £1,000 'to enable him to go through with a purchase which he heard he had a mind to' (Rowe 1709, p. x). Almost a hundred years later, Wheler reported this 'unanimous tradition' as an explanation for Shakespeare being able to 'purchase houses and land in Stratford' (Wheler 1806, p. 73). Among the many circles that make up any individual's life, oral history has an important place and currency, its own authority which needs to be analysed afresh as perspectives develop.

There are many things we should like to know more about. Shakespeare has come into sharper focus as a collaborative writer over the last thirty years. The precise nature and methods of collaboration are matters of on-going enquiry and discussion. As objectionable as George Wilkins was as a person, as far as Shakespeare was concerned collaborative and professional concerns did not have to coincide with moral judgement. Certainly Wilkins seems to have had a strain of romanticism which appealed to Shakespeare. Likewise, the romantically inclined John Fletcher was already writing plays for the King's Men before he started collaborating with Shakespeare. As difficult as *The Woman's Prize* (or *The Tamer Tamed*) is to date (possibly as early as 1610 and as late as the early 1620s), the fact that it is the earliest dramatic sequel to any Shakespeare play presents us with a fascinating model of collaborative endeavour. In Fletcher, Shakespeare was working with someone who both wanted to interact and think creatively with him and who clearly and profoundly admired his work. The more satirically inclined Thomas Middleton seems to have appealed to a different side of Shakespeare's creative instincts. Unlike Fletcher's, the plays he seems to have been involved with all appear in the 1623 Folio. Another writer, not usually thought of as a collaborator with Shakespeare, is Michael Drayton.

He worked on many plays, but scarcely any of his dramatic output survives. By 1598 Francis Meres classed him among 'the best for tragedy'. He is possibly one of Shakespeare's lost collaborators, working with him during his freelance years before the founding of the Lord Chamberlain's Men in 1594. The close links Drayton had with the Rainsford family a mile away from Stratford in the village of Clifford Chambers suggest that both he and Shakespeare may often have been in the area at the same time, possibly discussing their work with each other, and giving credibility to the story first recorded by the vicar of Stratford in the 1660s of how Shakespeare caught a fever and died after a 'merry meeting' with Drayton and Ben Jonson. We know much of what Jonson thought about Shakespeare, but it would be good to have Shakespeare's perspective on his friend and rival, and to know why the two never collaborated (except, as it were, posthumously on the 1623 Folio).

Where did Shakespeare's posthumous reputation begin and with what? Had he died in London, he would probably have been buried there, perhaps in Westminster Abbey, a possibility alluded to by both William Basse and Jonson. His memorial bust, produced in Southwark by Gerard Janssen, needed an inscription. Were the lines in Latin and English composed by London-based Ben Jonson, himself deeply involved with the Folio? The authorship of the Shakespeare family epitaphs (William's own and Susanna's, in English, along with Anne's and John's, in Latin) in Holy Trinity Church, Stratford, is unknown. They challenge us to speculate about the intentions of the family members who survived and how they wanted their dead relatives to be remembered. Shakespeare's final intentions are documented in his will. About that puzzling document there is much more to learn; the artefact itself bears further research. We want mainly to recall and to remark on Shakespeare's lack of a direct male heir. His envisaging and naming the 'fourth, fifth, sixth and seventh sons' of Susanna, as well as any male children of Elizabeth or, failing her, Judith, seems expressive of a longing and hope that had been lost and buried with Hamnet Shakespeare twenty years earlier. Entailments of this kind, though common, do not usually extend as far as the 'sixth and seventh'. Only Judith and Thomas Quiney would produce male children, three of them (Shakespeare, Richard and Thomas), all of whom died young. It is strange, given Shakespeare's obvious hope for male offspring by Susanna, that he should bequeath one of the most potent symbols of his gentlemanly status, his sword, outside the family circle. He left it to Thomas Combe, roughly the same age as Hamnet would have been. Perhaps he thought that neither of his sons-in-law was worthy of inheriting it.

The circles in this book help to indentify future research. Like René Weis, we find it difficult to accept that Shakespeare's personal papers and other belongings such as his books and coat of arms are irrevocably lost. Weis suggests that a full-scale tracing of all of the Barnards of Abington (from Elizabeth's step-children onwards), their direct and collateral descendants, could bear extraordinary fruit. Susan Brock has suggested that among Shakespeare's local associates, Francis Collins, Hamnet Sadler and Henry Rainsford are particularly worthy of further investigation. As we write these closing remarks, the Shakespeare Birthplace Trust's archaeological investigation of New Place is reaching its conclusion in time for the site to be re-presented to the public from 2016.

We hope that the chapters in this book provide fresh insights and play a distinctive part in the on-going conversation of Shakespearian biography. For us they are a welcome reminder that there are always new circles to explore, different stories to tell.

WORKS CITED

Rowe, Nicholas 1709. *The Works of Mr William Shakespeare*. London. Jacob Tonson

Wheler, R. B. 1806. *History and Antiquities of Stratford-upon-Avon*. London. J. Ward

Afterword

MARGARET DRABBLE

Shakespeare's circle

We shouldn't be surprised that Shakespeare's life is still full of surprises, but we are. Surely, we say to ourselves, there can be nothing left to discover. Surely everything has been examined and re-examined – every family document, every word he wrote or maybe didn't write, every artefact with which he was associated, every house or lodging he owned or lived in or may have lived in. And yet, each decade, each year, more is revealed.

This is partly thanks, as these chapters demonstrate, to the ingenious application of new technologies. Dendrochronology, now a comparatively venerable method of investigation, has demonstrated that Shakespeare's granddaughter Elizabeth Hall cannot have been born at the house known as Hall's Croft, and the more recent tools provided by DNA, hopes René Weis, may yet tell us more about her long and interesting afterlife. Search-able online databases have helped scholars to trace documents and refer-ences in her father's medical textbooks, and computer-aided stylistic analysis has shed compelling new light on Shakespeare's collaborations with Thomas Middleton – as Emma Smith challenges, in concluding her chapter on this subject, 'Watch this space.' Catherine Richardson suggests that research by Alan H. Nelson and William Ingram on the sales of Easter tokens in Southwark may tell us something about the otherwise obscure last year of Shakespeare's youngest actor brother Edmund, who was buried in Southwark 'with a fore noon knell of the great bell' on 31 December 1607. We now have searchable access to maps complete with 'placeography, personography [and] bibliography'. Materials painstakingly gleaned over the years from records of the Ecclesiastical Courts and the Parish Registers can now be made to give up their secrets almost effortlessly, at the click of a mouse, as we perceive new patterns, and add new pieces to the jigsaw.

But the new technologies are only aids to scholarship and imagination, and to receive interesting answers you have to ask interesting questions. In this volume, editors Stanley Wells and Paul Edmondson have gathered together a collection of essays that brilliantly encircles their immensely celebrated yet ever enigmatic central figure, William Shakespeare, and surrounds him with family, friends and colleagues, seen from many different perspectives. As we read through these varied and sometimes conflicting interpretations, we find ourselves engaging with questions that I at least had never thought to ask. Was Shakespeare's father a respected tradesman, who successfully employed his son William as envoy in the business of his London wool dealing, as David Fallow argues, or was he, as we more traditionally see him, a faintly disreputable 'brogger' who ended up in poverty, losing his wife's inheritance, as Michael Wood believes? Why did Shakespeare's brothers, unusually for the time, never marry? Were John Shakespeare and Mary Arden, Shakespeare's parents, literate? They must have been, argue some: no proof, answer others. Were they eager to follow the new religion, or did Mary in particular cling to the old? The evidence points both ways.

The lives of the women in Shakespeare's world have long been the object of scrutiny. Virginia Woolf, in her 1929 feminist essay *A Room of One's Own*, threw down the gauntlet, stating baldly that 'nothing is known about women before the eighteenth century', and inventing, to fill the gap, the cautionary tale of Shakespeare's gifted sister Judith, who ran away to London, committed suicide, and was buried at the crossroads at the Elephant and Castle. Since then, generations of feminist scholars have explored this alleged absence of hard information. Germaine Greer's 2007 defence of Anne Hathaway in *Shakespeare's Wife* (and, by extension, of many other ill-reputed wives) is here followed by her speculative account of his daughter Judith, and her marriage to the questionable Thomas Quiney. Several of the essays discuss what degree of literacy would have been expected of and attained by the girls and women of 'Shakespeare's circle' in Stratford, who would not have had the male privilege of a free education at an outstanding Grammar School. Their authors adduce evidence from seals and signatures and wills and, more curiously, from a witness at the London trial of a Stratford-born prostitute Elizabeth Evans, who had been 'to school' with the accused. We don't know what kind of school this 'petty school' was, but it seems that it taught its pupils a fair hand. Lachlan Mackinnon, in his piece on Shakespeare's other daughter, Susanna Hall, makes a good case for her literacy, and, delightfully and plausibly, imagines (or causes me to imagine) that she may have played chess with her father, on his visits home, as Miranda in *The Tempest* plays with Ferdinand. You need a good education to be able to play chess.

Mackinnon also gives a stirring and detailed interpretation of Susanna's mother Anne's extraordinary and much overlooked Latin epitaph, subject in this volume to differing readings: we don't know who wrote it, but Mackinnon's somewhat startling view is that it was written by Susanna herself, as a tribute to the one whose breasts gave her 'milk and life'. So, on this reading, she was not only literate in English, but also in Latin. Greer, in *Shakespeare's Wife*, had read this epitaph as a conventional example of 'uxorious' puritan piety, probably written by the physician John Hall, 'ventriloquising' for his wife: Mackinnon's more adventurous suggestion is endorsed, at least as a possibility, by Katherine Scheil in her essay on 'Anne Shakespeare and the Hathaways', although Scheil also proposes as the epitaph's putative author Thomas Greene, a so-called 'cousin' and Stratford friend who may have been Shakespeare's lodger at New Place. Greene has a section of his own here, although his place in the circle of Shakespeare's friendships remains, Tara Hamling admits, 'elusive'. But he surfaces favourably in Stanley Wells's account of the Combe family, appearing as compassionate, conscientious and humane – more committed to the public good, perhaps, than Shakespeare himself.

So the circles intersect, and the personal narratives overlap and are fleshed out, producing a colourful sense of the life of the small (and at times troubled) town of Stratford-upon-Avon, with which Shakespeare kept up such a close lifelong connection – a world of sheep and lambs and wool and oxen and enclosures, of husbandry and brewing and taverns – and also of the growing London of his professional career, with its theatres and its publishing industry and its pageantry. Both worlds, we read, were equally subject to the dangers of pestilence and fire. Because of the interlocking nature of the narratives, we have a clearer sense than usual of the relationship and distances between the Warwickshire town and the great city: so much coming and going, so many journeys, such close and important connections. The trajectory of Richard Field, Shakespeare's fellow townsman and, in London, his publisher, is traced by Carol Chillington Rutter, who perceptively notes possible echoes of the friendship and rivalry of Proteus and Valentine in what is probably Shakespeare's first play, *The Two Gentlemen of Verona*. The story of these two professionally successful school friends, or what we know of it, vividly demonstrates the interpenetration of town and city.

Each reader will find one or two particular threads to follow through this tapestry, and, as with all good Shakespeare biography, will be sent back with renewed interest and engagement to the poems and the plays. For me, the play to which I returned with a sense of illumination was *Pericles, Prince of Tyre*, now rarely performed, but in its day sensationally successful. We have long known that this was written in collaboration with another dramatist, and indeed this is evident from the text itself, even to a casual reader or theatre-goer. But the nature of that collaboration is stranger and more sinisterly suggestive than I had imagined. The name of George Wilkins runs through the pages of this volume like a dark thread. Introduced by the editors in their opening pages as 'the deplorable George Wilkins', he is a very different character from the more literary playwrights with whom Shakespeare is more commonly associated. He was a 'victualler' and brothel keeper, as well as, allegedly, the son of a 'Poett', and he was very much at home in the London underworld which features in several of Shakespeare's dramas: the neighbourhoods of Clerkenwell and Turnmill (or Turnbull) Street were a far cry from Stratford, full though Stratford was of taverns. There are several records of Wilkins's acts of violence, including the kicking of a pregnant woman in the belly, but there is also some testimony that he was by no means a negligible writer. He may have been 'a dreadful man', admits Duncan Salkeld in his portrait (Chapter 22), but he was also an inspiration to Shakespeare. He certainly played an underacknowledged part in the creation of *Pericles*, a play that was 'hugely popular' on stage, and much reprinted, although long erroneously ascribed solely to Shakespeare.

And what a play it is! In this volume, its themes of child-bed, childbirth and father–daughter reconciliation are convincingly linked to the birth of Shakespeare's granddaughter Elizabeth in February 1608, around the time of the play's composition, and there is also some discussion of earlier plausible speculations that the portrayal of the wise Cerimon, the physician who restores to life Pericles' wife Thaisa, is intended as a compliment to Elizabeth's physician father and Shakespeare's son-in-law, John Hall. But more striking, to me, than these possible biographical links, is the tone of the notorious brothel scene, Scene 16, in which Wilkins may or may not have had a minor hand. (He is usually credited with the first two acts of the play.) The dark shadow of Wilkins falls heavily on these brothel scenes, whether he wrote any of them or not. They are much more violent and sexually brutal than anything similar in the rest of Shakespeare: the bawdy tavern scenes of *Henry IV*, with Doll Tearsheet and Mistress Quickly, are positively pastoral in comparison, and even Mistress Overdone and Pompey in *Measure for Measure*'s disease-ridden Vienna seem relatively good-natured and healthy in spirit when we look at the language and behaviour of the Bawd, the Pander and their man Boult in *Pericles*. These are bullies beyond compare, and the pornographic prurience of their threats to Marina's virtue must have greatly titillated those Elizabethan audiences who enjoyed this play so much. We owe these scenes, we feel, to Wilkins, directly or indirectly, and through them we look into a grimmer world which Shakespeare rarely chose to enter.

Anyone who reads these collected biographical essays and sketches will come to know Shakespeare himself better. The indirect and circular approach has been a great success. These authors have drawn on the scholarship of others, each adding new research and insights, and creating, collaboratively, a fuller composite picture of the writer whose portrait will never be complete. The Shakespeare Birthplace Trust in Stratford-upon-Avon has been the base from which both editors have worked, and they take their subject from his Stratford birthplace, out into the world, and home again. We are all enriched by this literary journey, as it comes full circle, and as we enjoy the complementary findings of the archaeological explorations of New Place.

Index

Notes: Relationships to Shakespeare are indicated. Where two or more persons share a name they are identified by pointers such as relationship, birth date or as a last resort (1), (2) etc. (sr/jr refer only to parents and children).

Shakespeare's works are indexed by title. Other works (unless anonymous or of doubtful authorship) are indexed under the author's name.